THE
FAMILY MEDICAL REFERENCE BOOK

Consultant Editor

PHILIP EVANS

CBE, MD, FRCP,
Consultant Emeritus
Guy's Hospital
London

This edition published in 2001 by
SILVERDALE BOOKS
An imprint of Bookmart Ltd
Registered number 2372865
Trading as Bookmart Ltd
Desford Road, Enderby
Leicester LE9 5AD

ISBN 1-85605-604-X

Production by Omnipress, Eastbourne
Printed in Singapore

Little, Brown and Company (UK) Limited
Brettenham House, Lancaster Place
London WC2E 7EN

CONTENTS

PART I
The
Human Life Cycle

Sex and Reproduction

Men and women differ in obvious ways. Men are generally taller and heavier, have larger hands and feet, more body hair, hair on the face, and lower-pitched voices. Most men are physically stronger and can run faster and jump higher than most women, but women may have greater endurance. In most societies men are brought up to be more aggressive and dominating. In average intelligence men and women are equal but, owing to the roles they are expected to fill, their behaviour, tastes and pastimes often differ.

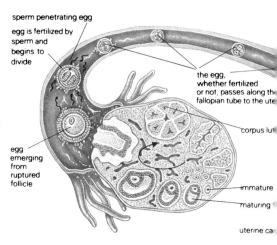

sperm penetrating egg

egg is fertilized by sperm and begins to divide

the egg, whether fertilized or not, passes along the fallopian tube to the ute

corpus lu

egg emerging from ruptured follicle

immature

maturing

uterine ca

endometr (uterine lir

myometri (uterine w

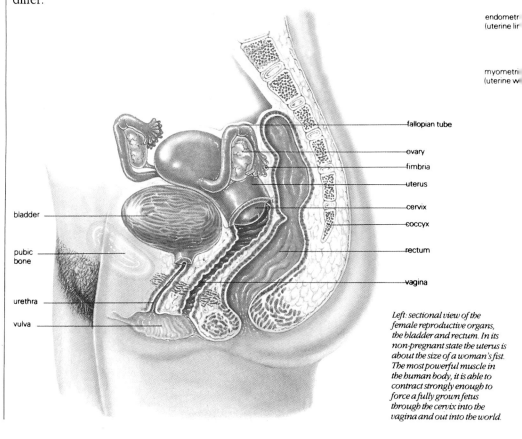

bladder

pubic bone

urethra

vulva

fallopian tube

ovary

fimbria

uterus

cervix

coccyx

rectum

vagina

Left: sectional view of the female reproductive organs, the bladder and rectum. In its non-pregnant state the uterus is about the size of a woman's fist. The most powerful muscle in the human body, it is able to contract strongly enough to force a fully grown fetus through the cervix into the vagina and out into the world.

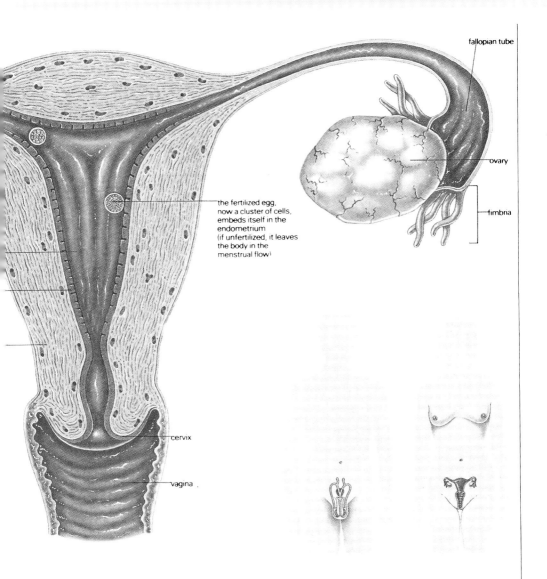

fallopian tube

ovary

fimbria

the fertilized egg, now a cluster of cells, embeds itself in the endometrium (if unfertilized, it leaves the body in the menstrual flow)

cervix

vagina

There is an enormous range of characteristics within each sex, so that there is much overlap between the sexes in many bodily aspects such as strength, weight and so on. In terms of health and illness, though, the most clear-cut differences between men and women are in the reproductive organs. In a woman these are the external genitals (the vulva), the vagina and the uterus (womb), the two fallopian tubes and the two ovaries within the abdominal cavity. In a man the reproductive organs are the penis, the two testes and their associated ducts and glands.

Above left: eggs are contained in the ovaries, which lie one on either side of the uterus, to which the fallopian tubes are connected. The sectional view of the left ovary shows the ripening of an egg, nourished by a follicle, and its expulsion into the fallopian tube through the fimbria. It is at this end of the tube that fertilization usually occurs. Whether fertilized or not, the egg travels along the fallopian tube to the uterus where it is either implanted in the uterine wall or is expelled during menstruation. Above: the position of the male and female reproductive organs. Other differences between men and women include body shape and fat distribution.

Female sexual anatomy

The female external genital organs are known collectively as the vulva. The vulva, the entrance to the sexual and urinary tracts, comprises the labia majora (two large folds of skin covered by hair after puberty), and within them the labia minora (hairless skin folds) which enclose the vestibule or entrance to the vagina and urethra. At the front of the vestibule is the clitoris, one of the main erotic zones in women, corresponding to the penis in men and becoming enlarged and stiff during sexual excitement. Round the entrance to the vagina is a ring of membranous tissue, the hymen, which is usually perforated and stretched at first intercourse.

The internal reproductive organs comprise the ovaries, fallopian tubes, uterus, cervix and vagina. The vagina is a tube about 8 cm (3 in) long, leading to the cervix or neck of the womb, which protrudes into its upper end. The vaginal walls are elastic and muscular and made up of numerous folds which enable it to expand to accommodate the passage of a baby during childbirth. The cervix has a small central opening which leads into the uterus. Blood passes out through this opening during menstruation, sperm pass in during intercourse, and during childbirth it dilates until it is wide enough to allow a baby's head to pass out of the uterus.

The uterus is a thick-walled, hollow, pear-shaped organ whose muscle fibres are the strongest in the human body. These fibres can stretch to accommodate a full-term fetus, contract to expel it at birth, and then shrink back to their original size in six weeks. The uterine walls are lined with glandular tissue containing a rich blood supply which undergoes changes during the menstrual cycle in preparation for receiving a fertilized egg. If it does not receive an egg, the lining is shed.

Joining the uterus on either side are the fallopian tubes which are about 10 cm (4 in) long. At their other ends are trumpet-shaped openings with fringe-like edges positioned very close to the ovaries. The ovaries, the egg-producing organs, are oval in shape and each one contains about 200,000 follicles, which are microscopic capsules. Within each follicle is an ovum, or egg cell. When an egg is released from an ovary it is gathered by the fringes of the end of the nearest fallopian tube and wafted into the tube to travel down to the uterus.

The breasts

The breasts, or mammary glands, a major secondary sexual characteristic, are modified sweat glands which after childbirth produce milk to feed the newborn baby. During most of a woman's adult life they are composed mainly of fatty tissue containing glands and ducts opening into the main duct in the nipple. The glands and ducts are usually very small and contain a little clear fluid, but enlarge and multiply under hormonal influence during pregnancy and childbirth so that milk can be produced. If the nipples were previously inverted or flat, as in about one in ten women, they usually evert, or stick out, by the time a baby is born so that breast-feeding can take place. After breast-feeding, or if a baby is not breast-fed, the breasts soon decrease in size.

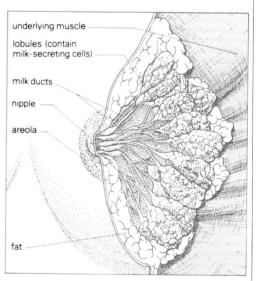

underlying muscle

lobules (contain milk-secreting cells)

milk ducts

nipple

areola

fat

The internal structure of the breast. Milk-secreting glands are grouped into about twenty lobules in each breast, and ducts from the lobules lead to the nipple, where they widen to form pouches for milk storage.

As a result of the hormonal changes of pregnancy and lactation, and to a lesser extent of the menstrual cycle, the breast varies in shape, size and consistency, becoming firmer in pregnancy and just before menstruation, and softer again afterwards. The breasts contain no muscle tissue, and their shape, which varies from woman to woman, depends on a suspensory system of ligaments across the chest wall. After a number of pregnancies or after the menopause these ligaments may stretch and cause the breasts to sag.

The female external genitalia, showing the relationship of the vagina to the urethra and anus.

mons pubis

clitoris

urethral orifice

labia majora
labia minora
vaginal orifice

hymen

anus

Female sexual development

The first stage of sexual development in girls occurs at around the age of ten or eleven when the breasts begin to develop. Their ducts grow to form a firm breast bud under the nipple, which also enlarges. The amount of fatty tissue in the breasts and hips increases. Hair begins to grow in the genital region, assuming the female pattern of a triangle with a clear-cut horizontal line at the top of the pubic bone; hair also appears in the armpits and sometimes around the nipples. At the same time both the internal and external sexual organs are growing, in readiness for the onset of hormonal changes which signal the menarche, the first period, which occurs at around the age of twelve or thirteen on average, but often later.

There is wide variation in frequency and regularity of menstruation during adolescence. There may be a break of several months after the first period before the second, and it may take up to three years for regular periods to become established. The amount of blood loss also varies between individuals.

The menstrual cycle

The hormones that distinguish women from men are progesterone and oestrogen, both of which are made by the ovaries. Their production is stimulated at puberty by two controlling substances, follicle stimulating hormone (FSH) and luteinising hormone (LH), both of which are made by the pituitary gland in the brain, under the influence of the hypothalamus. It is not known for certain what triggers the hormonal changes of puberty, but repeated small stimuli over the months before the menarche probably build up to release LH and FSH.

At the onset of a cycle, a rising amount of FSH is produced. This causes up to twenty eggs in the ovary to become mature. At the same time LH enters the bloodstream and reaches the ovaries, causing them to secrete the hormone oestrogen. This stimulates the lining of the uterus, or endometrium, to develop in order to receive a fertilized egg, and makes both uterus and breasts capable of development if conception occurs. The surge of LH and oestrogen causes release of an egg (ovulation). Usually only one egg, the one that has developed most quickly, is released, but if more than one is ready several may be released, giving rise to twins or multiple births if they are fertilized.

Once ovulation occurs, the follicle that contained the released egg develops into a temporary endocrine gland, the 'corpus luteum', within the ovary, and this produces the hormone progesterone. Progesterone acts on sexual tissues already under the influence of oestrogen, especially the uterus. The uterine lining thickens, with enlarged glands and blood vessels, which are necessary to nourish the developing baby if the egg is fertilized.

If conception does not occur the corpus luteum degenerates and disappears. The consequent lack of progesterone causes the uterine lining to be shed in the menstrual blood loss, or period, marking the end of one cycle.

The menstrual cycle lasts on average twenty-eight days, with the surge of LH and oestrogen occurring at mid-cycle and causing ovulation. If fertilization does not occur, menstruation begins fourteen days after ovulation and lasts

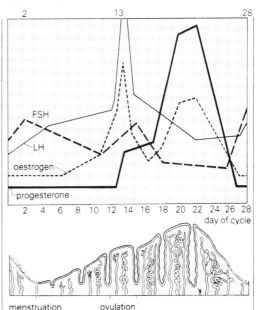

Top: variations in hormone levels during the menstrual cycle. The progesterone and oestrogen produced by the corpus luteum of the ovary influence the build-up of the uterine lining. Above: under hormonal influence, it increases during the menstrual cycle, reaches a peak after ovulation and breaks down at menstruation.

from two days to a week, varying from person to person. Even if a menstrual cycle is longer or shorter than the average, ovulation still usually occurs fourteen days before a period. For example, if a cycle lasts thirty-five days, ovulation probably occurs on day twenty-one (counting day one as the first day of the period).

Abnormalities of menstruation
Irregular periods

After the first menstruation it is normal for periods to be irregular for the first few months, or even longer, until the hormone patterns are fully developed. Later in life periods may become irregular again, as hormone levels become erratic towards the menopause. The level of the hormones causing the monthly cycle is also affected by the emotions, so that at times of stress periods may become irregular, although there is no such thing as an absolutely regular menstrual cycle.

Absence of periods (amenorrhoea)

In some girls periods may not start until much later than average, particularly if other members of the family have this tendency, but this is not considered abnormal unless the periods still have not appeared by the age of seventeen. The diseases which cause amenorrhoea are rare, however, and periods usually do start eventually. Sometimes the hymen across the vagina completely blocks the passage and the menstrual loss is unable to escape, but pain and swelling soon result from the trapped blood. Other causes of amenorrhoea are usually connected with imperfect development of either the uterus and/or vagina associated with hormone deficiency.

The commonest cause of periods stopping when they have been established for some years is pregnancy. Emotional upsets can also cause them to stop, as can rapid weight loss or prolonged illness such as a chronic infection. Less commonly, cysts of the ovary (see below) may cause amenorrhoea. The menopause (see below) is another cause, and occasionally it occurs early in an otherwise healthy woman in her thirties or early forties.

Heavy periods (menorrhagia)

A period lasting ten days or more and consisting of profuse, bright-red bleeding with clots is considered abnormal. It is usually caused by conditions in the uterus such as fibroid tumours. Fibroids are commoner in older women, especially after child-bearing, and cause heavy bleeding by distorting the cavity of the uterus. Infections of the uterus and fallopian tubes and the use of intra-uterine contraceptive devices (IUCDs) may also cause menorrhagia.

If a change occurs in the normal pattern of the periods it is a good idea to see a doctor, since there may be an underlying cause. If there is no obvious cause, the heavy bleeding is said to be 'dysfunctional'. This can be confirmed by dilatation and curettage (D & C), a minor operation under an anaesthetic in which the cervix is dilated and an instrument inserted into the womb to scrape away some of the lining which is then examined under a microscope. The D & C procedure may itself reduce blood loss for a while, but the relief is usually only temporary. Hormones such as those used in the contraceptive pill may be prescribed to control menorrhagia, and if a blood test shows anaemia iron tablets will also be given. If the condition persists despite all other treatment, surgical removal of the uterus (hysterectomy, see below) may be necessary.

Bleeding between periods

This may be anything from 'spotting', a very light loss of blood, to bleeding as heavy as a normal period. If irregular bleeding between periods occurs, however slight, a doctor should be consulted. It may be due to an IUCD, the oral contraceptive pill, fibroids or polyps in the uterus or cervix, or, more rarely, cancer of the cervix or the lining of the uterus. Treatment depends on the underlying cause.

Painful periods (dysmenorrhoea)

Painful periods are more common in women who have not borne children. Periods that follow ovulation may be uncomfortable or painful to some degree because of uterine contractions; in some women, particularly those who have heavy periods, the pain may be incapacitating. The first few periods after the onset of menstruation are usually painless; as they become more regular and ovulation occurs they may become painful. The pain may come on just before or at the start of a period, and last a day or so while the period is heaviest. Women who suffer severe pain may feel faint or sick at the same time.

Primary dysmenorrhoea (the type not caused by disease) results from overproduction of the chemical prostaglandin, and doctors are now able to prescribe prostaglandin inhibitors which usually cure the condition. Pain-relievers such as aspirin or paracetamol are also generally helpful, and one of the stronger types which has a specific action on the uterus may be prescribed. Relief will be greatest if you start to take pain-relievers a day or two before you usually get the pain, as well as during the period.

Another type of period pain, secondary dysmenorrhoea, starts two or more days before a period and gets worse during the period, lasting longer than the common type described above. This may be caused by pelvic infection or other disease, and a doctor should be consulted if this type of pain occurs. Occasionally, the only treatment for secondary dysmenorrhoea is hysterectomy (see page 15).

Premenstrual tension (PMT)

This is a common and increasingly publicized problem. Probably over half of all women have some degree of PMT, ranging from slight mood changes to severe symptoms. The main complaints are:

1 a feeling of fullness or bloating in the lower abdomen, sometimes causing considerable discomfort;

2 painful, swollen breasts;

3 weight gain, sometimes with puffy hands and feet;

4 headaches and migraine;

5 constipation and intestinal distension;

6 emotional instability, including depression, irritability, emotional outbursts and 'accident-proneness'.

Hormonal changes do lead to emotional disturbances and fluid retention in some women, but it is important to note down any mood changes and their relation to the menstrual cycle before assuming that irritability and depression are caused by PMT. Symptoms occur in the second part of the menstrual cycle, commonly for about a week but sometimes for up to two weeks before the period. Also, they are usually relieved by menstruation. If you are irritable all the time, or there is no clear premenstrual pattern with at least one week after a period when you feel well it is unlikely that you are suffering from true PMT.

Hormonal treatment may help PMT but may cause nausea or bloating, and is not suitable for everyone. Mild diuretic drugs often help if PMT is associated with fluid retention, and may be the only treatment necessary. More recently, vitamin preparations have been tried and many women appear to benefit from vitamin B6, either alone or in combination with one of the other remedies.

The menopause

The cessation of monthly periods is known as the menopause or 'change of life'. The climacteric, as it is called in medical terms, rarely occurs abruptly: the menstrual cycle first becomes irregular and eventually stops altogether. The menopause can occur at any age between thirty-five and sixty-five, but the average age is around fifty. Although fertility is greatly reduced by this time, it should not be assumed that pregnancy is impossible until periods have ceased for at least a year. Any symptoms accompanying the menopause result from the decline in the levels of oestrogen and progesterone, but many women have no symptoms.

Symptoms

There are two main symptoms of the menopause, one or both of which may be experienced. These are: hot flushes and night sweats; and vaginal dryness resulting from diminishing secretions, which can make sexual intercourse difficult. Palpitations are also sometimes experienced. Hot flushes are usually the most distressing problem, since they can occur at any time, leaving the skin bright pink and hot, which may be embarrassing and disturb sleep. They are also often associated with headaches and tiredness. Mood changes such as irritability and depression are common at this time, and these may also be caused by hormonal changes. As with PMT, however, it is important to distinguish these from depression caused by unhappy life events and stresses. Unfortunately the menopause occurs at a time when children may be leaving home and retirement from work is approaching, and these stresses may make menopausal changes even more distressing.

Symptoms of the menopause may persist for a few months or for several years, but if they are severe, treatment is available. Hormone-replacement therapy or HRT is usually very effective and free of side-effects, and the doses of hormones (oestrogen and progesterone) now given are so low as to be safe if taken correctly and under medical supervision to avoid overgrowth of the lining of the uterus.

Sexual responsiveness is not usually affected by the menopause, and women can be as sexually active and gain as much pleasure from sex after their periods stop as before. In fact, it has been said that twenty per cent of women have increased sexual desire after the menopause.

Breast disorders

It is important from time to time (preferably just after a period) for every woman to examine her breasts. Any lump found should be examined by a doctor. It may be a benign condition requiring no treatment, but if it is cancer, the sooner this is confirmed and treated the higher the chance of a cure. Never wait for a few months in the hope that a lump will disappear.

Mastitis

The commonest breast disorder is mastitis. There is usually tenderness and discomfort or pain in the breasts, sometimes with some enlargement, and the breasts feel nodular, with lumpy areas. The symptoms are often worse before a period. 'Mastitis' is a misnomer as the breasts are not infected or inflamed, but are responding to hormonal stimuli which make the glands enlarge and become tender. The condition is harmless, and can be eased by pain-relievers and sometimes by diuretics.

At times, one of these nodular areas may become a discrete lump that can be felt and sometimes seen. Usually such lumps are quite small, often pea-sized and hard, and just under the skin. These are caused by fibrous changes in the milk-producing glands, and are called fibroadenoma, or

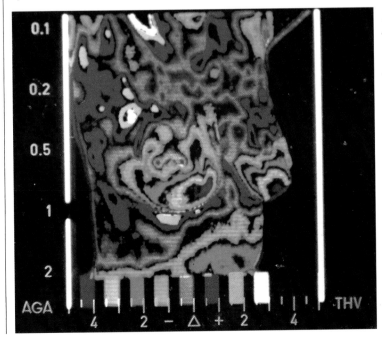

Thermography is the procedure of photographing the body with film sensitive to infra-red rays, in order to measure the heat emitted by different parts of the body. The resulting photograph, or thermogram, shows different temperatures in different colours, and may be used to detect cysts and tumours in areas such as the breasts, shown here, at an early stage, since slight alterations in normal temperature patterns may indicate the existence of such disorders.

'breast mice' and are harmless, often disappearing after one or two menstrual cycles. Larger lumps may be due to cysts in one of the glands; these are often tender and can be drained.

Breast cancer
Breast cancer is the commonest cancer in women, and can occur at any age. It starts as a painless lump in the breast, which may be very small or quite large, hard and irregular in shape. The presence of cancer is confirmed by taking a biopsy, small piece of suspect tissue for laboratory examination, and by mammography. Treatment of breast cancer may involve surgery, drugs and/or radiotherapy; the general approach nowadays is not to remove the whole breast but to conserve as much tissue as possible. In some cases a 'lumpectomy' (removing only the lump) may be sufficient. The exact treatment depends on the precise nature of the growth and the spread; for further information, see *Cancer*, pages 218-21.

Nipple discharge
There are various types of nipple discharge. It is common in pregnancy for a clear or milky substance to appear from the nipples as the breasts prepare to produce milk. After breast-feeding most women retain the ability to secrete milk, so if the nipple is squeezed a milky secretion is normal. In a few women who have never been pregnant, milk secretion occurs due to hormonal imbalance, and this should be investigated by a doctor. Other types of discharge should also be reported to your doctor. Infections in the ducts or papillomas (tiny tumours) inside the nipple may cause a thick or blood-stained discharge. Infections are usually treated by antibiotics, and troublesome papillomas may be removed by minor surgery.

Vaginal disorders
The commonest vaginal problem is discharge. It is normal for the nature and amount of the discharge to vary at different times of the month, in response to changing hormone levels. The usual vaginal secretions are colourless or whitish and have little or no odour. If the secretions have an unpleasant smell or cause soreness or itchiness an infection is probably present.

Thrush (candidiasis)
Thrush is caused by a fungus (*Monilia* or *Candida*) found under normal conditions but kept in check by the acid balance of the vagina. If the balance is upset the organism multiplies and causes the symptoms of thick, white discharge with irritation and soreness inside and outside the vagina. Thrush multiplication is encouraged by oral contraceptives or antibiotics; wearing tights, close-fitting trousers or synthetic underwear; and diabetes. Treatment involves Nystatin cream or pessaries in the vagina. It is important for the sexual partner of an infected person also to be treated.

Trichomoniasis
Trichomoniasis is caused by a protozoan parasite found in the vagina and the male urethra, and may be transmitted during sexual intercourse. Symptoms are uncommon in men but in women are an offensive, frothy, yellow vaginal discharge which causes irritation and burning on urination, especially if the bladder is affected. It is treated by drugs such as metronidazole taken orally; sexual partners must also be treated.

Prolapse
A prolapse occurs when part of the vagina and uterus descend from their proper positions, perhaps after a difficult childbirth or after the menopause, when the supporting ligaments are less strong and elastic. It is more common in overweight women. If the front wall of the vagina prolapses, the urethra may come down too, causing stress incontinence on coughing, sneezing or straining at stool, and possibly also the symptoms of cystitis. If the back vaginal wall prolapses discomfort is felt in the rectum; and if the uterus prolapses a dragging sensation or heavy pain may

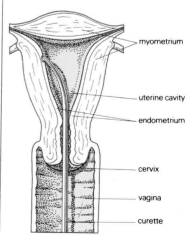

Left: polyps and fibroids in the uterus.

polyps   fibroids

Right: dilation and curettage (D & C) is a surgical procedure in which the cervix is dilated (stretched) so that a curette can be introduced into the uterus in order to scrape the uterine lining.

myometrium

uterine cavity

endometrium

cervix

vagina

curette

be experienced, and the cervix felt at the vaginal opening.

If the condition does not yet include incontinence, pelvic floor exercises (regularly tightening the pelvic floor muscles), stopping strenuous activity, losing weight and stopping smoking may arrest it. A vaginal supporting pessary may help, but the cure for prolapse is surgery, involving stitching up the tissues and ligaments or, if the prolapse is severe, vaginal hysterectomy (see below).

Disorders of the uterus and cervix
Fibroids and polyps
Some disorders of menstruation may be caused by fibroids, benign muscular growths in the uterine wall. They may be symptomless and are often found during a routine pelvic examination. They may give rise to heavy periods, however, and occasionally cause difficulties in pregnancy. Polyps, benign growths on stalks, also occur in the uterus and can usually be removed by D & C.

Endometriosis
In this condition fragments of the endometrium, the lining of the uterus, break off and develop elsewhere in the pelvic cavity, for example in the ovaries, fallopian tubes or within the uterine wall. Each month the fragments bleed like the endometrium, causing blistering and scarring. Hormone treatment may be advised if there is severe pain.

Cancer of the uterus
Cancer of the uterus is not a common cancer, and usually occurs in women over fifty-five. The first symptom is usually bleeding or abnormal discharge after the periods have ceased (post-menopausal bleeding), and should always be reported to a doctor. The usual treatment is surgical removal of the uterus (hysterectomy, see below), with or without radiotherapy.

Cervical erosion
Cervical erosion occurs when some of the cells forming the delicate lining of the inner cervix spread to cover the tip of the cervix, which is normally covered in stronger tissue. Though not a disease in itself, it makes the cervix more susceptible to infection, and may cause a heavy discharge and bleeding after sexual intercourse. Treatment involves cauterizing the affected area.

Cervical cancer
Apart from cervical erosion, the most well-known, and almost the only, disorder of the cervix is cancer. Cervical cancer is relatively common (second to breast cancer) and

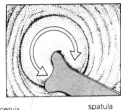

direction of movement

A cervical smear is performed with a specially shaped wooden spatula which is scraped round the cervix to remove some cells; these cells are then examined under a microscope to see if they are undergoing cancerous or pre-cancerous changes.

cervix   spatula

vagina

tends to occur before the menopause. In order to screen for the early stages doctors recommend all women over about twenty, and earlier if sexually active, to have cervical smears ('Pap' tests) taken regularly. Cancer of the cervix does not occur in nuns; and becomes more common the more sexual partners a woman has, and the earlier she begins sexual activity. The commonest symptom is bleeding between periods. Smears are taken by using a speculum to see into the vagina as far as the cervix, and its surface is scraped with a spatula to obtain a small sample of cells which is analyzed under a microscope. A number of microscopic changes may occur, many of which are not serious, but if so-called dysplasia or overgrowth is present you may be asked to have repeat smears every six months. The dysplasia may constitute pre-cancerous change in the cells, and further investigations may be required.

By taking cervical smears every three years early changes can be detected and treated, and cancer of the cervix prevented. All women should have smears taken regularly until after the menopause.

Disorders of the ovaries and tubes
Cysts
Cysts in the ovaries may be connected with hormonal changes and ovulation, in which case they may come and go without treatment (though they may be painful at the time). Larger cysts may cause symptoms of internal pressure, requiring their removal. Cancer of the ovary is rare and usually occurs in older women; the treatment is surgical removal of the ovaries, and often the uterus as well.

Infections
Infections of the fallopian tubes (salpingitis) may cause low abdominal pain, often nausea and vaginal discharge, and sometimes bleeding. Infections tend to occur in sexually active women, but are provoked by childbirth, operations such as D & C or abortion, or the use of IUCDs. They may need long courses of antibiotics, and leave some residual discomfort.

Ectopic pregnancy
Tubal or ectopic pregnancy is a rare but serious condition where a fertilized egg remains in a fallopian tube, develops there instead of in the uterus, and may rupture into the abdominal cavity. It is commoner if the tubes or surrounding tissues have been scarred by infection (such as appendicitis or salpingitis). See also page 28.

Hysterectomy
This operation consists of surgical removal of the uterus through a cut low in the abdomen, or through the vagina, leaving no outer scar. The ovaries are usually left intact unless diseased, so apart from having no periods, a woman's hormonal and sexual make-up is not affected.

A hysterectomy is a major operation, and most women need about three months off work afterwards, in which they should avoid lifting heavy weights.

Male sexual anatomy

The sexual organs in men are the penis and testes, associated ducts and small glands. The penis consists of the body (the shaft) and the sensitive cap-shaped tip, the glans penis, which is protected by a fold of skin called the prepuce (foreskin). Inside the penis is spongy tissue which becomes hard and erect when engorged with blood during sexual arousal. Along the length of the penis runs a tube, the urethra, that carries both urine and seminal fluid to the opening at the tip of the penis. Ducts open into the urethra from the prostate gland, which lies at the base of the bladder and manufactures substances which sustain the sperm.

The sperm (spermatozoa) are continually manufactured in the testes, two egg-shaped glands suspended in a bag of skin, the scrotum, that hangs behind the penis. Seminal vesicles, two small pouches next to the prostate gland, store the sperm until they are either ejaculated or die and are reabsorbed into the body. About 20 million sperm are released in each ejaculation.

The testes are held away from the abdomen in the scrotum which thus keeps them cooler than the rest of the body, a lower temperature allowing optimal sperm production. The scrotum contains contractile muscles which draw the testes up out of the way if it is too cold, or if injury threatens.

Male sexual development

Sexual development in males usually begins between the ages of ten and twelve. Hormones secreted by the pituitary gland stimulate the testes to produce the male hormone testosterone, which causes male sexual characteristics to appear: body contours change to the adult form; hair grows around the genitals in the male pattern of a triangular shape growing up towards the navel; hair also appears in the armpits and later on the face; the penis and testes enlarge, and sperm are produced. In addition, the voice 'breaks', that is, it becomes deeper in pitch as the vocal chords thicken. These changes take place gradually, over five or more years; and by the age of eighteen most boys are sexually mature.

After puberty, men remain fertile for the rest of their life, unlike women, who at birth have all the eggs they will ever have; there is no physiological equivalent of the female menopause. Sperm production decreases with age but continues to some degree throughout life.

Disorders of the male sexual organs

Undescended testicles

The testicles develop inside the body and normally descend into the scrotum before birth. Sometimes one or both testes do not descend fully, and cannot be felt in the scrotum. In most cases they do eventually descend by the time the child is a few years old, but otherwise an operation to lower them into position can be carried out. Surgeons prefer to operate before school age to give the best result. Undescended testes are, in addition, more prone to cancer, which is otherwise very rare. (It is important to differentiate between true undescended testicles and retractile ones. Retraction is normal, and may be induced by touching the inner side of the thigh.)

Cancer of the testicle

The testes normally differ slightly in size or shape or position, but if one becomes larger or heavier, a doctor's advice should be sought, to make sure that it is not malignant. The main symptom of cancer of the testicle is a slowly growing, usually painless lump, and unless this is treated at an early stage by surgical removal of the affected testis the cancer cells can spread to the rest of the body. Since the disease is unlikely to spread to the other testis, this is normally left intact and potency and fertility are not affected.

Torsion of the testicle

Usually one testis hangs slightly lower and more horizontally than the other. Occasionally, perhaps as a result of injury or sudden effort, but often for no reason, this testicle can twist, causing severe pain. The scrotum then becomes swollen and tender, as blood cannot flow through the veins leading from the testicle. In many cases the torsion comes undone of its own accord, but even so it is essential to see your doctor without delay because the probem can recur. Immediate surgery will be necessary, to untwist the gland and stitch it in place so that it cannot twist again. Untreated, the affected gland may die and shrivel.

Hypospadias

If the penis fails to develop properly, the urethra may open on to the undersurface. In this condition, known as hypospadias, the penis becomes bowed in shape and is usually shorter than normal. The problem can usually be corrected by surgery.

Circumcision

Circumcision is an operation to remove the foreskin (prepuce), the retractable skin covering the glans penis. It is often performed for religious reasons, but may be required if the foreskin is too tight to be drawn back comfortably over the penis. The condition may cause a painful constriction of the erect penis, or prevent the passage of urine. It is usually not detected until after the age of about five, or even until adolescence, since very young boys normally have a tight foreskin.

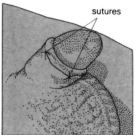

sutures

In circumcision, a simple operation in infants and young children, the foreskin is removed.

Right: the testes are packed with seminiferous tubules in which sperm are manufactured. When mature, sperm are released into the duct of the tubule and pass through the epididymis to the vas deferens. The head of the microscopic sperm contains the genetic material, and the body provides energy to drive the tail whose rhythmic beating enables the sperm to swim.

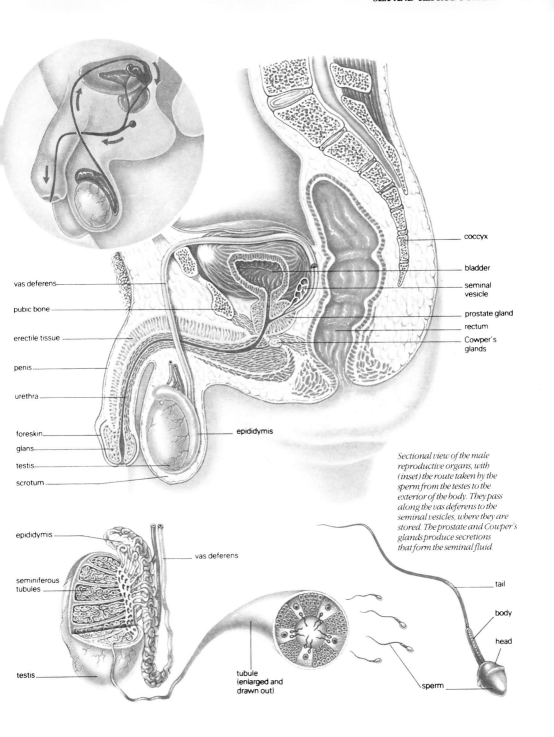

vas deferens

pubic bone

erectile tissue

penis

urethra

foreskin

glans

testis

scrotum

epididymis

coccyx

bladder

seminal
vesicle

prostate gland

rectum

Cowper's
glands

*Sectional view of the male
reproductive organs, with
(inset) the route taken by the
sperm from the testes to the
exterior of the body. They pass
along the vas deferens to the
seminal vesicles, where they are
stored. The prostate and Cowper's
glands produce secretions
that form the seminal fluid.*

epididymis

seminiferous
tubules

testis

vas deferens

tubule
(enlarged and
drawn out)

tail

body

head

sperm

Sexual reproduction

The biological aim of sexual intercourse is to continue the species and provide a wide variety of individuals. Every human body cell contains forty-six chromosomes, which contain genes specific to each individual. The thread-like chromosomes are arranged in pairs and one of the pairs carries the code for the person's sex. Women have two X-shaped chromosomes in each of their cells, while men have one X-shaped and one Y-shaped chromosome. The egg and sperm cells are formed from a parent cell which divides in half, so that sperm and egg cells each contain only half the usual number (twenty-three) of chromosomes. Sperm cells either have an X or a Y chromosome, whereas egg cells always carry an X chromosome.

After fertilization, the resulting zygote has the full set of forty-six chromosomes. Its sex depends on whether the sperm that fertilized the egg carried an X or a Y sex chromosome. After fertilization the new cell rapidly divides and forms a ball of cells which attaches itself to the uterine wall, and from this the fetus develops.

Abnormalities of chromosome division

Occasionally the 'original' division of the parent cell goes wrong and one or two of the chromosomes fails to divide. If the sex chromosomes fail to divide in the sperm-forming process, for example, one sperm will have both X and Y chromosomes and one will have none. The fertilized cell may then be XXY, XXX, Y only or X only. The Y-only cells are unable to divide and grow, but the others can. An X-only cell produces a baby with Turner's syndrome, who looks like a female but is short in stature and has no reproductive organs. Girls with XXX chromosomes are not much different from those with XX; those with XXY have Klinefelter's syndrome, appearing male but actually infertile because of poorly developed testicles.

If other chromosomes in the sperm or egg have failed to divide, the fertilized egg will have unevenly paired chromosomes which may mean that further development is impossible. This is the cause of many miscarriages in early pregnancy: in about a quarter of spontaneous miscarriages the fetus has some kind of chromosomal abnormality, compared to about two in every hundred induced abortions.

Down's Syndrome
Down's syndrome is one of the more common chromosomal abnormalities, affecting about one in a thousand live births. Its incidence rises sharply as maternal age increases, and about one in sixty births to mothers over forty results in a Down's baby. It is caused by the failure of the pair of number 21 chromosomes to divide, so that the fertilized cell has three number 21 chromosomes instead of two. For this reason, its technical name is trisomy 21. Physical characteristics of Down's syndrome include slanting eyes and a flat nose (which is why the disorder was formerly known as mongolism), abnormally mobile joints, a protruding tongue, short, stocky build, and an abnormal pattern of lines on the palms of the hands. Down's children are mentally handicapped to varying degrees and may also have heart, digestive tract and kidney abnormalities, but they are also loving, responsive and good-tempered.

Some people with Down's syndrome may eventually be capable of taking routine clerical and other simple jobs, while others may need help with such basic tasks as washing and dressing throughout their lives. They will always need a protective environment, either with a loving and supportive family or in a home for the mentally handicapped.

Genetic counselling

Many inherited diseases are caused by abnormal genes rather than chromosomal aberrations, and some become apparent only later in life. Families with a child or other relative with a genetic disorder may wish to know the likelihood of their passing on the condition to any subsequent children. First cousins who wish to have children together may also want to find out whether they carry any genetic disorder, as there is a higher rate of genetic and chromosomal abnormalities in the offspring of first cousins.

Common genetic disorders for which tests are available to determine carrier status (that is, whether a person, though healthy, carries a faulty gene) include sickle-cell anaemia, Tay-Sach's disease and thalassaemia. A couple requiring such information will usually be referred by their family doctor to a genetic counsellor who will carry out tests and calculate the risks of their having a child with the disease for which they are carriers. They will also be told about the severity of the disease, whether treatment is available, and any other information they need in order to make a decision. For example, a one in four chance means that for each pregnancy there is a risk of one in four that the baby will be affected, not that out of four children one would be affected. The risk of *any* baby being born with some kind of congenital abnormality is about one in forty.

Prospective parents will also be given the opportunity to discuss how they would feel if their child was a carrier like themselves, and, for certain sex-linked diseases, whether they would want to consider therapeutic termination of the pregnancy if the child was of the sex most likely to be affected by the disorder in question. (This applies to haemophilia: male children born to carriers have a fifty per cent chance of having the disease, while females have a fifty per cent chance of being carriers.)

Recent advances in prenatal diagnosis are making some of these decisions easier: some diseases can now be diagnosed early in pregnancy, by taking and analysing a specimen of the fluid surrounding the fetus (amniocentesis), or some tissue from the placenta. If the fetus is affected, the parents have the option of a therapeutic abortion; if it is not, they will have the peace of mind throughout the pregnancy that the child will not be affected.

Sexual intercourse

Sexual intercourse should be a pleasurable experience as well as the means of reproducing the species. Most people find it more enjoyable when combined with affection for their partner, and long relationships develop in which sex plays an important part, whether or not children are desired.

Sexual activity does not necessarily mean penetration of the vagina by the penis; it can take place without penetration or with penetration forming only one part of it. Foreplay, which helps build up excitement and arousal, means stroking and otherwise stimulating parts of the body in readiness for (but not necessarily preceding) full intercourse. Erogenous areas include the breasts, the ears, mouth, neck, insides of the thighs, and pubic and anal areas, but stroking or kissing any part of the body may be pleasurable. Oral sex is a part of foreplay that many people enjoy, and indeed it is important to realize that no part of sex is abnormal if it is enjoyed by both partners.

Sexual intercourse can take place when the man's penis is erect enough to penetrate the woman's vagina. If the woman is also aroused the vaginal opening widens and glands in the vagina secrete a lubricating fluid which makes penetration easier. Thrusting movements by both partners stimulate the penis and vagina, and the latter contracts. People vary in how long they take to come to orgasm, and if

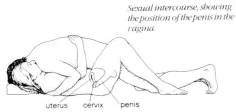

Sexual intercourse, showing the position of the penis in the vagina.

uterus   cervix   penis

one partner takes longer the other can learn to hold back so that orgasm is achieved together.

Positions during intercourse vary. The commonest is the so-called missionary position, whereby the woman lies on her back with the man on top of her. This is probably the most efficient way of introducing sperm high in the vagina when a couple wish to conceive.

Orgasm
Male orgasm is the ejaculation of sperm by muscular contractions of the seminal ducts and vesicles and penis. Female orgasm is experienced, together with uterine contractions, as muscular contractions either mainly in the clitoris or mainly in the vagina, or both, although the clitoris is the centre of maximum erotic sensitivity for most women.

It is normally intensely satisfying for both sexes. Unlike most men, many women do not always experience orgasm during sexual intercourse, for a number of complex social, physical and psychological reasons, not least the fact that many women take longer than men to reach the same level of excitement, and need more continuous stimulation.

After orgasm, people usually feel happy and pleasantly sleepy. Men need time after intercourse to build up their sperm supplies, so although they may be able to achieve erection soon afterwards, at least twenty minutes elapses before they are able to have another orgasm. Women, however, may find that they can experience several orgasms in quick succession.

Masturbation
Most people masturbate, especially during adolescence and at times when they are unable to have sexual intercourse with a partner. Many people achieve their first orgasm in

this way, and continue to find it an enjoyable method of achieving sexual satisfaction, with or without a partner.

Sexual problems
Most sexual problems arise as a result of sexual disharmony between partners: there may be different attitudes towards certain kinds of sexual activity, for example. Terms such as frigidity and impotence are vague terms, and to use such labels to describe sexual problems is not only meaningless but may be harmful. Given sympathy and understanding from a loving partner, most people can eventually overcome any difficulties. Simply talking about problems, either with one's partner or with a counsellor, may help to resolve them. Learning how to relax, changing sexual techniques, or simply improving a relationship by communicating more successfully can all lead to an improved sexual relationship. Stress and depression, which often occur after childbirth when a couple may be tired and have no time to relax and talk to each other, may also cause sexual difficulties to arise. Making the effort to be together in spite of all the demands on one's time is very important in sustaining a successful sexual relationship.

Fear of pregnancy may prevent a woman enjoying sex, and both partners should feel confident about their method of contraception. Common vaginal infections often cause soreness during intercourse, and if not treated may have a long-term adverse effect on sexual relationships as the woman subsequently tends to tense the vaginal muscles in anticipation of pain. Previous impotence in men, though cured, may also lead to loss of confidence in sexual ability.

For couples who are unable to resolve their sexual problems between themselves, counselling and therapy are available through hospitals, marriage guidance organizations and some family planning clinics.

Variations in sexual identity
A homosexual enjoys sex with a partner of the same gender; a lesbian is a female homosexual. Some people enjoy sex with both men and women, either together or separately, and either on a one-to-one basis or in groups. Similarly, transvestites are 'cross-dressers' who are stimulated by wearing clothes typical of the opposite sex; transsexuals wish to be physically members of the opposite sex.

All these variations on their own are (or should be) acceptable. Usually the greatest hurdle for someone whose sexual preference varies from the norm is other people's attitudes. When such variations produce deep emotional or psychological problems, there is often a place for some form of psychotherapy or psychosexual counselling. Some transsexuals insist on and obtain surgery to try and create the appearance of the opposite sex, and occasionally the results make the transsexual happier. However, in all these variations in sexual identity or preference, the watchword for everyone else should be tolerance.

Fertility
Most people take their fertility for granted, and a couple who decide to have a baby may be surprised when several months pass without a conception. In fact, one in ten couples has some difficulty in conceiving, although about

four out of five couples will have conceived after a year of regular unprotected intercourse. For conception to take place, several conditions must be fulfilled: the woman must be ovulating (see page 11); her fallopian tubes must allow the egg a clear passage through to the uterus; her partner's semen must contain plenty of normal spermatozoa; and the semen must be deposited close to the cervix at the time in the menstrual cycle when an egg has been released.

Obviously, the last condition is best achieved by the couple having regular frequent intercourse involving deep penetration of the vagina by the penis (see page 15). If the spermatozoa are deposited at the cervix during ejaculation, the distance they have to swim to reach the egg is reduced, and for the same reason, it helps if the woman stays in bed for at least an hour after intercourse.

Frequency of intercourse varies greatly between couples, and may be a factor in the ability to conceive: for most people intercourse two to three times a week is usually enough to ensure that conception occurs during the three or four days a month that the woman is fertile. Couples who are trying to conceive but who have intercourse only once or twice a month would have to time intercourse to co-incide with the fertile period. Most women show some physical sign that they have ovulated, the most obvious being a change in the cervical mucus (see page 22).

Sub-fertility
About ninety per cent of couples having intercourse without using contraception conceive within eighteen months; the other ten per cent are considered to be sub-fertile. This does not necessarily mean they will not be able to have a child together. It does mean that they would benefit from medical investigation, as about fifty per cent of infertile couples who seek help do eventually conceive.

Recent scientific advances have meant that it is now possible to remove a mature egg from an ovary, fertilize it with sperm in the laboratory and then return it to the uterus to continue its development. The minute embryo may even be frozen for a short time after fertilization.

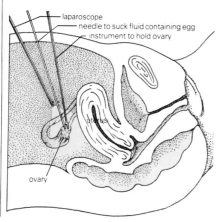

laparoscope
needle to suck fluid containing egg
instrument to hold ovary
uterus
ovary

Causes and treatment
Infertility in men may be caused by poor sperm production or obstruction of the route normally taken by sperm to the outside. Impaired sperm production may be due to the testes being at too high a temperature; and hot baths and tight-fitting underwear, particularly for men in sedentary jobs, should be avoided. As the sperm-production cycle takes about three months, however, such advice needs to be followed for a long time before any practical effect is likely. Male infertility may respond to hormone treatment or, if an anatomical abnormality is found obstructing the normal passage of sperm, to surgery. Some couples may be helped by artificial insemination by donor (AID).

Causes of infertility in women which are relatively easy to treat include spasm of the fallopian tubes, cervical narrowing, cervical mucus which is hostile to sperm, and fibroids. In ten to fifteen per cent of cases, infertility in women is caused by failure to ovulate, and in another twenty per cent by blocked fallopian tubes. Failure to ovulate can sometimes be corrected by hormone treatment, though such therapy can have side-effects, and may result in multiple pregnancies.

The commonest cause of blocked fallopian tubes is previous infection leading to the build-up of scar tissue, perhaps as a result of gonorrhoea, abortion, or using an intrauterine contraceptive device. It can sometimes be corrected by surgery, but the success rate is not high and better results have been obtained using the technique of *in vitro* fertilization. (*In vitro* is the Latin for 'in glass', another way of saying 'in the laboratory'.) This technique involves collecting the egg from its follicle in the ovary, using a needle and laparoscope under ultrasound guidance. The egg is fertilized in the laboratory using the partner's sperm, and replaced in the uterus, via the cervix. If all goes well, a normal pregnancy and birth will follow.

It has been found that, with this technique, the rate of implantation goes up if more than one embryo at a time is returned to the uterus. It is normally difficult to obtain more than one mature egg at a time, however, so hormonal drugs are used to induce 'superovulation' in which many eggs mature at the same time. Several can be fertilized and those that are not returned to the uterus on that occasion are, in some cases, frozen. This means that if a pregnancy does not become established immediately, more embryos can be thawed and returned to the uterus the following month.

Moral questions surrounding such recent advances in 'reproduction technology', as it is known, are now being raised. Some people are against fertilizing more than one egg at a time in the knowledge that some of them may never have the opportunity to develop; others wish to further medical knowledge by experimenting with the genetic material of the fertilized egg, in the hope of being able to prevent genetic diseases in future.

Sexually transmitted diseases
Anyone who thinks that they may have caught a sexually transmitted disease should seek medical advice urgently, preferably from a clinic specializing in the treatment of such infections. There is no need for a referral from one's general practitioner – just ring up and make an appoint-

ment. Clinics are usually found at local hospitals.

Clinic staff specialize in the diagnosis and treatment of genital infections and have laboratory facilities to hand. Patients are asked for a full history of their problems, and are given a comprehensive range of tests for all sexually transmitted diseases, in which samples are taken from the urethra, vagina and cervix or penis. Samples may also be taken from the throat and anus, if relevant, and blood and urine tests are carried out as well. The samples are examined under a microscope, and initial results may be obtained within half an hour or so. A second visit is usually needed after a week to find out the results of culture tests. Once the diagnosis is made, any drugs or medication prescribed are supplied there and then, free of charge.

Sexually transmitted diseases can be passed on through almost any kind of sexual activity, and it is important for people to avoid infecting others if they suspect they may have an infection. Equally, once they have had an infection diagnosed, they should inform all recent partners so that they too can be treated. In cases of gonorrhoea and syphilis, a clinic social worker may help in tracing previous contacts, vital when someone has had a symptomless infection for some time and may have unknowingly passed it on.

Gonorrhoea

Gonorrhoea, a bacterial infection caused by *Neisseria gonorrhoeae*, is one of the commoner sexually transmitted diseases: about one person in 1000 contracts it each year. It usually affects the urethra in men and the urethra and cervix in women. The rectum and throat may also be affected. It can also infect the eyes, especially those of infants born to infected mothers, unless precautions are taken.

Symptoms

The symptoms in heterosexual men, which appear within about a week or two of the infection being contracted, are a discharge of pus from the penis, and pain and burning on urination. The symptoms usually lead the sufferer to seek prompt medical treatment, but in about five to ten per cent of cases there are no symptoms at first, but the infection may progress to cause painful swelling of the epididymis. In homosexual men there may be a discharge of pus from the anus and pain during bowel movements.

As many as half of all infected women may have no symptoms. In the remainder there may be a slight vaginal discharge, and, less commonly, pain on urination. Rectal infection may occur in women even if anal intercourse has not taken place. Since a woman with gonorrhoea may not seek treatment because she has no symptoms, there is a risk that the infection will spread up the reproductive tract from the cervix to the fallopian tubes, and eventually cause sterility.

Treatment

Gonorrhoea is treated with antibiotics. It is important not to have any sexual contact until the infection has been successfully treated.

Syphilis

Syphilis is a potentially serious but rare disease caused by the bacterium *Treponema pallidum*. It affects about one person in 12,000 in any one year, ninety per cent of them

men, mainly homosexuals. The disease has three separate stages, the first two being highly contagious. As well as being transmitted through sexual contact, the infection can also pass through the placenta, causing congenital syphilis in an unborn child; but this no longer occurs in countries where antenatal screening is routine.

Symptoms

The first symptom is the appearance of a painless sore, or chancre, at the site of sexual contact, several weeks after exposure. In heterosexual men, the chancre is usually on the glans of the penis or inside the foreskin, though it may develop on the shaft of the penis. In homosexual men, the anus is the commonest site. In women, the chancre can occur on the vulva or cervix. Almost any mucous membrane can be affected, however, including the lips and mouth. The sore may not be noticed, and in any case disappears of its own accord within a few weeks.

About two months later the symptoms of the secondary stage appear: a pale, non-itchy rash develops, usually on the trunk but sometimes on the face and the palms of the hands and soles of the feet. There may also be a fever, swollen lymph glands, sore throat, headaches, nausea and possibly hair loss. Infectious ulcers (condylomata) often appear in the mouth or on the genitals. After several weeks the rash disappears spontaneously, and the disease enters a symptomless or dormant phase.

Tertiary syphilis, which appears up to twenty years later, may cause heart disease, brain damage, paralysis and personality deterioration or insanity. If cured in the primary or secondary stage, syphilis does not cause permanent damage, but tertiary syphilis can only be arrested and may ultimately prove fatal.

Treatment is with antibiotics, usually penicillin. Sexual relations should be avoided until the sufferer is cured.

Genital herpes

This is caused by the herpes simplex virus type II (HSVII) which is closely related to the virus HSVI which causes cold sores (see page 78) around the mouth. It behaves in a similar way, lying dormant after the primary attack, until reactivated by factors such as other infections, a rise in body temperature, immunosuppression or stress.

The first attack of genital herpes is always the most severe, with itching followed by painful ulcers on the penis in men and on the vulva in women. In women, there may also be severe pain on urination, sometimes leading to retention of urine, and the attack usually lasts about a fortnight. Secondary attacks are common, at variable intervals, although half of those affected suffer the condition only once. Recurrent attacks tend to be progressively milder and less frequent. Primary HSVII infection early in pregnancy may cause fetal abnormalities, and if the virus is active when the baby is due to be born, a Caesarean section may be performed so that the baby is not affected. Women who have had genital herpes should have regular cervical smears, as the infection may predispose to the development of cervical cancer.

There is no cure for genital herpes, though certain antiviral ointments appear to reduce the severity of attacks. To have any effect, these must be applied as soon as the first symptoms of pain or sensitivity in the skin develop.

Contraception

A wide choice of contraceptive methods is available, most of them for use by the woman. They are the means by which she can decide if and when she is going to become pregnant. The benefits and disadvantages of the different methods are outlined below.

Natural methods

The traditional ways of conception control are the 'safe period' and coitus interruptus, neither of which employs any artificial aids.

The safe period makes use of the fact that a woman's fertility is at its lowest in the first week or so after a period and immediately before the next one; intercourse is avoided at other times. There are three ways of calculating the safe period, one or all of which can be used (they are most effective used in combination). The calendar method involves finding the longest and shortest menstrual cycles over eight previous months, and using the chart (below) to find the fertile days of an average cycle. The temperature method involves measuring basal body temperature daily; the temperature drops and then rises for three days before ovulation. Intercourse is avoided at this time. The cervical mucus method depends on an awareness of the cyclical changes in vaginal secretions. On unsafe days the normally cloudy, sticky mucus becomes clearer, more abundant and slippery. Intercourse should be avoided as soon as the mucus changes in this way and for three days after its peak, until it becomes cloudy again.

Coitus interruptus is withdrawal of the penis from the vagina before ejaculation. It can be reasonably effective only if there is trust between partners, but has psychological disadvantages. This method also makes it impossible for the partners to enjoy simultaneous orgasm.

Advantages of natural methods are that there are no medical risks and they are inexpensive to use. Disadvantages are that they are not particularly effective when used alone, although some people use them for many years and limit their families successfully. They also curtail lovemaking more than any other method, and the safe period is complicated to use properly, particularly if cycles are irregular.

The sheath (condom)

A barrier method used by men, the thin rubber sheath is placed on the erect penis before penetration so that the sperm are contained in the tip. A new sheath should be used for each intercourse and should always be used with a spermicidal cream or jelly for added protection.

Advantages of the sheath are that it is effective if used correctly, it is readily available, and it is easy to use. There are no medical risks attached to its use apart from possible rare allergies to the rubber. Disadvantages are that it

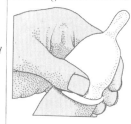

interferes with lovemaking to some extent, and some men find the loss of sensation it entails is too great, although this is minimized by the new thinner condoms available.

A sheath can only be put on once the penis is erect: air must be excluded from the teat, and the sheath unrolled along the length of the penis.

The diaphragm (cap)

A barrier method used by women, the diaphragm is a rubber dome with a flexible spring rim which is inserted into the vagina so that it covers the cervix and prevents sperm entering the uterus. The correct size of diaphragm is selected by a doctor who gives instruction in its correct use, which should be in conjunction with a spermicide. Once the technique is learned, most women find it easy to use.

Used correctly and checked regularly for fit and for holes, it is a very reliable method of birth control, equalling the

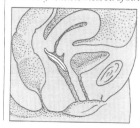

IUDC and mini-pill in efficiency. It poses no health risks apart from rare allergic reactions and can be inserted ahead of intercourse.

In its correct position, the diaphragm is tucked behind the pubic bone and covers the cervix completely.

Calculating the safe period

Finding the safe period by the calendar method involves taking the temperature every day, using a finely calibrated thermometer. Intercourse is relatively safe once the temperature has risen following ovulation.

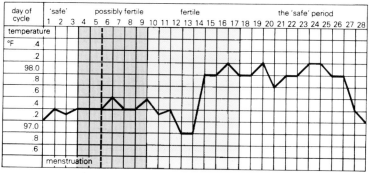

The coil (IUCD, IUD)

The intra-uterine contraceptive device (ICUD) is a small piece of moulded plastic inserted through the cervix into the uterus and left in place. Some devices contain copper which improves their efficiency; these should be changed every two to three years. Other types can be left in place indefinitely. Coils should be inserted and removed only by trained personnel (insertion may cause discomfort), and the wearer should regularly check that it is in place by feeling for the plastic string attached to it.

The coil is an effective contraceptive method, second only to the Pill. It does not interfere with lovemaking or hormone balance, but may cause heavy periods and bleeding between periods. Rare complications include perforation of the uterus and pelvic infection including salpingitis which may lead to infertility. Ectopic pregnancy is more common in coil users. About ten per cent of coils are accidentally expelled.

are at increased risk of these disorders, and should not use the pill. The mini-pill has fewer side-effects than the regular pill and can be used by women who are breast feeding since it does not affect milk secretion. In a small percentage of those who have been on the pill, fertility is delayed for several months, particularly in those whose periods were previously irregular.

A contraceptive pill packet.

Sterilization

Sterilization, the only permanent method of birth control, may be performed on both men and women. In men it involves cutting and tying the vas deferens (which transport sperm from the testicles to the penis) in a quick, simple, safe operation – vasectomy – done under local anaesthetic. Recovery is rapid and there is no change in hormone levels or libido. In women sterilization involves closing the fallopian tubes so that fertilization is impossible. It is usually done with a laparoscope, a telescopic device introduced into the abdominal cavity through tiny incisions, under an anaesthetic. It is a more complicated procedure than vasectomy, as it involves abdominal surgery and the small risk that this entails. While not 100 per cent effective, it is far more effective than any other method of birth control. Both male and female sterilization should be regarded as irreversible, since reversal, though occasionally successful, cannot be guaranteed.

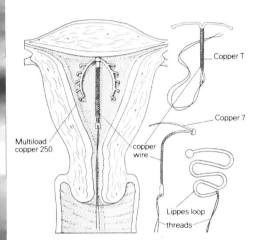

Different types of intrauterine contraceptive device, one shown in position in the uterus. The device is passed into the uterus via a narrow tube, and expands once it is in position.

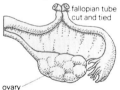

In male sterilization – vasectomy (right) – the vasa deferentia are cut and tied. In female sterilization (above) the fallopian tubes are cut and tied or sealed off by cauterization.

Oral contraceptives (the pill)

The most effective reversible method of contraception, the pill contains hormones that prevent ovulation (or, in the case of mini-pills, partially suppress it). The combined pill contains oestrogen and progestogen and is taken for three weeks out of four, the period occurring during the pill-free week. The mini-pill contains no oestrogen and is slightly less effective than the regular pill. It must be taken every day.

The pill gives the best chance of avoiding pregnancy of any reversible method, it does not interfere with lovemaking, and periods are light and painless. Side-effects may include nausea, bloating, weight gain and headaches, all of which may be overcome by changing the brand. More serious side-effects are rare, but may include high blood pressure, venous thrombosis, liver damage and severe depression. Women over thirty-five and those who smoke

The contraceptive sponge

This recently introduced device is a disposable sponge impregnated with spermicide, inserted into the vagina so that it expands to cover the cervix. The sponge can be bought over the counter like the sheath, and is inserted before intercourse like the diaphragm. Unlike the diaphragm, it does not need to be fitted by a doctor. Rarely, women may have problems with allergy to the spermicide, and it may be slightly less effective as a contraceptive than the diaphragm.

Prenatal Development and Birth

Each human being begins life as a fertilized egg, formed by the union of sperm and egg (ovum) at the moment of conception. This cell contains all the information required for its development into a highly complex human being. The process leading to conception starts at ovulation, when a minute egg is released from the surface of an ovary and passes into the fallopian tube nearest it. Spermatozoa which have entered the uterus following sexual intercourse swim upwards to enter the fallopian tubes, moving at a rate of about 3mm (⅒in) a minute. Of the many millions of spermatozoa reaching the ovum, only one will fertilize it.

As soon as the wall of the ovum has been penetrated by one sperm it immediately becomes impenetrable to others. The genetic material in the nuclei of the two cells then fuses. Fertilization usually occurs in one of the fallopian tubes; the fertilized egg then passes into the uterus, where it becomes embedded in the lining membrane and begins to develop until finally, after about thirty-eight weeks in the uterus, the child is fully developed and ready to be born.

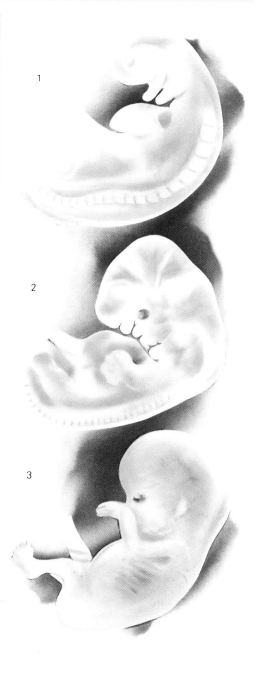

1

2

3

1 *Four weeks after conception, the embryo is about 6mm (¼in) long. It has a head and tail and a rudimentary brain, as well as a beating heart. Limb buds are just beginning to form.*

2 *Six weeks after conception, the 22mm (⅞in) embryo has rudimentary internal organs, and the eyes and ears are forming. Limb joints and facial features are recognizable.*

3 *Three weeks later, the fetus is recognizably human. About 50mm (2in) long, its head is large in relation to its limbs, and fingers and toes are still webbed.*

4 *After twelve weeks of pregnancy the uterus has enlarged so that it can be felt through the abdominal wall. The fetus is already moving, although the mother will not yet be aware of it.*

5 *By the twenty-eighth week of pregnancy the movements of the fetus are usually very noticeable, even from the outside. There is still enough room in the uterus to allow the fetus to move around.*

6 *By the fortieth week the baby is fully developed and ready to be born. Its head has usually settled into the pelvis, and its movements are less vigorous as it fills the uterus completely.*

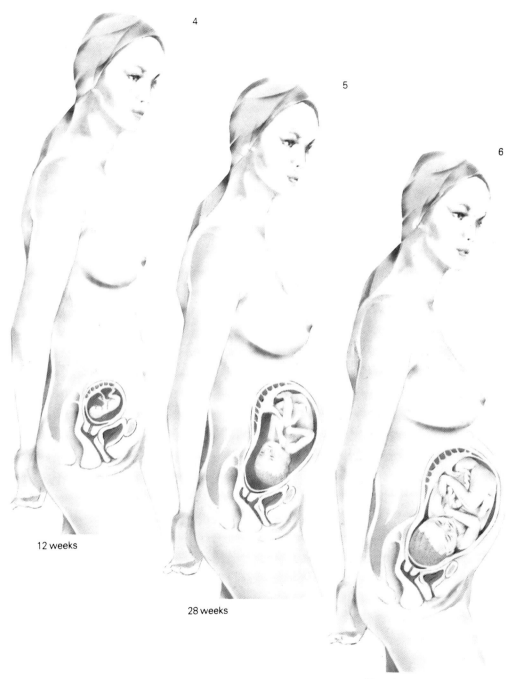

4

5

6

12 weeks

28 weeks

40 weeks

Development before birth

The first of the embryonic systems to become fully functional is the cardiovascular system (heart and blood vessels) for, without an efficient circulation, the embryo would be unable to obtain the food and oxygen it requires for growth. Essential substances are supplied to the embryo via the placenta and the maternal blood supply, but it requires its own efficient vascular system and heart in order to use them. The embryo's blood starts to circulate at the beginning of the fourth week after conception, and by the end of the eighth week all the other internal systems are established too. The umbilical cord is properly developed, and the eyes are beginning to appear. The embryo is now approximately 25mm (1in) long, and looks human.

During the third month, growth is still extremely rapid, and the fetus almost doubles in length. Throughout the fetal period the head is large and the body and legs relatively small. These proportions remain to some extent in the newborn baby. Early in the third month the eyelids develop and the rudiments of hair start to appear. By the end of the third month this hair has formed a very fine soft down called lanugo. The limbs, which first appeared in the embryonic stage as paddle-shaped protuberances – the limb buds – from the trunk are now recognizable as human arms and legs, and the finger- and toe-nails are beginning to appear.

The fetus floats in a bag of amniotic fluid enclosed in a membrane, and the uterine contents are sealed off by a plug of mucus in the cervix, so that the baby is contained within its own sterile, warm, shock-proof capsule. At first the embryo is nourished by the lining of the uterus, but by the third month the placenta has formed, and it transports oxygen and nourishment to the developing fetus, and carries waste products from the fetus back to the mother's bloodstream. The fetal and maternal bloodstreams are completely separate, kept apart within the placenta by a fine membrane which lets through dissolved gases, food and waste.

By the fourth month the length of the fetus, excluding the legs (as in a sitting position), is about 10cm (4in). The mother now becomes aware of the movements of the fetus for the first time. At five months the head and trunk measure about 12.5cm (5in) long, and the lower limbs are growing rapidly. From the seventh month onwards, the alveoli in the lungs (see pages 85-7) begin to develop, a process that continues even after birth.

At about the seventh month the baby usually turns round so that its head is pointing downwards. By this time, too, the mother will be feeling the baby's movements more and more strongly. Towards the end of pregnancy, particularly a first pregnancy, the baby's head descends into the pelvis, but sometimes the head does not 'engage' in the pelvis until labour starts. This is most common in second and subsequent pregnancies.

During the eighth and ninth months the hair on the head becomes more prominent than the lanugo, which gradually disappears. Fat continues to be laid down and growth is even more rapid. When the baby is ready to be born, it usually weighs about 3kg (7lb) and has an overall length of about 50cm (20in).

Twins and multiple births

Twins happen about once in 100 pregnancies. There are two types of twins: identical and fraternal. In identical twins, the ovum divides into two shortly after fertilization, and the two fetuses that result each carry identical genetic material, and are the same sex. If the ovum does not separate fully the result can be Siamese twins who are joined together at some point, though this is very rare. With fraternal twins, two separate ova are fertilized and develop individually in the uterus. Fraternal twins may be of different sexes and will have the similarities of any other brother or sister relationship.

Triplets, quadruplets and quintuplets are rarer than twins and commoner in women who have been given 'fertility' drugs because of difficulties in conceiving. Such multiple births may also result from 'test tube' fertilization when several fertilized eggs are returned to the uterus; usually not all the offspring of multiple births survive but as many as six have been known to do so.

The course of pregnancy
Early pregnancy

One of the first signs of pregnancy is a missed menstrual period. At that stage the embryo has probably been developing for only about two weeks, since conception is most likely around ovulation in mid-cycle, when a ripe ovum is released from the ovary. Pregnancies are therefore usually calculated from about fourteen days before the first missed period, and birth is expected 280 days (40 weeks) from the first day of the last period. Other signs of pregnancy are enlargement and tenderness of the breasts, and increased development of the small nodules on the surface of the areola (the brown skin around the nipple). Veins in the breasts may show through a fair skin. Some women experience nausea and vomiting in the early stages, and this may continue throughout the first three months. It is often relieved by food, and if it occurs in the early morning, one of the best treatments is a cup of tea and dry toast or crackers soon after waking and while still in bed. Early-evening nausea may be helped by resting in the afternoon. If nausea and vomiting persist after the first twelve weeks, or if they are severe, medical advice should be sought.

Various tests can be used to diagnose pregnancy. Most tests are based on the fact that the hormone human chorionic gonadotrophin (HCG), secreted by the placenta, can be detected in urine as early as the tenth day of gestation. However, for a reliable result, two to seven days should elapse after the date of the first missed period (that is, sixteen to twenty-one days of gestation). False results do, however, sometimes occur.

In the first few months of pregnancy some women feel tired, and may find that they need more rest. The body is undergoing enormous changes and first-time mothers also have to get used to the idea of having a baby. In addition, adjustments must be made by the prospective father and other relatives, which means that the expectant mother is caught up in the complications of changing relationships.

As the uterus enlarges it presses against the bladder – after even a few weeks of pregnancy you may need to urinate more frequently.

Mid-pregnancy

Women usually feel particularly well during pregnancy, especially during the fourth to eighth months. Eating a sensible diet, including vitamin-rich foods and extra iron, contributes to this sense of well-being and also benefits the skin, eyes, nails and hair. The skin stretches over the area where the baby lies and wherever extra fat deposits are being laid down, and this stretching of tissue may cause marks to form around the breasts, hips, buttocks, abdomen and thighs. Such stretch marks usually appear as reddish-purple streaks, eventually fading after childbirth to faint silvery lines. Creams said to prevent stretch marks probably do little good, though massaging cream or oil into the skin will help prevent the dry skin common in pregnancy.

Darker pigmented patches may appear on the face, making a kind of mask. This is thought to be caused by changed hormone levels in pregnancy, and disappears afterwards. The vulva, nipples, umbilicus, and the line down the middle of the abdomen (the linea nigra) also darken during pregnancy. These changes in pigmentation fade but do not disappear after delivery.

The 'bump' will not usually be obvious until the fourth or fifth month of pregnancy, and may not be noticeable till the sixth month. The waist expands first and, because tight waist-bands or belts can add to feelings of nausea, clothes should be loose and comfortable.

As weight distribution changes, the sense of balance is often affected. As the uterus grows heavier the posture must be altered, but it is easy to allow the small of the back to cave

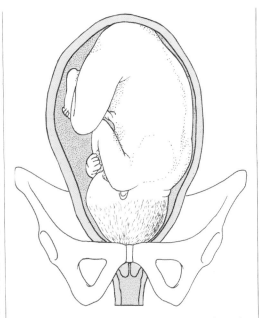

At about the thirty-sixth week of pregnancy in a woman having her first baby, the baby's head usually 'drops' into the pelvic cavity, and becomes 'engaged'. In subsequent pregnancies this does not usually happen until labour starts.

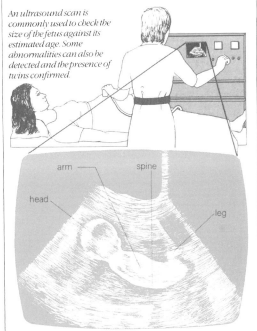

An ultrasound scan is commonly used to check the size of the fetus against its estimated age. Some abnormalities can also be detected and the presence of twins confirmed.

arm   spine

head

leg

in, the buttocks to stick out and the shoulders to be thrown back to balance the weight. The result is a leaning gait which can cause fatigue and strained muscles. If the buttocks are tucked in and care is taken to stand and walk with a straight back, there will be improved well-being and less fatigue.

The muscles of the floor of the pelvis – those around the vagina, urethra and anus – are important in pregnancy, both because they support the internal organs and because it is through them that the baby is born. Slackness of these muscles can cause backache, involuntary passing of urine during coughing or laughter, and a feeling that one's insides are dropping out. An expectant mother should learn how to contract these muscles so that they are strengthened and firm, not only to help maintain the correct posture but also so that she is aware enough of them to be able to relax them during childbirth.

Late pregnancy

Later in pregnancy the uterus extends upwards into the abdomen, gradually filling the abdominal cavity and pressing on other organs – particularly those of the digestive system – often causing indigestion and heartburn. At around thirty-six weeks, the uterus starts pressing on the diaphragm and lower ribs, resulting in shortness of breath and discomfort, particularly when sitting down.

When the baby's head is engaged towards the end of pregnancy breathing is easier, since the baby is no longer pressing against the ribcage and diaphragm, but there may be a feeling of having something hard between the legs, especially when sitting on a hard chair or standing for any length of time. There may also be a buzzing sensation at the top of the vagina, as the baby's head presses against the nerves in the pelvis.

It is safe to take one's usual exercise during pregnancy, but avoid becoming over-tired. Leisurely swimming and walking are both excellent exercise. Sitting still for any length of time can result in pelvic engorgement, as the circulation of blood in the pelvis and legs is restricted, so during long journeys, for example, change position frequently. Sexual intercourse during pregnancy is safe unless the doctor advises otherwise (as he or she may do if there is a history of miscarriage). In late pregnancy, an orgasm can set off contractions of the uterine muscles but these have no ill-effects and soon pass. At the very end of pregnancy, when the baby's head is low, intercourse may be uncomfortable in the conventional position and couples may find sex easier lying on their sides – either facing each other or with the man behind.

Once the head has engaged in the pelvis, most of the baby's kicking is felt at the top of the abdomen, with less vigorous movements coming from the arms below. Rolling movements of the baby's trunk, as it squirms from side to side, produce a wave-like movement across the abdomen. With a breech presentation, when the baby sits head-up in the uterus, most of the kicking is felt low down, and the hard round head is felt beneath the ribs.

Inside the uterus, the baby not only moves its limbs, but also sucks its thumb, uses its breathing muscles (although of course it takes into the lungs not air but amniotic fluid), swallows, and can even have hiccups. It responds to noise (including music), sometimes with a great deal of activity, and can hear its mother's heartbeat and other internal noises.

In the three or four weeks before the expected date of delivery (EDD) morale may be low, and the prospective mother may feel she has been pregnant for years, not months. Sleep may be restless and during the day backache, cramp and other vague aches and pains may occur. There may also be powerful and sometimes even painful contractions but unless they gradually become not only stronger but also longer and closer together, these are unlikely to mean the start of labour. In the few days before labour, the thighs, the area of the pubis and the small of the back may ache. It may be necessary to empty the bladder frequently, as the baby's head presses against it.

Antenatal care

For the sake of your own health and the baby's, it is essential to visit the doctor or antenatal clinic regularly, starting after the second period is missed, and then once a month until the last three months of pregnancy, when you may be examined every two weeks, and then every week. A physical examination, including measurement of blood pressure and blood and urine tests, is carried out. The position of the uterus and, later in pregnancy, the way the baby is lying, are determined by feeling through the mother's abdominal wall, and can also be seen using the technique of ultrasound scanning, where an image of the baby can be seen on a screen. After about twenty-four weeks the baby's heart can be heard with the fetal stethoscope (much earlier if ultrasound is used).

Nicotine and carbon monoxide (from smoking) are among the harmful substances that can cross the placenta. Though easier said than done, giving up smoking and avoiding drinking alcohol during pregnancy are advisable. It is also important not to take any drugs except under medical supervision.

Screening for fetal defects

Certain disorders such as Down's syndrome (see page 18), Tay-Sachs disease and spina bifida (see page 195) can be diagnosed in pregnancy. In the case of the latter an initial blood test may be followed by amniocentesis (see page 18) and by ultrasound (see above).

Problems during pregnancy

High blood pressure

In the later months of pregnancy, some women develop high blood pressure (hypertension), protein in the urine (proteinuria), and an excess of fluid in the tissues (oedema). It used to be thought that these symptoms were due to a toxic substance in the blood, hence the diagnosis of 'toxaemia' of pregnancy. Rarely, fits can follow these signs, and the term eclampsia is used to distinguish them from convulsions caused by other conditions such as epilepsy. For the diagnosis of pre-eclamptic toxaemia, at least two of the above three symptoms must be present. Other symptoms include headache, blurring of vision, a sensation of spots before the eyes, and nausea, which are all directly related to raised blood pressure.

Good antenatal supervision is vital for the prevention and alleviation of toxaemia. Treatment varies but above all bed-rest, if necessary in hospital and often with sedation, is essential. It may be necessary to induce labour prematurely, and in more severe cases Caesarean section may be considered. A woman with simple toxaemia of pregnancy returns to normal health within days of the birth. Similarly, once her baby has survived birth and the early days of life it will progress normally.

Hydatidiform mole

One rare disease which may give rise to pre-eclamptic toxaemia, or eclampsia, is hydatidiform mole. Normally, the fertilized ovum develops a network of tissue which eventually becomes the placenta; if the ovum dies but does not miscarry, the placenta continues to grow and develops into many small cysts, causing hydatidiform mole. This occurs in perhaps one in 2000 pregnancies, and must be removed to avoid the complications of infection and bleeding. Occasionally a mole develops into a malignant choriocarcinoma and a woman who has had a hydatidiform mole should be kept under observation for up to two years.

Ectopic pregnancy

This rare but serious complication occurs when the fertilized ovum develops in a fallopian tube instead of in the uterus. The tube will eventually rupture, causing severe pain and haemorrhage. Treatment involves surgically re-

Backache in pregnancy is a common problem, and may be relieved by this simple exercise: in the all-fours position, as shown, curve the back upwards several times from the straight-backed position, lowering your head at the same time. (Do not allow the small of the back to sag.)

Good posture in pregnancy means guarding against the tendency to lean backwards to compensate for the extra weight in front (as shown by the dotted line); keep the small of the back pushed out and the abdomen pulled in, the shoulders and jaw relaxed.

moving the affected tube; this does not necessarily affect the chances of a normal pregnancy in the future.

Placenta praevia

This condition, in which the placenta develops low down in the uterus rather than high up as is normal, occurs in about one in every 200 pregnancies. As the uterus stretches in late pregnancy, the placenta is pulled away from its original position and bright-red bleeding results. The diagnosis is confirmed by ultrasound, and the mother is usually advised to stay in hospital in case further bleeding develops. When a complete placenta praevia is present – one in which the placenta covers the cervix – delivery usually has to be by Caesarean section, to prevent damage to the placenta by the emerging baby, so depriving the baby of oxygen.

Miscarriage

A pregnancy that ends spontaneously before the 28th week is termed a miscarriage. As many as one in six pregnancies of up to twelve weeks' duration end in miscarriage. Probably the true figure is even higher than this, since miscarriages can occur before a woman is aware that she is pregnant. Early miscarriages are usually due to abnormality of the fetus; those that occur later in pregnancy may reflect a defect in the placenta or cervix. The first sign of miscarriage is usually vaginal bleeding, which may be heavy or slight. A 'threatened' miscarriage, which is often painless, is not uncommon in early pregnancy, but after a small amount of bleeding the pregnancy proceeds normally. Some miscarriages are inevitable, however, since the fetus has died in the uterus. The uterus will begin to contract and pain will be felt, perhaps for several days.

At the first sign of a possible miscarriage, tell your doctor and rest in bed. This may succeed in stopping any light bleeding, but nothing can be done medically to prevent an inevitable miscarriage. After a miscarriage, dilatation and curettage (D&C) may be necessary if any products of the pregnancy have been retained. In this minor operation, the cervix is dilated and the lining of the womb scraped.

A single miscarriage does not significantly affect a woman's chances of a successful subsequent pregnancy. However, repeated miscarriages usually require a gynaecologist to discover their cause.

Preparation for childbirth

Until relatively recently, women underwent virtually no preparation for childbirth. Until the late nineteenth century, few women would think of consulting a doctor before going into labour, and childbirth was regarded as too natural a process to warrant interference. Nowadays, in developed countries at least, it is rare for a woman not to have antenatal care.

Preparation for childbirth is extremely important, and includes regular antenatal examination so that the expectant mother goes into labour in the best possible state for having a healthy baby. In many countries, preparation classes are held for expectant mothers, where they can learn exactly what is happening to them during pregnancy and what will happen during childbirth. Care of the newborn baby is also covered, and the classes provide an opportunity to ask questions, as well as to meet other expectant mothers. Fathers are usually encouraged to attend as well. The prospect of childbirth can be frightening but knowledge of what is involved is a major factor in alleviating this fear.

Preparation for childbirth includes learning methods of relaxation to help to relieve tension and pain during labour, and special exercises that build up the muscles of the abdomen and pelvis involved in labour. The classes also teach special ways of breathing which can be used during labour to help control pain. The National Childbirth Trust in the UK is one organization that caters for such classes, as do most hospitals and local health clinics.

Labour and birth

Labour is divided into three stages. The first stage begins at the onset of labour, and lasts until the cervix (neck of the womb) has widened to its maximum of about 10cm (4in), at which point the baby's head can pass into the vagina. The second stage lasts from the full dilatation of the cervix till the birth of the baby, and the third stage follows between birth and expulsion of the placenta. The bag of fluid surrounding the baby may rupture at the start of labour, or may remain intact until labour is well established. This event is popularly known as the 'waters breaking'.

The first stage

The first stage is the longest part of labour, though its duration varies greatly. For someone having her first baby, it can last fifteen hours or more, but can be much shorter for women who have given birth before.

At the beginning of the first stage of labour, contractions are mild and may be twelve to fifteen minutes apart. They gradually become stronger and more frequent. In hospital, a midwife, nurse or doctor will ask for a brief history of the symptoms – how long and how often the contractions are coming, whether the waters have broken, etc. Blood pressure is measured and an abdominal examination performed to ascertain the position of the baby and the contractions felt with the hand. A stethoscope or ultrasonic device is used to listen to the baby's heartbeat and measure its rate. An enema or a suppository may be administered to empty the bowels and some of the pubic hair shaved for reasons of hygiene. (Until recently, these measures were routine practice in most hospitals, but it is now not always thought necessary, and the mother will in any case be asked for her consent.) Finally, a bath or (if the waters have broken) a shower may be taken. The woman in labour will probably be asked not to eat anything, in case an anaesthetic is needed later. After this, it is a matter of waiting as the first stage continues its course.

It is reassuring to have a close companion during labour, to provide moral support, as well as helping in more practical ways, such as massage or relaxation exercises. During the first stage, there will probably be little restriction on

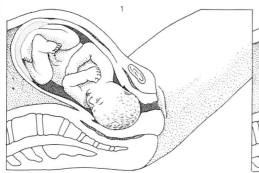

During the first stage of labour, the purpose of the contractions is to widen the cervix so that the baby can pass through it: the cervix and vagina together form the birth canal.

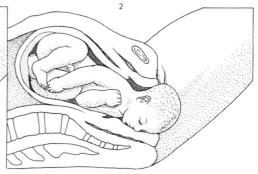

Crowning during the second stage of labour, the actual birth. At this point the top of the baby's head is visible, and the mother needs to push only very gently until the rest of the head is born.

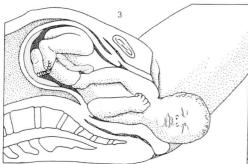

After the head has emerged, the birth of the rest of the body is usually simple, and may be aided by the midwife or doctor. Usually only a few more contractions are needed before the birth is over.

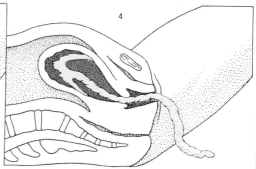

The third stage of labour involves the expulsion of the afterbirth, or placenta. This usually occurs about ten minutes after the birth, or sooner if an injection is given to make the uterus contract.

movements or position. Even if a fetal heart monitor has to be attached it may be a portable one, so that the woman can still lie on her side, kneel or walk around – whichever is most comfortable.

An examination is usually carried out from time to time to discover how widely the cervix is dilated. Vaginal examinations are kept to a minimum to avoid infection, and rectal examinations may be performed instead. A check will be kept on the baby's heartbeat, as this is a good indicator of the baby's condition. This may be done with an ear trumpet or stethoscope, or an ultrasound probe, and sometimes an electronic hearing device may be strapped to the mother's abdomen, which allows a permanent record to be kept of the baby's heart rate. If labour is likely to be complicated, a fetal heart monitor may be attached to the baby's head, and this will bleep with every heartbeat. In some hospitals, blood samples taken from the baby's scalp will be tested to discover whether the baby is getting enough oxygen.

Towards the end of the first stage of labour, the contractions occur about every two or three minutes, and may last for a good minute or so. A sedative may be given if the pains are severe. A change in the type of pain and an involuntary desire to push or 'bear down' usually indicates that the cervix is fully dilated, and that the second stage of labour has started or is about to start.

The second stage

The second stage is short compared with the first. Exactly how long varies greatly: in a woman having her first baby it is usually about an hour or so; in others it may be much shorter. Until the start of the second stage, it would have been pointless to try to bear down; now the urge to push down hard with each contraction intensifies and with each push the baby moves a little farther down the birth canal. Between contractions the mother can rest and conserve her energy. This stage is hard work, though not always thought of as painful.

It is important to find a comfortable position for the second stage, within the constraint that the midwife and doctor need to be able to see what is going on. Propped up in a semi-squatting position means that, unlike lying flat on her back, the woman is aided in the birth by the force of gravity. Some hospitals have reverted to using old-fashioned birthing couches or chairs which help maintain this kind of position. Other maternity centres encourage women to squat or kneel or adopt virtually any position in which they feel comfortable and confident.

By a combination of pushing with the abdominal muscles and uterine contractions, the baby's head is slowly forced down the birth canal until it becomes visible at the opening of the vagina. After a few contractions, the widest part of the baby's head appears. This is called 'crowning', when the top of the baby's skull is pushed out of the vagina, leaving the face still unborn. At this point the woman will be advised to stop pushing. Most midwives suggest that at this stage it is best to concentrate on taking small panting breaths, to prevent the urge to push. When the next contraction comes, the mother is normally asked to bear down very slightly and gently. This is in order to push the rest of the baby's head out slowly without damaging the vaginal tissues.

In the next minute or two, the doctor or midwife may help by holding the baby's head and then the shoulders and, when the next contraction comes, carefully guiding the infant's body out of the vagina. Often, the baby is placed on the mother's abdomen before the cord is cut, although it is quite common for the doctor to have to clean mucus and liquid out of the baby's respiratory passages before handing him or her to the mother. In twin deliveries, after the first child has been born there is a pause of five or ten minutes before contractions start again, and the second twin is often born after no more than half a dozen contractions.

Episiotomy

If the baby's head and shoulders are too large to pass through the mother's vagina without tearing the skin of the perineum, the area between the vagina and the anus, a small incision, known as an episiotomy, is made in the perineum. Where the baby is relatively small, the doctor or midwife can usually help ease the head and shoulders through the vagina in such a way as to avoid tears. The larger the baby, however, the greater is the risk of a tear.

Once an episiotomy is carried out the baby's head can advance rapidly, which usually shortens the second stage. The cut is so placed that it cannot extend to the rectum and thus avoids a perineal tear. Opinions are nevertheless divided as to whether this procedure should be performed except in very rare cases. It may be that a tear heals more quickly than an episiotomy. Episiotomies were routine in many hospitals until recently but mothers are now normally asked for their consent before one is performed.

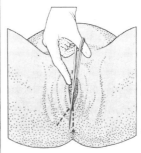

An episiotomy, in one of the positions shown, may be thought necessary to avoid tearing the perineum during the birth of the baby's head and shoulders.

The third stage

This involves the expulsion of the placenta, or afterbirth, from the womb. The umbilical cord from the placenta runs down through the vagina and is still connected to the baby.

Two clamps are placed on the cord which is then cut between them to prevent blood loss. There may be a return of contractions but these are milder than before. The midwife may help deliver the placenta and its membranes by pulling gently on the cord. The placenta and membranes will then be checked carefully to make sure they are complete, since any fragments retained in the womb could cause troublesome bleeding and necessitate a dilatation and curettage (D&C) postnatally (see page 14).

Sometimes the placenta does not readily separate (retained placenta). The doctor will then remove it manually, usually under a general anaesthetic.

Pain relief during childbirth

Drugs given to the mother during labour may pass to the baby and affect it after birth, so pain-relieving drugs and anaesthetics must therefore be used carefully. The drug pethidine is often given as a pain-reliever, but may cause drowsiness and nausea in the mother. The baby's breathing may be affected too. Towards the end of the first stage a mixture of the gases nitrous oxide and oxygen ('gas and air') can be inhaled by the mother through a face mask; this has no side-effects on baby or mother, although if taken in excess can also cause drowsiness and nausea.

Neither gas nor pethidine abolish pain completely. An alternative is an injection of local anaesthetic either by the epidural route, in the small of the back, or by the caudal route, in the lower end of the backbone. These anaesthetics often result in a completely painless labour but have the disadvantage that the muscles used to expel the baby may also be partly paralyzed, delaying delivery. Administering an epidural anaesthetic is a skilled procedure and, in the unlikely event that something should go wrong, there is a risk of permanent paralysis. Such a risk, small though it is, should be borne in mind by the mother when she is deciding which methods of pain relief she will accept.

Complications of childbirth

Forceps

Although most births are normal there may be complications. By far the most common procedure is the forceps-assisted delivery where, towards the end of the second stage of labour, some good reason arises for speeding the delivery of the baby; for example, prolonged labour may lead to signs of distress on the part of the mother or baby. The forceps, which have handles and a pair of blades curved to the shape of a baby's head, are slid into the vagina, one blade on each side of the baby's head, and used to pull the baby out of the birth canal. A local anaesthetic is given unless an epidural has been administered. Red marks may be seen on the baby's head as a result but these soon fade.

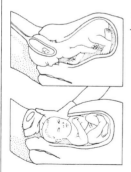

Delivery may be assisted by forceps, which fit neatly on either side of the baby's head and allow the doctor or midwife to guide the baby out.

In a Caesarean delivery the baby is delivered through an incision in the abdominal wall.

Ventouse

A similar process to forceps delivery involves applying a shallow metal suction cup, the ventouse, to the baby's head and pulling on it gently. This has the advantage that it can be used at an earlier stage of labour than forceps. The resulting swelling on the baby's head soon goes down.

Caesarean section

When it is unsafe or impossible for a baby to be born via the birth canal, an incision known as a Caesarean section is made in the abdomen and uterus through which the baby is delivered. This may be done either under general anaesthetic or with an epidural, which has the advantage that the mother is awake during delivery – although she is usually screened from the surgical procedure – and can hold her baby immediately afterwards.

A Caesarean section is a safe operation and may be elective, that is, agreed to by the mother and performed before labour begins, perhaps because the pelvis is not wide enough for the baby to pass through it or because of breech presentation (see below). Other reasons include severe pre-eclampsia or eclampsia or repeated haemorrhage. Emergency Caesarean section may be performed during labour because of haemorrhage or signs of distress in the baby, and in most cases of the condition known as 'placenta praevia' when the placenta is situated in front of the fetus and blocks the exit from the womb either partially or completely. A Caesarean will mean a longer stay in hospital, and it is important to do special postnatal exercises after having one.

Malpresentation

The most common position (presentation) of a baby just before birth is head down and facing the mother's back, and this is the easiest position for the baby to pass down the birth canal. In breech presentation, which occurs in about three per cent of deliveries, the baby is born buttocks or feet first instead of head first, and because the baby's head comes last it has to pass through the cervix quickly. Another type of malpresentation is called occipito posterior, when the baby's head is facing the mother's front instead of her back. Labour is likely to be more prolonged than with the most common, back-facing presentation. Most babies delivered in this way by a skilled obstetrician come through none the worse, but if there is any difficulty a Caesarean section may be performed.

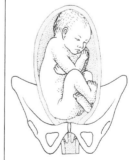

Breech presentation. It is sometimes possible for the doctor to turn the baby into the head-down position before birth, or it may be decided to deliver by Caesarean section. For breech delivery to be safe, the mother's pelvis must be wide enough to ensure that there will be no delay in the birth of the head since this could deprive the baby of oxygen.

Prematurity

Prematurity is another complication of childbirth. A baby is premature when labour starts after twenty-eight weeks' gestation but before the thirty-seventh week. The premature baby will usually survive but may have to be looked after in an incubator or in a neonatal intensive care unit (a ward specializing in the emergency care of very young babies). In this case, it is important for the parents to be with their child as much as possible, and to touch, hold, and help to feed him or her as far as is practicable. The weight of the baby is taken as indicating prematurity – 2.5kg (5½lb) or less – and this will include babies who are not premature but are small at birth. Disease in the mother, malformation of the uterus or twin pregnancy can all be causes of premature labour.

Induction
For some mothers, the problem may be not prematurity, but failure to go into labour at the expected time. In this case, if there is any risk to the baby's or the mother's health (maternal high blood pressure, for example) then labour is induced. The doctor will normally discuss this decision with the mother. Methods of inducing labour include inserting a vaginal pessary to 'ripen' the cervix, breaking the waters, or setting up a hormone 'drip' into the mother's bloodstream. All these procedures will usually set off contractions.

Postnatal problems
Many women experience problems of varying kinds and magnitude in the days immediately after childbirth. Some of these may be physical, some psychological. Adjusting to fast bodily changes after the physical trauma of childbirth, and coping with the demands of a new baby, make this one of the most stressful times in many women's lives. For some mothers, there is a definite 'let-down' after delivery. These feelings are very common and a talk with a sympathetic doctor, nurse or friend will often help resolve them. Some people do, however, suffer severe postnatal depression, and medical help may be necessary.

Physical illnesses that may develop during the weeks after giving birth (the puerperium) include postpartum haemorrhage, or PPH. This vaginal bleeding can occur at any time in the two weeks after delivery, or occasionally even later. The condition is potentially serious unless treated promptly, so it is important for the doctor or nurse to be informed immediately if any bleeding is noticed. Many women develop a slight fever after childbirth, and the causes must be sought and eliminated as rapidly as possible. Among the possible reasons for a high temperature is thrombosis in a leg vein and, although this is still a common condition, it is less common now that women are encouraged to get up and move around in the days following childbirth.

Birth defects
Simple tests are carried out on every newborn baby so that any congenital defects can be detected. There are several kinds of congenital defect, most of which are genetic in origin, but many conditions may have environmental causes such as disease, radiation and drugs. Most notorious is German measles, or rubella. If a mother-to-be contracts rubella during the first sixteen weeks of pregnancy, there may be resultant cataract, blindness, deafness and heart malformations in the infant. About thirty per cent of rubella-infected mothers bear defective children, and possibly as many as fifty per cent abort naturally. To safeguard against this infection, girls are now routinely vaccinated against rubella at school: women who did not have the benefit of this should ask their doctors for a blood test which will show if they are immune. If they are not, they can be vaccinated, but it is essential not to become pregnant for at least three months after vaccination.

Temporary breast enlargement occurs in about half of all newborn boys and girls, as a result of hormones from the mother crossing the placenta before birth. The degree of enlargement varies considerably. Sometimes a little milk (colostrum) comes out of the nipple. It is quite normal, however, and no treatment is required. Baby girls may also have a blood-stained vaginal discharge for a few days after the birth, due to withdrawal of the maternal hormones; this is also normal.

An umbilical hernia is a common birth defect, and requires no treatment; it is harmless and nearly always cures itself. On the other hand, inguinal hernias – in the groin – must be operated on when diagnosed because of the risk of later obstruction.

Women who smoke during pregnancy tend to bear children lighter than those born to non-smokers. Smoking is also associated with increased spontaneous abortion (miscarriage), stillbirth, or fetal death soon after birth. Even at the age of seven, the children of smokers may be smaller and their reading ability slightly below average. In one survey, 0.73 per cent of children of smokers were found to have congenital heart disease, compared to 0.47 per cent of children of non-smokers.

A stillborn baby is one born dead after the twenty-eighth week of pregnancy. (If the baby breathes at all, however briefly, he or she is said to be liveborn.) The parents, especially the mother, should be able to see and hold the dead baby, as this helps them to adjust to the bereavement.

Birth injuries
Several types of injury may occur during birth. Cephalhaematoma is a bruise over the skull which, although unsightly, is harmless. Forceps injuries are usually minor cuts on the face or scalp. The pressure of forceps blades may cause a temporary paralysis of the nerves of the face. Other nerve injuries may also occur, particularly to the nerves supplying the arm, but after a few weeks recovery is usually complete. Fractures of bones are uncommon; when they do occur, healing is usually rapid.

Brain injuries are among the most common, as well as the most serious, birth injuries. The baby's head is subjected to considerable stress as it passes down the birth canal, and the bones of the skull are constructed so that the head can change its shape by 'moulding' as is seen in virtually every newborn baby except those born by Caesarian section. The shape of the head returns to normal within a few days, but in some cases the stresses on the skull are such that internal bleeding occurs. If the injury is great, or if the haemorrhage is gross, the injury may prove fatal within hours but normally the injury is rather less severe. The baby may be born in a state of shock, known as white asphyxia, with shallow and weak respiration and limp, flaccid arms and legs. In mild cases, the infant is merely irritable.

Care of the newborn

Babies must be kept warm–but not too warm. Sweat rashes often occur as a result of overheating. On the other hand, hypothermia occurs in young babies who are not kept warm enough. The face and extremities go red, the baby becomes drowsy and goes off its food, and the temperature is found to be subnormal. An affected child must be warmed very slowly, under medical supervision, over a period of twenty-four to forty-eight hours, as sudden reheating may be fatal. There is a thirty per cent mortality rate in this condition.

Skin care

Care of the skin is important, and the baby should be bathed regularly, though not necessarily every day; on days a bath is missed, it is enough just to wash the face and genitals. On no account should a baby ever be left alone in the bath; many have tragically drowned when left for even half a minute. The hair should be washed regularly, but if the scalp becomes scurfy this can usually be treated by rubbing the scalp with olive oil or one per cent centrimide, an antiseptic detergent. Facial spots are common, perhaps due to the baby dribbling, lying with its face against a pillow, or bringing up milk which remains on the skin. A simple baby cream is usually sufficient to deal with the problem. Many newborn babies have whitish-yellow spots the size of pinheads on the face, particularly the nose; these are called milia, and are caused by blockage of the glands in the skin. No treatment is required. For a septic spot, dabbing with surgical spirit four or five times a day is usually sufficient. Spottiness on the body is probably due to a sweat rash.

Most babies get some degree of nappy (diaper) rash at some time. By far the most common form is ammonia dermatitis which is a diffuse reddening of the skin of the nappy area. The rash is caused by ammonia produced by bacteria acting on urine after it has been passed. It follows that the longer a wet nappy is left in contact with the skin, the more likely a rash is to develop. As young babies are likely to pass urine about twenty-four times a day, no parent can change the baby sufficiently frequently to prevent the skin being exposed to urine some of the time, so sensitive babies frequently have the condition (while others seem immune). Numerous skin creams and lotions deal effectively with the complaint, and there are various brands of disposable nappy with special linings which keep a baby's skin dry, and liners for ordinary terry nappies that allow the urine to pass through them so that the material next to the skin remains dry.

The baby's nails must be kept clean and short, otherwise they may infect the skin when the baby scratches. Finally, every care must be taken to avoid sunburn by exposure to sunlight for long periods.

Minor problems

In the first few weeks of life babies sneeze frequently, but this is normal and does not necessarily indicate a cold. They often hiccup after a feed, though this does not mean indigestion. The nose may get blocked, and this is best dealt with by cleaning with moistened buds of cotton wool. There

is no need to worry about tongue tie: the fold of tissue under the tongue is attached near the tip of the tongue in young babies, but the tip itself grows forward as the baby gets older. Sometimes there is also a fold of tissue under the upper lip – the alveolar frenum – which may be attached to the gum margin, and if necessary a dental surgeon may perform a minor operation on it when the child is six or seven.

About one baby in 2000 is born with a tooth or teeth, but usually the first tooth appears at about six months. Teething is a natural process, and does not cause a rash, fever or convulsions, as is often thought, though it may cause red gums and irritability. The eyes of the newborn baby may water because the tear ducts have not opened completely, but they almost always open in a few weeks without treatment.

A programme of immunization against infectious diseases should be started during the baby's first year, when vaccine is given against diptheria, pertussis (whooping cough), tetanus and polio. The possible risks of whooping cough vaccine have been widely debated, but the risks of the disease are generally thought greater than the risks of the vaccine. However, children with a history of fits or convulsions should not receive this vaccine; nor should a child with fever or other illness be vaccinated until it has passed.

Feeding babies and infants

For the first few months of life, babies need only milk – either breast milk or a special preparation, usually modified cow's milk. Solid foods are gradually introduced until the infant is eating a diet very similar to that of its parents (minus sugar and salt) by the time it is a year old.

Breast-feeding and bottle-feeding both have advantages and disadvantages, and much depends on the needs of both mother and child. Most doctors would nowadays support the slogan 'breast is best', although breast-feeding may take some time to establish successfully and may be inconvenient for mothers who wish to return to work soon after the birth.

Breast-feeding

Changes in the breast occur during pregnancy but the secretion of milk does not begin until after birth. The beginning of lactation coincides with the end of pregnancy as a result of the high level of hormones associated with reproduction, particularly prolactin which is secreted by the pituitary gland. The first fluid produced by the breast after birth, colostrum, is rich in vitamins A and E, in proteins, and in antibodies which help protect the baby from infection during the first days of life. Colostrum is produced for about four days after birth, until milk production takes over.

Milk is made in the glands of the breasts, and production continues until it is inhibited by a build-up of pressure from the stored milk. To relieve this pressure and maintain lactation, the milk must be fed to the baby and this only happens when there is a 'let-down' of milk in response to the baby sucking the nipple. This stimulus causes the release of oxytocin, another pituitary hormone, into the blood, which in turn causes the milk to be forced to the nipple. This 'let-down' reflex often occurs when a mother hears the baby cry in anticipation of being fed.

The production of sufficient milk is essential for good breast-feeding. The best results are achieved when feeding takes place frequently, as there is then less interruption of milk production. Infants who are given milk whenever they demand it will build up the milk supply to match their needs, and gain weight rapidly. Only about four per cent of women produce too little milk at the beginning of lactation, although older women breast-feeding for the first time generally produce less milk than younger women. Successful breast-feeding is also determined by several other factors. Undoubtedly the most important is the attitude of the mother and those around her. Hospital and nursing staff and health visitors will help with sympathetic advice and encouragement. The flow of milk can be affected if the mother is tense or physically or emotionally disturbed.

The main problems with breast-feeding include cracked, sore or inverted nipples, engorged breasts and blocked ducts. It is important to keep the nipples clean and dry and to avoid using irritating substances on them, such as soap. Swelling and tenderness may be relieved by expressing milk manually and feeding the baby more frequently.

Some drugs may affect lactation, and all forms of medication should be avoided during nursing if possible. Where drug treatment is necessary, the doctor will be able to advise on which are safe.

Sexual intercourse does not affect lactation and there is no reason to refrain from sexual activity as soon as the mother has recovered from the birth. But it must be remembered that a woman can conceive while breast-feeding; although it is true that lactation delays menstruation, ovulation (egg release from the ovary) can occur before the first period after the birth. It is usually preferable for contraception other than the oral contraceptive to be used, as the oestrogen in the combined oestrogen-progestogen pill suppresses lactation. If oral contraception is preferred, a progestogen-only 'mini-pill' should be used. If a further pregnancy does occur during lactation, it will not affect the quality or quantity of the milk.

Bottle-feeding

A wide range of manufactured baby milk is available. Almost all brands are modified cow's milk, either heat-dried to a powder or reduced in volume by evaporation. Cow's milk is modified to make it more like breast milk, which contains less milk protein (casein) and more milk sugar (lactose), and only this sort is suitable for a very young baby. When reconstituted with boiled water, most brands of dried or evaporated milk have about twenty calories per 30 ml (1 fl oz), which is roughly the same as breast milk. Provided that the makers' instructions are exactly followed when dried or evaporated milk is made up, the baby will usually thrive on any reputable brand. It is essential that all utensils and bottles used in the preparation of feeds are kept sterile with a non-poisonous disinfectant (usually a hypochlorite).

Useful guidelines about how much milk to give in the early weeks are supplied by the manufacturers of baby milk, but it is important to remember that babies are individuals with different needs, some of whom will be content with more, and others with less, than the recommended amounts. A healthy baby will usually need 150 ml of breast or reconstituted milk per kg (about 2½ fl oz per lb) of body weight per day during the first five months. No baby should be encouraged to take more than it wants as this can cause obesity. After the first two weeks of life, the expected weight of babies can be calculated by knowing that they put on about 175 g (6 oz) per week for the first five months. If, because of illness, weight gain has been delayed, the baby should still be offered enough to satisfy expected needs as if the weight gain has continued uninterrupted. This will help to regain the lost weight.

Since every baby is different, the best system of feeding is often found by trial and error. Rather than trying to adhere to fixed feeding times it is better to feed the baby when he or she wants to be fed. The baby will eventually settle into a routine, asking for a feed every two or three hours in the initial few weeks. After that, four-hourly feeds will probably be sufficient.

When they are between four and six weeks old, babies may be given small supplements of vitamins C, A and D, either as drops or in the form of fruit juice (C) and cod liver oil (A and D). It is important not to exceed the recommended dose of vitamins A and D since they are stored in the body; babies should not receive more than 400 units of vitamin D per day from all sources. Most dried milk powders contain added vitamin D.

Mixed feeding

For up to six months, breast milk alone supplies all the baby's nutritional needs, but mixed feeds can be introduced as early as the third month, if the baby seems to need them.

It is usual to start mixed feeding with small quantities of puréed fruit, vegetables, or precooked cereal and milk at one of the feeds, gradually increasing the amounts until by about five or six months the food can be given at two out of three daytime feeds. Milk only is still given in the early morning and late in the evening, until the number of milk feeds is reduced to three or four per day by six to eight months. It is usual to wait until the baby is six months old before changing from breast or bottle milk to cow's milk. If cow's milk is given at too early an age, health problems such as allergies may arise in later childhood. In families where some members have allergies the health centre or clinic can advise about avoiding cow's milk preparations.

Between about six and eight months, the baby may gradually be integrated into family mealtimes. Most plainly cooked foods can be given, and with adjustments the best mixtures of purees for the individual baby can be found. Introducing a new food every few days will identify any food that upsets the baby. Obviously, it is important to give a balanced diet with the right proportions of carbohydrates, protein, fat and vitamins. Babies should not be given fried food, highly spiced or salted food. There are several brands of manufactured baby food, made with advice from nutritionists. They may taste very bland to adults because no salt is added to them, but they should be given just as they are.

At home with a new baby

The first few weeks at home with a new baby can be the most difficult time of a mother's life. Frequent periods of physical tiredness combined with the emotional turmoil that often arises in this novel situation can make the practical problems of caring for a new baby as well as running a household seem insurmountable. During this period it is important to make as few extra demands on yourself as possible; by accepting help with chores from family and friends, by making sure that you have adequate rest, even if this means forgetting housework or putting off visitors, and by having regular nourishing meals, you will be better able to attend to the baby in a relaxed, happy state. No two babies are alike, and it is only through observation and experience that you can begin to get to know your baby's own particular needs and rhythm. Take things as they come for a while, and bear in mind that the problems and worries you have at first will quickly become easier to deal with, as you and your baby get to know one another, and adapt to each other and to your life together.

Babies should be bathed regularly, though not necessarily every day. On the days that they do not have a bath, they can be 'topped and tailed'. This means washing the face with water-soaked cotton wool, paying particular attention to the eyes which should also be wiped with damp cotton wool, a new piece for each eye. The bottom should then be washed in the same way and dried carefully. Baby powder is optional; make sure that the skin is quite dry before applying it.

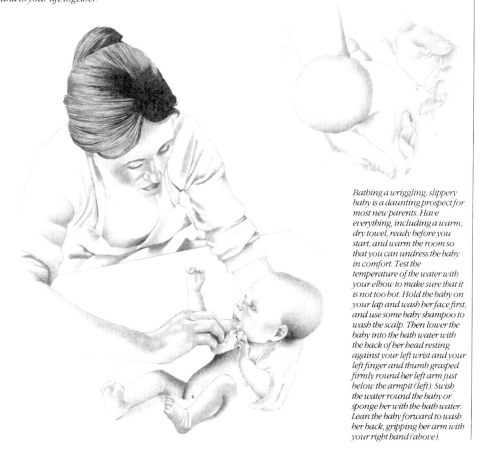

Bathing a wriggling, slippery baby is a daunting prospect for most new parents. Have everything, including a warm, dry towel, ready before you start, and warm the room so that you can undress the baby in comfort. Test the temperature of the water with your elbow to make sure that it is not too hot. Hold the baby on your lap and wash her face first, and use some baby shampoo to wash the scalp. Then lower the baby into the bath water with the back of her head resting against your left wrist and your left finger and thumb grasped firmly round her left arm just below the armpit (left). Swish the water round the baby or sponge her with the bath water. Lean the baby forward to wash her back, gripping her arm with your right hand (above).

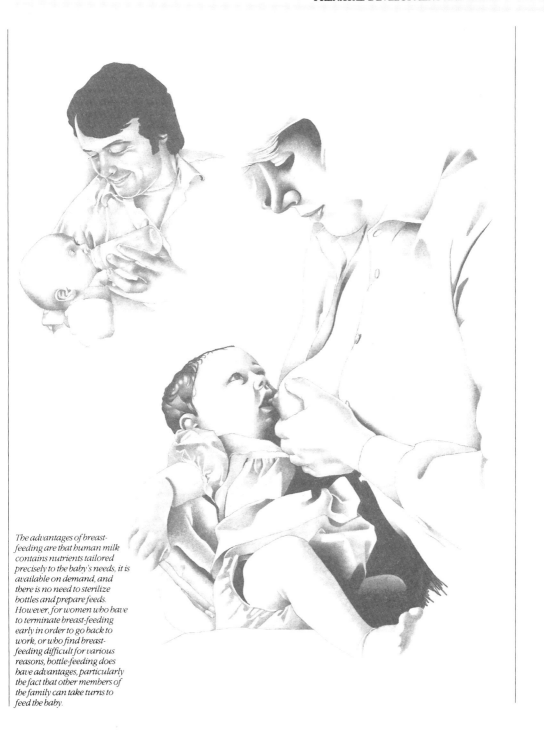

The advantages of breast-feeding are that human milk contains nutrients tailored precisely to the baby's needs, it is available on demand, and there is no need to sterilize bottles and prepare feeds. However, for women who have to terminate breast-feeding early in order to go back to work, or who find breast-feeding difficult for various reasons, bottle-feeding does have advantages, particularly the fact that other members of the family can take turns to feed the baby.

Growth

Growth of the human body begins at
conception, and continues until the end of
adolescence. After that time, the skeleton will
still grow by about two per cent, and all parts
of the body change and develop – or
sometimes regress – until the end of life.
Taking an average of all the cell divisions in
the body, the fertilized egg divides about
forty-four times before birth; but only about
four more times between birth and
adulthood.

*A child's rate of growth and eventual height depend on many
factors, from a good diet and happy family life to the heights of his
or her parents. Children do not usually grow steadily: they grow in
spurts, and one of the most noticeable is that which takes place
around puberty (at age ten or eleven in girls, and two or
three years later in boys). At this time pubic hair
appears, followed, in girls, by breast development
and the first period and, in boys, by the
growth of the penis and testicles and the
ability to ejaculate. By the age
of eighteen differences in body
shape are obvious: women have
wider hips and more
subcutaneous fat; men have
wider shoulders and are
more muscular.*

nine months   two years   nine to ten years

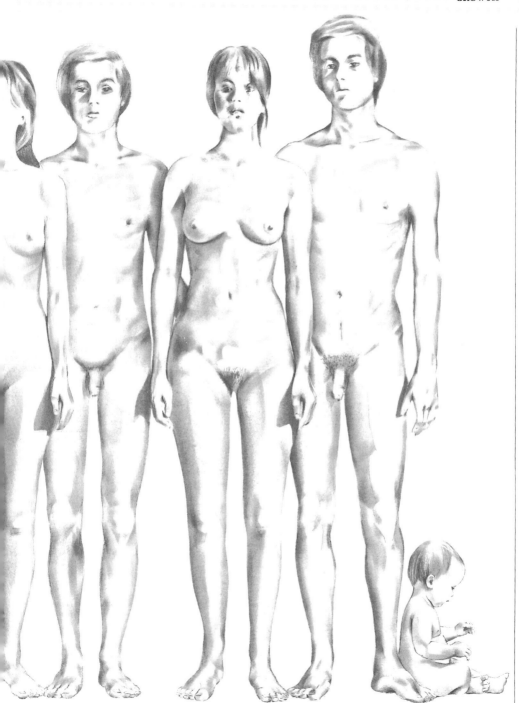

fourteen years   eighteen years   six months

Recording growth

One obvious way of recording growth is to plot height against the age of a child; this produces a gradually rising curve with some uneven parts. Another, and more interesting, chart is one showing the increase in the height of a child from one age to the next. The first type of graph shows the stage at which a child is, while the second type shows how fast he or she is growing, or the rate of growth.

After about four years of age the rate of height gain decreases rapidly and becomes more or less steady until adolescence. Then there is a rapid increase in height until the peak of the adolescent growth spurt, when height is increasing as fast as it was at the age of two. After this point, growth gradually slows down until it stops at between the ages of about sixteen and eighteen.

The type of information obtained by measuring a child on different occasions is called longitudinal. Other information can be learned by measuring many children on one occasion only and repeating this for different ages; this is called cross-sectional. If one hundred children of the same age were measured and arranged in order of height, there would be a height with fifty children above it and fifty below it. This height is called the fiftieth centile for this age. By measuring many children at different ages a series of fiftieth centile heights may be obtained over the whole growing period and an average growth curve drawn. To find out if a child is growing normally, several measurements at different times are needed. A child's position on the growth curve depends mainly on genes inherited from the parents, but is also influenced by the individual's own rate of development. There is nothing abnormal in being a late or an early developer: everyone is different and no one is average. Nevertheless, a striking feature of human growth is its regularity. Most children follow a remarkably constant and similar course, not only in height but also in all features of the body. Although all diseases slow down growth, even if only for a short time, the child soon catches up unless the disease is lasting and severe.

Patterns of growth

Almost all organs show a pattern of growth similar to that of height, but certain organs grow more rapidly at certain times. The brain, for example, is almost fully grown by the time a child is three or four, while the reproductive organs grow only slowly before puberty and much faster during adolescence. These are the extremes of development and most parts of the body grow at an intermediate rate. For example, fat beneath the skin begins to appear in the fetus at about five or six months after conception and the amount rapidly increases until the end of the first year of life. Then, until adolescence, there is a slight loss of fat in both sexes. In adolescence the average boy loses fat, although there may be a rapid increase just before adoles-

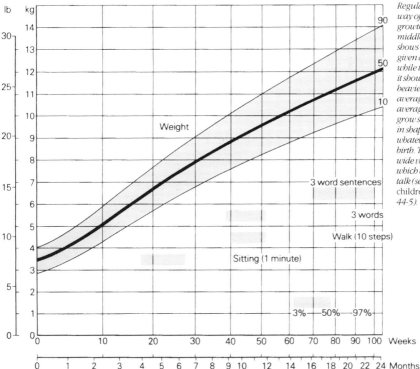

Regular weighing is a simple way of checking on a baby's growth and development. The middle curve on this graph shows the average weight at a given age, or fiftieth centile, while the ones above and below it show the growth curves for heavier and lighter-than-average babies. No baby is average, of course, but should grow steadily in a curve similar in shape to those shown, whatever his or her weight at birth. The chart also shows the wide variation in the age at which babies first sit, walk and talk (see also Milestones in children's development, pages 44-5).

cence, resulting in obesity ('puppy fat'). Girls tend to lose less fat in childhood and normally gain fat in adolescence. The average woman has more fat tissue than the average man.

Although growth of the skeleton is almost complete by the end of adolescence, fat continues to be laid down during the middle years of life – a possible reason for 'middle-aged spread'. This phenomenon, which is due to more fat being packed into existing fat cells rather than new fat cells being formed, stops later, and during old age there is a gradual loss of fat.

Some children grow rapidly from birth and stop growing early, while others take much longer to complete their growth. Similar variations may occur in intellectual growth. The idea, therefore, that a child's growth can be categorized by his or her chronological age is clearly wrong and the concept of developmental age has therefore been established as a measure that can be used throughout the whole period of growth.

Developmental age

There are four ways of arriving at a child's developmental age: by assessing skeletal age, dental age, size or shape age, and secondary sex character age. The last, based on the appearance of pubic hair and changes in the reproductive organs, is useful only after puberty. Dental age has the opposite disadvantage: it is only useful before puberty, because by that time nearly all the teeth have erupted.

Most people subconsciously use size or shape age as a guide to developmental age. The use of shape as a guide is subtle, since it is based on the change in the proportions of the body. In a baby there is proportionally a large head, long body and short legs, while in an adult body and leg length are approximately equal and the head is proportionally much smaller. The main difficulty in applying these changes is in defining shape accurately.

infant   5-6 years   18 years

Bone age is a closer indication of physical maturity than height, and an X-ray can provide reassuring evidence that a slow developer has not yet finished growing.

Skeletal age is the most commonly used indicator of physical maturity. It is possible to study an X-ray of one part, a hand, for example, and then to make an informed judgment about the whole skeleton. An individual will not grow after the bones are fully mature. There is a marked difference in the rate at which the skeletons of boys and girls progress to maturity: the average girl passes through the various stages of bone development one or two years ahead of the average boy, and the average woman is shorter than the average man by about 12 cm (5 in). The height of a child at any one time does not show how far he or she has progressed to maturity, because in a fast-maturing child the bones are advanced for the age and less time will be needed for growth than for a slowly developing child, who will enter puberty later and continue to grow for longer. By using special tables, however, it is possible to predict, from

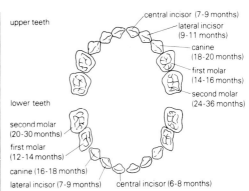

upper teeth

central incisor (7-9 months)
lateral incisor (9-11 months)
canine (18-20 months)
first molar (14-16 months)
second molar (24-36 months)

lower teeth

second molar (20-30 months)
first molar (12-14 months)
canine (16-18 months)
lateral incisor (7-9 months)   central incisor (6-8 months)

The milk (first) teeth, and the average ages at which they appear.

the skeletal age, what part of a child's growth has passed and what the final height will be. For children over five years old, these predictions are accurate to within 5 cm (2 in) in ninety-five per cent of cases and they can be used, for example, to predict the height of children who enter ballet schools.

Many educational systems are based on the division of children by their chronological age and, although intellectual development is less tied to skeletal age than other types of growth, there is evidence that children maturing early have a higher score in intelligence tests than later-maturing children of the same age, even though, when finally mature, their ratings may be the same.

Factors affecting growth

Many factors affect growth, of which some of the most important are heredity, the time of year, nutrition, the state of health or disease, emotional factors, and the so-called 'secular' trend – the changing trend in growth rates over the years.

Genetics

Tall parents tend to have tall children, and these children are taller at all stages of growth. Genetic influences occur not only in height but also in, for example, skeletal maturity, and there is in addition a strong link between the age at which menstruation starts (menarche) in mothers and daughters, in sisters and, particularly, in identical twins. The relationship between the height of parents and their children is much stronger than that for weight, which is often influenced by environmental factors. Although genetics plays a part in the growth of some other organs, not all growth is genetically controlled.

The seasons

Children tend to grow more in the spring, although they put on weight mainly in the winter months. The speed of height increase in spring is about twice what it is in winter, although this varies a great deal from child to child. It appears that the length and strength of daylight is an important factor in these seasonal variations in height increase.

Seasonal changes in weight are probably caused by different patterns of activity and eating.

It is unlikely that climate has any effect on growth or development. For example, there is evidence that climate has no effect on the age at which the menarche occurs: girls in Alaska and Nigeria start to menstruate at the same average age (although see *Secular trends*, below).

Nutrition

Malnutrition may either delay or have a permanent effect on growth, depending on when it occurs and how severe it is. If it occurs before adolescence it may delay the beginning of puberty. The long-term effects of malnutrition in the period immediately after birth are not fully understood. Children who are overfed in the early months of life, on the other hand, may remain permanently heavier than other children and their chance of being obese later in childhood and as adults is much higher. Such children are taller than average at this early stage, and have advanced skeletal maturation. Consequently, the final height of obese children is the same as, or even slightly less than, that which might be predicted.

Although adequate nutrition is necessary for normal growth, over-nutrition is not a way of improving it and brings all the disadvantages of obesity, including physical and emotional problems in childhood, and illness and earlier death in adult life.

Illness

The effect of illness on growth depends on how the disease affects skeletal maturation. If the development of the bones is affected as much as the growth in height, then the final height after recovery and catching up is likely to be normal. However, if skeletal maturation continues during the illness while the growth in height has stopped, then the child will not grow as tall as he or she would otherwise have done.

Emotional factors

As well as good health and adequate nutrition, a child needs a stable emotional environment in order to grow normally. A study of nutrition and growth in Germany just after the Second World War found that children in one institution, where the food was good, grew less well than others in a home with poorer food. The first institution was run by a matron who made the children's lives a misery, and they failed to grow as well as the others, despite the better food. Some children, then, fail to grow because relationships in their family or surroundings are unstable or unhappy. In some cases this is because the growth hormones are not produced. When the child is removed to a better environment, these hormones are produced again and the lost growth is recovered.

Studies have shown that children from the most privileged social classes grow faster and are taller than children from lower social classes. The reasons for this difference include better nutrition and housing; regular meals and parental care are probably also important. Another factor may be that lower-income families tend to be larger than higher-income ones so that each child receives less attention from its parents.

Secular trends

A secular trend is one occurring over a long period of time: in the last 130 years, for example, the age at which puberty is reached has decreased and the whole rate of growth has been progressively speeded up. The average height of children in the West today is greater than that of the most well-off children in the nineteenth century. In girls, the age when menarche occurs has decreased over the last hundred years in all countries where the statistics have been examined; this trend seems now to have stopped in the most affluent parts of the world, and was probably the result of gradually improving standards of nutrition and environment.

Tallness and shortness

Tallness is regulated by genes and tends to run in families. Two tall parents are much more likely to contribute a genetic mix which will produce tall children. However, tallness genes will only be fully effective if all the other factors necessary for normal growth are present. The one most likely to be lacking is an adequate diet. Bones and flesh cannot respond to the stimulus to grow which the genes provide unless there are ample raw materials for cell production. On the other hand, the healthiest diet will not make a child grow beyond the limits his or her genes have ordained.

Abnormal growth: dwarfs and giants

Some people who are much taller than average may be tall naturally as a result of genetic influences, but although they may sometimes be called giants, they are not abnormal. A true pathological giant results when the pituitary gland oversecretes growth hormone, often as a result of a tumour. If this happens in a young person, normal growth of all the tissues in the body is greatly accelerated, and the affected person (it is more common in boys than in girls) can grow to between 2 and 2.5 m ($6\frac{1}{2}$ to 8 ft) tall. This is the condition known as gigantism. The pituitary tumour continues to grow larger, and finally, by sheer pressure, begins to destroy cells which should be producing other hormones. Sexual function commonly fails and the thyroid and adrenal glands stop secreting their essential hormones. The enlarging pituitary may also cause severe headaches, and by pressing on the nerves supplying the eyes, may produce blindness.

If a tumour of the growth-hormone-producing cells does not develop until adult life, height is not affected, since the long bones of the limbs are no longer capable of growth. The extra growth hormone acts elsewhere, to cause distorted growth of the head, hands and feet. Most noticeably, there is an overgrowth of the lower jaw, and of the ridges of bone above the eyes. This disease, called acromegaly, may progress slowly, over many years.

Tumours of the pituitary may be treated by radiotherapy (see page 220) or surgical removal; certain drugs can also control the secretion of growth hormone.

An absence of any of the factors needed for normal growth, including adequate food, produces some degree of dwarfism. A major requirement for normal growth is thyroxine, the hormone produced by the thyroid gland in the neck. Some infants are born with congenital thyroxine deficiency (cretinism).

Achondroplasia is a form of dwarfism involving stunted limbs, a large trunk, small face, and relatively large head. These individuals are mentally alert, sexually normal, and physically strong. Their condition is due to congenital failure of bone formation, for which there is no treatment.

Less common causes of dwarfism include some disturbances of the kidneys, liver, heart, lungs and pancreas, which result in the inadequate absorption, distribution, or utilization of the nutrients needed for growth. Treatment of these cases depends upon the underlying condition.

Pituitary dwarfs have pituitary glands which do not produce enough growth hormone. Unlike pituitary giants, they do not die in early life. They have a normal, or better than normal, intelligence and they lead healthy lives of good or better than average length. Pituitary dwarfs are often referred to as midgets, to distinguish their condition from the more common type of dwarfism, achondroplasia (see above). Most midgets fail to develop sexually, because the pituitary which produces growth hormone is also the source of sex hormones. Pituitary dwarfs respond to growth hormone but until recently it had to be made from human pituitary glands, which limited its use.

Some success has now been achieved in manufacturing human growth hormone by genetic engineering, that is, by substituting suitable genetic material into bacteria which will produce the required protein. The bacteria can be easily grown and harvested, and when this method has been fully developed and tested, human growth hormone will become freely available for the treatment of pituitary dwarfism. (For further information on hormones and the glands that produce them, see *Hormones*, pages 180-88.)

Growth and development in infancy and childhood

The senses

At birth, human babies are helpless, dependent and vulnerable. Babies can cry, suck, swallow, sneeze and move their eyes. Although they can perceive light, it usually takes a day or so before the eyes remain still enough to make rudimentary vision possible. This fixation of the eyes develops at feeding times. Around the third or fourth week the baby begins to look at objects, usually faces. Three to four months after birth, both eyes turn together, and can focus by about six months.

Newborn babies can distinguish sound and silence, but cannot attach significance to what they hear. They can feel in a crude way but, because many of the nerve pathways are still developing, it is doubtful if they are aware of pain: for example, young babies will frequently put their fingernails in their corneas, the most sensitive part of the eye, without crying. Infants do not respond to needle pricks or electric shocks in the first four of five days of life but do so by the eighth or tenth day.

Newborn babies can also taste and smell: they will suck and lick their lips if a finger dipped in syrup is put in their mouth, but if the finger is covered with a salt solution, they will grimace and not suck very much. Probably the most significant 'sense' present at birth is that concerned with movement; unless the baby is hungry, rocking is more likely to hush crying and soothe irritability than anything else. The next strongest perceptions are the sensations of feeling and warmth – the gentle pressure, contact, stroking and snuggling which are the essence of early care. Apart from crying, the baby does not usually begin to make sounds such as babbling until about five months old.

Different types of giant and dwarf, showing their characteristic physical attributes, compared with the proportions of normal tall and short individuals. Except for achondroplasia, which is caused by a failure of bone formation, height is affected by disorders of the pituitary gland, which produces growth hormone. Acromegaly and pituitary dwarfism and gigantism can now be treated, provided they are detected early enough.

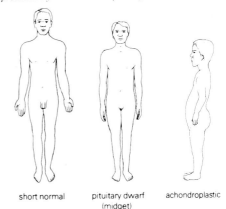

tall normal   pituitary giant   acromegalic   short normal   pituitary dwarf   achondroplastic
                                                                        (midget)

Milestones in children's development

It is an exciting and rewarding experience to watch your child acquiring new skills as he or she grows. Children learn more in their first two years than they ever will in any other comparable period, and at the same time develop a personality and physique which are unique. All children develop their mental and physical skills in much the same order (for example, learning to sit before being able to stand or crawl), but vary enormously in the rate at which they learn these skills. Some babies may be advanced in some areas, such as muscular development, but slower than average in others, and the chart on these two pages is intended to be only a rough guide to the ages at which skills are acquired. Try not to compare your baby with others too much: no child is average, and will progress at a rate that is largely predetermined by genetic factors, although progress may be held up by illness or accident (in which case the child will catch up afterwards). If you are at all concerned about your child's lack of progress, consult a doctor. It is important that any defects (deafness, for example) are diagnosed early so that development is not impeded. Parents are often the first people to spot any signs of slowness because they know their baby better than anyone.

While your baby will not do anything until he or she is ready, you can do a great deal to encourage development by providing the right toys and praise when something is achieved. By giving your baby the confidence to try new skills in spite of the inevitable bumps and falls, you can make sure that your baby enjoys reaching each milestone.

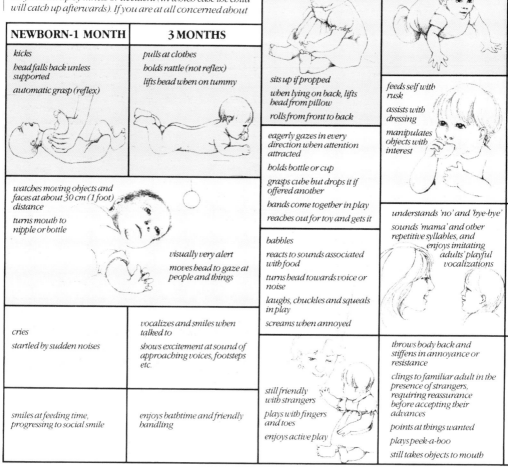

NEWBORN–1 MONTH	3 MONTHS	6 MONTHS	9 MONTHS
kicks head falls back unless supported automatic grasp (reflex)	pulls at clothes holds rattle (not reflex) lifts head when on tummy		sits unaided; may crawl pulls self up to standing
watches moving objects and faces at about 30 cm (1 foot) distance turns mouth to nipple or bottle	visually very alert moves head to gaze at people and things	sits up if propped when lying on back, lifts head from pillow rolls from front to back eagerly gazes in every direction when attention attracted holds bottle or cup grasps cube but drops it if offered another hands come together in play reaches out for toy and gets it	feeds self with rusk assists with dressing manipulates objects with interest
		babbles reacts to sounds associated with food turns head towards voice or noise laughs, chuckles and squeals in play screams when annoyed	understands 'no' and 'bye-bye' sounds 'mama' and other repetitive syllables, and enjoys imitating adults' playful vocalizations
cries startled by sudden noises	vocalizes and smiles when talked to shows excitement at sound of approaching voices, footsteps etc.	still friendly with strangers plays with fingers and toes enjoys active play	throws body back and stiffens in annoyance or resistance clings to familiar adult in the presence of strangers, requiring reassurance before accepting their advances points at things wanted plays peek-a-boo still takes objects to mouth
smiles at feeding time, progressing to social smile	enjoys bathtime and friendly handling		

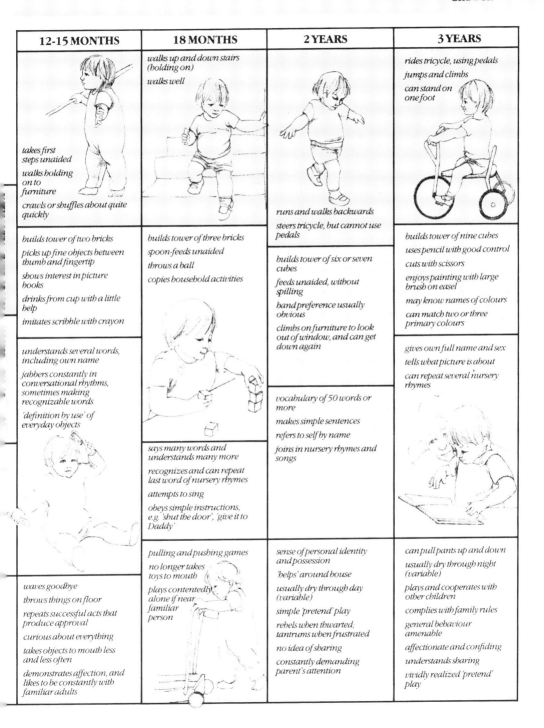

12-15 MONTHS	18 MONTHS	2 YEARS	3 YEARS
	walks up and down stairs (holding on) *walks well*		*rides tricycle, using pedals* *jumps and climbs* *can stand on one foot*
takes first steps unaided *walks holding on to furniture* *crawls or shuffles about quite quickly*		*runs and walks backwards* *steers tricycle, but cannot use pedals*	
builds tower of two bricks *picks up fine objects between thumb and fingertip* *shows interest in picture books* *drinks from cup with a little help* *imitates scribble with crayon*	*builds tower of three bricks* *spoon-feeds unaided* *throws a ball* *copies household activities*	*builds tower of six or seven cubes* *feeds unaided, without spilling* *hand preference usually obvious* *climbs on furniture to look out of window, and can get down again*	*builds tower of nine cubes* *uses pencil with good control* *cuts with scissors* *enjoys painting with large brush on easel* *may know names of colours* *can match two or three primary colours*
understands several words, including own name *jabbers constantly in conversational rhythms, sometimes making recognizable words* *'definition by use' of everyday objects*			*gives own full name and sex* *tells what picture is about* *can repeat several nursery rhymes*
	says many words and understands many more *recognizes and can repeat last word of nursery rhymes* *attempts to sing* *obeys simple instructions, e.g. 'shut the door', 'give it to Daddy'*	*vocabulary of 50 words or more* *makes simple sentences* *refers to self by name* *joins in nursery rhymes and songs*	
waves goodbye *throws things on floor* *repeats successful acts that produce approval* *curious about everything* *takes objects to mouth less and less often* *demonstrates affection, and likes to be constantly with familiar adults*	*pulling and pushing games* *no longer takes toys to mouth* *plays contentedly alone if near familiar person*	*sense of personal identity and possession* *'helps' around house* *usually dry through day (variable)* *simple 'pretend' play* *rebels when thwarted; tantrums when frustrated* *no idea of sharing* *constantly demanding parent's attention*	*can pull pants up and down* *usually dry through night (variable)* *plays and cooperates with other children* *complies with family rules* *general behaviour amenable* *affectionate and confiding* *understands sharing* *vividly realized 'pretend' play*

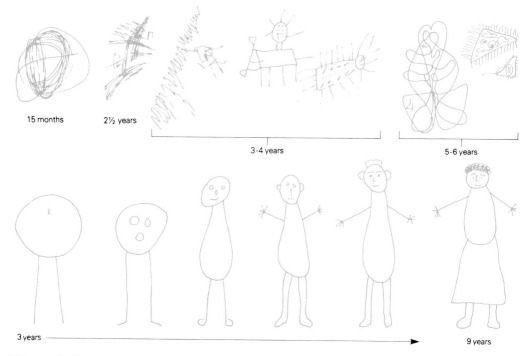

15 months   2½ years

3-4 years

5-6 years

3 years ———→ 9 years

Motor skills

Control of the hands follows a fairly standard pattern of development. Babies are born with a grasp reflex which is so strong in the first few weeks of life that they can support themselves hanging from a fixed point. The grasp reflex is largely lost by the time the infant is eight weeks old. At twelve weeks, on average, babies can hold on to a rattle and pull at their clothes, but cannot usually play for any length of time with a rattle placed in their hand until they are sixteen weeks old. By twenty-four weeks they can hold a bottle, and grasp a cube in their palm, although they will drop it when given another. The ability to hold two cubes is apparent at twenty-eight weeks, as is that of transferring objects from one hand to another. Soon after this, the child learns to pick up a pellet between fingers and thumb. A baby will offer a block to his or her mother at this stage but cannot let it go: the ability to release an object, and perhaps offer it to someone, comes later, at about eleven months, and by the age of one year, he or she is happily throwing things on the floor.

At fifteen months a baby can imitate a scribble, or scribbles spontaneously, but does not imitate strokes until about eighteen months. Vertical and circular strokes can be imitated at two years, and horizontal strokes at two and a half, at which age a pencil can be held between fingers and thumb for the first time, instead of in the fist. At this age the infant can make two or more strokes for a cross. Children of three years old can copy a circle and imitate a cross. At four they can copy a cross, six months later a square, and six

A child's drawing ability develops as he or she gets older: at fifteen months a baby can scribble spontaneously, but does not copy strokes until about eighteen months. Children aged five can usually copy a triangle, but not a diamond.

months after that a triangle; but they cannot copy a diamond until aged six or seven. If colour is introduced to the child, it is the sunny colours, yellow and red, which are most popular, and after that blue and green.

Babies' body movements also follow a fairly standard pattern: by sixteen weeks they can usually hold their head up and can sit up by about six or seven months. By nine or ten months they can pull themselves up to a standing position, and can also crawl at this stage. The next stage is walking (by about fifteen months), by which time they are also speaking their first words, and by two years they have mastered three-word sentences and have learned to run. At three they can climb and ride a tricycle and at four they can walk downstairs one at a time. These are only approximate times, however, and each baby will vary in the age when he or she first carries out these activities.

Measuring ability

Intelligence tests are one way of predicting potential ability. Tests are graded in difficulty so that, for example, most five-year-olds can successfully do all the tests done by younger children and those for their own age, but cannot do the more difficult set managed by most six-year-olds. The age in years at which most children can do a set of tests of given difficulty has been called the mental age. Sometimes it is found that an exceptional young child is able to pass tests usually passed only by older children. For instance, if a six-year-old passes tests that most children cannot do until they are nine, he or she has a mental age of nine, in spite of the fact that his or her chronological age is only six. The ratio of mental age to chronological age is the mental ratio: in this example 9/6, which equals 1.5. In order to avoid decimal points, this is multiplied by 100 to give the intelligence quotient (IQ) which in this case would be 150.

There are several ways of testing and measuring IQ, and there is much debate on how useful these tests are in predicting and determining intelligence. They may be useful, however, for detecting abnormalities which need special treatment.

Behaviour in infancy and childhood

Babies are born with certain reflexes which are important for survival. Some of these reflexes, such as the sucking reflex and the startle reflex, help them to obtain food and protect them from harm; others are a preview of what will become normal later in life. For example, the standing reflex is present in a young infant: if the baby is held so that the feet touch a surface such as a table top, the legs may straighten up as if to stand. This reflex soon disappears, however, until the baby is several months old and beginning to be able to take its own weight on its feet.

What is more usually considered to be behaviour is the response of the infant to its surroundings and to other people. By the second and third months of life, for example, the infant smiles at certain stimuli. Gradually, the baby will take more and more interest in his or her surroundings, recognize his or her parents and begin to understand things in a limited way. Even some individual character traits may begin to be recognized.

During the early months of life, many aspects of behaviour are a result of external factors. A baby who cries frequently may do so because of hunger, pain or discomfort, or because it needs loving. The way the infant is treated is an important factor in determining behaviour at this stage, although personality also plays a part: even under identical conditions, babies will give different reactions. The emotional atmosphere of the home also affects a baby's behaviour.

At the age of about nine or ten months, the average infant is mobile, crawling on all fours, shuffling on his or her buttocks, walking while holding on to furniture, or even walking independently. The baby can say some words, but is unlikely yet to know what they mean. Nevertheless he or she is learning extremely rapidly, and daily develops new skills. At this stage babies still accept the authority of their parents and their behaviour usually does not present any problems.

The next stage in a child's life is one of rapid advancement in all spheres, and one in which individual behaviour becomes much more evident. The child learns to walk, speak and feed himself or herself, and becomes conscious of this new-found freedom. The child's subconscious mind begins to appreciate his or her own individuality. As a result

of this ego development, and depending on how the parents deal with situations that arise, the child will exhibit different types of behaviour which might be interpreted as 'good' or 'bad'.

Behavioural problems
Toddlers
Behavioural problems do not normally start before the age of about twenty months, when toddlers realize their separateness and independence, and often try to draw attention to it, by rebelling against parents. This is frequently seen as defiance or disobedience, and parents may respond to it with discipline; this may not be the best reaction, however, since it reinforces the reason for the behaviour, which is that the child wants attention. It is better to ignore this kind of behaviour, and reward more acceptable behaviour with praise. At this stage, correct management by the parents is important, since the foundations of future behaviour are being laid. Most small children will show some sort of 'behaviour problem' at this stage.

One of the most common problems of this type is refusing food. It is difficult to ignore a child who will not eat, but this is the best way of avoiding mealtime battles. Offer food at mealtimes but do not make a fuss if it is rejected. No food should be given between meals because this will only take away the appetite for the next meal. No normal child will voluntarily starve, so the problem will pass.

Another common problem is pot refusal. Many babies, after being trained to sit on a pot after feeding, will suddenly begin to reject the pot. Again, the correct reaction is completely to ignore the pot until the child has forgotten the battles that have taken place and is no longer gaining attention by this behaviour (see *Toilet training*, below). Indeed, it is probably best to wait for the child to ask for it.

Sleep problems are also common: the child either will not go to sleep in the evenings, or wakes in the night, demanding attention. To ignore a child crying at night is not easy and often impracticable. Allowing the child into the parents' bed may help to stop the crying and allow the parents to sleep, but may also make the problem last longer. A warm milk drink just before going to bed or a low-power light in the room may help. If the problem persists, a doctor should be consulted.

Breath-holding attacks which express frustration are less common: these are harmless and should be ignored.

A sense of insecurity may arise directly from the attitudes of the parents. Parents who favour one child and neglect another will harm both. In the same way, when parents are over-ambitious for their children, anxious about their health or over-protective, behavioural problems can result. When a child has to go away from home for a limited period, perhaps to go into hospital, there may be behavioural problems on his or her return home. Tantrums, bedwetting and a less mature pattern of behaviour are often encountered, and are a result of the child's insecurity. Understanding and patience are usually all that are needed.

Three to five years
During their third, fourth, and fifth years, children continue to acquire many new skills, and learn very quickly. They

become integrated into various social groups such as the family and, as this happens, behaviour becomes more socially acceptable again. All toddlers should be given every chance to develop their potential both physically and emotionally, and to advance their skills. They should have plenty of opportunity to mix with their peers, and should also be taught respect for other people's feelings and property. Exactly when and what punishment is required must be agreed by the parents, and this decision adhered to, otherwise the child will become confused. Any punishment should be given at the time of the offence and not later.

Starting school
By the time the child starts school he or she is usually well integrated into the community. The first few weeks of school may be accompanied by tantrums or other unruly behaviour at home, and the child may suffer from various emotional upsets such as nightmares. For most children, however, the problems of starting school are minor, and settle within a few weeks. Most children of average or high intelligence enjoy the prospect of school, whereas dull children may have difficulty in accepting it, as they take less pleasure in learning. Such children's behaviour is likely to be more difficult, as their poor concentration means that they are less able to benefit from school, unless they are specially provided for.

Serious behavioural problems at this stage are uncommon, but occasionally do need paediatric or psychiatric aid. Some degree of school phobia is common and merely needs sympathetic handling, but when severe, this seems to be caused by some basic sense of insecurity, most often starting from an unhealthy emotional atmosphere at home or school. Persistent truancy usually arises for similar reasons. Persistent stealing of valuables, deliberate destruction of property or the causing of accidents may indicate the child's desire to improve his or her status among peers at school. Genuine psychiatric disease is very uncommon before adolescence, but occasionally depressive or schizophrenic disorders (see pages 64 and 67) do occur.

Certain medical problems can also cause emotional difficulties. Examples are dyslexia (specific reading disability), epilepsy, diabetes mellitus and various physical defects. However, the emotional atmosphere in the home is probably the most important factor of all, and if parent-child relationships are happy and harmonious, difficulties are less likely to arise.

Toilet training
Control of the bladder and the bowels requires a certain amount of muscle power and this is not reliably developed until a child is two or three years old. Not until the age of two can a child be properly trained to anticipate events before an 'accident' occurs. Children are generally bladder-trained at a later stage than they are bowel-trained. By the age of three most children are dry day and night, apart from the occasional mishap – although, of course, different children develop at different rates. Boys usually become dry later than girls.

To teach a child to be 'clean', and about hygiene, parents should first talk to the infant about his or her nappies as they are changed so that gradually he or she will come to associate the soiled and wet nappies with faeces and urine. It is a good idea to accustom children to the potty before they start using it, by talking about it and letting them examine it. It is also possible to get a special child's seat to put on the lavatory. Imitation is a very good learning process and it is useful to let the child watch brothers, sisters, young friends and parents using the potty or lavatory. For the first few attempts, it may be better if the child is held, but do not force him or her to sit there alone. Gradually, the child can be allowed to sit alone but never for too long since he or she may just want to play and will not come to associate the potty with its real purpose.

It is important not to scold a child who refuses to sit on the potty because it may become associated with being told off. For the same reason, try not to show disappointment if the child does not urinate or have a bowel movement when first tried on the pot. The opposite is just as important, for with too much praise he or she may show the excreta to everyone. When the child does urinate or have a bowel movement, show how it is disposed of and the different hygienic procedures such as hand-washing.

Once it can be predicted that the child is going to have a bowel movement or wants to urinate, the child should be placed on the pot, and will begin to associate the potty or toilet with bowel movements and urination. The child will also master, with time, the function of releasing and retaining. Success in leaving off nappies is a matter of trial and error and it is advisable to leave the nappy on at night at first.

Lack of bladder control
Lack of bladder control at night after the age of about four is referred to as enuresis. Constant dribbling of urine may be a sign of disease but may also be the result of poor early training, a disturbed relationship between parent and child, or parental hostility during the toilet-training period.

Bed-wetting at night may be due to too small a bladder to hold the urine until morning. An electrical alarm which wakes the child as soon as he or she starts to urinate is useful for older children.

Growth and development during adolescence

Adolescence spans the time between the start of sexual growth and the completion of physical growth, or maturity. It is a period of rapid development, when the body needs plenty of nourishment. Protein foods are particularly important for building tissues, and about fifteen per cent of the calorie intake should be protein. Carbohydrates are needed for energy but over-indulgence in bread, cakes, sugar and sweets should nevertheless be avoided as this can cause obesity and dental decay. In general, an adolescent needs about the same amount of food as a moderately heavy manual worker, usually between 2500 and 3000 Calories a day, sometimes rising to 3300 Calories for seventeen- and eighteen-year-olds. This will vary to a certain extent according to the amount of physical activity being undertaken. A good diet for normal growth in adolescence is based on three balanced meals a day. For more information on nutrition.

The adolescent growth spurt

Almost all the body is affected by the adolescent growth spurt, though not all to an equal degree. Most of the spurt in height is in the trunk rather than the legs, although a spurt does occur in the legs. The hands and feet mature first, then the legs, then the trunk, so that children stop growing out of their trousers about a year before they stop growing out of jumpers and jackets.

In addition to the changes in height and in the genitals, breasts and body hair (see *Sexual development*, pages 11 and 16), there are changes in body composition. Boys gain in muscle bulk and strength, while they tend to lose body fat; girls gain fat during adolescence and have a much smaller growth spurt in muscle bulk. These changes account for much of the difference in appearance between the sexes, but there are also differences in the way the skeleton grows. A boy has wider shoulders and a girl wider hips. The bones stop growing in girls on average before the age of sixteen, and in boys by eighteen. A few continue to grow until their early twenties.

Diseases related to adolescence

Adolescence should be, and usually is, a period of good health. However, the rapid growth and increased physical activity of adolescence may increase the demands on the body and hence its requirements. For example, there is an increased need for iron and there can be a tendency for anaemia to develop unless there is enough in the diet. There is also an increased need for iodine by the thyroid gland; and pubertal goitre may occur, particularly in regions with less natural iodine (see page 183).

The rapid growth of the bones and teeth requires increased calcium, and adequate amounts of this mineral, from food, are important in preventing dental decay. The benefits of fluoride in water or in toothpaste are also well proven. Regular inspection of the teeth by a dentist is particularly important during adolescence.

Because of the extra demands made on the endocrine glands, hormone-related disorders may arise (see *Hormones*, page 180). For example, the insulin-secreting cells of the pancreas may be affected, causing diabetes. The hormonal changes occurring also affect the skin, and acne is a common problem of adolescence, but usually clears up by the twenties (see *The Skin*, page 72).

During early adolescence there is often fatty enlargement of the breasts in boys; nodules in the breast may be felt, similar to those of interstitial mastitis in girls. They are harmless and eventually disappear. In a very few cases this increase in breast size is permanent. It is called pseudo-gynaecomastia, and differs from true gynaecomastia, which occurs in some males because of hormone or chromosome defects, or perhaps as a reaction to certain drugs. Boys may also have the condition of undescended testicles (see page 16).

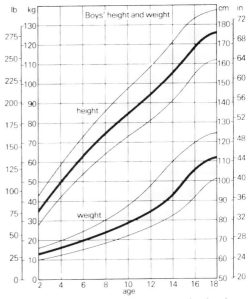

Average growths curves for height and weight of children from age two to eighteen (the heavy lines), along with curves for larger and smaller children. The growth rate of ninety-seven per cent of children falls within these outer curves in the blue bands, which show that the range widens as adolescence approaches; they also show that height and weight increases level off sooner in girls than in boys, since the bones stop growing on average before the age of sixteen in girls, and not till eighteen in boys.

The developing personality in adolescence
Emotions

Adolescents are faced with some years of emotional upset which add to the other loads they have to bear. Although they are learning to live their lives with greater independence and responsibility, which they might be eager for, they may at the same time feel unready for this. They have to learn to accept adult emotions and must also make decisions about their future career, but are not yet entitled to adult privileges. This period of transition can be made smoother if the adolescent is given encouragement and sympathy by parents and teachers, but unfortunately this period is also the time when pressures at school are often strongest. The physical strains of growing up affect emotional reactions, and for some the whole process may be too much; rarely, breakdowns can occur and can even lead to suicide. The adolescent's life has to be simplified and parents and teachers must help to reduce some of the pressures.

Increasing independence and the longing for adult responsibility accelerate towards the end of adolescence and account for much of the aggressive rebellion encountered at this age. This is part of normal development and has to be accepted to some degree. It is similar to the period of ego development during the second year of life when the child presents all manner of rebellious behaviour problems.

One of the most important aspects of adolescence parents have to face is finding the correct balance between punishment and praise in the management of their children during this difficult period. In trying to help adolescents through this emotional transition, it is important to realize their great need to be accepted by their associates. In an effort to be accepted, both boys and girls become concerned with their appearance and this must not be ridiculed by parents. Worries over relationships with the opposite sex, or their absence, can seriously affect school work and emotional reactions. Boasting and bluffing are common features of this period, and should be accepted as normal behaviour.

Sexual feelings

Ideally, children should be prepared early for their own sexual development during adolescence. Parents should answer their questions about sex frankly from an early age, and children will normally also have reproductive biology lessons in school. If sex education is not given early enough, a girl may be confronted with her first period without knowing what it is, and the first a boy may know of this aspect of his development is a sexual dream and nocturnal emission ('wet dream').

Half-truths and tall stories circulate rapidly among adolescents who are not sure of their facts, and mothers and fathers should try to ensure that their children know about contraception and the risks of sexually transmitted diseases. Parents often worry about early sexual activity, particularly in girls, and may become over-protective, setting excessive restrictions on their offspring's social life. Developing a mutual trust does not always come naturally, and is something both parents and sons and daughters need to work at developing.

Identity

The adolescent's fight to establish his or her identity may involve extreme criticism of his or her parent's views and way of life. This is often expressed in different fashions and hairstyles and by following cults associated with a particular kind of music, diet or politics. Such tendencies are often encouraged by commercial pressures and powerful advertising. This can lead the adolescent to sometimes quite unjustified dissatisfaction with his or her physical attributes, abilities or prospects, until he or she comes to understand the powers at work.

Though it may seem difficult to find time for activities involving all the family, especially when children who are growing up and moving away tend to fragment rather than unite it, a supportive and caring family provides a good foil to the conflicting pressures and demands on the adolescent. Of course, this is not always available.

Special problems of ethnic groups

Second-generation immigrant children have particular problems in adolescence. After a relatively integrated childhood attending school and making friends with other children from different backgrounds, they may suddenly come under tremendous pressure to conform to the standards and customs of their parents, who are often insulated to some extent from the society in which they live. A tradition of arranged marriages, and much stricter codes of sexual conduct often form a focal point for such conflicts.

*Adolescence is a time of
internal conflict: teenagers
suddenly realize that they have
their own lives to lead, but no
power or resources to effect the
changes that they would like.
They may not see the point of
working for examinations
which seem to do little to
prepare them for a society with
high unemployment levels, and
start to rebel against authority
figures such as parents and
teachers. They may find
relationships with the opposite
sex difficult to establish, and
their self-confidence may be
undermined by such problems
as acne or greasy hair. Such
difficulties, so easily forgotten
once they have passed, need
sympathy and understanding –
not necessarily overt – from
everyone who has dealings with
young people.*

Ageing

The growth phase of the human body ends on average between the ages of sixteen and eighteen, slightly earlier in women than in men. Although the development and laying down of fat may occur much later in life, the cessation of bone growth is the most significant indicator of ageing. However, not until the late thirties does noticeable ageing occur.

In terms of calendar years, 'middle age' is a very nebulous period, but can be taken to mean the period between the mid-forties and mid-sixties. Different parts of the body age at different rates in different people, but it is remarkable how uniform the process is: a skilled observer is seldom more than ten per cent out in estimating a person's age.

The signs of ageing

The first quality to show deterioration is the mental ability to formulate completely new concepts. The physical theories of Newton and Einstein and most new discoveries in pure mathematics were made by men under thirty, usually under twenty-five. Along with this deterioration – but some years later – goes an increasing difficulty in

Right: the development of osteoporosis, a condition of thinning brittle bones. It is commoner in women than men, mainly because the reduced levels of oestrogen following the menopause affect calcium metabolism. Not only does the condition make the bones more prone to fracture, but loss of calcium from the vertebrae weakens the backbone, resulting in a gradual loss of height and rounding of the shoulders (centre). Unless the process is checked by taking oestrogen, as the individual ages the ribs may drop down almost to the level of the pelvis and a hump back develops, the 'dowager's hump', often due to collapsed vertebrae (far right). A diet rich in calcium may help reduce the tendency to osteoporosis.

Left: one of the most obvious signs of ageing is a gradual wrinkling and sagging of the skin, as a result of the degeneration of the elastic fibres just under the skin. This process is faster in people who have spent their lives in the sun.

 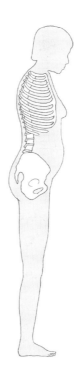 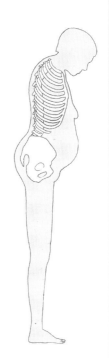

learning new facts and, more particularly, in appreciating their significance and relating them to previous knowledge. For many years this difficulty is compensated for by the benefits of increased experience. The balance of this equation between difficulty with new ideas and better appreciation of the familiar depends a great deal on a person's job. For example, a forty-five-year-old manager faced with new techniques in a rapidly expanding company may be unable to cope, while a judge of more than seventy years old may remain an excellent administrator of the law which changes very slowly.

The other common mental difficulty of middle age is deterioration in memory, but this does not often become a problem till the late fifties, or later. The normal pattern is difficulty in remembering new things and in recalling recent events; skills learned in the past remain unimpaired. In very old people there is often a complete lack of recollection about the events of yesterday, while they remember clearly things that happened fifty years ago.

Changes in appearance

The most obvious signs of ageing are in the physical appearance. The degree of greying of the hair is one guide, and so is loss of elasticity of the skin which shows itself by wrinkles, particularly on the neck and at the corners of the eyes. Baldness, particularly in men, is another common sign of ageing. The teeth decay, and have to be filled or

extracted, particularly in those who consume a high-sugar diet. Changes in posture are common, with round shoulders, a forward stoop and generally flaccid muscles, though much of this is due to a sedentary way of life and is not seen in manual workers or those who take care of their bodies.

Ageing bones become smaller, thinner and more brittle, particularly after the age of fifty-five, and there is a measurable decrease in height. Movements may be slower and more deliberate. Reaction time becomes slower; for example, it takes fractionally longer for a middle-aged car driver to stop in an emergency than for someone in their twenties.

Changes in internal organs

The organs of the body and the chemical constituents of the blood also alter with age. Total lung capacity decreases by about 0.7 per cent a year in nonsmokers due to the effects of age and, perhaps, atmospheric pollution. In those exposed to chronic poisoning from smoking tobacco, the rate is higher at 0.8 per cent. Blood pressure rises with age, the heart enlarges and the arteries become more rigid. The available iron in the blood, contained in the haemoglobin of red blood cells, decreases with age, as does the protein albumin in blood. With increasing age the amount of calcium, the mineral responsible for the structure and strength of bones, gradually decreases in both women and men, but begins about ten years earlier in women who at the time of the menopause lose calcium more rapidly than men. The blood level of urea (a waste product) rises with age, suggesting ageing of the kidneys, and other changes reflect deteriorating liver function.

Degeneration of the nervous system – the brain, spinal cord, and peripheral nerves – may cause difficulties in co-ordination of the arms and legs. Balance may also be affected by a stroke, Parkinson's disease or lack of muscle tone. Loss of feeling in the feet and limbs, through a nervous condition such as peripheral neuritis, is another possible problem in the elderly. Temporary faintness or loss of consciousness through reduced brain circulation from atherosclerosis, anaemia, heart disease and temporarily lowered blood pressure, may add to balance and co-ordination difficulties.

Progressive visual difficulty is commonly part of the ageing process. Refractive errors – difficulty in focusing on objects at different distances – may appear or become more noticeable. Lens opacity, cataract and retinal changes may also occur in the elderly. Hearing, too, deteriorates with age. As early as the twenties the ability to hear very high-pitched sounds is already deteriorating.

Diseases of old age

As people age they become more liable to disease. In north-western Europe and the USA mortality statistics are very similar. In the age group twenty-five to thirty-four the chances of dying in any one year are 9 per 10,000 for men and 5 per 10,000 for women. The most common cause of death is accidents, nearly all of them preventable. In the next decade, the thirty-five to forty-four age group, the rates are around 18 and 12 per 10,000 respectively. In this age group, coronary heart disease accounts for over a quarter of male deaths, while probably less than half that proportion of women die from this disease. Perhaps because of this, the relative difference in total death rates between the two sexes increases, being – in the forty-five to fifty-four age group – 61 per 10,000 for men and 38 per 10,000 for women. In the next ten-year age group, strokes, coronary heart disease and related conditions account for about half the total male death rate of about 188 per 10,000. By retiring age, in the sixty-five to seventy-four age group, the chances of dying in any one year are quite considerable, at 239 per 10,000 for women and 455 per 10,000 for men.

In the western world, atherosclerosis (see page 160) is so common that it has become accepted as an inevitable part of ageing. However, diet and way of life are also partly to blame. The level of cholesterol in the blood is considered one of the factors related to the development of atherosclerosis. In women, average blood cholesterol levels rise steadily with age after the menopause; in men this is true up to the fifties, but cholesterol levels then stabilize, or even start to fall.

The commonest causes of death in middle age are cancer and coronary heart disease, and respiratory illnesses are the most common form of non-fatal sickness. Several simple measures will help people avoid these illnesses, and enjoy middle age and the retirement that follows. The most important single measure is to stop smoking. A thirty-five-year-old non-smoker has about an eighteen per cent chance of dying before sixty-five; for a light smoker (less than fifteen cigarettes a day) it is twenty-five per cent; for a heavy smoker (fifteen to twenty-four a day) it is thirty-one per cent; and for the very heavy smoker (twenty-five or more cigarettes a day) it is forty per cent (more than twice as high as for the non-smoker). Put another way, the thirty-five-year-old light smoker is throwing away four-and-a-half years of his average life expectancy, and the very heavy smoker six years. Quite apart from bringing death nearer, cigarettes cause illness. Very heavy smokers have, on average, twice as much sickness absence from work as the non-smoker (see pages 164-7).

Three common conditions of middle age which are closely related to cigarette smoking are lung cancer, bronchitis and coronary heart disease. In western Europe and the USA chronic bronchitis and emphysema are the biggest single causes of sickness absence from work, and coronary heart disease is the biggest single killer in the middle-age group.

Diet and exercise

More than fifty per cent of middle-aged people are above the desirable weight for their age, so their diet is of great importance. For every ten per cent extra weight above the norm, mortality increases by about fifteen per cent. To put this in perspective, however, one has to be fifty per cent overweight to have the same chance of death as someone who smokes twenty cigarettes a day.

Other dietary factors are important as well as Calories. Over ten per cent of middle-aged people in developed countries have high blood cholesterol levels and probably ninety per cent have levels above what is desirable. This is due to a combination of factors including lack of fibre in the diet and excessive consumption of sugar and fat, particularly animal fats. Obesity and lack of exercise also predispose people to having high blood cholesterol.

Exercise maintains the mobility of joints, increases muscular strength, and, most importantly, exercises the heart and lungs, by increasing the pulse and breathing rates. Anyone who has been sedentary for a long time should begin exercising carefully and gradually, and is advised to have a medical examination first.

Social problems of ageing

In western countries, where people over sixty years old may represent round twenty per cent of the total population, ageing presents a number of social as well as medical problems. These problems are increasing as the proportion of retired to working people increases, since the working population undertakes the economic support of those who are retired, either indirectly through taxation which pays for pensions and welfare benefits, or directly by material and physical help from relatives and friends, or both. Most old people try to remain physically if not economically independent in their post-retirement years, but by the age of eighty or so most people depend to some degree on the physical support and help of neighbours, family and friends, and the social services.

Loneliness in the older age group is a major problem: the death of friends and spouses and the decreased ability to make new friends, along with physical disabilities, may contribute to a feeling of isolation which in turn may lead to apathy, rigid attitudes, introspection, and increased dwelling on the past, its lost opportunities and pleasures. A physical illness or increasing frailty may also make depression worse, and even lead to true clinical depression. Anti-depressant drugs as well as treatment for any physical complaints may often be prescribed for old people.

Retirement from employment is another major problem of ageing. A fixed retirement age in many companies means that physically active and mentally agile people with a wealth of employment experience behind them are discharged into a life of leisure that may last twenty or thirty years or more. Useful advice on adjusting to retirement is given on the following two pages.

Geriatric medicine

Geriatric medicine is that branch of the subject concerned with the medical, psychological and social aspects of illness and disability in old people. A number of important principles underlie the geriatric approach, the main one being the existence of a 'geriatric team' of different specialists who pool their talents in the interests of the patient's recovery and return to reasonable independence within the community. For example, if an elderly woman falls at home, fractures her hip and develops a chest infection, she will be admitted to hospital. Here the medical team will include: the orthopaedic surgeon who operates on the broken bone; the nurse who attends to the general well-being of the patient; a physiotherapist, who will give the appropriate exercises for muscle strengthening, heat therapy for pain relief and massage if required; and the occupational therapist and the medical social worker, who deal with the patient's return home and any associated difficulties involved.

The second important principle of geriatrics is that, where possible, elderly patients should be examined and treated in their own homes, and admission to hospital should be avoided if possible. The third, and perhaps most important, principle is that old age is not a disease. Much can be done to relieve the problems of old age; there is no need for older people to lose their independence and entitlement to reasonable health.

Drug treatment of old people follows the usual rules of treating the disease as well as the symptoms, and using the appropriate drug for the particular illness. Doses may need to be adjusted in elderly patients whose tolerance is decreased or whose ability to break down and excrete drugs may be impaired. Sedatives, for example, may accumulate in an old person's bloodstream and produce increasing drowsiness and confusion.

In addition, old people may be forgetful or confused during an illness; it helps if a relative or other assistant sets out clearly which pills should be taken and when. Child-proof containers may also cause difficulties for the elderly.

The treatment of mental disorders calls for care in assessment and diagnosis and, where required, voluntary or compulsory admission to mental hospitals or nursing homes. The full range of modern psychiatric treatment may be used in treating mental illness in the elderly.

Hospice care

One difficulty for elderly patients and their relatives, especially for those who are terminally ill, is coming to terms with their own death. The hospice movement has been developing rapidly in several countries in order to meet this need; many of those who pioneered it are motivated by religious beliefs, but admission is not restricted on those grounds. Patients and their families are helped to accept the inevitability of death and understand their own feelings. An important component of hospice care relates to the relief of pain in terminal illness: analgesic drugs are given in regular doses large enough to eliminate pain and before the pain recurs, with none of the usual precautions regarding addiction.

Accidents

Deteriorating hearing and vision increase the risk of accidents, whether in the home, crossing the street, driving a car or attending machines at work. Poor balance and slowness of movement and reaction also contribute to the increased likelihood of an accident. Outside the home there is little an individual can do to guard against an accident apart from observing safety rules such as using crossing points and taking extra care, but in the home many precautions can be taken to prevent falls and other accidents.

Safety in the home
The following guidelines for safety in the home are worth considering at any age, but are particularly important for the elderly.
1 Make sure that all rooms, halls and stairways are adequately lit. Dark corners can also be lightened if painted white.

2 Do not allow electrical flexes and other wires to trail across the floor; secure them to walls and skirting boards.
3 Make sure carpets and other loose floor coverings are secured in position; those with worn out patches should be removed. Do not polish floors until they become slippery; mop up spills in bathrooms and kitchens as soon as they occur.
4 Fix handrails to staircases, outdoor steps, near the bath and lavatory, and use non-slip mats in the bath or shower.
5 Minimize clutter in rooms used by the elderly: make sure that there is a place for everything and that things used by an elderly person are always kept in the same accessible place.
6 Have all electrical appliances checked regularly; burns and electric shock from faulty appliances are common in the elderly.
In addition if elderly people are at all unsteady on their feet, a walking stick with a rubber tip or a frame should be used, along with well-fitting shoes with non-slip soles.

Living longer and living well

The decade between the ages of sixty and seventy is one of adjustment to retirement from full-time paid employment, and for many people it is a period of great anxiety. The life one has led for so long is over and one's skills and experience seem no longer needed by society. Retirement appears to create five major problems, all of which are interrelated: loss of status, lack of companionship, drop in income, feelings of uselessness, and boredom. Without adequate preparation, retirement can be damaging to both health and morale. However, it can also be a new chapter in a full and active life, and a fulfilment of the all the previous years' efforts and ambitions.

Planning for retirement

A positive attitude to the future rather than regrets about the past is the key to a happy retirement, and this means making plans well in advance of the event. Since it is quite possible to spend a quarter of one's life in retirement while remaining mentally and physically fit, it is sensible to make appropriate financial arrangements for this major period of life and to decide on ways of filling the abundance of free time. For some people retirement offers the opportunity to move to an area with a better climate, perhaps to a place where holidays have been taken, but care must be taken over such a decision: friends and neighbours will become more important than ever, and it is therefore advisable to choose an area where some social contact is already established, since it is harder to make new friends as one gets older. It is also important to consider the suitability of a new home for a future when physical disabilities may arise, and to make sure that shops and other amenities are nearby and readily accessible.

Retirement offers the opportunity to devote more time to existing interests and hobbies and to take up new ones. For those whose job was their main interest in life, some form of part-time or voluntary work may prove enjoyable, whether related to previous employment or not. Further education courses may also be an ideal way of developing new interests and meeting people. Retirement is also a time for renewing old friendships, taking an active part in looking after grandchildren and being a useful member of the community.

Maintaining health and fitness

In order to enjoy retirement to the full, it is vital to make sure that health is maintained. This means eating a healthful, varied diet containing plenty of fruit and vegetables and dietary fibre, not smoking or drinking too much, taking regular exercise, and avoiding unnecessary stress. For all age groups, it is unfitness that poses more problems than exercise, and for the elderly exercise probably brings more rewards than at any other period of life: exercise will improve and maintain muscle power and increase mobility, thereby delaying the effects of the ageing process with its decline in bodily strength. The more active you are the more independent you can remain – a vital aspect of enjoying retirement. Many keep-fit activities can enhance social life as well as fitness. For more information on achieving and maintaining good health.

The right kind of exercise taken regularly helps keep the body mobile, the joints supple and the muscles strong. Make exercise part of your life, perhaps by taking up an outdoor activity such as gardening.

Exercise can be an enjoyable way of meeting new people, particularly if you join a social club for dancing or a walking or cycling club. Group support can also make it easier to sustain physical activities.

Physical activity keeps both body and mind alert, and brisk walking is excellent exercise that can easily be incorporated into the daily routine. Grandparents can share this and many other pursuits with their grandchildren, thus bridging the generation gap.

Dying, Death and Bereavement

Only a minority of people die suddenly; for most people dying is a gradual process lasting weeks or months. For a dying person's relatives this is in some ways preferable to an unexpected bereavement, because they have time to adjust to their loss and to make preparations for the practical arrangements that have to be attended to following a death. The word death means different things to different people, but in practical terms, a doctor has to be able to sign the death certificate. Cremation formalities require special additional certification.

The diagnosis of death

A doctor has several criteria by which to judge when a person is dead. The first is absence of the heartbeat, examined by feeling the pulse and listening for heart sounds in the chest. However, if the blood pressure is low, or the arteries are diseased, it may be impossible to feel the pulse.

The second test involves determining whether breathing has stopped by listening at different points on the chest for the characteristic breath sounds, and putting a cold metal surface or mirror near the mouth and nose to see if mist forms on it as a result of moisture in expired air. This test is not definitive either, since recovery is possible from respiratory arrest – for example, after drowning, or an overdose of sleeping tablets – provided that the heart has not stopped beating.

In the third test the surface of the eyes is examined to see if they have a glazed appearance. This appearance is probably caused by the evaporation of water from the surface of the unblinking eyes, but is sometimes also seen following an epileptic fit or dehydration. The fourth criterion is dilated pupils, but these are also seen in some types of brain injury, and after an overdose of some drugs.

The fifth criterion is pallor or blueness of the body, as a result of the tissues using up the oxygen in the blood, and the redistribution of the blood by gravity to the lower parts of the body. But these features are also found in hypothermia and exposure. A sixth criterion of death is coldness of the skin, but climate, clothing and physical build can all maintain the core body temperature which may not fall drastically until some time after death, unless the person died of cold. Another important factor is whether there has been a recent history of disease or an accident, which would, in the normal course of events, be expected to result in death.

The general surgeon uses the same criteria as the physician to ascertain whether death has occurred. However, a different view is taken by a neurosurgeon or transplant surgeon who is advising whether organs of a dying patient should be taken for transplantation once death has occurred. The neurosurgeon knows that the sooner the organ is taken from the donor, the healthier it will be when transplanted into the recipient. On the other hand, no patient who would have even the slightest chance of survival must be operated on as a donor. So the neurosurgeon needs separate and detailed criteria of death. These are: loss of reflexes; clinical evidence of irrecoverable brain damage; and complete absence of any signs of improving consciousness.

Stages of death

The process of death is essentially due to a lack of blood (and therefore oxygen), first in the brain and spinal cord, and then in the rest of the body. The nervous system is most sensitive to lack of oxygen: at normal body temperature, the brain can remain without oxygen for only about four minutes before irreversible damage occurs to its specialized cells. If, by the use of artificial respiration and artificial circulation, a person is revived, any slight brain damage will be shown by loss of concentration, memory or reason; more severe damage will result in unconsciousness, although the heart may be beating normally and respiration may be quite regular. If such patients are unconscious, their cough reflexes are usually weak or absent. They therefore have no defences against foreign matter, and often inhale bacteria which can cause infections, such as pneumonia, that may prove fatal.

Fear of being buried while still alive is widespread. There have been cases of wrong diagnosis of death, usually following drug overdosage and exposure to extreme cold: there are many cases of drunkards who have suffered prolonged exposure to cold and appeared dead but who survived. It is exceedingly rare for anyone to be taken to a mortuary while still alive.

One problem that surrounds the question of death is that today the majority of the dying, however feeble or weak, may be kept alive artificially and indefinitely. If their hearts are failing, they may be connected to an external perfusion system; if their kidneys are failing, there is a dialysis machine; if they are losing blood, it may be replaced; if they are too weak to breathe, they can be put on a ventilator. In fact, all the vital functions can be sustained by machines in the intensive care unit of a hospital, where patients are under the constant supervision of specialist medical and nursing staff.

With enough resources available it would theoretically be possible to support indefinitely an increasing number of terminally ill people. In countries where people pay for their own medical treatment, this could lead to the gradual reallocation of vital medical resources from poor, acutely ill young patients, to the rich, failing, chronically ill few. In countries where health care is financed by the state, such a trend creates a dilemma which is not easily resolved for those who have to allocate resources, or where resources are limited.

After death

Several days usually elapse after death before a body can be removed from the mortuary for burial or cremation. Strict laws govern the certification of death, and doctors are acutely aware of the professional and legal problems that premature removal of a patient could cause.

The death of a loved one is one of life's worst events, and we probably fear it, when we dare to think of it, more than our own death. The sudden loss of those we love tends to cut off all motive for any activity or pursuit and sometimes, at least temporarily, the taste for life itself. The emotion which follows loss of love is depression, one of the most unpleasant experiences that human beings may have to endure.

The grief of bereavement is something which has to be suffered, expressed by mourning and, more especially, shared. A bereaved person is vulnerable and isolated, and needs the support of family and friends. Normally, after a period of mourning, the loss is accepted and eventually fresh attachments will be made. A bereavement is one of the most significant events in anyone's life, and the future of the bereaved person often depends on how it is dealt with (see below).

Bereavement reactions

The death of a spouse usually has considerable medical and psychiatric effects. There is an increased chance of physical illness during the following year, and the death of a spouse increases by six times the chances of a person requiring admission to a psychiatric hospital within six months of the bereavement. The emotional loss and sudden loneliness are of course important, but a sudden drop in income, which frequently occurs when a husband dies, is also an important factor. The mental health of a widow or widower and the children depends greatly on the support of relatives and the community at this time, and the relief of any financial crisis often makes all the difference between coping or breaking down.

To an adult, the death of a loved brother, sister or parent, or the death of a son or daughter can all cause a reaction as profound as the loss of a spouse. Sometimes the first reaction of a bereaved person is to deny that the death has happened. This is normal for a while, but if continued for long it amounts to a morbid state, approaching the formation of delusions (see page 65). An emotional, tearful reaction to bereavement, in which sorrow can be shared, is more conducive to recovery than denial. It is particularly unsatisfactory for a surviving parent to try to deny the other parent's death to the children.

Psychotherapy directed towards bereavement and death is often very effective in the treatment of adults suffering from various fears and depressions, more so sometimes than the old sex-oriented psychotherapy. The patient is given an opportunity of discussing fully his or her bereavement experiences, and situations of loss and death, and may relax, break down and show reactions which can then be therapeutically handled and carefully used for his or her benefit. Fear of death and separation is more primitive and fundamental, and begins earlier in life, than any sex urge.

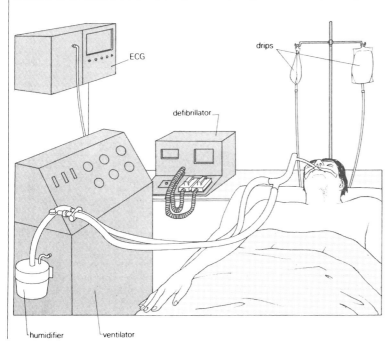

The role of a hospital's intensive care unit is to monitor and support a patient's vital functions round the clock. This is usually required after severe injury, serious illness such as a heart attack, or major surgery, when death would otherwise ensue. The patient is linked to a ventilator which assists breathing, while an electrocardiograph (ECG) continuously observes and records heart performance. A defibrillator may also be used, to give a measured electric shock to the heart in order to restore its regular beat. Drip-feeds are given to replace lost blood or body fluids, or for intravenous feeding.

This kind of analysis is appropriate not only for psycho-neuroses, but also for some of the behaviour difficulties in adults.

The bereaved child

It used to be thought that children were too young to appreciate the facts of death. But in fact many children think a great deal about death from the age of three onwards; many of their most intense fears are about their own deaths and those of their parents. Death of parents is to a child the severest form of bereavement: it involves not only the loss of loved ones but also of the care they would normally receive, and the disorganization of his or her subsequent life. Fortunately the death of both a child's parents is an extremely rare occurrence. The most common causes of orphanhood in industrial societies are the death of a parent in a road traffic accident, and from heart disease or cancer.

In handling a bereaved child and his or her anxiety, it should be realized that much of the anxiety is associated with guilt. The child will probably previously have shown or felt antagonism, anger or even death wishes against the deceased parent; after the parent's death the child frequently feels very guilty at the memory of these thoughts, and imagines that they may have been instrumental in bringing about the death. The ghost of the parent may return in dreams, much to the terror of the child, who then develops a fear of his or her own death happening as a punishment for previous thoughts. He or she also tends to fear the death of the surviving parent. Reassurance about this, and dream interpretation, is often very effective in relieving the guilt anxiety of bereavement.

The bereaved schoolchild may become, at least temporarily, backward at school. This is often because of depression, and also the lack of the motive of pleasing the deceased parent. It is important that teachers should appreciate the difficulties of the bereaved child at this time, and give him or her special and sympathetic encouragement.

The long-term effects of bereavement in childhood can be considerable, and depend largely on how the lack of a parent is compensated. If accompanied by physical and mental deprivation, and perhaps institutional upbringing, orphanhood can have a damaging effect on any child. The effects of orphanhood vary according to the culture pattern and traditions of child care in a community. Where there is a large family of uncles, aunts and other relatives, the problems of orphanhood are probably fewer than where the social services of the state have to be relied upon completely.

The practicalities of death

Before a funeral can be held, various legal formalities must be attended to by the dead person's next of kin or executor (whomever the dead person has appointed to carry out his or her wishes, as set out in a will). These formalities include obtaining a death certificate and registering the death. If the death has occurred at home a doctor must be called, since only a doctor can certify that someone is dead. If the doctor has not seen the dead person within fourteen days of the death he or she is legally obliged to examine the body to determine the cause of death, and also if it is to be cremated. Most people die in hospital, however, and the doctor in attendance at the time of death will issue the death certificate and may also organize the registration of the death. Otherwise the duty to inform the registrar usually falls on a relative; the doctor will provide, along with the certificate, a document listing those who can register the death and the procedure for doing so.

In the event of an unexplained or accidental death, the doctor informs the coroner who will issue the death certificate, usually after a post-mortem examination has been performed. If the post-mortem fails to reveal the cause of death, or if there are grounds for suspecting that the death was due to unnatural causes, an inquest – a public court hearing – will be held. Only after the inquest is over can a death certificate be issued and the death actually registered with the authorities.

Once the death has been registered and a certificate of disposal has been issued, definite arrangements for the funeral can be made. The services of a funeral director or undertaker can greatly ease the burden of organization, either by arranging the basic funeral or by seeing to everything including press notices and the actual burial service or crematorium arrangements. The funeral itself, usually held between three and six days after the death, is in two parts if performed by the Church – the religious ceremony and the burial or cremation. A non-religious ceremony is also possible.

Coping with bereavement

The following ways of helping a bereaved person come to terms with his or her loss have been shown to be useful:

- *Offer practical assistance to the bereaved, particularly if they are organizing the funeral, helping with such day-to-day tasks as shopping and cooking.*

- *Allow the bereaved person to talk freely about his or her loss. Expression of grief is an important part of the mourning process.*

- *Continue to offer support and sympathy even after the shock of the first few weeks or months has passed. This is especially important at anniversaries of the death and other significant times such as Christmas and birthdays,*

- *when loneliness and memories are likely to be most strongly felt by the bereaved person.*

- *Encourage the bereaved person to avoid sedatives and other drugs unless they are felt by a doctor to be absolutely necessary.*

- *Enlist professional support from the bereaved person's doctor, lawyer and priest if necessary.*

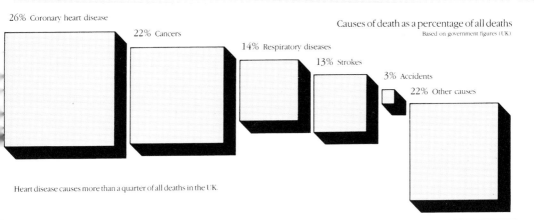

26% Coronary heart disease

22% Cancers

14% Respiratory diseases

13% Strokes

3% Accidents

22% Other causes

Causes of death as a percentage of all deaths
Based on government figures (UK)

Heart disease causes more than a quarter of all deaths in the UK.

Main cause of death in each age-group with death rates per million population* 1983

Age	All causes	1st	2nd	3rd
Under 1 year*†	10.2	Perinatal causes 3.8	Congenital anomalies 2.7	Signs, symptoms and ill-defined conditions 1.8
1-4	438	Congenital anomalies 97	Accidents 95	Cancer 49
5-14	228	Accidents 85	Cancer 46	Congenital anomalies 20
15-34	616	Accidents 218	Cancer 110	Suicide 65
35-44	1,441	Cancer 485	Heart disease 312	Accidents 139
45-54	4,623	Cancer 1,740	Heart disease 1,569	Cerebrovascular disease 274
55-64	13,406	Heart disease 4,908	Cancer 4,892	Respiratory diseases 1,052
65-74	33,637	Heart disease 12,380	Cancer 9,906	Respiratory diseases 3,825
75 and over	98,260	Heart disease 32,827	Respiratory diseases 19,787	Cancer 15,665

*Deaths under 1 year per 1,000 live births.
†Provisional.

Based on government figures (UK).

PART II
The Body in Health and Illness

Mental Health and Illness

Mental illness usually begins after a period of emotional stress, but may have other causes. It is not easy to find a neat identifiable reason for most mental illness, much of which is caused by several factors. Some are related to physical disorders, such as epilepsy, which can cause hallucinations, while others can be linked to circumstances, including difficulties with relationships or to dependence on alcohol or other drugs. Some, such as schizophrenia, are partly inherited.

Some psychiatrists divide mental problems into: neuroses, where the patient is reacting overemotionally or unreasonably to everyday stresses; psychoses, where the patient loses contact with reality and may not realize he or she is mentally ill; addictions, which have both a mental and a physical component; and a few others such as personality disorders and psychosexual problems. Some of these distinctions are technical and are by no means universally accepted, so this section deals with problems in a terminology that is familiar to us all – anxiety, depression, alcoholism, and so on. Also, since one or more treatments may be used, depending on the person's circumstances and the type and severity of the problem, the various methods of treatment are grouped together on pages 68-9.

Anxiety

This is probably the commonest of all psychological problems, and in one form or another it accounts for a significant proportion of all visits to GPs. For most people, anxiety is a temporary response to stress. It becomes an illness only when the symptoms persist so that they dominate one's whole life. Symptoms of anxiety are a feeling of fear or apprehension for no apparent reason, and outward signs of this include flushing of the face, dilation of the pupils, rapid heartbeat (palpitations), sweating and muscular tension that may lead to pain, as in a tension headache (see page 194). This mental and physical state is in fact a readiness to run away or fight for one's life, called the 'fight or flight' response, and is the same in all animals. For some people, this feeling of anxiety is prolonged, while others have frequent so-called 'panic attacks' without warning, when symptoms are intense. These 'anxiety states' may be related to emotional problems or to circumstances, even though the sufferer may not realize it. Some people react more strongly to stressful situations such as exams or changing jobs than others, and are thus more prone to anxiety.

To treat anxiety, it is possible to help yourself in several ways. If there is a specific reason for the anxiety it may be possible to remove it. Some sufferers think their symptoms may be caused by physical problems such as heart or stomach trouble (and worrying about this may be enough to bring on an attack of anxiety), so it is a good idea to consult a doctor in order to rule out any physical illness. There are various methods of relaxation which may reduce the severity of symptoms, and setting aside a period in which to 'unwind' each day, perhaps by sitting down with a book or going for a walk, can in many cases be beneficial. If professional help is needed, the doctor may prescribe drugs or psychotherapy (see pages 68-9).

Phobias

Some people with excessive anxiety are afraid of harmless objects and activities such as cats or shopping. These specific fears are called phobias, and can usually be treated. For example, agoraphobia (literally, fear of the market-place) is the commonest phobia, and may make normal life extremely difficult, since the sufferer fears public places such as shops and streets. It may start with a slight feeling of anxiety in a certain place such as a supermarket checkout, and gradually get worse until the sufferer has a 'panic attack'. The situation is then avoided, and activities become more and more restricted until the agoraphobic is afraid of leaving home altogether. The usual treatment for this condition is behaviour therapy (see page 68). Sometimes tranquillizing drugs may help in the short term (but they may create problems of their own).

Social phobia, a term meaning excessive shyness accompanied by anxiety, is also a common phobia. It is more difficult than agoraphobia to treat with behaviour therapy, but not impossible. There are also many specific phobias, often fears of a particular animal. To go through a phase of being afraid of animals is normal in preschool children, and it is possible to develop a phobia of almost anything, for example snakes or spiders, but it is simple to avoid these objects without disrupting one's life. It is the severity of the fear and the degree to which it interferes with normal life that determine whether it is an illness.

Depression

Depression and anxiety often go together; people with depression have low self-esteem and do not feel capable of worthy of doing normal day-to-day activities. Usually, though, they keep trying, but everything seems more of an obstacle than it would to someone who was not depressed. The world seems threatening, and this causes anxiety. Similarly, chronic anxiety can lead to depression.

The basic feeling of depression is one of low spirits. This can vary in intensity from a transient 'blueness' or mild sadness, which most people experience at some time in their lives, to a severe and even life-threatening disease. Because the spectrum is so wide, psychiatrists (and others) have classified depression into two types – depression without physical symptoms and depression with physical symptoms – each type responding to different treatment.

Depression without physical symptoms is sometimes termed 'neurotic' or 'reactive' depression. It occurs in response to a particular event, such as a bereavement, but is more intense and prolonged than one would normally expect, and leads to depressed feelings about life in general rather than just the sad event that first caused it.

The feeling of worthlessness caused by depression leads to an inability to cope. You may, for example, feel that you are a bad person or a failure in some way, that the future looks bleak and that things will never get better. Depressed people often see only the negative side of the world around them, such as tragic events in the news. Predisposing factors to depression if any emotional blow occurs are: being female; being unemployed; having three or more children under the age of fourteen; having lost your mother before you were aged about eleven; and having no close confiding relationship. While depression may be set off by a specific traumatic event, some people have mild reactive depression all their lives; it seems to be a part of their personality to respond in this way to the world around them. This might be partly hereditary and partly learned in childhood. Depression without physical symptoms sometimes responds to psychotherapy.

A smaller number of people suffer from endogenous depression, that is, depression originating from within rather than resulting only from external circumstances. As well as feelings of depression, the sufferer has physical symptoms which are probably due to a malfunction of the part of the brain (the hypothalamus) related to emotion. The hypothalamus (see page 182) regulates not only emotion but also sleep, eating and hormonal secretions. Symptoms may include loss of appetite (and therefore loss of weight, which can be dramatic), sleeping difficulties and a tendency to wake very early in the morning. Concentration is often impaired, and movement can be affected, becoming either very slow or agitated, with pacing, for example. This type of depression can, however, also be precipitated by external events, and it is known that hereditary factors play a part.

People with this type of depression may also experience delusions – such as a belief that they are fatally ill or have no money – or hallucinations that are usually voices (not visions) saying derogatory things about them. This condition, called psychotic depression, is the most severe form of depression and usually requires hospital treatment, and

unfortunately may recur.

Very rarely, people who suffer severe depression at some time in their lives develop at other times what appears to be the opposite – mania. Someone who has experienced both states at different times is termed a manic-depressive. In the manic phase, the person becomes rather grandiose and overactive, and may seem happy but is often aggressive and irritable. It is for this group of patients that antidepressant drugs or electroconvulsive therapy is most helpful.

Suicide

Most people who try to kill themselves are severely depressed, although not all of them sincerely wish to end their lives, but use the attempt as a way of asking for help. Nevertheless, anyone talking about or actually making any sort of attempt on their life must be taken seriously. Many people find it difficult to talk about suicidal feelings, and a proportion of those who kill themselves have been to their doctor shortly before their death but been unable to mention their depression and suicidal thoughts.

Those at greatest risk of committing suicide tend to be male, middle-aged, in poor health, and single, divorced or widowed. Alcoholics are at much greater risk than others, and so are people with certain medical conditions such as epilepsy.

If someone you know talks of ending his or her life, or if you yourself are thinking seriously of it, it is vital to talk to someone about the problem: a sympathetic member of the family, a trusted friend, your GP or the Samaritans, who are on call 24 hours a day and are experienced in dealing with this problem. Nearly everyone who attempts suicide and fails is relieved afterwards to be still alive.

If you find someone unconscious or semi-conscious, send for medical help immediately, and meanwhile apply first aid. Any tablets or pill bottles nearby should be kept and shown to medical personnel.

Anorexia nervosa

Our society places great value on physical attractiveness, which largely depends on being slim. A desire for fashionable slimness (rather than healthy slimness) leads many people, particularly young women and adolescent girls, to go on a reducing diet. It is when the dieting continues even

---

Many people, including doctors, find the field of mental health and psychological/psychiatric medicine difficult to understand. One area of misunderstanding is the role of the various professionals. The following definitions may be useful:

A psychiatrist is a doctor who specializes in mental disorders and, being medically qualified, can prescribe appropriate drugs.

A psychologist is not medically qualified, cannot prescribe drugs, but does have training in clinical psychology, and uses psychological techniques such as behaviour therapy.

A psychoanalyst may or may not be medically qualified but does have a qualification in psychoanalysis (delving into the subconscious and unconscious to look for the root causes of mental problems).

A psychotherapist is anybody who uses 'talking treatment' to help people.

Most of these practitioners are highly qualified but there are no regulations about people calling themselves by certain titles (especially in psychotherapy). General practitioners may use psychotherapy in treating mental illness, and of course may prescribe whatever drugs they consider advisable.

after the healthy weight is reached, and the dieter continues to eat very little or nothing, that problems arise. Anorexia nervosa is defined as loss of more than a quarter of normal body weight coupled with a refusal to eat and a belief that the sufferer is still too fat. The extreme loss of weight leads to hormonal disturbances and subsequent loss of periods (amenorrhoea) and, if untreated, will eventually be fatal.

Anorexia nervosa is often a symptom of an underlying psychological problem connected with family relationships. Anorexic girls often have parents who seem to be domineering and over-controlling, and it may be that a refusal to eat is the only way of achieving some control over their lives. Another theory is that anorexia is the result of a subconscious desire to remain a child: for some reason the sufferer fears adulthood and physical maturity.

A condition related to anorexia nervosa is bulimia nervosa, in which the sufferer fasts most of the time but then craves food so much that she goes on a binge, eating any and every food available, in huge quantities. This gorging engenders feelings of guilt and so the sufferer induces vomiting and uses laxatives excessively to purge the body of the food. All this can lead to an imbalance of blood chemistry which in turn can cause dangerous irregularities of heart rhythm.

With treatment, most sufferers recover, but may have eating problems for many years, even into middle age. Far fewer males than females have anorexia; those that do follow the same pattern. If you suspect someone of anorexia nervosa, it is important to persuade them to see a doctor. There is no scope for self-help in this condition; it is best treated in hospital, possibly with psychotherapy as well as attention to diet under close supervision.

Alcoholism

The stereotypical picture of an alcoholic – an old man living rough who drinks cheap sherry or methylated spirits – is, in fact, very rare. Most alcoholics are young men and (increasingly) women with responsible jobs who are supporting a family. It is more common in people with alcoholic parents, in those who make or sell alcohol, and in those such as the self-employed who have little or no supervision at work, and no one can see that they are drinking. Alcohol is one of the major health hazards of modern society.

Signs and symptoms

People who become alcoholics usually begin drinking heavily in response to stress. The temporary relief from stress that drinking brings gradually leads to a habit, where any feeling of tension can only be dissipated by alcohol. Eventually the person finds that he or she needs a drink just to feel normal, even on waking. Often the change from social drinking to alcoholism is imperceptible, occurring over several years, although it can occur very quickly. Early signs and symptoms are frequently unnoticed, even by friends and family. The following signs are indications of alcohol dependence:

1 Repeated withdrawal symptoms
These include feeling unwell with a headache (hangover) on most days; feeling sick or retching when, for instance, cleaning teeth; tremors (the DTs) in the morning so that it is difficult to hold a cup without shaking.

2 Drinking to relieve withdrawal symptoms
This includes drinking in the morning, and waiting outside pubs before they open.

3 Craving for alcohol
If a few days have passed without a drink, the alcoholic has an urgent desire to drink, and perhaps goes on a 'binge' of drinking over two or three days. Drinking may become secretive.

4 Increasing tolerance of alcohol
More drinks or longer and stronger drinks are needed for the same effect.

5 Uncharacteristic behaviour
The alcoholic may become aggressive and irritable, and have bouts of depression or jealousy. Loss of memory, even blackouts, may occur, and an increasing lack of ability to concentrate will mean that the demands of a job become more difficult to meet.

Health risks

Heavy drinking eventually damages the body, and leads to many serious physical diseases, including cirrhosis of the liver (see page 107), gastric ulcers and other problems of the digestive tract causing internal bleeding, and brain damage. A pregnant woman who drinks excessively, that is, more than six measures of spirits or large glasses of wine a day, has a one in three chance of having a physically or mentally handicapped baby. Since alcoholics rarely eat adequately, vitamin deficiencies often occur.

Treatment

For treatment to be effective, the alcoholic must recognize that he or she has a problem and be highly motivated to overcome it. It may be possible for some people to control their drinking successfully, but most alcoholics have to abstain for the rest of their lives. They usually need help to overcome the problem, and a counselling service such as Alcoholics Anonymous may be invaluable. Treatment is based on a combination of psychological and psychiatric counselling, detoxification programmes in hospital with tranquillizers used to suppress withdrawal symptoms, and eventual social reintegration into family and work environment. The exact form of treatment will be varied to suit the individual, and its success largely depends on the alcoholic's determination to be cured.

Drug addiction

People become addicted to drugs either because they have been prescribed them by a doctor for use over some time, or because they enjoy the pleasurable effect a drug gives and go on to take it habitually and in increasingly large amounts. So-called soft drugs, those that are only mildly addictive, such as codeine, or apparently non-addictive, such as cannabis, may be used without serious psychological effects. It is the so-called hard drugs such as heroin that can lead to severe addiction, since they must be taken in bigger doses to maintain the pleasurable effect. The mortality rate among heroin addicts is very high. Some prescribed drugs are also addictive. They include the benzodiazepine drugs, such as the tranquillizers Valium and Ativan, and sleeping tablets such as Normison and Mogadon. For a short time these drugs are very effective, but tolerance and then dependence can occur after a month or so, without one realizing. Volatile substances such as glue, if inhaled, may also lead to addiction. Drug addiction leads to physical and mental breakdown, since the body's chemistry is disturbed.

Treatment

Drug addicts need help but are unlikely to seek it if their addiction is to an illegal drug such as heroin. It is important, therefore, to recognize drug addiction early if possible, and act quickly. Generally the best action is to consult your doctor who, if the problem seems to be some prescribed drug, will recommend steps that you can take to break the habit. If, on the other hand, the problem arises in a young person whose drug abuse is related to emotional problems, it is important first to gain his or her confidence so that the problem can be discussed openly. Hospital treatment will be necessary, first to break the habit and then to prevent renewed addiction by psychiatric treatment.

Senile dementia

Dementia in the elderly is a common problem, and becoming more common as the proportion of elderly people in the population increases. In this disorder the brain ceases to function normally and the mind gradually deteriorates. This may be due to multi-infarct dementia, in which many small strokes due to hardened arteries affect brain function. Severe depression in an elderly person may be confused with dementia.

Although dementia is usually a disease of the elderly, rare forms of pre-senile dementia occur in younger people, some of which are hereditary. (Alzheimer's disease, an abnormal degeneration of the brain of unknown cause, usually arises between the ages of forty and sixty, causing loss of memory, often with hallucinations, and progresses within a few years to a helpless state for which no treatment is known.)

Symptoms

The early signs of dementia are a slight forgetfulness of recent events (for example, what was eaten at the previous meal). Frequently, however, forgetfulness is a normal accompaniment of ageing and does not necessarily mean that the person is becoming demented, so it is not always possible to make the diagnosis early in the course of the illness. As the disease progresses, other intellectual functions decline: as well as loss of memory there is a confusion, a loss of reasoning powers and an apathetic withdrawal from the real world. Sometimes the sufferer behaves in antisocial ways, and may even become violent.

Treatment

There is no cure for this condition, and treatment is mainly supportive. In the early stages it may be possible for a senile person to continue living at home if there is a companion or friends to help with daily tasks, and if help from the social services and other community services is available. Eventually the demented person will probably need the constant care that only the geriatric ward of a hospital can provide.

Schizophrenia

It is not known what causes schizophrenia; several factors are normally involved in its onset. The condition is known to be partly inherited, but this does not mean that children of schizophrenics inevitably get schizophrenia. It is likely that a biochemical defect in the brain predisposes some people to schizophrenia, and that when people with this defect are subjected to external stresses, they break down with schizophrenic symptoms. Worldwide, about one per cent of the population suffers an attack of schizophrenia at some time in their lives.

Symptoms

The symptoms of schizophrenia are of two kinds: positive, where some abnormal element appears in the mental state; and negative, where something normal disappears from a person's make-up. The positive symptoms are hallucinations (usually hearing voices) and delusions (false beliefs which seem very important to the sufferer). The voices usually say things with little emotional content, such as echoing thoughts, or a running commentary on actions. The delusions may be persecutory or grandiose and are often bizarre. The negative symptoms include loss of the richness of emotional life: the victim becomes apathetic with no ability to interact with people, and withdraws socially. These may be the only symptoms of schizophrenia but they are very difficult to treat.

Treatment

Hallucinations and delusions are normally controlled by antipsychotic drugs. These do not improve negative symptoms, however. A long course of rehabilitation is often necessary, with a slow re-entry into the community. Even so, a proportion of schizophrenics are so ill that they must remain in hospital for long periods, and relapse each time discharge is attempted.

Obsessional neurosis

Another term for this condition is obsessive-compulsive neurosis, because there are two kinds of symptoms. The first are obsessional thoughts, which are intrusive and repetitive. They may be very unpleasant for the sufferer, often taking one of two themes – aggressive thoughts towards a loved one, or thoughts about being dirty or contaminated. The sufferer tries to resist the thoughts but the more he or she resists them the more they return. The second group of symptoms involves compulsive acts. These are usually related to the thoughts, because for a short time the act reduces the anxiety associated with the thought. For example, an anxiety about being contaminated would be reduced by washing the hands, but since the anxiety soon returns the act needs to be repeated, and so becomes a compulsion. In addition, many sufferers are also depressed.

Some people are called 'obsessional' by their friends. These are usually people who are never late for appointments, who are particular about tidiness and cleanliness and who may be very careful with money. Such people have only a very slightly increased risk of becoming truly obsessive; the vast majority continue to lead productive and trouble-free lives.

Hysteria

It is almost impossible to describe or diagnose hysteria without making assumptions about the unconscious state of the person concerned – a state which is not directly observable. The term is applied to people who develop physical symptoms (such as paralysis or numbness of a limb) that are not due to physical disease. A large percentage of people diagnosed as hysterical go on to develop true physical disease, so hysteria is a difficult and sometimes dangerous term to use. Nevertheless there are some people who complain of symptoms in many parts of their body and who are also profoundly disturbed psychologically, and these people clearly come into the category of hysteria. With modern investigations it is fairly easy to determine that there is no physical cause of the illness, but diagnosing the underlying psychological conflict responsible for the symptoms is much more difficult.

As with obsessional problems, there are normal people who are labelled as 'hysterical' by their friends. Such people are usually overdramatic in their personal relations, and generally over-emotional (the emotions are felt to be fraudulent by others). These people do not appear to be at any greater risk of developing true hysteria than others.

Treatment for mental and psychological problems

Treatments for the conditions discussed in the previous pages fall into two main groups: the 'talking treatment' of psychotherapy; and drug therapy (chemotherapy).

Psychotherapy

This term includes many types of treatment. Behavioural psychotherapy aims to change a person's behaviour in specific ways, using techniques specific to the problem. This approach is best used for phobias and obsessions.

A phobic person is usually introduced into the frightening situation by the therapist, either in reality or in fantasy. At this point, the anxiety increases and the patient does what he or she has always done – tries to avoid the anxiety by withdrawing from the situation. However, the therapist encourages the patient to resist until able to remain in contact with the situation without anxiety. This is called desensitization or 'flooding'.

Obsessive-compulsive neurosis can be very successfully treated by behaviour therapy. The therapist finds out what triggers off the obsessional thought (such as going to the lavatory) and then puts the patient in contact with that situation for long periods of time and prevents, by persuasion, the carrying out of the compulsion. At first this is

very frightening but eventually the patient learns to cope and the anxiety diminishes.

Behaviour therapy also includes aversion therapy in which someone is punished (often by receiving a small electric shock) for a detrimental behaviour. This technique has been used to help sex offenders give up such behaviour as exhibitionism or paedophilia.

Psychotherapy also includes psychoanalysis – as practised by Freud and Jung, and also including a wide range of methods that have grown out of their pioneering work. Psychoanalysis assumes that a large part of our daily behaviour, including some mental problems, is based on unconscious processes – that is, we may not always be aware of our motivation. The treatment aims to uncover these processes and thus to give the person being analysed more control over his or her life. Such techniques are sometimes called 'insight therapies' because analysts believe the new insight gained through treatment is crucial to improvement. Analysis is a very slow process, taking many years, although shorter versions, of twelve to eighteen months, have been developed and used in some cases.

As well as the two extremes of psychotherapy – behavioural and analytic – there are a number of other types of therapy. One of these is family therapy. Its practitioners say that it is impossible to understand a psychological problem in isolation from the person's family (if they have one), so they treat the whole family as being in need of help. During sessions with the family they try to recognize patterns of family interaction that disturb one or more members, and then try to change this by discussion, or by getting the members to play different roles for a while, or even by behavioural means (reward for a good response).

Cognitive therapy is used to treat depression and anxiety. Cognitive therapists maintain, not unreasonably, that our mood depends upon what we think. Therefore, if we concentrate on negative aspects of our life we will become depressed; if we see everything as a threat we will become anxious. Cognitive therapists collaborate with their patients to help them decide which of their thoughts about themselves and the world are real and which distortions. Various techniques are then used to help the patient gain a better perspective and thus control the mood disorder.

Drug treatments

Drugs have a limited but valuable place in the treatment of mental and psychiatric disorders. There is no doubt about the effectiveness of many drugs, although there is also a large placebo effect – people get better because they are expecting a drug to work or because of the therapist's interest. We know about many of the chemical actions of these drugs but not yet which ones are crucial.

Antidepressants

Antidepressant drugs have a specific application to depression accompanied by physical symptoms. They usually relieve depression after several weeks. Side-effects may include a dry mouth, slight difficulty in focusing, constipation, low blood pressure and sedation.

Tranquillizers

Tranquillizers are drugs which reduce anxiety. The barbiturates have been replaced by the benzodiazepines like

Tranxene, Valium, Ativan, Frisium and Librium which are safer, with fewer side effects. However, they can create problems of dependence – it is difficult to stop taking them if they have been taken for a long time – and there is some doubt about whether they continue to be effective over long periods of time. They also slow reactions so that driving under their influence can be dangerous, and in old people they may cause confusion.

Probably the best way to take tranquillizers is when needed – up to a maximum number of times per day. Some days only one tablet may be necessary; on other days it may be difficult to stay within the limit. This method prevents dependence and allows the patient to identify things which make them anxious because they have to think whether they need a tablet before taking one. Your GP will advise when and for how long such drugs should be taken when they are prescribed. If he or she does not, then ask.

Hypnotics

Hypnotics induce sleep. Most tranquillizers are also hypnotics if taken in a high enough dose. Some of them, like tranquillizers, belong to the benzodiazepine group. The longer-acting ones are not suitable for people who want to be fully active the following day, since they take longer to be eliminated from the body. Shorter-acting types are eliminated more quickly so, while inducing sleep, they are no longer active later in the night, or by the morning. This is usually better for the patient, especially if he or she is elderly.

Antipsychotics

Antipsychotics are drugs which are often sedative but also have an action against psychotic symptoms such as hallucinations and delusions. They are used in schizophrenia and manic depression. Largactil, Melleril, Orap, Sparine and Stelazine are antipsychotics. These are powerful drugs and are not used for trivial conditions. They have side-effects such as dry mouth, sedation and low blood pressure and also a wide range of interactions with other drugs. One particular side-effect is abnormality of movement, which can include the symptoms of Parkinson's disease, fidgety legs and sudden twisting movements of the neck and limbs. In the long term, some patients develop repetitive movements of the mouth and lower face.

Lithium, given regularly, has been found to prevent manic depression as well as to reduce the symptoms of mania. It has some side-effects: the patient passes a lot of urine and so needs to drink more, for example, and it is important that people on lithium have regular blood tests to measure the amount of the drug getting into the blood.

Electroconvulsive therapy

Electroconvulsive therapy (ECT) is used for severe depression. First, a general anaesthetic and muscle relaxant is given, then an electric current, just enough to cause a temporary epileptic-like fit, is passed between two electrodes placed on the temples. Although the brain goes into a momentary seizure there is no risk of damage to the body of the patient because it has been totally relaxed by the anaesthetic. ECT is a rapid, safe and effective treatment, but most doctors prefer to try antidepressant drugs first and progress to ECT only if the patient remains ill.

Measuring stress levels

The table below lists the amount of stress involved in various life events. Too many life changes within a relatively short time are often followed by some form of illness, physical or mental, within the ensuing year. To estimate your risk of a health change in the future, add up the scores of the events listed in the table that have occurred in the last year.

Below 80: your stress level is probably average or below average.

Between 80 and 150: you are under too much stress and should look at ways of reducing it. Consult the following two pages.

Over 150: your chances of future serious illness are more than fifty per cent, and it is important to identify the problem and do something about it by changing those aspects of your life that are causing stress.

1 Death of a spouse 100
2 Divorce 73
3 Marital separation 65
4 Jail sentence 63
5 Death of a close family member 63
6 Personal injury or illness 53
7 Marriage 50
8 Sacking or redundancy 47
9 Marital reconciliation 45
10 Retirement 45
11 Change in health of a family member 44
12 Pregnancy 40
13 Sex difficulties 39
14 Gain of a new family member 39
15 Business readjustment 39
16 Change in financial state 38
17 Death of a close friend 37
18 Change to a different line of work 36
19 More or fewer arguments with spouse 35
20 High mortgage or loan 31
21 Foreclosure of mortgage or loan 30
22 Change in responsibilities at work 29
23 Son or daughter leaving home 29
24 Trouble with in-laws 29
25 Outstanding personal achievement 28
26 Spouse beginning or stopping work 26
27 Beginning or ending school or college 26
28 Change in living conditions 25
29 Change in personal habits 24
30 Trouble with the boss 23
31 Change in working hours or conditions 20
32 Change in residence 20
33 Change in school or college 20
34 Change in recreation 19
35 Change in church activities 19
36 Change in social activities 18
37 Moderate mortgage or loan 17
38 Change in sleeping habits 16
39 More or fewer family get-togethers 15
40 Change in eating habits 15
41 Holiday 31
42 Christmas 12
43 Minor violations of the law 11

Keeping mentally fit

Most people, even those who are outwardly extremely placid and easy-going, experience periods of great stress, when mental health may be at risk. Bereavement, divorce, losing or changing one's job, money worries, sexual difficulties and domestic upheavals such as moving house may all be triggering factors in depression or other mental illness, especially if several such crises occur at the same time. Since stress often cannot be avoided unless one totally changes one's way of living, it is a good idea to learn how best to cope with stressful situations. This means cultivating a certain attitude of mind that leads to increased mental resilience. It also means knowing how to relieve any tension that builds up.

Relieving tension

By employing one or a combination of the following methods of relieving tension several times a week, you will find that you gradually acquire the ability to unwind. By using this ability regularly, not just in times of severe stress, you will find yourself better able to cope with problems.

Muscle relaxation
Learning to relax the muscles
can be done by means of an exercise similar
to that taught in yoga classes.

1 Wearing loose clothing, lie face up on the floor
with your arms by your sides, palms up and feet apart.

2 Starting with your feet and legs, stretch the muscles taut
for a moment, then relax them.

3 Tighten the buttocks and lift them from the ground,
feeling the spine stretch as you do so. Then relax them.

4 Stretch out your arms and fingers, then relax them.

5 Press your shoulders and neck down to the floor, then
relax them.

6 Lift up your head and feel the back
of your neck stretching. Let it fall slowly
back to the floor.

7 Screw up your face muscles,
then relax them. Drop your jaw so
that your mouth is slightly open.

8 Lie totally limp, and feel your
body weight completely supported
by the floor, as if it is sinking into
the ground. After a few minutes,
roll over slowly and lie on your
side for a few more minutes before
getting up.

Deep breathing

Breathing deeply is a useful weapon against the onset of tension and also helps to combat existing tension. To develop the habit, sit or lie comfortably and take deep slow breaths through the nose at about half the normal breathing rate, for up to five minutes. If you consciously slow your breathing in this way whenever tension begins to build up, you will notice an immediate relaxing effect.

Meditation

There are many ways of meditating, all of which aim to achieve mental peace by emptying the mind of thought, and therefore worry. The following method may be effective. In a quiet room, sit comfortably upright with the eyes closed. Choose a word with no emotional connotations – or alternatively, choose something visual such as a candle flame or wall pattern – and focus your attention on it. Give your full attention to the word or image – in the case of the word, repeating it under your breath – so that your mind is emptied of all other thoughts. Gradually increase the meditation period until you can easily do the exercise for about twenty minutes per session.

Exercise

Physical exercise – jogging, cycling, swimming or gardening, for example – is an excellent way of aiding mental fitness. In fact, any activity that makes you breathless and sweaty, if performed regularly, say two or three times a week, will make you less likely to have major health problems, mental as well as physical.

Exercise reduces fatigue because it helps people sleep better and awake more refreshed, it increases alertness and the ability to concentrate, and it releases tension. All these psychological benefits mean that your ability to relax and to respond to stress with equanimity is enhanced.

Increasing mental resilience

Learning to modify your behaviour in the following ways will help you to deal with stress more effectively.

1 Live in the present

Concentrate on things as they are now. Try not to dwell on the past or think about future events over which you have no control.

2 Talk things over

Discuss problems with friends and relations, but do listen to their opinions or advice rather than merely burdening them with your difficulties.

3 Act positively

Once you have made a decision about a problem, act promptly and positively rather than doing nothing.

4 Don't take problems to bed with you

Try not to think about your troubles or about work less than two hours before going to bed. Allow yourself time to unwind first, perhaps by going for a walk or reading a light, escapist novel.

5 Keep busy

Don't brood about your problems – engage in social activities or a hobby rather than sitting about worrying.

6 Learn to relax

Teach yourself at least one of the techniques described above under the heading Relieving tension.

The Skin

The skin is one of the largest and most important organs of the body. It covers about 1.7 square metres (2 square yards) and weighs around 3 kg (6 lb). Its functions include protecting the body against water loss, injury and infection, and helping to regulate the body's temperature. The skin is also a sensory organ that monitors the body's surroundings, and it plays a role in sexual attraction. Both the hair and nails form part of the skin.

The structure of the skin

The skin is composed of two main layers, the epidermis and the dermis. The epidermis is the outer layer, and consists of dead cells covering a layer of living cells. The living cells are continually dividing and producing new cells which move towards the surface of the skin, where they form the outer layer. During this process the cells die and fill with keratin, a tough waterproof protein which also forms the hair and nails. The outermost layer of epidermis is continually being worn away, by friction and washing.

The second main layer is the dermis which is below the epidermis and consists of a network of blood and lymph vessels, nerve endings and fibres of the proteins collagen and elastin, which support the skin. Sweat and sebaceous glands and hair follicles are also present in the dermis. Beneath the dermis there is a layer of fat which acts as insulation and as a cushion and shock-absorber.

Skin and hair colour depend on the amount of brown pigment, called melanin, in the epidermis. People of all races have the same number of melanin-producing cells – melanocytes – in the epidermis but because of genetic differences the amount of melanin actually produced varies. Sunlight also causes more melanin to be produced, since it helps to protect the skin from the damaging effects of sunlight, and results in a sun-tan. Albinos have no melanin because they lack an important enzyme required for its production.

There are important glands in the dermis and the tissue below it. These are coiled tubes, opening to the outside of the body through pores in the epidermis, and are mainly either sebaceous glands or sweat glands. Sebaceous glands open into the hair follicles and produce a secretion – sebum – which oils the hair and skin. There are two main types of sweat glands: eccrine and apocrine. Eccrine sweat glands produce a mixture of water, salts and urea; they are important in temperature control and excretion. The apocrine glands are found mostly in the skin around the nipples, in the armpits and in the pubic region. Controlled by the sex hormones (see *Growth*, pages 38-51), they are much more numerous in women than in men. These glands produce a thicker secretion which, when broken down by bacteria, produces body odour. The wax glands in the outer ear canal are specialized sweat glands.

The skin varies greatly in structure from one region of the body to another, but there are only two principal types: hair-bearing skin and smooth skin. Hair-bearing skin occurs over most of the body surface, producing varying amounts of hair from one person to another and from one area to another, from one sex to the other and from one age group to another. Smooth skin is present on the palms of the hands and soles of the feet, and its surface is patterned with continuously alternating ridges and grooves forming distinctive prints, such as the fingerprints, peculiar to each individual. Smooth skin has a relatively thick and compact epidermis, designed to provide additional protection in these areas from buffeting, and to bear pressure. It has sweat glands but no sebaceous glands, and gives a powerful grip at the places where this is most needed. It is also well supplied with nerve endings for extra sensitivity to touch and pain.

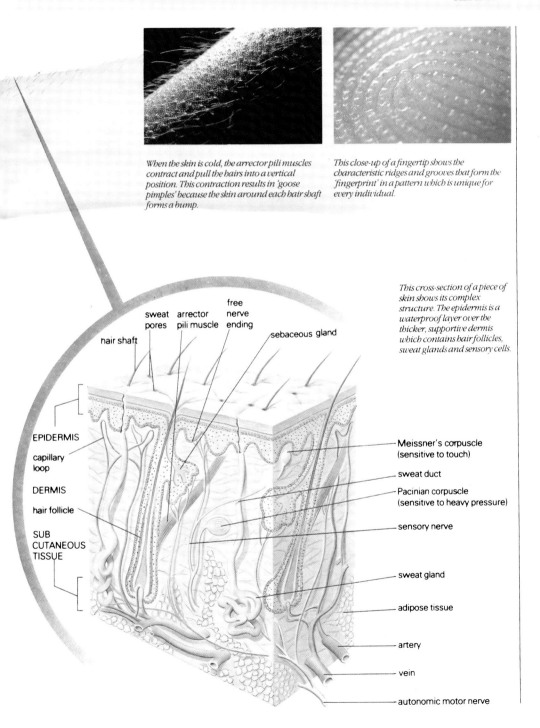

When the skin is cold, the arrector pili muscles contract and pull the hairs into a vertical position. This contraction results in 'goose pimples' because the skin around each hair shaft forms a bump.

This close-up of a fingertip shows the characteristic ridges and grooves that form the 'fingerprint' in a pattern which is unique for every individual.

This cross-section of a piece of skin shows its complex structure. The epidermis is a waterproof layer over the thicker, supportive dermis which contains hair follicles, sweat glands and sensory cells.

hair shaft

sweat pores

arrector pili muscle

free nerve ending

sebaceous gland

EPIDERMIS

capillary loop

DERMIS

hair follicle

SUB CUTANEOUS TISSUE

Meissner's corpuscle (sensitive to touch)

sweat duct

Pacinian corpuscle (sensitive to heavy pressure)

sensory nerve

sweat gland

adipose tissue

artery

vein

autonomic motor nerve

Hair and nails

Hairs are produced by the hair follicles, which are tubes within the dermis. Hair consists of dead cells full of the protein keratin. The base of the hair follicle continually produces new cells which, as they are pushed up the follicle, gradually die and harden to produce the hair. Hair colour depends on the amount of pigment melanin present in the hair; grey and white hairs have little or no pigment.

All a person's hair follicles are present at birth but not all are functioning. Some become active in later life as the result of hormone action, as, for example, at puberty. If the base of the follicle is destroyed, a new hair will not grow again in that particular spot, whereas if another area of the follicle is damaged, hair growth may still continue.

There are about 100,000 to 140,000 hairs on the average person's head, and they usually last between two and four years; every hair is shed and replaced after this time. Normal hair loss is rarely noticed because hairs are shed a few at a time, and new hairs are growing constantly. On average, between forty and a hundred scalp hairs fall out each day. It has been estimated that the growth rate of hair on the head is about 0.5 cm (0.2 in) every ten days, or 1.5 cm (0.6 in) a month. The shape of the hair follicle probably determines whether a hair is straight or curly; if the follicle is oval in section the hair will be curly, whereas if it is circular the hair will be straight.

Each hair follicle is attached to a small muscle that can contract to raise the hair upright. In animals the raised fur helps to trap air which acts as an insulating layer. In humans this heat-retaining function is less important but the hair can still stand on end, particularly after a fright.

The nails develop from a special layer of cells underneath the cuticle. These cells fill with the hard protein keratin and, as they are forced along by the growth of new cells, they die and form the nail. Apart from the lunula, the crescent-shaped white area near its base, a nail is transparent and the pink colour reflects that of the nail bed beneath.

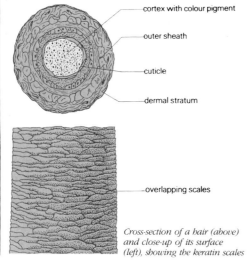

Cross-section of a hair (above) and close-up of its surface (left), showing the keratin scales

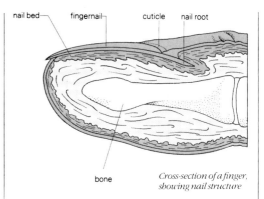

Cross-section of a finger, showing nail structure

Temperature control

The skin helps to control body temperature in two different ways: by changes in blood flow through the skin, and by sweating. The hypothalamus in the brain (see page 182) has overall control over body temperature, and both nervous and hormonal messages from the brain to the skin control the amount of heat lost.

Overheating causes an increase in blood flow through the blood vessels in the dermis, and heat is then lost from the blood through the skin surface. At the same time, sweat glands increase their secretion, and the evaporation of water in the sweat on the skin causes the body to cool.

A fall in body temperature leads to a reduction both in blood flow through the skin and in sweating. The erector muscles attached to the hairs contract, causing the hair to stand on end, trapping air which also helps to conserve body heat.

Skin disorders and diseases

Skin problems fall into several different groups. Inherited and congenital disorders are a result of abnormalities in the genes or a malfunction during fetal development. The skin also reacts to many substances in the environment and can become infected by a variety of different organisms. There are also tumours of the skin, either benign or malignant. Finally, there are the minor but irritating skin problems that afflict many people. Some skin conditions are contagious but most – such as psoriasis and eczema – are not. These disorders, though mild and of little danger to general health, affect the appearance and may cause psychological problems.

Inherited and congenital disorders

Inherited abnormalities may be relatively mild, such as dryness of the skin (xeroderma), or more serious conditions that may involve not only the skin and related tissues (hair, nails and sweat and sebaceous glands) but also the teeth and, more importantly, the nervous system.

Anhidrosis

The absence or deficiency of sweat-gland secretion (anhidrosis) may be a congenital defect (caused by their abnormal development), but it can also be a complication of an infectious skin disease or another disorder such as diabetes. A form of anhidrosis that occurs in the tropics often follows one or more attacks of 'prickly heat'. In this condition, the sweat glands appear to be blocked by plugs of keratin and the sweat fails to escape to the surface of the skin. Heat exhaustion is a consequence of this type of anhidrosis, and the only effective treatment is to move the person to a cool environment where the skin can recover.

Epidermolysis bullosa
Epidermolysis bullosa is an abnormality of the skin in which large blisters (bullae) appear, either spontaneously or as a result of very mild injury. The condition usually becomes evident within a year of birth, and has an hereditary basis.

Psoriasis
Psoriasis, an inherited disease of the skin, nails and joints, can appear at any time of life. The characteristic feature is the appearance of well-defined red raised patches, called plaques, covered by silvery scales. These plaques vary in size and in their location on the body. Normally there is no itchiness, and since the condition is not infectious the main problem is one of appearance. Treatment with ultra-violet light, application of ointment containing coal tar or dithranol or corticosteroid cream, and drug therapy often help clear the condition in severe cases

Birthmarks
A birthmark, or naevus, is a type of skin discoloration due to an anomaly in intra-uterine development. There are many types of naevus and their cause is usually unknown, although it is known that the fetus is at greatest risk during the early stages of pregnancy. Certain drugs taken by the mother, virus infections, and serious nutritional problems may all lead to such abnormalities. Two types of naevus are the 'Port-wine stain' and the 'strawberry mark'. Both are caused by growths of small blood vessels just under the skin (angiomas) which give the characteristic red colour. Port-wine stains (capillary angiomas) tend to occur on the head, face and neck. The affected area is not distorted, although the overlying skin is usually very thin. A port-wine stain on the face is usually treated by destroying the cells within it, but those on less obvious parts of the body may be left and camouflaged with cosmetic cream when necessary. Strawberry marks or cavernous angiomas are raised areas formed of blood-filled spaces under the skin. They are frequently not apparent at birth but develop during the first few months of life. Although disfiguring, especially if the angioma is on the face, the mark often disappears of its own accord, and treatment is seldom necessary.

Other naevi are brown, due to overproduction of normal skin pigment. They are the familiar brown round or oval birthmarks (moles) which last a lifetime unless removed by a doctor using a process such as cautery or curettage.

Dermatitis and eczema
Dermatitis, inflammation of the skin, has many different causes ranging from infection to allergy. When not due to infection it is also known as eczema. It may begin at any age,

and outbreaks often follow mental stress. Poor hygiene encourages dermatitis in the skin creases, as in the groin, toe clefts and anal regions; and it may start as the result of chapping, from frequent contact with water, or as the result of irritation caused by a wide range of detergents, solvents and other chemicals. Constant scratching of the infected areas leads to thickening of the skin (lichenification). Dermatitis may also result from bacterial or fungal infection of the superficial layers of the skin.

Atopic dermatitis (atopic eczema, or eczema)
Atopic dermatitis is partly inherited and is sometimes associated with allergic disorders such as asthma or hay fever. It often starts in infancy although it may commence at any age. The rash usually starts on the face, with itchy patches that weep and become encrusted. Later the rash spreads to involve the insides of the elbows and knees, the sides of the neck, wrists and ankles. Dryness of the skin is common. About half the cases clear during adolescence, but if the dermatitis is severe in childhood it is likely to continue in some degree throughout life. There is evidence that the problem stems from an abnormality in the immune system.

To treat the condition, all possible irritating factors which cause itching, such as rough clothing, should be avoided. Some soaps may prove irritating, so emulsifying ointments and creams should be substituted when washing. Your doctor may prescribe a steroid cream or ointment to ease the itching and inflammation.

Contact dermatitis
Contact dermatitis has two main causes: the development of an allergy to something that has been in contact with the skin, or irritation from a toxic substance. It is relatively common in industry, from contact with chemicals or oil. Many species of plants may also be responsible, notably primulas, chrysanthemums, poison ivy, tulips and hyacinths. Cosmetics may cause contact dermatitis; various components of rubber may cause a rubber allergy; and nickel sensitivity may give rise to a rash under earrings, fasteners and other metal fittings which irritate the skin. Medical applications such as ointments and eye drops may also cause trouble, particularly those containing mercury, as may antihistamine drugs, local anaesthetics and antibiotics. Even some textiles can cause contact dermatitis.

The distribution of the rash will often give a clue as to the cause; for instance, an allergy to the rubber in rubber gloves will show as a rash which includes the fingers and hands but ends in a fairly sharp line at the wrists. Once dermatitis has started, it may spread to areas of the body that have not been in contact with the substance in question. Familiarity with a substance does not help develop a resistance to contact dermatitis, and a person may suddenly become allergic to something which has been handled constantly for many years without causing trouble.

Seborrhoeic dermatitis
Seborrhoeic dermatitis is a scaly rash which often starts on the scalp, giving dandruff, and then spreads to the eyebrows, ears, chest and back. In obese people the armpits and other skin folds may be affected.

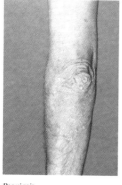

Psoriasis

Birthmark 'strawberry mark'

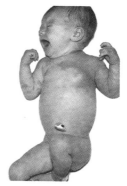

Birthmark: 'port-wine stain'

Atopic dermatitis (eczema)

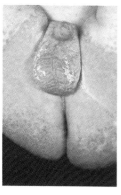

Nappy rash

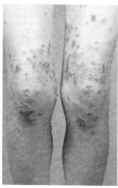

Impetigo

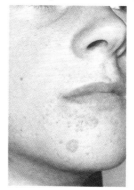

Warts

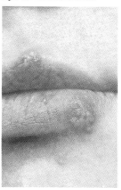

Cold sores

Lichen simplex

Lichen simplex is a type of chronic dermatitis in which the skin lesions are thickened, and kept open by the patient's constant scratching. Prescription drugs may relieve this condition.

Stasis dermatitis

Stasis dermatitis and varicose eczema are due to a malfunction of the veins in the legs interfering with blood supply, and causing oedema (a build-up of fluid) in the tissues. Varicose eczema is often seen before a varicose ulcer develops, particularly when the leg is injured. The most effective treatment is compression with a carefully applied elastic support bandage over an antibiotic or antiseptic cream. The bandage must be worn throughout the day and, when sitting, the patient should aid circulation by always having the legs raised on a chair. Associated varicose veins usually require treatment.

Nappy rash

In infants, nappy rash is a common form of dermatitis, and it can spread to involve the rest of the body. It may be a reaction to the chemical ammonia formed by the urine, to drugs, or as a result of other disease. Allergic eczema in infants is also common and, as its name suggests, may be an allergic reaction to some foods, particularly cow's milk, or other irritating substances. The eczema usually begins as red pimples on the face. If untreated, these can form small blisters which break to form a crust. Treatment involves finding the cause, and either avoiding it or using a hypo-allergenic alternative (a substitute which is extremely unlikely to trigger allergy). Creams and ointments can help soothe the rash. The eczema usually clears up by the second year of life, even if untreated.

Skin infections

Many harmless organisms naturally live on the skin. The skin is one of the body's defences against infection but in some circumstances it can be invaded by infectious organisms such as viruses, bacteria, fungi and parasites.

Impetigo

Impetigo is a common bacterial skin condition, particularly in children. It begins with a slight redness of the skin, followed by small blisters which burst and discharge to form a golden-coloured crust on the skin. Staphylococcal bacteria cause most cases of impetigo, and prompt treatment with antibiotics is usually effective.

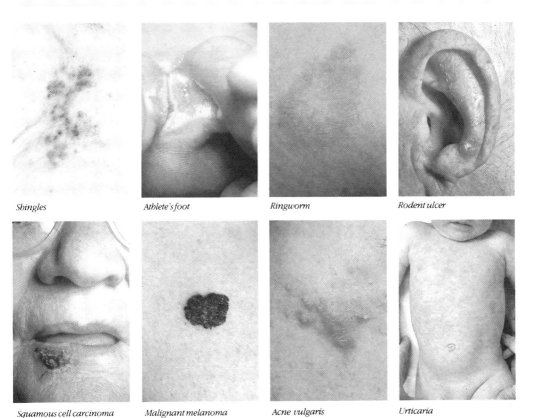

Shingles *Athlete's foot* *Ringworm* *Rodent ulcer*

Squamous cell carcinoma *Malignant melanoma* *Acne vulgaris* *Urticaria*

Boils

A boil is an infection of a hair follicle, usually with staphylococci. If several hair follicles in the same area are affected, this may produce a carbuncle. The bacteria are often already present on the skin and multiply to cause infection when resistance to them is lowered for some reason. Antibiotics and the local application of antiseptics are usually effective in treating boils, but when they occur frequently the underlying cause of the reduced resistance to infection should be investigated by a doctor.

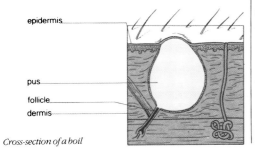

epidermis

pus

follicle

dermis

Cross-section of a boil

Erysipelas (cellulitis)

Erysipelas is caused by infection with a type of streptococcal bacteria through a crack in the skin. The skin is reddened and raised with a defined ridge; there may also be a high temperature and shivering. Antibiotics are effective treatment for the infection.

Warts

Warts are caused by a virus and can affect the skin on different parts of the body such as the hands, feet, buttocks and genital region, and face. Although the same virus is probably responsible for all these types, their appearance varies according to which area is affected. Warts are infective, but many people seem to be resistant to them. There are many folklore cures surrounding the treatment of warts, such as the use of charms or burying meat under a stone, and occasionally warts do disappear after these cures and after hypnosis. There is no known reason for this, and all warts eventually clear up with no treatment. You can usually destroy a wart with a chemical wart paint or cream bought from the chemist. If this fails, the doctor is usually able to remove the wart with chemicals, by freezing or by electrical cauterization. Sometimes repeated treatment may be necessary.

Cold sores

Cold sores *(Herpes simplex)* are common and unpleasant viral infections, usually affecting the skin around the lips. A small blister forms and then bursts to leave a crust. Infections may occur again and again at the same location, the virus probably remaining dormant until another infection, often the common cold, precipitates another attack. The virus is not easy to kill but there are antiviral drugs that help to control attacks. An antiviral ointment is available on prescription that prevents cold sores developing, but must be applied at the beginning of a bout of infection.

The herpes virus is also responsible for genital ulcers, which are sexually transmitted either during sexual intercourse with an infected person or after oral sex with someone who has cold sores. An attack of herpes genitalis lasts about two weeks and can recur over many years. Antiviral creams may relieve attacks.

Shingles

Shingles *(Herpes zoster)* is caused by the same virus as chickenpox. The virus attacks one or more sensory nerves on one side of the body, and there may be severe pain along the area of the affected nerve. The pain is followed by the eruption of small, deep blisters at the same site, and these eventually burst and dry into crusts. If the eyes are affected, the cornea can become scarred, causing problems with vision. Use of antiviral ointments in the early stages of the infection helps to control the disease.

Thrush (monilia)

The yeast-like organism *Candida albicans* (monilia) can infect various parts of the body. On the skin it is found in warm, damp areas such as the mouth, genitals and between the buttocks. In adults, the infection is most common in women in the vagina and vulva where it causes thrush. In babies it can affect the mouth and nappy area. In some individuals who have a low resistance to infection, *Candida* can cause serious problems, but in most cases treatment with a suitable fungus-destroying antibiotic soon clears the condition.

Athlete's foot

Athlete's foot *(Tinea pedis)* is a common fungal infection associated with conditions that produce hot, sweating feet. It is highly contagious and can be transmitted in public or communal baths, showers and locker rooms by walking around in bare feet. The fungus lives in the soft skin between the toes and can spread to the sole and upper surface of the foot, causing small blisters which may crack, and severe itching. Sometimes in hot weather the hands can also be affected. Though it causes discomfort, it is not harmful unless the damaged skin becomes infected by another organism.

Treatment involves keeping the skin dry and clean, and going about barefoot (in dry places) as much as possible to allow air to circulate. Socks or stockings should be changed frequently, and fungicidal ointments or medicated foot powders used. To avoid transmitting the disease an infected person should use their own bathmat and towel, kept away from those used by others. Socks should be boiled to kill the fungi. Synthetic fibre socks should be avoided, because they tend to make the feet sweat more profusely, and shoes and boots made of plastic or rubber are inadvisable for the same reason.

Ringworm

Ringworm *(Tinea)* is a common fungal infection of the skin, caused by a group called dermatophyl, particularly among children. The fungus lives on the skin or scalp, producing circular bald patches or rings covered with greyish scales. It may be carried in combs and brushes, hats and headscarves, and is also transmitted to humans by animals. It is usually treated by an antifungal drug, taken by mouth, which protects the keratin of the hair against further infection. After a while the diseased hair may be cut off; new growth should be unaffected.

Ringworm of the smooth skin usually appears as round areas with a spreading edge, and can also be contracted from animals. The fungus may also infect the nails. Again, it can be treated with antifungal preparations available from your doctor.

Insects and mites

Parasitic infection can be transmitted by sleeping in the same bed as people infected with mites or ticks, or occasionally simply by contact with infected bedding or clothing. People may also become infected by close personal contact or sexual intercourse with an infected person.

Scabies

In scabies the fertilized females of the itch mite burrow in the skin to deposit their eggs, while the males and young live on the surface or in the openings of hair follicles. The burrow appears as a fine, zigzag discoloured line beneath the skin. The sites usually affected are the hands, between the fingers, the inside of the wrists, the armpits, groin and under the breasts; the face and neck are never affected. The eggs hatch in four to eight days, the larvae leave their burrow and eventually mature into adults.

The burrows cause intense itching, particularly when the host (and therefore the mites) is warm in bed; scratching the site may lead to infection with other organisms, and the formation of pustules. The diagnosis is usually made from the symptoms of intense itching, the appearance of the burrows and the microscopic identification of the mite or its eggs in scrapings from the skin.

Scabies mite (greatly enlarged)

Treatment is straightforward. After taking a hot bath or shower, with thorough soaping and scrubbing of the infected areas, the whole body below the neck must be painted twice with an insecticide lotion, and a further application made the following day. All those who have been in contact with an infected person should be treated at the same time, to avoid reinfection. Itching may continue after this, even though all the mites have been killed. Clothes and bedding which might be infected should be left unused for three weeks, after which time all the mites in them should have died.

Another mite, *Demodex folliculorum*, lives within the hair follicles, particularly on the face, and may cause pimpling or inflammation in the external ear.

Lice
There are three types of lice that infest different parts of the body: head lice, body lice and pubic lice. Lice can be seen with the naked eye and the eggs (nits) of the head and the pubic louse attach themselves to the hairs in these regions. The eggs take about eight days to hatch. Body lice live in the seams of clothing and infest the skin only when they are actually feeding. Lice feed on blood and their bites cause intense itching, which is not harmful unless the damaged skin is infected with other organisms. A pesticide in the form of a shampoo or lotion is effective, but treatment must be repeated to kill any lice that may have hatched since the first treatment. Clothes must be washed and ironed to kill the lice in them.

Human louse (greatly enlarged)

Fleas
Animal fleas frequently bite humans, and some people are more susceptible than others. Pets and their bedding should be regularly treated with an antiflea powder. Fleas are only a serious health problem in the tropics, where they are dangerous carriers of much disease.

Insect bites
Bites from mosquitoes, midges, ants, horse flies, bees and wasps can often cause skin irritation, but are rarely serious unless bacterial infection follows or the person is allergic to the venom injected by the insect.

Tumours
Skin tumours or neoplasms can be either benign or malignant (cancerous). Benign growths take many forms and, although a few give rise to malignant tumours, most are harmless. If there is any doubt about a growth on the skin, medical advice should be sought.

Rodent ulcer
Rodent ulcers (basal-cell carcinoma) are the commonest malignant skin disease, and are usually found in people over fifty, on the face around the nose, neck, ears and at the edges of the scalp. The ulcer starts as a small raised patch of scaly skin which grows again when it is picked off, eventually producing a raw patch which slowly increases in size. The ulcer can be removed surgically or by radiotherapy. It is only locally malignant and does not spread to other parts of the body.

Solar keratosis
Excessive exposure to sunlight, particularly in fair-skinned people, can result in solar keratosis. The skin becomes freckled and scaly wart-like lesions occur, the skin becoming dry and thin. After some years these growths can become cancerous and invade other areas, and therefore should be treated in the early stages.

Squamous cell carcinoma
This type of skin cancer is commonly caused by prolonged exposure to sunshine over many years, although certain chemicals and X-rays are other causes. The tumour grows quickly and can invade other tissues, but early treatment by surgery or radiotherapy is usually successful.

Malignant melanoma
This is a rare but serious form of skin cancer. It can arise spontaneously or from pre-existing dark moles on any part of the body. It is not known what causes the change, but sunshine and hormonal changes may be involved. Any changes in a mole, such as itching, growth or discharge should be treated with suspicion; although these do not necessarily indicate a malignant change, medical advice should be taken quickly, since early treatment is the most successful.

Other skin disorders
A variety of skin disorders can occur when the normal functioning of the skin goes wrong. In most of these conditions the actual cause is obscure, and consequently some are difficult to treat.

Acne
This is a common skin disease in which spots and pimples occur on the face, neck and body. Several forms of the condition are known and the type that occurs in adolescence, known as acne vulgaris, is common; three out of four adolescents suffer from it at some time.

Acne vulgaris appears at puberty and is caused by an increase in the secretion of sebum by the sebaceous glands, which are under the influence of the sex hormones. The sebaceous glands open into the hair follicle and it is blockage of these follicles that causes acne. This can begin as a blackhead (comedone) followed by the gland swelling to produce a whitehead. This may then burst into the surrounding tissue, causing irritation. Infection with skin bacteria can aggravate the condition.

In the most severe forms of acne the inflammation extends deeply into the sebaceous glands and destroys the walls of the glands. This results in pus-filled cysts in the tissue which can join together to form cavities. Although these do eventually burst and heal, scarring can result.

It is little consolation to the adolescent sufferer that acne almost always disappears with maturity; it can cause severe psychological problems and deserves sympathetic attention. Treatment is aimed at removing the blockages as well as reducing the amount of sebum produced. Careful attention to washing the face, using soap and mild antiseptics, helps to remove grease and keep the skin clean. Degreasing lotions and abrasive soaps or powders can be used to dry the skin and to remove blackheads.

It is thought that some foods, particularly chocolate, cocoa and coffee, can aggravate acne; lack of vitamin C may also have an effect. Modern drug therapy, though by no means offering a certain cure in every case, is effective and a doctor should be consulted before one of the many over-the-counter preparations is tried. Severe scarring caused by acne can be treated by cosmetic surgery.

Chilblains
These are red, itchy swellings, usually on the fingers, toes, nose and ears, caused by cold damaging the blood vessels of the skin. They may be associated with poor circulation to the extremities. Chilblains can be prevented by keeping warm and dry by adequate clothing in cold weather.

Ichthyosis
This is abnormal dryness of the skin caused by insufficient secretion of the grease (sebum) that prevents the skin losing water. The condition is usually inherited and is most prominent on the legs, where the skin may look scaly and dirty. Creams and oils used daily can help to restore suppleness to the skin, which should be protected from cold.

Urticaria (nettle rash; hives)
The symptoms of nettle rash are raised weals with a pale centre surrounded by a red flare, and they may occur in many shapes or sizes, sometimes accompanied by swelling (oedema). There can be many causes, from food or drug allergy to emotional stress. In some people, a weal can even be produced when the skin is stroked or written on (dermatographia). Antihistamine drugs are usually used as treatment until the cause of the problem is found (by means of various tests); remove the cause if possible.

Pruritus
Pruritus is the medical term for itching. It is most often applied to itching in the female genital region (pruritus vulvae) or in the area of the anus (pruritus ani). The causes include both local and general disorders. Very often pruritus is due to excessive drying out of the skin as a result of the over-use of soap, hot water or detergents. Reactions to certain chemicals in cosmetics, deodorants or ointments, and in medicines taken by mouth may also cause itching. So, too, may plants, such as poison ivy and members of the Primula family, and insect bites. General disorders such as eczema and urticaria can cause pruritus, as can various types of dermatitis, including the common contact dermatitis. Other conditions that may cause general itching

include jaundice and Hodgkin's disease.

Pruritus vulvae has many possible causes. The urine should be tested for the presence of sugar (indicating possible diabetes), or a urinary infection. Swabs should be taken from the vagina, particularly if a discharge is present. Very often laboratory examination reveals the presence of *Candida* or of *Trichomonas vaginitis*, both of which can infect the vulva and vagina. Threadworm and ringworm may also cause vulval irritation, and allergy to contraceptive creams and foams, and to vaginal deodorants, is also a common cause. Treatment of infections is usually fairly straightforward, in the form of vaginal pessaries or tablets. The patient's partner may also require treatment to prevent reinfection from him.

Causes of pruritus ani, which is usually found in men, include inflamed haemorrhoids and eczema of the anal region, which is very common and which responds well to steroid ointments. Parasites (particularly threadworms) and fungi can produce intense anal pruritus, and so can antibiotics taken by mouth. Faulty sanitary habits – either failure to wipe the anus properly, or over-vigorous wiping – may also lead to irritation. Excessive sweating can contribute to the problem, and synthetic underwear should be avoided.

Diseases affecting the skin

Many illnesses produce symptoms affecting the skin. For example, viral infections such as measles and chickenpox produce a rash; and disorders of the endocrine glands, diabetes mellitus, and pituitary, thyroid, parathyroid and adrenal disorders may all show their presence with changes in the skin and hair.

Liver disease can cause skin changes such as sensitivity of the skin to light. Acne rosacea is often, but not always, associated with alcoholism and cirrhosis of the liver, and seems to occur most commonly in middle-aged women. Redness of the facial skin due to enlarged small blood vessels is the first sign, followed by the appearance of pimples. In advanced cases the nose may become purple, and bulbous and cystic nodules appear.

Emotional disorders may aggravate existing skin conditions or activate new ones. Some people damage their own skin, by scratching or pinching, often as a way of expressing excessive aggressive feelings. Anxiety and insecurity are sometimes expressed, and probably to some extent relieved, by scratching or rubbing. Occasionally, mentally disturbed people actually make their own skin seem diseased by injuring it in some way, usually with heat or chemicals. Others have delusions about their skins, usually of parasitic infestation which does not exist, although they bring samples to the doctor to try to prove it. Some hypochondriacs are morbidly anxious about trivial, harmless changes in the skin, some of which may be barely visible to the observer.

Hair diseases

Several of the skin diseases described elsewhere in this chapter, such as ringworm, can affect the scalp and therefore the hair. There are also several disorders which affect the scalp and hair alone.

Baldness (alopecia)

Total or partial loss of hair is usually found in men, and is called male-pattern alopecia. The hair stops growing first on the temples and the top of the head, and the hair loss gradually extends to the back of the head. The hair at the sides and back of the head is not normally affected. Male-pattern baldness is probably partly inherited and there is no known method of preventing or stopping the process, although transplanting hair from the sides and back of the head can have limited success in covering the bald areas. However, most men accept this type of baldness as a natural part of the ageing process.

Hair loss can occur during illness or after pregnancy, but growth is usually restored during recovery, or after treatment of the underlying condition. Drugs given in the treatment of leukaemia may cause baldness. The child may need to wear a wig until regrowth occurs.

Alopecia areata, where well-defined round patches of complete baldness develop, can affect any part of the body. The condition may be hereditary. The hair often grows again after a few months, but the baldness can recur. There are many possible treatments, but none is especially effective.

Ingrowing hair

If a growing hair turns back on itself and penetrates and grows into the skin an irritating reaction can occur. This can be a particular problem with very tightly curled hair, particularly in negro men after shaving. The ingrowing hair can be removed with a needle, and one way to prevent the condition recurring is by growing a beard.

Hirsutism

This is increased hair growth on areas which normally do not have much hair, such as the face and chest in women. This may be a genetic trait and although in a few people hormonal disorders may be the cause, no underlying abnormality can be found in most cases. It is really a cosmetic problem but nevertheless can cause great emotional distress. There are various depilatories on the cosmetic market, but electrolysis is probably the most effective method of removing unwanted hair, by passing a small electric current to the root of the hair follicle. This can be very time-consuming if there are many hairs, and scarring can result if the process is not skilfully carried out.

Cosmetic surgery

Some people have psychological problems which a new appearance can help to overcome. Worry over an apparently minor disfigurement or abnormality can build up over a period of years into quite serious mental ill-health. The wrinkles and sags of ageing can cause considerable distress, and the outlay of a substantial sum of money on a face-lift operation may seem to be a worthwhile investment. A cosmetic surgeon cannot create an entirely new appearance, only modify and improve existing features, and should explain to the patient before the operation just how much can be achieved, so as to avoid disappointment.

There are many surgical techniques for altering appearance, some of them of doubtful efficacy. The standard face-lift is one of the most popular of all cosmetic surgery operations. The operation may take as long as three-and-a-half hours, using injections into the skin of the face to reduce bleeding and produce local anaesthesia, as well as general premedication to sedate the patient. The aim of the operation is to tighten up the skin across the face and neck by removing sagging or slack skin round the chin and jaws, and softening the lines of the face. A good face-lift lasts several years and a general rule is that the younger the patient, the longer the face-lift will last, since younger skin and tissues are softer and more easily stretched. But eventually the sagging and wrinkling of age will occur again.

Surgical techniques are also available to improve a complexion damaged by pitted acne scars. A 'sand-papering' technique called dermabrasion is normally used, where the outer skin is rubbed away completely, along with the scars, and new skin grows in place of the old. Finally, there are the surgical methods used to restore features as a result of a congenital deformity (such as a hare lip), or following accidental injury, ulceration or tumour growth.

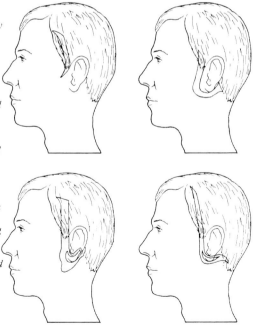

These drawings show places where the skin may be removed to tighten the skin of the face, an operation known as a face-lift. After removal of the shaded portion, the remaining skin is pulled up and rejoined, thereby removing the looseness that was present.

Keeping the skin healthy

A healthy-looking, attractive skin is not only an asset to the appearance but also a sign of good general health. A sensible lifestyle, which means a balanced diet, adequate exercise and fresh air, good sanitation and cleanliness, and avoiding contact with harmful substances, will help to keep the skin in good condition and enable it to carry out its important functions.

Routine skin care

Routine skin care includes washing with soap and water, which not only helps to remove dirt and grease but also prevents the spread of infection. Too-frequent washing, however, can be harmful because soap does remove the skin's natural protective oils. Excessively dry or chapped skin should be protected with a mild cream or oil, while very greasy skin may be washed frequently with soap and wiped with an astringent lotion to keep it free of excess oil. Hair should be washed with a mild shampoo at least once a week, and hair driers, rollers and curling tongs should be used carefully to avoid over-drying the hair; the best way to dry hair is to allow it to dry on its own. Too-vigorous brushing can damage the hair, and chemicals such as perming and tinting agents should be used carefully and not too frequently.

Cosmetic products such as face creams, eye shadows, after-shaves and anti-perspirants are usually carefully tested for irritants which may cause skin damage to ensure that they are safe, but their abuse (by use on the wrong part of the body) or overuse can nevertheless cause problems. If these arise, use of the product involved should be discontinued immediately. Cosmetic skin preparations should never be used on broken areas of skin. Every person's skin is different, and what is safe for one person may be harmful to another.

Many of the common disorders and infections affecting the skin can be prevented by careful attention to personal hygiene and cleanliness. Frequent changes of clothing, especially underclothes, particularly in hot weather, and clean towels, will help reduce the risk of infections spreading. Tight clothing and artificial fibres can cause excessive sweating, chafing and irritation, which lead to skin problems. Some infections are spread by contact with infected people or clothing, and these can be avoided by careful attention to hygiene in public places or where there is communal living. People who have a skin infection should always have their own towel and their clothes should be washed separately from those of other people.

In the environment there are many factors, both natural and artificial, that can be potentially harmful to the skin and hair. Ultra-violet light in sunlight and sun-lamps is one example; a commonsense attitude to sunbathing by avoiding excessive exposure and by using a suitable sun-tan lotion is important. A tan may look attractive but is the skin's way of protecting itself against the sun's harmful rays. Sunlight actually destroys skin by breaking up its collagen, which gives skin its elasticity, and so exposure to the sun has an ageing effect. Excessively hot, cold or wet conditions can also harm the skin, and protective creams and clothing can

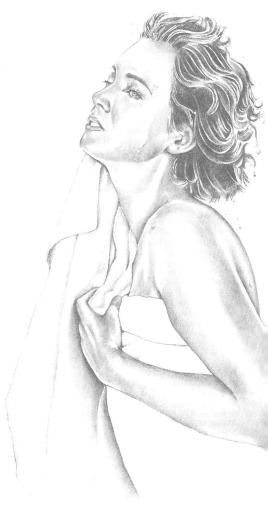

Although showering or bathing is pleasant, water has a drying effect on the skin; unless your skin is greasy use a moisturizer.

help prevent damage.

Both at home and at work the use of harmful chemicals such as cleaning products, paints and oils, is common, and some sort of protection, such as barrier creams or protective clothing, should be used to prevent contact with them and guard against irritation and the skin being damaged, perhaps permanently. Many of these harmful substances can be absorbed through the skin, to cause damage to other parts of the body, and they should be avoided wherever possible.

Diet and exercise

Regular exercise, especially in the open air, contributes to a healthy and attractive skin by keeping the muscles beneath the skin firm and by maintaining good blood circulation. Diet also has an important effect on the skin: too much greasy food, for example, can lead to greasy skin, encouraging acne (see page 79). A balanced diet with the correct proportions of carbohydrates, fats, proteins, vitamins and minerals will contribute to healthy skin, hair and nails. Fresh uncooked fruit is a rich source of vitamin C, important for healthy skin. It is essential for the manufacture of connective tissue, necessary for the skin's elasticity. Vitamin A is also essential for a healthy skin as it aids growth and tissue repair and maintains normal mucous membranes.

Effects of drugs and stress on the skin

Many commonly used drugs for both internal and external use can affect the skin, causing allergic rashes or abnormal sensitivity to sunlight, and in such cases moderation, or abstinence if possible, is desirable. Such drugs include antibiotics, aspirin, tranquillizers and sleeping pills, and germicidal agents such as hexachlorophene. Abnormal stress (see page 69) from pressures in the home or at work, can also affect the skin and hair, or aggravate existing skin problems, and the causes of stress should therefore be dealt with and controlled by means of observing a pattern of living where relaxation and leisure pursuits are as much a part of one's day as more stressful activities.

Leafy green vegetables, fruit and nuts all contain vitamins we need to maintain health; vitamin deficiency can lead to dry, rough skin, sore lips, mouth and tongue, dermatitis, and easily bruised skin and bleeding of the gums.

The skin and food

The western diet removes the possibility of malnutrition and its resulting skin changes, unless there is malabsorption of food due to disease. In other parts of the world, however, dietary deficiencies usually cause alterations in hair and nail growth, and can lead to dryness and darkening of the skin. For example, shortage of vitamin A or niacin causes roughening of the skin, shortage of riboflavine leads to sore lips and clogged pores, and deficiency of vitamin C causes rough, dry skin. In the West people at risk of such deficiencies include old people who do not eat a varied diet including fresh fruit and vegetables, alcoholics, and those on strict diets such as vegans.

Safety in the sun

Always use a sunscreen. Use one with a protection factor appropriate to your skin type: for example, if you tan without burning a protection factor of four is suitable; if you always burn use one of between twelve and fifteen. Reapply after bathing.

Start slowly. Build up from a few minutes' exposure on the first day of a holiday, gradually increasing the time over several days. Avoid the midday sun, which is stronger at this time.

Wear a hat at least some of the time. Children are particularly susceptible to sunstroke and should be encouraged always to wear a wide-brimmed hat. Wear sunglasses if necessary.

Dealing with skin problems

1 If a skin problem develops, and is not resolved by taking the preventive steps described above, first consult your doctor who will advise on appropriate treatment, perhaps referring you to a dermatologist (skin specialist).

2 Tell the doctor full details of the problem: identification of the cause of a skin disease often means the irritant or cause of the allergy can be removed.

3 Rest the damaged or injured area to promote faster healing, and find out whether or not a rash should be covered.

4 Use only the medication you have been prescribed, and do not overuse it. Don't use anyone else's ointment or lotion: what works for someone else may not be suitable for you. Cortisone creams help all rashes but do not cure them and can spread the infection; other preparations could make the condition much worse.

The Respiratory System

Breathing, so vital to life, occurs automatically without us even thinking about it. It is the only way that the cells in the body receive oxygen, itself vital for converting sugars and other food products into energy. The various parts of the respiratory system – the nose, throat, larynx, bronchi and lungs – are designed to get the maximum amount of oxygen out of the air and into the bloodstream.

The respiratory system is centred on the lungs. Air is inhaled through the mouth and nose, and passes into the lungs where oxygen from the air is taken up by the blood passing through them. At the same time, the blood releases carbon dioxide, the waste product of some of the cells' activities. The bloodstream takes oxygen to the rest of the body where it is used in cell respiration.

The upper respiratory system

Air enters the lungs through the upper air passages, first through the nose and mouth and then the pharynx (throat), larynx (voicebox) and trachea (windpipe). This part of the respiratory system acts as a filter and cleanser of the inhaled air, by means of a hairy mucous membrane lining the nasal passages. This membrane contains many tiny blood vessels that warm the air as it is drawn into the system.

The nose and sinuses

The first 13 mm (½ in) of the inside of the nose, divided into two cavities by a septum of bone and cartilage, is lined with coarse hairs (vibrissae) which trap large particles in the inhaled air. The nasal passages are lined by a mucous membrane, with cilia (tiny hair-like structures) on its surface, that produces a thin layer of mucus. Foreign particles such as dust and bacteria are trapped on the mucous layer which is continually being moved towards the throat by the waving of the cilia; the mucus is then usually swallowed and digested. As the air moves through the nose it is warmed and humidified by small blood vessels very near the surface of the nasal cavity, to prevent it damaging the delicate membranes of the lungs.

The nasal sinuses are linked air spaces within the bones of the skull surrounding the nasal cavity, and opening into it through small gaps. The sinuses, lined, like the nose, with mucous membrane, are paired on either side of the face. The two largest, the maxillary, are in the cheeks, the frontal sinuses are in the forehead, and the ethmoidal and sphenoidal sinuses are at the side and back of the nose. The sinuses have no known function, although they help to give the voice resonance.

The throat

The back of the nose opens into the pharynx, which is hidden from view by the soft palate. At the top of the pharynx are the adenoids, which are collections of lymphoid tissue (see *Blood and Lymph*, page 142), similar to the tonsils on each side of the throat. Both the adenoids and tonsils play a role in combating infection. The throat leads into both the oesophagus (gullet), down which food and drink pass on their way to the stomach, and the trachea which leads to the lungs. When food or drink is swallowed, the epiglottis closes off the larynx and trachea by folding over the aperture.

At the top of the trachea is the larynx containing the vocal chords, and the gap between them, the glottis, allows air to pass through the larynx to the lungs. At the top of the glottis is the epiglottis, a valve which stands up like a stout leaf and prevents food and drink entering the trachea. The vocal cords are stretched pieces of tissue which resonate when air passes over them like a reed in the mouthpiece of a wind instrument. These can be tightened or loosened, and moved together or separated by muscles, to vary the tone and pitch of the voice, which is amplified by the cavities of the throat and mouth. The larynx is also a fundamental part of the cough mechanism, by which excessive secretions of mucus from the respiratory tract, as well as small foreign bodies, can be expelled.

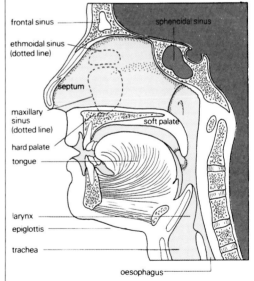

Sectional view of the upper respiratory tract, showing the close connection between the mouth, nose, trachea (windpipe) and oesophagus (gullet). The function of the epiglottis, a large, leaf-shaped piece of cartilage lying on top of the larynx, is to ensure that food goes down the oesophagus and that only inhaled air enters the trachea en route to the lungs; it does this by closing over the aperture to the larynx and trachea when food or drink are swallowed.

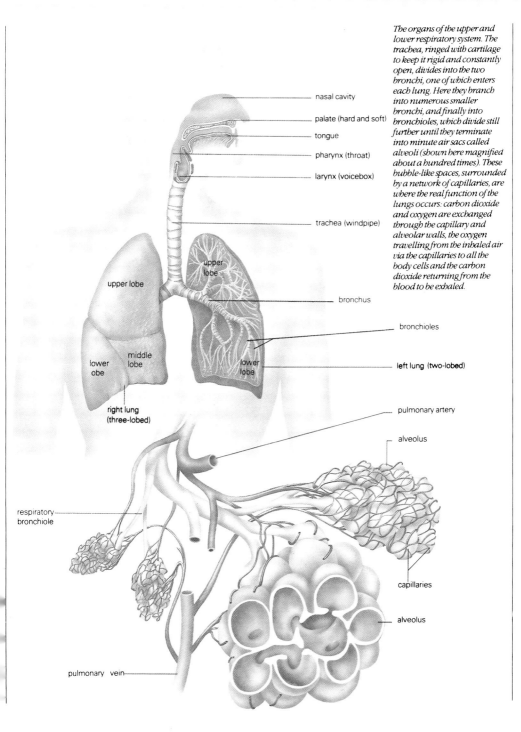

The organs of the upper and lower respiratory system. The trachea, ringed with cartilage to keep it rigid and constantly open, divides into the two bronchi, one of which enters each lung. Here they branch into numerous smaller bronchi, and finally into bronchioles, which divide still further until they terminate into minute air sacs called alveoli (shown here magnified about a hundred times). These bubble-like spaces, surrounded by a network of capillaries, are where the real function of the lungs occurs: carbon dioxide and oxygen are exchanged through the capillary and alveolar walls, the oxygen travelling from the inhaled air via the capillaries to all the body cells and the carbon dioxide returning from the blood to be exhaled.

nasal cavity

palate (hard and soft)

tongue

pharynx (throat)

larynx (voicebox)

trachea (windpipe)

upper lobe

upper lobe

bronchus

bronchioles

middle lobe

lower lobe

lower lobe

left lung (two-lobed)

right lung (three-lobed)

pulmonary artery

alveolus

respiratory bronchiole

capillaries

alveolus

pulmonary vein

The lower respiratory system

The trachea is a tube about 12 cm (5 in) long, joined to the bottom of the larynx. It is prevented from collapsing by C-shaped rings of cartilage spaced along its length. Soon after entering the chest (thorax), the trachea divides into the right and left bronchi, the main branches of the bronchial tree inside the lungs. Like the trachea and upper airway, the larger bronchi are lined with cilia and a layer of mucus. These help prevent particles of dust and large bacteria from entering the lungs. Very small particles are allowed through, however. Each main bronchus divides again into several branches and each of these subdivides again and again, some twenty times. At every division each branch becomes narrower, forming bronchioles, of which there are about a million terminal bronchioles. These divide into delicate short tubes (respiratory bronchioles); and it is these that form the first part of true respiratory tissue of the lung. The respiratory bronchioles are connected to clusters of passages whose walls consist of a single layer of thin, flat cells. The respiratory bronchiole and the space into which it leads is called a lung lobule. Each lobule consists of a large number of shallow pouches or alveoli, and it is here that the exchange of gases with the blood occurs.

How the lungs work

There are about 300 million alveoli in the human lung, all of microscopic size. Each one is in close contact with a rich network of blood capillaries, forming a huge and extremely thin surface for the transfer of gases between air and blood.

The total surface area of this membrane is about 70 sq m (83 sq yd), or forty times the whole surface area of the body, and the membrane is less than one thousandth of a millimetre (0.000039 in) thick.

Blood is supplied to the lungs by the pulmonary circulation (see *The Heart and Circulation*, page 152). From the right side of the heart, blood low in oxygen is pumped from the rest of the body to the lung through the pulmonary artery. This artery divides many times to provide an enormous number of thin-walled capillaries which surround the alveoli. After the blood has passed through the capillaries and exchanged carbon dioxide and oxygen with the air in the alveoli, it returns to the left side of the heart through the pulmonary vein, to be pumped around the body. The extremely thin walls of the capillaries, in close contact with the alveolar walls, allow the rapid exchange of gases between the blood and air. The process has to be very fast because each red blood cell takes less than a tenth of a second to pass through the capillaries.

This final exchange of gases between the air in the alveoli and the blood takes place by a process called molecular diffusion. The blood entering the lungs has a high concentration of carbon dioxide, the waste gas from cell respiration, which it has absorbed from the tissues. But the blood does not have much oxygen left since it has been used by the cells in the body. The transfer of oxygen into the blood, and carbon dioxide out of it, takes place across the alveolar walls as a result of these differences in concentration between the blood and air: the gas molecules move in the direction of decreasing concentration.

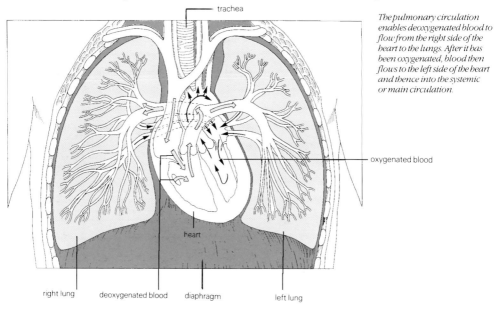

The pulmonary circulation enables deoxygenated blood to flow from the right side of the heart to the lungs. After it has been oxygenated, blood then flows to the left side of the heart and thence into the systemic or main circulation.

trachea

oxygenated blood

heart

right lung   deoxygenated blood   diaphragm   left lung

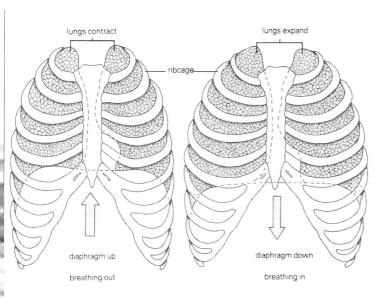

lungs contract

ribcage

lungs expand

diaphragm up

breathing out

diaphragm down

breathing in

During breathing, the diaphragm, the dome-shaped muscle that separates the lungs and heart from the abdominal organs, moves up and down in order to increase and decrease the volume of the lungs. As the diaphragm rises and the ribs contract, air is forced out of the lungs. When the diaphragm is lowered other muscles pull the ribs and sternum upwards and outwards, and air is forced into the lungs to maintain their internal pressure.

Breathing

The lungs fill most of the chest cavity. They are elastic structures, returning to their normal size after stretching, which helps the movements of breathing. On inhaling, fresh air is drawn into the lungs by increasing the volume of the thorax and making the pressure inside less than outside. The outer surface of each lung is covered by the pleura, a double layer of membrane also lining the inside of the rib cage. A fluid secreted between the layers lubricates the breathing movements.

The main muscles of breathing are the diaphragm and the intercostal muscles between the ribs. Muscles in the neck, shoulders and abdomen can also be used in certain circumstances, such as during exercise. The diaphragm, the most important muscle, is a dome-shaped sheet that separates the thorax from the abdomen. As it contracts it becomes flatter, and this increases the volume of the thorax. Air is then drawn into the lungs.

Expiration, the expulsion of air from the lungs, normally requires no muscular activity owing to the elastic nature of the lungs, which return to their resting size when the respiratory muscles relax. During exercise, more active expiration can be produced by using the intercostal muscles and the muscles of the abdomen.

At rest, the respiratory rate in an adult is about twelve times a minute; a healthy baby will breath at twice this rate. A normal breath takes in 500 cc (30 cu in) of air, but only 350 cc (21 cu in) of this is fresh air as the first 150 cc (9 cu in) is 'dead' air already in the nose, trachea and bronchi, which is not exchanged with air from outside. The total amount of air that can be inhaled is increased by more forceful

inspiration and expiration. Some air is left in the lungs, known as the residual volume. The lower parts of the lungs are more fully ventilated than the upper parts.

Control of breathing

All the complex mechanisms of breathing are regulated and controlled by the nervous system. Inspiration and expiration result from the rhythmical contraction and relaxation of the respiratory muscles and normally a person is unaware of these processes, which continue during sleep and even under anaesthesia. The nervous impulses controlling the contractions originate in the respiratory centres of the brain (see *The Nervous System*, page 188).

Impulses from the inspiratory centre pass to the diaphragm and the intercostal muscles of the chest wall. As a result, inflation of the lung occurs and special cells called stretch receptors within the lung are stimulated; impulses from these receptors pass to the expiratory centre. The strength of this stimulus increases as inflation goes on, until the expiratory centre causes the inspiratory centre to stop its drive; expiration, a passive process, then begins. Stimulation of the stretch receptors decreases and the cycle is repeated.

The level of carbon dioxide in the blood is an important stimulus to respiration. Special nerve receptors close to the respiratory centre, in the aorta near the heart and in the carotid artery that goes to the brain, monitor changes in carbon dioxide in the body. If the amount of this increases, both the rate and depth of breathing increase. Changes in oxygen levels are also monitored, but the receptors are not as sensitive to changes in oxygen as to carbon dioxide.

Disorders of the respiratory system

Respiratory diseases are usually the result of inhaling toxic particles or infectious agents from the air. The mucosa of the upper respiratory passages may become inflamed as a result of infection, allergy or irritation by chemicals. This gives rise to complaints such as rhinitis, hay fever (where the nose is mainly affected), sinusitis, pharyngitis, laryngitis and tracheitis. Diseases of the lower respiratory tract, for example, asthma, bronchitis, emphysema and tuberculosis can all cause permanent damage and be debilitating and prolonged. (Some infectious diseases of the respiratory tract are dealt with in *Infections and Infestations*, page 202.)

Rhinitis

Rhinitis is inflammation of the membrane lining the nose. Strictly speaking, anyone who has a cold has rhinitis, but the use of the term is usually restricted to the conditions of hay fever, perennial rhinitis and vasomotor rhinitis.

When the nasal membrane becomes inflamed, its cells respond by producing large quantities of mucus, which is why one of the main symptoms of any type of rhinitis is a 'runny nose'. Other symptoms include sneezing and intense itching within the nose. Often the blood vessels inside the nose become swollen, and block the airway. If the narrow entrances to the sinuses are blocked as well, sinusitis may follow rhinitis.

Hay fever

Hay fever is a form of allergic rhinitis brought on by exposure to pollen. Symptoms include a streaming nose, sneezing, watering and reddened eyes, and intense itching of both the nose and the eyes. For many sufferers, the annual pollen season becomes a nightmare. The time of this season varies from country to country. In the USA the principal plant responsible for hay fever is ragweed, which produces pollen between the beginning of August and the end of October. Grass pollen sufferers find that May and June are the worst months in the northern USA, while in the south grass may produce pollen all year round. In Britain and Europe, June and July are usually the worst months for grass pollen, but there is not likely to be much ragweed pollen in the air at any time of year.

In treating hay fever, skin tests are used to determine the precise type of pollen causing the allergic reaction. Depending on the results, a course of desensitization injections may be given over a period of several months (see *Allergy and Hypersensitivity*, pages 204-5). Antihistamine drugs are also useful for most cases, but often have to be taken in quite large doses to produce relief of symptoms. Some may cause drowsiness, but other drugs are available which are equally effective without producing side-effects. A doctor may also prescribe a steroid nasal spray which can prevent an allergic attack occurring.

Perennial rhinitis

Perennial rhinitis is similar to hay fever, except that it occurs all the year round. The allergens responsible are house dust, house mites, scales from skin or pet fur, tiny particles of feathers, or mould spores. Food particles and face-powder may sometimes be responsible. The treatment is similar to that for hay fever.

Vasomotor rhinitis

Vasomotor rhinitis is much less common. The symptoms are similar to those of perennial rhinitis but there does not appear to be a clearly defined allergic cause. It is thought that psychological stress may play a part in the development of the condition.

Sinusitis

Sinusitis is inflammation of the sinuses. If the mucous membranes lining the nose become congested and swollen, the tiny openings into the sinuses become blocked, and no air can get in or out. These are ideal conditions for germs to multiply within the sinuses, resulting in sinusitis. Sinusitis may follow a cold or hay fever, or even be provoked by rapid changes in air pressure (as occurs in air travel and underwater diving). Infection of the maxillary sinuses may be caused by sepsis of the upper teeth, which lie just under the floor of these sinuses, or by fractures of the upper jaw. After frequent attacks of acute sinusitis, the lining membrane can become thickened and hypersensitive to quite minor irritants such as cigarette smoke, spicy foods or thick fog. Attacks then become more frequent and difficult to control.

Symptoms

The symptoms of sinusitis depend both on the severity of the infection and the sinuses involved. In acute sinusitis there is almost always intense pain, due to the accumulation of pus in the affected sinus, and the sufferer feels very ill with a high temperature. In chronic sinusitis the pain is often more of a dull ache, but is far more persistent. Maxillary sinusitis causes pain in the upper region of the cheek bones, the forehead and the upper teeth. Ethmoid sinusitis may cause pain whenever the eyes are moved. Frontal sinusitis can cause a vague morning headache, which may be mistakenly attributed to migraine, eyestrain, or some other cause. Sphenoid sinusitis is liable to cause a persistent discharge of pus down the back of the throat (a 'post-nasal drip') with a cough and possibly chest complications. Of the various forms of sinusitis, maxillary sinusitis is the most common.

Treatment

Treatment involves pain-killers and antibiotics such as penicillin or tetracycline. Nose drops are used to shrink the congested and inflamed membranes, and so allow the sinuses to drain. Examination by an ear, nose and throat specialist may be necessary, and the inflamed sinuses may be washed out. Very occasionally, surgery is required. An operation for chronic maxillary sinusitis, the Caldwell-Luc procedure, involves cutting bone away under the upper lip, to allow the maxillary sinuses to drain.

Laryngitis and pharyngitis

Laryngitis, inflammation of the larynx, causes partial or complete loss of voice; the sufferer cannot speak above a whisper, if at all. Laryngitis is usually caused by infection such as a common cold or by strained vocal cords. Recovery will usually follow if the voice is rested for a few days. Frequent attacks of laryngitis, without infection or voice strain, may be psychological in origin, affecting the nerves of the larynx.

Pharyngitis, inflammation of the pharynx, frequently accompanies an upper respiratory tract disorder that may also affect the nose, larynx and trachea. Bacterial and viral infections such as tonsillitis or the common cold usually cause this condition. Sometimes the inhalation of irritating substances may cause a reaction in the delicate mucous membrane of the throat. Pharyngitis also accompanies infections such as measles, scarlet fever and whooping cough (see *Infections and Infestations*, page 206). The throat becomes dry, red and swollen, and swallowing is painful. Treatment includes a light diet of nourishing soft foods and liquids, rest and warmth. Gargles help ease soreness, and antibiotics are often used for bacterial infections.

Adenoids and tonsillitis
Overgrowth of the adenoids, known simply as 'adenoids', afflicts children of all races, usually between the ages of three and twelve. The reason for the excessive growth of the adenoids in some children is unknown, in spite of the commonness of the condition. It seems that the growth of the lymphatic tissue that occurs with normal development simply progresses too far.

The enlarged adenoids partially block the nasal passage and result in open-mouthed breathing and the inability to pronounce nasal consonants so that 'nose' becomes 'doze' and 'mud' becomes 'bud'. Victims of adenoids may have difficulty with eating, and tend to drool and snore during sleep. As well as obstructing respiration, adenoids often block the ends of either or both of the Eustachian tubes. These are the narrow passages that lead from the middle ear to the back of the throat and serve to maintain equal atmospheric pressure on the two sides of the eardrums. Common consequences of this are deafness and earache. A more serious result, however, is infection of the middle ear (otitis media) which may lead to perforation of the eardrum, a discharge from the ear, and sometimes permanent damage

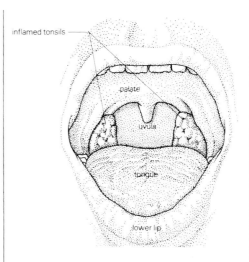

In tonsillitis the infected tonsils become inflamed.

to hearing. Surgical removal of the adenoids is required in severe cases, but most clear up by themselves.

Inflammation of the tonsils – tonsillitis – is usually caused by bacterial or viral infection. Symptoms include a sore throat, difficulty in swallowing, and fever; and there may be a white coating over the surface of the tonsils, which are redder than usual. Although many types of microbe can cause tonsillitis, infection with streptococci is one of the commonest causes, and treatment with antibiotics, particularly penicillin, is usually effective. In some children the tonsils become infected repeatedly, and their surgical removal is then considered. Slight enlargement of the tonsils is normal in most children and both they and the adenoids will normally shrink in size as the child grows.

Coughing
Coughing is a reflex action, an automatic response to a particular stimulus, and it usually occurs involuntarily. It is sometimes possible to suppress a cough; it is always possible to cough on purpose; but even an unconscious person can cough.

Anything which irritates the pharynx or the larynx, or tickles the nerve endings inside the lungs or in the pleura can stimulate a cough. Irritation of the pharynx or larynx is the usual cause. When a foreign particle is inhaled it inevitably hits the sensitive wall of the throat or some other part of the upper air passages.

This touch of the foreign body on the lining membrane causes a nervous impulse to travel to the brain. In the brain the message is distributed to a number of control centres, each of which sends off a pattern of impulses to cause several things to happen. First, there is a rapid contraction of both the chest muscles and the diaphragm, which results in a sharp intake of air. Next, the glottis, the opening at the back of the throat guarding the entrance to the windpipe,

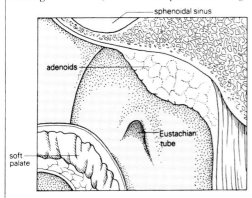

The adenoids are situated at the back of the nasal cavity.

closes. Then the muscles of the chest and abdomen contract again to squeeze the chest cavity. This produces a steep rise in pressure of the air inside it. The glottis is then opened suddenly, and the air under pressure in the chest escapes forcefully, expelling, in most cases, the offending material.

Sneezing

A sneeze serves the same function as a cough, but for the upper parts of the air passages, and is produced by the same mechanism.

Choking

Choking occurs when blockage of the throat or windpipe prevents air reaching the lungs. The most common cause of choking is the accidental inhalation of a piece of food or quantities of liquid, which 'go down the wrong way'. In most cases the resulting fit of coughing dislodges the material, and after the initial spluttering the person regains breath and no harm is done. Occasionally, swallowed foreign bodies which have entered the trachea become stuck, creating a life-threatening situation. A less common cause of choking is inflammation and swelling of the throat, caused perhaps by infection.

The symptoms of severe choking are sudden and intense coughing, followed by violent but ineffective attempts to breathe in, together with congestion of the neck veins and increasing blueness of the face.

Choking caused by a foreign body is common among children who often put small objects such as beads in their mouths. It is wise to avoid giving infants toys of this sort to play with. Adults sometimes choke when trying to swallow pieces of poorly chewed food, when broken teeth or dentures fall back in the throat, or following inhalation of vomit; here the greatest risk is among people who have had too much alcohol to drink.

Croup

Croup refers to any kind of childhood inflammation of the larynx or voice-box and is not a single disorder in itself. The characteristic features are a harsh, barking cough and noisy inspiration (stridor) caused by the vibration of air as it passes through the narrowed, inflamed larynx. If a child develops these symptoms medical advice should be sought since he or she may have inhaled a foreign body.

The most common type of croup, known as catarrhal croup, is usually not very serious, although it may be alarming for parents. The child often has had a slight cold for a day or so, but has felt well and had no high temperature. The onset is sudden, the child often waking in a fit of violent coughing. There is a loud 'crowing' noise as the child breathes, the chest heaving with the effort of drawing in air through the narrowed larynx. At this point, parents often become very worried but there is rarely any danger, though a doctor should be consulted. It is important not to panic, but concentrate on reassuring the child. As he or she calms down, the respiration rate will slow, and breathing will become a little easier. Meanwhile, the child should be kept in a moist atmosphere provided, perhaps, by keeping a

boiling electric kettle in the room (make sure this is safe) or taking him or her into the bathroom to breathe in the steam from a hot shower. A towel over the head can be used to direct the vapour towards the mouth and nose (taking care that the child is not scalded by the steam). These measures should produce relief within minutes.

Severe croup with fever can be much more serious. In its most dangerous form, called 'laryngotracheobronchitis', there is extreme breathlessness, very loud stridor, and increasing duskiness of the face. Medical help should be sought immediately.

Hiccups

This sharp sound accompanied by spasm is the result of an involuntary contraction of all or part of the diaphragm and sudden closure of the glottis as air is drawn into the chest. Hiccups can be caused by eating too quickly: rapid eating produces stomach distension which, in turn, produces stimulation of the nerves of the intestine, triggering hiccups. As the distension subsides, so does the stimulus, until the hiccups die away. Hiccups can also be caused by drinking alcohol, which produces stomach irritation. Persistent hiccups are more serious, sometimes reflecting an underlying illness, such as pericarditis (irritation of the covering of the heart) or disease of the lungs or diaphragm.

Procedures designed to interrupt the cycle of hiccups, such as deliberately holding the breath or drinking a glass of cold water from the far side, will often stop simple hiccups. More persistent hiccups may respond to a pull on the tongue or to pressure applied to the phrenic nerve in the neck. Breathing in and out of a paper bag is a popular and effective method; the build-up of carbon dioxide in the air in the bag affects the 'hiccup centre' in the nervous system. In very severe cases drugs, or even a small surgical operation, may be necessary.

Asthma

Asthma is a chronic condition characterized by frequent bouts of breathlessness. In an asthmatic attack the bronchi become narrowed because their walls contract, and the resulting partial obstruction causes difficulty in breathing, often accompanied by wheezing. The narrowing can occur suddenly, sometimes in a few minutes, and there may also be a slow swelling (oedema) of the mucous membrane lining the bronchi, along with the secretion of a thick and sticky mucus.

Symptoms

A common type of asthmatic attack begins with a feeling of tightness in the chest, sometimes preceded by a dry irritating cough or blocked nose. During an attack, the depth of breathing increases and may reach the maximum level of full inspiration. This stretches the narrowed bronchi so that the necessary amount of air can enter the lungs. Wheezing is caused by the turbulence of the air as it passes through the narrowed air passages. If the attack is severe the sufferer has to devote all his or her energy to the task of breathing, is unable to sleep or eat, and can drink only a little. The symptoms often subside of their own accord: breathing gradually becomes easier, the wheezing declines, and a little sticky colourless sputum may be coughed up.

The development, duration and severity of attacks varies between individuals. The attack may develop in minutes or take hours to reach its peak; it may cause only minor discomfort and breathlessness or may be severe enough to cause total incapacity and require hospitalization. Intervals between attacks can vary from a few days to many months. In any one person the pattern tends to be consistent, although it may change over several years. Death from an asthmatic attack is rare except in elderly people who have other diseases as well.

Causes

There is sometimes no obvious cause of asthma, but in many cases attacks are triggered by an allergic reaction to a substance harmless to most other people (see *The Immune System and Allergies*, page 202). Such substances, called allergens, include airborne particles such as pollen, house dust and animal fur or feathers. People who have allergies, for example hay fever or eczema, are also more likely to have asthma.

Asthma may occur mainly at home because of house dust, or mainly at work because of dust from occupational materials. Pollen grains and mould spores are often an important source of asthma in a similar way to hay fever. In house dust the main cause is the house mite which feeds principally on tiny scales of human skin shed from the body. The mite is microscopic and occurs in great numbers in the dust on the surfaces of mattresses, and in carpets and soft furnishings. Anything that throws house dust into the air, such as bed-making or cleaning, is likely to bring on an attack of wheezing in an asthmatic sensitive to house dust. These mites thrive in warm, damp conditions, and their numbers increase in August, September and October. Also present in house dust, but less important in causing asthma, are mould spores, algae, bits of feathers, kapok, and horse-hair. Dandruff and hair from animals, especially from cats and dogs, are a common cause, and other pets such as rabbits, hamsters, mice and birds may also be allergenic.

Certain foods and drinks can in certain people provoke an asthmatic attack. Milk, eggs and wheat may be the cause, particularly in children, and at any age, fish, eggs, chocolate and nuts may be responsible. Although drugs can cause allergic reactions they rarely cause asthma.

A wide range of dusts, gases, vapours and fumes emitted by industrial processes may be responsible for asthma: polyurethane paint sprays, toluene diisocyanate (used in making polyurethane foam), sulphur dioxide, phtalic anhydride (used in PVC production) and platinum salts (used in electroplating) have all been suspected of causing asthma.

Emotional and psychological stresses may also provoke asthmatic attacks in certain people; for example parents may be over-protective or over-ambitious towards their children and this can contribute towards the development of asthma. Physical stress, for example in some forms of exercise, is also a possible triggering factor for asthma.

Treatment

The first stage of treatment is to find the cause of the asthma, by taking a detailed history of the affected person, which will include information on the environment at home and at work, allergies, chest infections and emotional stresses. Skin tests, which involve applying small amounts of different allergens to the skin by pricking or scratching the surface, may be carried out. It is possible to make up to twenty-five tests on the skin of the arm or the back at one session. If the patient is sensitive to a substance a small reaction, in the form of a weal or flare, will occur at that particular site, thus indicating the cause or causes of the asthma.

Once the allergen has been identified, treatment involves avoiding exposure to it. In any case, most asthmatics are helped if the amount of dust in their house is reduced, by limiting carpets or soft furnishings, and by vacuum-cleaning thoroughly. Any dampness in the structure of the home should also be repaired, so as to reduce the possibility of mould spores in the air. Feathers in pillows and quilts should be replaced by plastic foam. Pets and domestic animals, if shown to be the cause, should be removed. If certain foods, drinks or drugs are the cause of the allergy, it is important to make sure that mixtures containing them are avoided.

There are many drugs available which will prevent attacks occurring or reduce their severity. Bronchodilators, drugs which relax the muscles of the bronchus when it has gone into spasm, can bring relief during an asthmatic attack. Drugs which have this effect may be inhaled or swallowed and new types are constantly being developed. Relief is most rapid when the drug in the form of a fine spray is inhaled through the mouth, since this is the fastest way for the drug to reach the lungs. Several types of inhalers are available but if you find them difficult to use (because the release of the spray must coincide with taking a deep breath), devices are available to make this easier. Alternatively, these drugs may be swallowed. For severe, recurrent attacks of asthma there are steroid drugs that help to prevent attacks. These are also usually inhaled. In a particularly severe or life-threatening attack, the drug may be injected.

Where anxiety is a main cause of asthma, tranquillizers may help, and psychotherapy has been used when emotional problems are responsible. In severe cases, hospital treatment with oxygen and mechanical breathing aids may be needed.

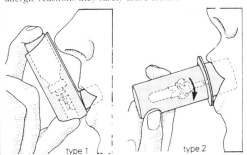

type 1   type 2

Two types of inhaler used to treat asthma. The top of type one is depressed while the contents are inhaled, while in type two the act of inhaling automatically releases the drug by spinning a propeller inside the device.

Bronchitis

Bronchitis is inflammation of the mucous lining of the bronchi. If the air we breathe contains irritating particles and gases, the bronchi can gradually become inflamed. The amount of air pollution in the environment can be an important factor in causing bronchitis; exhaust fumes from motor vehicles, smoke from fires and factories, and other chemicals released in the air can all irritate the bronchi. Cigarette smoking is a potent self-inflicted irritant and is a major cause of bronchitis.

Acute bronchitis

Acute bronchitis usually begins as a viral infection such as a cold that spreads down into the bronchi and is followed by bacterial infection. The larynx and trachea are often also affected. Anyone with a respiratory infection may develop acute bronchitis, but most cases are mild and clear up by themselves. However, the infection may spread to the lungs, causing bronchopneumonia.

Symptoms

The first symptoms are a dry cough and a feeling of soreness in the centre of the chest, and also hoarseness if the throat is involved. After two or three days, yellow or green sputum containing pus is produced, and there may be a slight fever. About a week later, the sputum becomes either clear and colourless or, in smokers, grey from inhaled smoke. People with healthy lungs recover from mild bronchitis in about two weeks, when the cough ceases, but smokers may continue to cough for up to six weeks and are much more likely to have recurrent attacks and eventually the chronic form of the disease (see below).

Infants, because of their narrow airways, are affected more severely by bronchitis than adults, especially if the small branches of the bronchi, the bronchioles, are involved. Wheezing during an attack of bronchitis sometimes means that asthma (see page 90) may develop later in childhood.

Treatment

Most cases of acute bronchitis do not require treatment with antibiotics. Aspirin may be useful if there is fever, and any cough linctus may be taken to soothe the cough. Symptoms should begin to lessen two or three days after their onset, if you rest and keep warm at home. If you do not improve in this time and instead become breathless or wheezy or begin to run a high temperature, over 38.5°C (101°F), consult your doctor, who may prescribe an antibiotic and perhaps a bronchodilator drug to be inhaled.

Chronic bronchitis

Chronic bronchitis is an insidious disease in which repeated infections of the bronchi eventually damage the tissue permanently. Symptoms – a persistent cough with sputum and shortness of breath – develop gradually, often over a period of many years. The disease may start at any age, but most commonly between the ages of thirty and sixty, recurring every winter.

People with chronic bronchitis are very susceptible to infection, and every cold or bout of influenza will cause a flare-up, so that the affected person may have several attacks a year. Each repeated infection further damages the lungs, making them more susceptible to yet another infection. The disease can eventually lead to pneumonia (see below), hypertension in the lungs (see page 163), emphysema (see below) or even heart failure (see page 157).

In industrialized countries the mortality rate for bronchitis in men is between two and four times higher than that for women. The difference may be due to men's higher exposure to pollutants in their jobs, or their greater tobacco consumption. The incidence of bronchitis increases after the age of forty-five, and in the age group fifty-five to sixty-four the death rate is double that for all other ages. Prevention of bronchitis requires the elimination of tobacco smoking, a reduction in atmospheric pollution, and prompt and effective treatment of chest infections in people most at risk.

Symptoms

The amount of sputum and the duration of the cough gradually increases, until it is continuous throughout three months of the year or more. The sputum, at first colourless or grey from the presence of inhaled smoke or soot, eventually becomes frothy, with a thick and sticky consistency. As the disease progresses, breathlessness and wheezing are additional symptoms, and the affected person will notice that he or she can no longer keep pace with other people of the same age and build, or climb stairs without gasping for air. In the severest cases, breathlessness may occur even at rest. The shortness of breath is due to the narrowing of the bronchi and to the inefficient exchange of oxygen and carbon dioxide in the lungs. In the advanced stages, there may be cyanosis (blueness of the skin) due to the lack of oxygen.

The severest form of chronic bronchitis and the most deaths occur among heavy smokers. Many smokers regard the 'smoker's cough' as normal, but it is actually an early symptom of chronic bronchitis. Another factor is air pollution: the disease is more common in urban, industrial areas.

Treatment

To treat bronchitis, there are several possible self-help measures: give up smoking, and avoid smoke-filled rooms and people with colds. If possible, move to a rural area away from the pollution of a town or city. Drugs which help to expel mucus (expectorants) can be helpful, as can drugs which dilate the bronchi, as used for asthma. Antibiotics may be given for a bad attack with signs of infection.

Emphysema

This disorder is normally the result of underlying lung disease, such as chronic bronchitis or asthma, which has destroyed the delicate alveoli of the lungs. Shortness of breath is the main symptom, and bronchodilator drugs may be given to help the patient breathe. The condition gradually worsens over several years and may eventually lead to respiratory failure.

Pneumonia

This is a general term used to describe any lung inflammation, usually conditions in which fluid is discharged into the alveoli. The different types of pneumonia can be divided into two main groups: the specific type, in which the disease is caused by a specific harmful organism, either a bacterium or a virus; and the aspiration, or secondary, type, in which some abnormality in the respiratory system predisposes the lungs to infection by otherwise fairly harmless organisms.

Pneumococcal pneumonia (sometimes called acute lobar pneumonia), caused by pneumococcus bacteria, is a specific type of pneumonia. It affects one or more lobes, or segments, of a lung; if both lungs are affected it is commonly known as double pneumonia. The affected lobes become congested and the blood vessels distended, causing the lung to be enlarged and heavy.

Another type of specific pneumonia is caused by staphylococcal-type bacteria. It resembles pneumococcal pneumonia and may be confused with it. It is often a complication of influenza.

The aspiration types of pneumonia are not caused by bacteria or viruses; the infection generally reaches the lungs by being breathed in from other parts of the respiratory tract. It may occur as part of another infection such as tuberculosis, or after major surgery, an accident, or breathing in some poisonous chemical. Whenever there is an excess of secretions in the respiratory tract and the mechanisms for preventing these accumulating in the bronchi are ineffective (if the person is too weak to cough, for example), the secretions and any organisms within them are carried deeply into the lungs and may cause infection. Acute pneumonia (or bronchopneumonia) is the most common type of aspiration pneumonia, and is a result of a spreading bronchial infection.

Symptoms
Pneumonia, which can occur at any age, most commonly in winter, begins suddenly, with a fever which may rise to 38.8° to 40°C (102° to 104°F) in a few hours. There is a cough, and may also be a headache and general feeling of chill. A sharp pain in the chest, shoulder or abdomen develops, and breathing is fast, shallow and painful. The cough, dry at first, becomes productive, and the sputum may be a distinctive rust colour, sometimes containing blood. The pulse is rapid, and sometimes the blood pressure drops. The skin is hot and dry and the face flushed, with a slightly blue tinge (cyanosis). The severity of symptoms depends on the size of the area in the lung that is affected.

Treatment
Even though many cases of pneumonia are mild in otherwise healthy people, admission to hospital is usually advised because the disease can suddenly become severe. Close medical supervision is therefore desirable, particularly if the sufferer's health is generally poor. Treatment is with antibiotics chosen to deal with the specific cause of the inflammation, as detected by laboratory tests. Analgesics may also be given for any pain in the chest. In severe cases of breathlessness and cyanosis oxygen may be given.

In nearly all cases the chances of rapid recovery are good. Within one or two days the temperature, pulse and breathing rate drop rapidly, and the lung inflammation is dramatically relieved. Other symptoms may take longer to disappear, but a healthy young person will normally recover completely within a week or two. However, in the very young, very old, heavy smokers and those suffering from a chronic illness or alcoholism, the outlook is less

good. A person in one of these high-risk groups may rapidly weaken and die of circulatory failure or hypoxia (insufficient oxygen in the bloodstream).

Legionnaire's disease

This is a relatively new disease, producing the symptoms of pneumonia. It is named from the original outbreak of infection in 1976 when 200 American ex-servicemen developed serious respiratory infection and twenty-nine died. An organism since named *Legionella pneumophila* was isolated. Since then there have been several outbreaks which have originated mainly in hotels and hospitals, where it is believed the source was contaminated water vaporized and fed into the air-conditioning system. The symptoms include nausea, vomiting, sweating, malaise, fever and cough. It is treated with the drug erythromycin. Full recovery usually follows in about three weeks, but there may be residual lung and liver damage.

Tuberculosis

Tuberculosis (TB) is an infectious disease usually caused by the bacterium *Mycobacterium tuberculosis* (or, rarely, by other species of *Mycobacterium*). In western countries tuberculosis is no longer a major problem, as it was a century ago, but in many developing countries it is still a prevalent disease; every year about two million people still die of it.

Tuberculosis can be prevented by vaccination, and the introduction of BCG vaccine some forty years ago has contributed considerably to the decline in incidence of TB. Vaccination can be carried out at birth or between the ages of ten and thirteen if a skin test shows a person is not immune.

Although tuberculosis may affect most organs of the body, by far the most common form of the disease involves the lungs. It is spread almost entirely by organisms coughed out of the lungs of people harbouring the tubercle bacillus. Until relatively recently the majority of people became infected with tuberculosis before reaching adulthood, although very few of them were actually ill. Cow's milk used to be a common source of infection but milk is now pasteurized and tested for the tubercle bacillus, and most herds are now free from TB.

When a person first inhales tubercle bacilli an infection may be set up. A small area of tuberculous pneumonia then develops, but this is nearly always overcome by the body's natural defences (see *The Immune System and Allergies*, page 202). A small scar remains, sometimes visible on X-rays. In many cases the disease never develops beyond this first stage, but occasionally natural resistance is unable to overcome the infection, which may spread from the lung through the bloodstream to other organs of the body. Even when the infection appears to have been overcome, a small number of living tubercle bacilli may remain dormant in the apparently healed lung, and the infection recurs, perhaps years later. It is likely that most cases of tuberculosis of the lungs in adults represent a secondary stage of an infection present since childhood.

The adult with tuberculosis, whether a reactivation of a childhood infection or a new infection, develops a new area of pneumonia, usually in the upper part of the lung. This behaves differently from other kinds of pneumonia because the tubercle bacillus has the ability to destroy lung tissue, leaving cavities which may grow larger until much of the lung has been destroyed. The effects of tuberculosis in an adult result partly from loss of lung tissue and in part from the general ill-effects of a serious infection.

Other common sites of tuberculosis are the bones (particularly the spine), the kidneys, the fallopian tubes and lymph nodes. When infection spreads through the bloodstream, minute tuberculous abscesses may develop in nearly all the organs of the body (miliary tuberculosis) and, most dangerously, in the membranes surrounding the brain (tuberculous meningitis).

Symptoms
There are often no symptoms during the primary stage of the disease; or there may be a flu-like illness not associated with TB at the time. If the disease progresses, the destruction of lung tissue causes a dry cough and bleeding, so that the phlegm becomes bloodstained. Coughing up blood is the most common reason for patients with tuberculosis to consult their doctor. Breathlessness occurs only when a large amount of lung has been destroyed and the disease is at an advanced stage.

Diagnosis
One method of detecting tuberculosis is to carry out a tuberculin skin test. In this, a small amount of a protein extracted from the tubercle bacteria is injected into the skin; those who have, or have had, tuberculosis develop a small painless red lump at the site of the injection. To diagnose a case of pulmonary tuberculosis, the sputum is examined under a microscope so that the tubercle bacilli can be seen and identified. Tuberculosis is also diagnosed with X-rays. Many of those who have an abnormal X-ray or a positive tuberculin test have a disease which has been overcome by the body's defences and may be considered inactive. These people require no treatment with antituberculous drugs, but may be kept under observation in case the disease flares up later.

Treatment
Before the discovery of antituberculous drugs, the main treatment was bed-rest, nourishing food and other treatments aimed at slowing the spread of the disease. Today drug therapy is the main treatment, usually given over a long period – a year or more. Unfortunately the tubercle bacilli can become resistant to antituberculous drugs, so that a drug that at first seems to be curing a particular case may become ineffective after a few months. However, it is very unusual for resistance to develop against two or three drugs at once, and for this reason several different antituberculous drugs are usually given together. If resistant organisms do develop, they may infect other people who will then start their disease with resistant organisms which cannot be treated with that particular drug.

Pneumoconiosis

Pneumoconiosis, meaning dust in the lungs, is caused by inhaling particular forms of dust over a long time, leading to irreversible changes in the lung tissue. There are several different forms, depending on the dust inhaled – almost all of them related to occupation. One form is coal-miner's pneumoconiosis, caused by daily exposure to coal dust over many years; others are silicosis (caused by silicon dust), asbestosis and byssinosis (cotton-workers disease), to name just a few. All these ailments cause fibrosis, the formation of scar tissue in the lungs, and consequent breathlessness.

The disease begins when microscopic particles are inhaled and reach the alveoli. Although scavenging cells called macrophages pick up some of these particles and carry them into the lymphoid system, the deposited matter encourages the formation of fibrous tissue, usually in nodules. Although to begin with they are small, these fibrous nodules can fuse into larger masses. The nodules are usually not malignant, but asbestosis may lead to lung cancer.

Asbestosis is one of the forms of pneumoconiosis which has increased in recent years. Asbestos bodies, tiny fibres with cell material deposited on them, have been found in the sputum and lungs of people who have been exposed to asbestos during their work. The mineral has also been associated with abnormally high rates of gastrointestinal cancer, bronchial carcinoma, and mesothelioma, an otherwise rare cancer of the membranes surrounding the lungs. Other mineral silicates like mica and kaolin (white clay) can also cause pneumoconiosis, and the dust from mouldy hay can cause the form of pneumoconiosis known as 'farmer's lung'. Those affected are allergic to mould spores in damp hay, usually in districts with heavy rainfall, resulting in the harvesting and storage of damp hay. Symptoms include chills, muscle pain, vomiting and disturbed lung function. If diagnosed soon enough, the irreversible fibrosis formation which follows a few weeks later can be avoided.

There are also many non-fibrotic dust diseases. Dust from compounds of manganese, vanadium, cadmium and beryllium can all cause inflammation of the lungs with symptoms resembling pneumonia.

Prevention
Cleanliness and good ventilation are among the simplest means of reducing atmospheric dust. Particles can be damped down with water; stonemasons can use a water spray. Powders should be handled in a solution or paste. Special ventilation methods can suck dust away from the tip of a pneumatic drill, and exhaust ventilation will remove particles from the workbench or factory. Respirator masks with filters are widely available to prevent workers inhaling dangerous dusts.

Dust-caused diseases are particularly dangerous because their effects may not show for many years after the initial exposure and only a short exposure may cause disease.

Lung cancer

As with cancer of other organs (see *Cancer*, page 218), lung cancer can be of two kinds. It may be primary, arising in the lung tissue or bronchus, or secondary, where the cancer has started somewhere else and spread to the lungs.

There are two main types of primary lung cancer. One is adenocarcinoma of the lung, which arises in glands in the bronchi. This is usually slow-growing and sometimes not even malignant. The second form, bronchogenic carcinoma, or 'smoker's cancer', is extremely malignant and becoming more common. Smoking is a major cause of this form of lung cancer. Other causative factors include air pollution, especially from coal smoke; and certain occupations such as working with asbestos and mining certain metallic ores, carry a greater risk of this sort of cancer.

Symptoms
Lung cancer can show itself in several ways. Often it is not discovered until late in the course of the disease, when there is an attack of bronchitis or pneumonia which does not get better, or the spitting of blood. Sometimes the primary cancer in the lung is discovered as a result of the effects of secondary cancers elsewhere.

Treatment
If diagnosed early, the affected lobe or part of the lung may be removed surgically. This gives the best chance of recovery. Most cancers are not diagnosed until they have progressed too far for this, however. Radiotherapy or anti-cancer (cytotoxic) drugs may be used in these more advanced cases with varying degrees of success.

Pleurisy

The pleural membrane which surrounds each lung normally has a thin layer of lubricating fluid in between its two layers (the pleural cavity) which allows the membranes to slide across each other smoothly as the lungs expand and relax. In pleurisy, the pleura becomes inflamed and congested, losing its smooth surface. In primary pleurisy the inflammation may arise from injury, exposure to cold, or infection. Secondary pleurisy is due to spread of disease, such as pneumonia, tuberculosis, bronchitis or pulmonary abscess, from the lungs.

Symptoms
In dry pleurisy a coating of the protein fibrin, varying in thickness from a thin film to a thick pasty coating, forms between the layers of membrane. The inflamed membranes then rub together, causing a sharp chest pain as the rib-cage moves during breathing. In pleurisy with effusion, or wet pleurisy, the two layers become separated by fluid and there is no pain, although there may be shortness of breath as the lung is compressed by the fluid. A sample of this fluid can be taken and used for diagnosis.

Treatment
Treatment usually consists of antibiotics and bed-rest. If the amount of fluid is large and makes breathing difficult, even causing the lung to collapse, it can be drained.

Pulmonary embolism

Some lung disorders are associated with disorders of the circulation. Pulmonary embolism occurs when clots of blood formed in the veins pass through the right side of the heart to lodge somewhere in the branches of the pulmonary artery. Those with deep vein thrombosis are most at risk of pulmonary embolism, so treatment is important (see *The Heart and Circulation*, page 152). The clot causes a blockage which means that the part of the lung supplied by that branch of the artery may die (pulmonary infarct). Severe or recurring infections, such as bronchitis, can also cause obstruction to the flow of blood to the lungs. This may begin as interference with the oxygen supply to the alveoli,

causing the arteries in the region to become narrowed. If the condition persists and becomes permanent the vessels may eventually be destroyed, causing increased blood pressure or even heart failure.

Treatment
Hospital treatment may be necessary, and consists of using drugs that dissolve the clot (thrombolytic drugs) and/or drugs that prevent further clotting (anticoagulants). The condition can be fatal, depending on the site and size of the clot, but if the patient survives the first few days satisfactory recovery is likely.

Bronchiectasis

Bronchiectasis is the term given to abnormal dilatation of one or more bronchi, usually following frequent childhood infections, perhaps beginning with an attack of whooping cough or measles and gradually leading to permanent damage of the bronchial tree in adulthood. The disorder has become something of a rarity since the introduction of antibiotics.

Symptoms
The main symptom is a persistent chronic cough which worsens in winter and produces large amounts of green or yellow sputum, often blood-stained. Evident since childhood, the cough gradually becomes more troublesome over many years, and is often made worse by a change of position and on getting up in the morning. The inflamed and damaged bronchi also cause increased breathlessness, loss of weight and general debility, and repeated lung infections and bad breath are additional symptoms of the disease.

Treatment
Recurrent respiratory infections in childhood, which may lead to bronchiectasis, should be investigated and treated before they have a chance to damage the lungs. If the disorder is diagnosed (usually by X-ray examination and bronchoscopy), the main treatment is the administration of antibiotics at the first sign of infection. In addition, the technique of postural drainage may be indicated, in which the patient is taught how to lie in such a position that the force of gravity drains the bronchial secretions from the lungs. In certain cases surgical removal of the affected part of the lungs may be advisable. All bronchiectatics should take especial care to avoid catching colds and throat infections, and should also keep away from smoke-filled rooms. As long as their damaged bronchi remain uninfected, people with the condition should be able to live relatively normal lives with few if any symptoms.

Pneumothorax

Pneumothorax occurs when air enters the pleural space between the membranes covering the lung, and causes the lung, or part of it, to collapse. One cause of this is chest injury; another is air escaping into the pleura from the lung itself. The main symptoms are breathlessness and chest pain, the severity of which depends on the size of the damaged area and on general health. A small pneumothorax is often self-healing, but if treatment is required it usually consists of inserting a catheter into the pleural space to suck out the air.

The dangers of smoking

Smoking is the only cause of epidemic disease to which humans have ever deliberately and knowingly exposed themselves. Smoking can kill; and when it does not kill it encourages the progress of disease. Even one puff on a cigarette significantly impairs bodily functions for longer than it takes to exhale.

Cancer (see page 218) is the most dramatic of the ailments which can afflict the respiratory system and which are caused or aggravated by smoking. Chronic bronchitis (see page 92) and emphysema (see page 92) are many times more common among people who smoke, and so are coughs and chest infections. After repeated attacks of

bronchitis the passageways of the lungs narrow, making breathing more difficult. The accompanying emphysema involves a breakdown of the alveoli, the minute sacs in the lungs through whose membranes oxygen is transferred to the bloodstream. Besides causing breathlessness and coughing, the general breakdown in lung function is likely to lead eventually to heart disease, since a greater strain is put on the heart. A middle-aged man who smokes cigarettes is two or three times more likely to have a heart attack than a non-smoker or pipe-smoker of the same age, and although women have fewer heart attacks, their risk increases equally with smoking. Smoking also encourages dangerous blood clotting in the blood vessels and hardening of the arteries, which may cause strokes (see page 196).

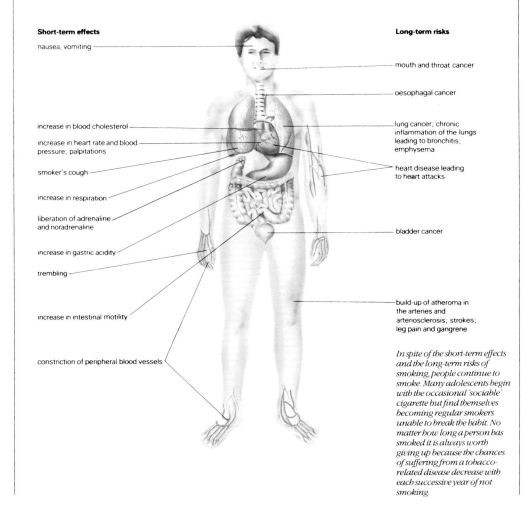

Short-term effects

nausea, vomiting

increase in blood cholesterol

increase in heart rate and blood pressure; palpitations

smoker's cough

increase in respiration

liberation of adrenaline and noradrenaline

increase in gastric acidity

trembling

increase in intestinal motility

constriction of peripheral blood vessels

Long-term risks

mouth and throat cancer

oesophagal cancer

lung cancer; chronic inflammation of the lungs leading to bronchitis; emphysema

heart disease leading to heart attacks

bladder cancer

build-up of atheroma in the arteries and arteriosclerosis; strokes; leg pain and gangrene

In spite of the short-term effects and the long-term risks of smoking, people continue to smoke. Many adolescents begin with the occasional 'sociable' cigarette but find themselves becoming regular smokers unable to break the habit. No matter how long a person has smoked it is always worth giving up because the chances of suffering from a tobacco-related disease decrease with each successive year of not smoking.

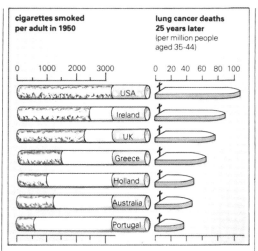

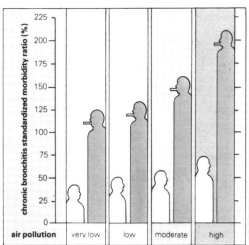

This table shows lung cancer deaths and adult smoking habits in different countries, clearly demonstrating the strong correlation between the two.

This figure shows that the effect of cigarette smoking is considerably stronger than air pollution on the prevalence of chronic bronchitis. Non-smokers (the white figures) run much less risk of bronchitis, even in a highly polluted environment, than do smokers (the shaded figures).

Dusts and fumes that are dangerous if inhaled

There are many chemicals which, in the form of dust or fumes, may cause lung damage and even cancer in the long term. Other possible harmful effects include damage to the liver, kidneys and brain.

Dusts
- *Asbestos dust, especially blue asbestos*
- *Glass fibre (silica) dust*
- *Dust and particles from pets, especially parrots, cause mainly allergies but can also cause disease*
- *Smoke particles, coal dust*

Fumes
- *Household bleach (sodium hypochlorite). Dangerous in itself, and if mixed with acid it produces deadly chlorine gas.*
- *Ammonia*
- *Solvents, including acetone, dry-cleaning fluids such as carbon tetrachloride and fluorocarbons, plastic glues and impact adhesives*
- *Carbon monoxide, combined with lead in car fumes*
- *Photographic fixer (sodium thiosulphate)*
- *Battery acid (sulphuric acid – H_2SO_4)*
- *Petrol, lighter fuels, paraffin, kerosene*
- *Cigarette fumes*
- *Aerosols*
- *Typewriter correction fluid*
- *Some paints, especially those for sealing damp areas, when being applied*
- *Paint stripper*

Keeping the lungs healthy

There is impressive evidence that people who take frequent exercise of the right kind are less prone to the major diseases of western society, which include bronchitis and lung cancer as well as heart disease and strokes. Exercises which are good for the lungs also help to keep the whole body healthy, by building stamina through rhythmic movements of the limbs. Such movements create a demand for oxygen, so the heart works a little harder and the lungs are fully used, pumping oxygen into the bloodstream so that it passes through the heart and reaches the working muscles. Sometimes this is called aerobic exercise; and jogging, cycling, rowing, swimming and rope-skipping are all excellent forms of aerobics. As well as increasing the body's stamina and strength, such exercises boost suppleness and flexibility, increase muscle tone, help to control blood pressure and weight, improve sleep and relieve tension and depression.

With all forms of exercise, it is important to start slowly and build up gently. Doing too much too quickly can put a strain on muscles and joints that have not been used to hard work. If you have not exercised for some time, or if you are in doubt about taking up exercise for any other reason, consult your doctor first.

Running and jogging

Running, known as jogging when performed at a slower pace, is the most natural form of aerobic exercise: it is impossible to run and not raise the pulse rate. Its great advantages are that it is flexible and capable of meeting individual needs. You can choose when and where to run, and you do not need special equipment except for suitable shoes. The only precautions are that you should start gradually, as with any sport; and you should not run within two hours of eating a meal. Warming up and cooling down with a few stretching exercises before and after running will help prevent stiffness and muscle injuries. Three runs a week of about twenty minutes each are enough to improve fitness.

Cycling

For cycling to have a beneficial effect, it should be a regular pursuit: aim to make at least two or three journeys of between three and six miles a week, increasing your time in the saddle as you become fitter. Changes in gradient, wind speed and traffic conditions will mean that you naturally change pace frequently in the course of a journey, and it is therefore difficult to be precise about the effects of time and distance. The aim should be to keep up a reasonable level of effort within a cycling session of twenty to thirty minutes: cycle hard enough to sweat a little and get slightly breathless but not so hard that it makes you feel ill or in pain (in which case stop and take a rest).

As well as having health advantages, cycling can also be a pleasant, sociable activity that the whole family can enjoy— or it can be pursued alone, depending on your preference and your circumstances. It can easily be fitted into daily routines and can also save you money and time on travelling.

Swimming

Swimming is an ideal form of exercise, promoting stamina, strength and suppleness without putting a strain on the joints (making it suitable for those with back or joint problems and also for people who are overweight). The crawl is the most effective stroke for its health benefits, because it is the most arduous, although other strokes such as backstroke and breaststroke are also beneficial. In order to improve the condition of the lungs, heart and muscles you need to be able to swim continuously for at least ten minutes, two or three times a week, building up gradually to this level of activity.

Rowing and canoeing

Rowing and canoeing are effective forms of aerobic exercise, but both pursuits require a degree of skill, particularly rowing which is also essentially a team sport. Both activities exercise the upper body more than the legs, but are ideal for those who enjoy the challenge of competition and learning a specific skill.

Skipping

A convenient form of aerobic exercise which can be done indoors is skipping, which needs no equipment apart from an ordinary skipping rope. Start off with a slow and rhythmical flat-footed skip, progressing gradually to variations such as hopping and double jumps. A five-minute session three times a week can be increased over three months or so to a daily twenty-minute session.

The Digestive System

Eating is a vital, and to most people pleasurable, part of life. Food provides the body with a supply of energy and with nutrients necessary for proper growth and development. Food is needed to keep the body healthy and functioning correctly, but to do this food has first to be broken down into its basic constituent parts and then absorbed. The digestive tract is designed to do this efficiently and without conscious control.

Digestion begins the moment food enters the mouth. After being chewed by the teeth to a pulp and moistened by saliva, the food is pushed to the back of the throat by the tongue and swallowed. It is driven down the oesophagus (gullet) by muscular contractions and into the stomach, where the digestive juices liquidize it and begin to break it down into simpler chemical compounds. The liquid then passes into the first part of the small intestine, where enzymes from the pancreas and small intestine break it down further. The process of absorbing the nutrients in digested food into the blood occurs in the small intestine, and the waste products that remain pass into the large intestine; here the water is absorbed back into the body, to leave semi-solid faeces which are expelled through the rectum and anus. The liver, the largest single organ of the body and the one with the most complex functions, is responsible for processing the products of digestion that have been absorbed into the blood. The whole process of digestion is controlled both by nervous impulses and by hormonal influences (see pages 188-92 and 180-87).

Digestion and absorption

The digestive tract is essentially a hollow tube with the mouth at one end and the anus at the other. Although the tract is continuous, it can be divided into distinct parts, each of which has a different structure and function.

The mouth

The digestive tract begins at the mouth, where food first comes into contact with the teeth. These chew up the food, with the front teeth tearing it and the molars at the back of the mouth grinding the food down into smaller pieces. The teeth mix the food with saliva which softens and lubricates it and also starts to digest starches. Saliva is secreted into the mouth by three pairs of salivary glands, one pair under the tongue (sublingual), one in the lower jaw (submaxillary) and one in the cheeks (paratoid). These glands begin to secrete saliva when a person sees and smells food, but the

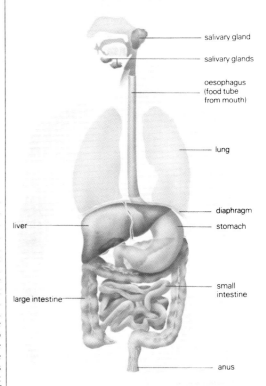

salivary gland

salivary glands

oesophagus (food tube from mouth)

lung

diaphragm

liver

stomach

small intestine

large intestine

anus

The organs of the digestive system, showing their relationship to the lungs and diaphragm and the approximate position in which they lie in the body. The digestive system comprises the alimentary tract – the tube that runs from mouth to anus along which the food passes – and its associated organs.

greatest flow of saliva is produced by a reflex triggered by the physical sensation of food in the mouth and also by the taste of the food.

Saliva contains mucus, rich in a slimy protein called mucin, which lubricates the food in the mouth and helps in swallowing; and amylase, an enzyme which acts on the starch in foods rich in carbohydrate, breaking it down into the sugar, maltose. In the brief period before food is swallowed, up to five per cent of starches can be broken down into sugar in this way.

Food is moved around the mouth by the tongue, a muscular organ which, as well as being involved in speech, is important in taste; the rough upper surface of the tongue is covered in papillae, small projections containing the taste buds.

*Here, the organs of the digestive tract from the stomach onwards
have been spread out to show their relationship to each other. Parts
have also been cut away to show their internal structure. The
kidneys and bladder are not part of the digestive system: they
excrete the waste end products of digestion.*

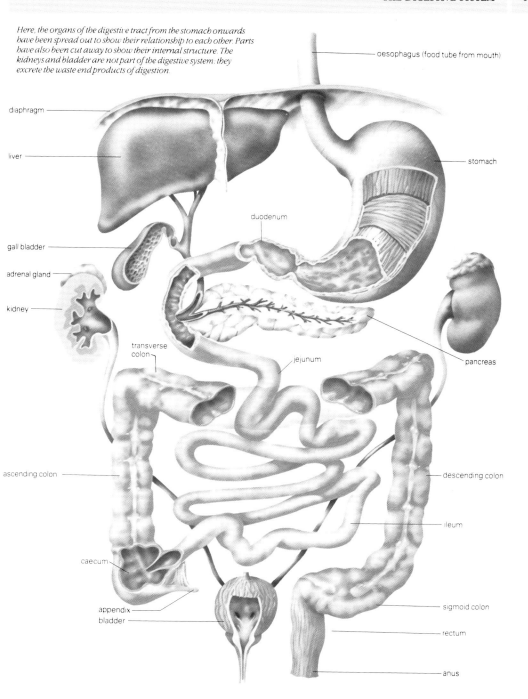

oesophagus (food tube from mouth)

diaphragm

liver

stomach

gall bladder

duodenum

adrenal gland

kidney

transverse colon

jejunum

pancreas

ascending colon

descending colon

ileum

caecum

appendix

bladder

sigmoid colon

rectum

anus

The oesophagus

Once a mouthful of food has been worked by the teeth and saliva, it is moulded into a soft mass or 'bolus'. The touch of the bolus against the back of the throat then starts a series of swallowing reflexes, whereby the diaphragm and chest wall stop moving so that breathing is impossible, and the bolus is forced into the oesophagus (gullet) that connects the mouth to the stomach. Waves of muscular contraction and relaxation, a movement called peristalsis, produce pressure that forces the bolus down the oesophagus into the stomach.

At the entrance to the stomach there is a ring of muscle called the cardia. Except during eating, this ring is kept shut to prevent the acid in the stomach passing back up into the oesophagus, where it might cause damage. When peristalsis begins in the oesophagus, the cardia relaxes to allow the food to enter the stomach. The cardia also relaxes and opens by a reflex action to allow vomiting and belching.

The stomach

The stomach is a J-shaped muscular bag situated on the left side of the body just under the lower ribs. It can hold about 1½ litres (2½ pints) of fluid at a time. The stomach produces and mixes gastric juice with food to start the next stage of digestion. Gastric juice is secreted by about 35,000,000 glands in the stomach wall; up to two litres (four pints) a day can be produced. This juice consists of mucus, hydrochloric acid and the enzyme pepsin, the first enzyme in the system to start digesting protein. The acid converts iron in food into a form in which it can later be absorbed, and provides the acid conditions which pepsin needs to be able to act. The acid also stops the action of the amylase that was secreted in the saliva, but only after about forty per cent of starches have been converted into sugars by this enzyme. The lining of the stomach protects itself from attack by the acid by producing a thick layer of mucus. The stomach lining also produces a substance called intrinsic factor, which is essential for the absorption of vitamin B_{12}.

Young babies' stomachs produce one other protein-digesting enzyme, rennin. This curdling agent converts the protein in milk, caseinogen, into casein, causing it to clot. As an infant is weaned, the enzyme pepsin takes over the role of rennin.

As food is digested in the stomach it is turned into a thick liquid called chyme. A muscular valve, the pyloric sphincter, controls the exit of chyme into the first part of the small intestine, the duodenum. The length of time that food remains in the stomach depends on the type of meal eaten. A meal with a lot of fat will tend to stay in the stomach longer than a meal rich in carbohydrate; and this is one reason why carbohydrates can supply energy to the body more quickly than fats. A small amount of chyme is squirted towards the pyloric sphincter each time peristaltic waves pass through the stomach and, although most of it is swished back at first, significant amounts of semi-liquid food begin to leave the stomach half an hour after a meal.

The small intestine

The bulk of the breakdown and absorption of food takes place in the small intestine, so called because of its narrow

diameter of 4 cm (1½ in). The first 25 cm (10 in) forms the duodenum, followed by the jejunum and then the ileum.

The duodenum is linked by hollow ducts to the liver and pancreas. Both these organs produce secretions essential for digestion.

Bile production

The liver produces bile, a thick, green, bitter liquid which is stored in the gall bladder between meals. As soon as food enters the small intestine, bile is secreted from the gall bladder through the common bile duct. Bile contains no digestive enzymes but consists mainly of chemicals known as bile salts. These act like strong detergents and break down fats into small globules, making them easier to digest. Within the intestine, however, as much as ninety-five per cent of all bile salts are re-absorbed, combined with fats. The bile salts then pass into the blood and are returned to the liver where they are secreted again in bile. It has been estimated that between their original manufacture (from cholesterol) in the liver and their eventual secretion in faeces, the bile salts recirculate from liver to intestine about eighteen times. (Other functions of the liver are described on the next page.)

The pancreas and pancreatic enzymes

The pancreas plays a vital role in digestion, and its activities can be divided into two main types. Firstly, it produces pancreatic juice which contains enzymes that break down proteins, carbohydrates and fats. Secondly, the pancreas secretes two important hormones, insulin and glucagon, which control the level of sugar in the bloodstream.

Trypsin, the chief protein-digesting enzyme in pancreatic juice, breaks the protein units into their smaller components, polypeptides, then peptides, and even into some of the smallest units, amino acids. The pancreas also secretes large amounts of the enzyme amylase (also present in saliva), which reduces starch to sugars. However, amylase from the pancreas is stronger than that in the saliva, being able to digest uncooked starch and tough plant cells.

A third pancreatic enzyme, called lipase, acts on the fats which have already been emulsified by the bile salts and breaks them up into their components, glycerol and fatty acids, which can then be absorbed into the bloodstream.

Enzymes and other secretions that play a part in digestion are produced by the cells lining the small intestine. These cells also produce thick mucus to protect the intestine from being digested by its own juices. In the small intestine, enzymes are released from microscopic tube-shaped glands in response to the stretching of the intestinal wall as chyme enters. In addition to trypsin, the intestinal secretion also contains three carbohydrate-digesting enzymes: lactase, which splits lactose (the sugar in milk) into galactose and glucose; sucrase, which splits sucrose (cane sugar) into galactose and glucose; and maltase, which reduces maltose (the end-product of amylase action on starch) into glucose. All these final substances are called monosaccharides and are now ready for absorption.

The small intestine has an important role in absorbing nutrients; much of this is carried out in the jejunum, the second part of the small intestine. The inner surface of the small intestine consists of a mucous membrane which is pleated and folded and covered with millions of small, finger-like projections called villi. These increase the surface area of the lining of the intestine about twenty times, making a total of 550 sq m (660 sq yd), for the purpose of secretion and absorption. Each of the villi is covered by a single layer of cells with pores between them: small molecules pass through these into the bloodstream to be transported to the liver in the portal vein.

The end-products of the digestive processes in the small intestine are: amino acids from animal and plant proteins which are used to build human protein; the simplest sugars (glucose, fructose and galactose) which come from vegetable starch, milk sugar and other sources but which are used to build human starch (glycogen) and to provide energy; and fatty acids and glycerol, which are the basic material of fats, of which some go to the liver and most are reconverted into fat in the villi. These minute fat globules are then transported in the vessels of the lymphatic system to the neck, where they are emptied into the bloodstream.

By the time chyme reaches the end of the ileum, only half a litre (1 pint) of the original ten litres (17 pints) present at the beginning of the small intestine remains. The remainder contains indigestible matter such as cellulose and fibre.

The large intestine

At the end of the small intestine there is a valve, the ileocaecal valve, which controls the movement of material into the large intestine. The first part of this is called the caecum which is followed by the ascending, then the transverse and finally the descending parts of the colon. The descending colon is joined by the sigmoid colon to the top of the rectum, which opens to the outside through the anus. The appendix, a narrow, blind tube 5 to 30 cm (2 to 12 in) long, opens into the caecum but plays no part in the digestion or absorption of food.

The main function of the large intestine, the last part of the alimentary tract, is to remove water as well as any useful substances in the remains of the food and to store the waste material, the faeces, until it can be expelled from the body. No enzymes are secreted by it.

Millions of bacteria, called the 'intestinal flora', are always present in the intestine and are most dense in the transverse colon. They cause no harm and in many ways are useful; they can digest small amounts of cellulose which comes from plant cells, and also produce vitamins K and B.

In the colon, 'mass movements' propel faeces towards the anus. These movements begin with a constriction at the point where the colon is already distended. Next, the part behind the bulge contracts, forcing the contents forward. In this way, faeces are pushed into the rectum. When the rectum fills, a person will experience the desire to pass a stool. If circumstances are suitable, the brain sends a message to a nervous centre in the spinal cord and, with assistance from the muscles in the abdomen and the sphincter muscles around the anus, the faeces are ejected from the body. The waste products discharged in the faeces, which average about 100 g (3½ oz) a day, are three-quarters water and one quarter solids, the latter consisting of dead bacteria, fat, protein and undigested roughage.

The liver

The liver is an important organ in the digestion of food and the processing of absorbed materials. It is a large wedge-shaped organ which lies under the diaphragm, protected by the ribs. It is unusual in that it has two sorts of blood supply, one from the hepatic artery which carries oxygen to the liver, and the other from the portal vein which brings blood that has passed through the spleen, stomach and intestines where it has absorbed the products of digestion. Some of these are stored in the liver for future use; others are converted into forms that the body can use straight away. From the spleen the liver receives the end-products of old blood cells, mainly the pigment bilirubin, formed from haemoglobin in red blood cells. The cells in the liver process bilirubin and excrete it into minute channels, or bile canaliculi, which join up to form bile ducts. These, in turn, emerge and join the common bile duct which discharges bile into the duodenum (see page 102). Besides bilirubin (a waste product, in fact), bile also contains the bile salts, other salts and water. Bilirubin is converted in the intestine into stercobilin which gives faeces their brown colour. Bile salts are important in breaking down fats but are also required for the absorption of vitamin A.

Through the stomach and intestines the liver receives the end-products of digestion. Amino acids can pass through the liver and are transported in the blood to other organs in the body to build protein. But the proteins that are part of the blood, such as albumin, globulin and prothrombin, are made in the liver. Many other essential enzymes are also produced here.

About ten per cent of the fatty acids and glycerol present in the intestine also go through the liver which makes important lipids (fatty substances) from them. One lipid, cholesterol, is found in almost all the tissues of the body, especially in red blood cells and in nerve cells.

Glucose and the other simple sugars are converted into glycogen, which is stored in the liver and can be broken down to release glucose in order to maintain the blood-sugar level. Many cells and tissues take up glucose from the blood and use it to produce energy. Muscles produce glycogen from blood glucose and store it until energy is needed quickly, when it is broken down again.

Another important function of the liver is to convert and dispose of harmful substances, such as alcohol and certain drugs.

Examining the digestive system

A range of special tests and techniques can be used to examine the digestive tract for the diagnosis of disorders.

An endoscope is an instrument used to examine the inside of body cavities and organs. The modern fibre-optic endoscope is a flexible tube made up of many glass fibres which transmit light and images. This makes it possible to visualize the digestive tract from the oesophagus to the anus. Still and cine photographs and video-films can be made and, by attaching other instruments to the endoscope, tissue samples can be removed or small operations carried out. The proctoscope and sigmoidoscope, which are rigid hollow endoscopes with a light source, are used to examine the anal canal and colon respectively. Laparoscopy is a surgical operation involving piercing the abdominal wall (usually under a local anaesthetic), and examining the contents of the abdomen with an endoscope. It is used mainly to examine the Fallopian tubes and ovaries.

A tube can be passed down the throat and into the stomach and intestine to collect samples of their contents. Specimens of liver tissue can be obtained by biopsy, a procedure in which a hollow needle is inserted through the skin and abdominal wall into the liver and a small core of tissue removed for microscopical examination.

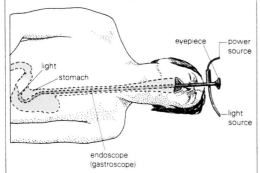

Endoscopy is often the investigation of choice in someone complaining of severe indigestion. The endoscope is passed down the oesophagus while the patient is lightly sedated, so that the doctor can inspect the stomach and duodenum, and examine any abnormalities such as ulcers.

X-ray examination of the different parts of the digestive tract can be used alone or in combination with other procedures such as endoscopy. It may be necessary to use a substance opaque to X-rays (radio-opaque) to show up the outline of the intestines. Barium is most commonly used, given either by mouth in the form of a barium meal, or as an enema.

Much information can be gained by examining the faeces. A fresh sample must be collected in a clean container, and detailed analysis of the contents carried out using chemical and bacteriological tests.

Disorders of the digestive system

Mouth disorders

Infection and inflammation
Stomatitis is the term for general inflammation of the mouth. Glossitis (inflammation of the tongue) and gingivitis (inflammation of the gums) are both kinds of stomatitis. The characteristic features include redness, swelling and tenderness, together with foul-smelling breath (halitosis) and excessive production of saliva. An extreme stage is gangrenous stomatitis (cancrum oris).

Aphthous stomatitis (mouth ulcers) is a troublesome condition in which small white blisters appear. It may be caused by a virus and is often related to stress, or being generally run down. Mouth ulcers can also be caused by damage to the delicate lining of the mouth as a result of scratching or other injury. Mouthwashes and creams are available to help alleviate the pain caused by such ulcers. A doctor should be consulted if aphthous ulcers persist.

Thrush is caused by a fungus *(Candida albicans)* and appears as little white patches. It is most common in infants and the elderly, and after treatment with steroid drugs or antibiotics. It is not a serious condition and is normally treated with antifungal lozenges.

There are also several skin conditions which appear as an inflamed mouth, such as lichen planus. Steroid drugs may alleviate this harmless but irritating condition.

Halitosis, popularly known as 'bad' or offensive breath, is usually linked to decomposition in the mouth of deposits on the teeth, septic gums or decayed teeth (caries). Infections of the nose, throat and chest can also cause halitosis. X-rays of the teeth may show the cause to be an abscess at the base of a tooth.

Parotitis, or inflammation of the largest salivary glands, the parotids, is usually the first sign of the virus infection, mumps. Septic parotitis is common in the elderly and bed-ridden. Recurrent parotitis occurs mainly in children but becomes less frequent as they grow up.

Salivary calculus consists of a stone composed of calcium carbonate or phosphate that forms in a salivary gland or duct. The gland becomes swollen because saliva cannot pass down the duct normally. Once the stone has been located it can be removed by simple surgery under local anaesthetic.

Cleft palate
Cleft palate is a congenital defect of the roof of the mouth where the two halves have failed to fuse, and is often accompanied by hare lip, a congenital defect in the front of the upper lip. Both conditions are caused by failure in the development of the structure of the face before birth. The repair of hare lip is a relatively minor operation which can be carried out at about three months of age. Cleft palate repair is a more difficult operation and is not usually carried out until the child is one to one-and-a-half years old, but before he or she learns to speak.

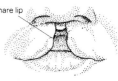

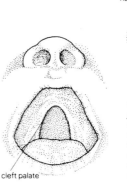

Cleft palate and hare lip result from a failure of the two halves of the face to fuse during fetal development. Though parents may find it a shock that their child has been born with such a defect, the results of surgical correction are good.

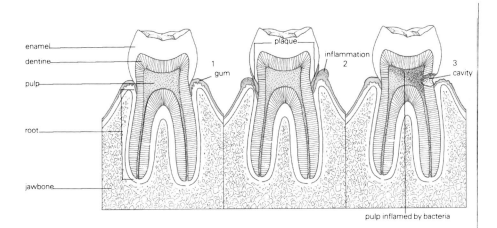

enamel
dentine
pulp
root
jawbone

plaque
inflammation
gum
cavity

1
2
3

pulp inflamed by bacteria

Above: the development of tooth decay. In order for decay to occur, both bacteria and sugar need to be present, and both these can be removed by regular brushing. If plaque, a sticky residue containing bacteria, is allowed to build up next to the gums (1), these will become inflamed and bleed when the teeth are brushed (2). The bacteria in the plaque produce acid which destroys the

enamel of the tooth, creating a cavity. If this is not filled by a dentist, bacteria can inflame the pulp of the tooth (3), eventually causing its death.

Below: a painful abscess may result if bacterial infection travels down to the root of the tooth.

Disorders of the teeth and gums

Diseases of the teeth and gums are often closely related. Many can be easily avoided, however, by proper cleaning and care of the teeth, and regular check-ups by a dentist.

Dental decay (caries) is extremely common, both in children and adults. The first stage in the process is the build-up of plaque around the teeth and gums. Bacteria in the plaque produce acid which starts to erode the tooth. If not treated, bacteria can invade the central cavity of the tooth, the pulp, and the tooth will die.

Abscesses are the painful result of infection of the pulp or the jawbone around the tooth. Pus builds up in the cavity and may eventually burst out, with infected pulp getting into the bloodstream. A dentist can usually drain the pus from an abscess without removing the tooth, and antibiotics may be given to prevent the infection spreading.

When teeth have to be taken out because of decay or disease, or if they fall out, they can be replaced by false teeth, usually attached to a plate in the form of dentures, or on a bridge cemented on to adjacent teeth. However, these can present their own problems if they do not fit well or if the gums are not kept healthy. The most common problems are mouth ulcers and, occasionally, gum disease.

Inflammation of the gums, gingivitis, is caused by plaque that sticks to the base of the teeth. The gums are swollen and red, and bleed easily. If not treated (by getting rid of all plaque), the condition may worsen to cause destructive gum disease. The best remedy is scaling, a procedure whereby a dentist or dental hygienist removes all plaque and hard deposits (calculus).

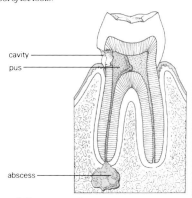

cavity
pus

abscess

Disorders of the oesophagus

Dysphagia, difficulty in swallowing, may be caused by many disorders of the throat and oesophagus. An infection of the throat will often cause swelling and soreness, with resultant dysphagia and enlargement of the lymph glands near the throat. Damage to nerves, due to diseases such as poliomyelitis or diphtheria, can lead to paralysis of the muscles used in swallowing. In myasthenia gravis (see page 128), muscular weakness can cause dysphagia, and it is also common after a stroke.

Damage caused to the lining of the oesophagus, as when a corrosive or foreign body is swallowed, may, if severe, make swallowing impossible. Tumours in nearby tissues or in the oesophagus itself can obstruct the passage of food.

Disorders of the stomach and duodenum

Ulcers

Peptic ulcers are a common cause of abdominal pain and discomfort. About one in ten people will have an ulcer at some time in their life. There are two main types of peptic ulcer: duodenal ulcer, which is the commonest and seems to occur especially in men; and gastric or stomach ulcer, which tends to affect both men and women. Ulcers of the lower oesophagus or the pylorus are much less common.

All ulcers produce pain in the upper abdomen. With a duodenal ulcer, pain comes on when the stomach is empty and is relieved by small meals; with gastric ulcers pain is brought on by eating; oesophageal ulcers are often more painful when lying down, as the gastric juice washes against the opening of the oesophagus into the stomach; pyloric ulcers cause spasms in the pyloric sphincter (so that the stomach cannot empty normally) and severe vomiting. The mainstay of treatment for peptic ulcers is drugs to reduce acidity. Antacids such as aluminium hydroxide, magnesium trisilicate and magnesium hydroxide are often used. Over the last decade, drugs that selectively reduce gastric acid and pepsin secretion have been introduced and shown to be very effective in healing ulcers. These drugs, such as cimetidine and ranitidine, work by blocking histamine receptors on the cells lining the intestine and stomach (see pages 102-3). Peptic ulcers are rarely permanently cured, however, and in most sufferers they tend to be a lifelong problem. Smoking, in particular, and heavy alcohol consumption hinder healing and are likely to cause ulcers to recur. Those who have a peptic ulcer should therefore avoid cigarettes and alcohol.

In serious cases bleeding may occur, with vomiting of blood (haematemesis) and shiny-tar-coloured stools due to the presence of blood, causing shock and anaemia. An ulcer may perforate the wall of the stomach or oesophagus, allowing the contents of the organ to escape, causing peritonitis (inflammation of the membrane lining the abdominal cavity). Surgery is essential to drain and close the perforation. A surgical operation may also be necessary when there is haematemesis or when gastric ulceration is frequent.

Duodenal ulcer is five times commoner than gastric ulcer, and both types produce abdominal pain.

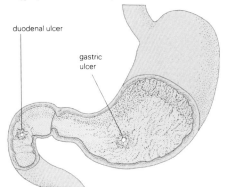

duodenal ulcer

gastric ulcer

Gastritis and heartburn

Gastritis, or inflammation of the lining of the stomach, can be caused by several things. Alcohol, aspirin, some food-poisoning bacteria, and corrosive substances such as acid or poison may cause severe gastritis with bleeding of the stomach. Symptoms include nausea, abdominal discomfort and vomiting and usually appear within a few hours of swallowing the irritating substance. Gastritis caused by acid or alcohol may be felt very soon, while gastritis caused by food poisoning may take five hours or more to develop.

Heartburn is a sharp, burning sensation in the lower chest, usually in the centre, which occurs about an hour after eating. It is usually associated with indigestion and lasts for only a few minutes, although it may continue for longer. It is caused by acid from the stomach entering the lower oesophagus, and often occurs in cases of obesity, pregnancy or hiatus hernia. Sometimes pyrosis (water-brash) occurs, when the acid fluid from the stomach comes up into the mouth, giving a bitter taste.

Flatus

Flatus is gas in the gut, and excess flatus, which leads to flatulence, has several causes. The type of food eaten affects the amount and types of gases produced, although this also varies with the individual. Beans, peas and other leguminous vegetables are a well-known cause of flatulence; they contain an unusual carbohydrate, stachyose, from which the bacteria in the gut produce gas. Flatulence can be a serious problem after operations on the abdomen, and discomfort arising from expansion of the gas in the gut can develop as a result of travelling at high altitudes in an unpressurized aircraft.

A major cause of flatulence is the swallowing of air, or aerophagia, and about seventy per cent of the gas in the intestine is caused by it. Since eighty per cent of air is nitrogen which cannot be absorbed, it must be expelled as flatus. Aerophagia is often an unconscious habit and may be caused by certain diseases, such as infections or disorders of the digestive tract which encourage the swallowing of saliva. Swallowing air in order to belch seems to relieve discomfort in cases of peptic ulcer, gall bladder disease, and angina (see page 155). Eating too rapidly, chewing gum, sucking on sweets, and poorly fitting false teeth are other causes of aerophagia.

Cancer of the stomach

Stomach, or gastric, cancer is most common in the middle-aged and elderly. This type of cancer seems to be influenced in some cases by the type of food eaten. It is more common in some countries than others, which may be due to differences in diet. The symptoms produced by stomach cancer fall into three main groups: those of the first group are caused by the tumour itself, such as pain (often similar to that produced by a peptic ulcer), vomiting, and sometimes difficulty in swallowing; the second group of symptoms includes more general ones such as loss of weight and appetite; and the third group occurs when secondary cancers, arising originally from the stomach, spread to other parts of the body and produce symptoms there.

Treatment might involve total or partial removal of the stomach (gastrectomy). The death rate from stomach cancer is high, however.

Pyloric stenosis

There are few congenital abnormalities or deformities of the stomach; hypertrophic pyloric stenosis is the only common one. It is usually diagnosed in the first one to three weeks of life. In this condition, the pylorus (the opening connecting the stomach to the duodenum) is narrowed, or stenosed. The narrowing is caused by overgrowth of the pyloric sphincter. This means that little or no food can pass from the stomach, and the baby vomits violently after feeds.

Pyloric stenosis occurs in three or four of every 1000 births. Boys are affected more than girls and it seems to run in families. The main form of treatment is a simple operation to expand the passageway of the pylorus to allow food to pass through it.

In adults pyloric stenosis (without hypertrophy) can occur as a serious complication of peptic ulcer or cancer affecting the pylorus.

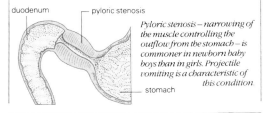

duodenum   pyloric stenosis

Pyloric stenosis – narrowing of the muscle controlling the outflow from the stomach – is commoner in newborn baby boys than in girls. Projectile vomiting is a characteristic of this condition.

stomach

Gastrectomy

The stomach can be partly or completely removed by an operation called partial or total gastrectomy. After the operation the patient can survive in good health, eat adequate-sized meals, enjoy food and lead an almost normal life. However, because the stomach is involved in the absorption of vitamin B_{12} and iron, injections of the vitamin may be required after the stores in the liver have been exhausted, and extra iron may also have to be given by injection or in food.

Liver disorders

Hepatitis

The most common disease of the liver is viral hepatitis. The liver can be attacked by a number of viruses, but the term is normally reserved for an illness caused by at least two closely related viruses which are transmitted in different ways.

Infectious hepatitis (type A) is spread by the oral-faecal route, either by contact with an infected person or by contamination of food or water; children and young adults are most at risk. The time between exposure to the virus and development of symptoms, the incubation period, is from eighteen days to six weeks, and the disease lasts for about three weeks. It is nearly always a mild illness, beginning with gastro-intestinal symptoms. The urine becomes dark brown, and the faeces become pale because of obstruction to the flow of bile from the liver. At this stage jaundice appears and the patient usually begins to feel better. No special treatment is required, apart from bed-rest in the early stages, but drugs and alcohol should be prohibited for at least six months. The type A virus is found in faeces for several months after an attack, but rarely remains infectious after a month.

Serum hepatitis (type B), as its name implies, is spread by infected blood serum contaminating syringes, needles and instruments. For this reason no person with a history of hepatitis should give blood for transfusion. Drug addicts and homosexual men are at a high risk of contracting hepatitis B. Hospital staff, particularly those who come into contact with blood samples, are also at risk. The incubation period for serum hepatitis is long – from two to six months. Its symptoms and treatment are similar to type A virus, although it is a more serious disease, beginning insidiously, with jaundice often the first sign of infection. Prolonged, chronic hepatitis B can eventually lead to cancer of the liver. Vaccines to protect against hepatitis B, because of the potential seriousness of the disease, are recommended for anyone in the high-risk groups.

Another type of viral hepatitis, 'non-A non-B', occurs but its relationship to the other types is not fully understood.

Cirrhosis

Cirrhosis is a chronic disease of the liver found in many parts of the world. In cirrhosis, dead cells are replaced by scar tissue (fibrosis) while surviving liver cells multiply to form clumps or nodules of liver tissue. The liver is permanently and progressively damaged, but continues to function for varying lengths of time, sometimes indefinitely if the cause of the damage (such as alcohol) is removed. The flow of blood is impeded by scar tissue and as a result the pressure in the portal vein increases as it attempts to overcome the obstruction, causing hypertension (high blood pressure) in the portal circulation.

In western Europe and the USA alcoholism is a major cause of cirrhosis, while in underdeveloped countries and the Far East infections and toxic substances in the diet are more common causes of the condition. Some diseases, such as hepatitis and malaria, can lead to cirrhosis. Only one in eight alcoholics develops cirrhosis, however, and there may be an innate sensitivity in some people, perhaps related to the activity of certain enzymes in the liver. A number of other diseases that may lead to cirrhosis include diabetes mellitus, schistosomiasis (a tropical worm disease) and ulcerative colitis.

Cirrhosis is diagnosed by taking a specimen of the liver for examination (biopsy). Chemical tests on how certain liver enzymes are working are also used to detect cirrhosis.

As portal hypertension is a common complication in all forms of cirrhosis, various surgical methods such as a by-pass operation have been developed to overcome this. However, once the symptoms of cirrhosis develop the outlook is poor. The usual cause of death is liver cell failure. In the future, liver transplantation may offer a cure, but at the moment many technical problems need to be overcome before it can hope to provide a worthwhile treatment.

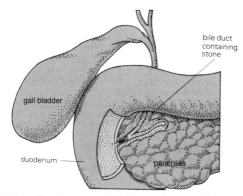

bile duct
containing
stone

gall bladder

duodenum

pancreas

Pain and jaundice may result if gallstones obstruct the bile duct.

Gall bladder disorders

Gallstones
Gallstones are the commonest condition associated with the gall bladder. The gallstones may form in the gall bladder or common bile duct. Pain can occur if the stone cannot get through part of the biliary system and, if the bile duct is blocked, jaundice may occur. Drugs can be used to dissolve the stones but in general they are removed by surgery. The whole gall bladder can be removed without harmful effects: bile from the liver passes straight to the duodenum.

Cholecystitis
Cholecystitis, inflammation of the gall bladder, is usually associated with gallstones, and may be acute or chronic. In the acute type there may be severe pain, vomiting and fever, with slight jaundice in some cases. Chronic cholecystitis is seen most often in overweight middle-aged women. Eating fatty foods causes an attack of abdominal pain (with belching and distension), which patients may have suffered intermittently for years.

Disorders of the pancreas
In acute pancreatitis, the pancreas becomes inflamed, and its enzymes are activated within the gland so that it begins to 'digest' itself and the surrounding tissues. The patient develops severe abdominal pain and is often extremely ill but, despite the damage to the gland, usually recovers.

Chronic pancreatitis causes the pancreas to become fibrosed and functionless: food is not digested properly and malnutrition occurs. The condition can be alleviated to some extent by adding extracts of animal pancreas (containing the necessary enzymes) to the food. Patients also need powerful painkillers and treatment with insulin because of the associated diabetes (see pages 185-7). Animal pancreas is also used to treat cystic fibrosis, a congenital disorder in which a failure of the pancreas to produce sufficient enzymes results in malabsorption of nutrients. The disease also causes a malfunctioning of the glands lining the bronchi, leading to recurrent respiratory infections. Cancer of the pancreas, a condition that is becoming more common, calls for complete removal of the organ.

Disorders of the small intestine
Crohn's disease (regional ileitis)
Crohn's disease is inflammation of the part of the small intestine called the ileum. The cause of the inflammation is not known, but the disease causes disturbances in bowel function (usually intermittent diarrhoea) and abdominal tenderness and pain. The patient usually has a fever, loses weight and appears chronically ill. The colon and rectum may also be involved. There is no totally reliable treatment for Crohn's disease. Corticosteroid drugs are often given to reduce the inflammation. It is important that people with this disease eat a high calorie diet, and special liquid food can be taken to supplement the normal diet. The diseased part of the intestine may require surgical removal and a colostomy (see page 111).

Paralytic ileus (adynamic ileus)
Paralytic ileus is obstruction of the bowel, caused by paralysis of the muscles of the intestinal wall. The symptoms are abdominal distension, vomiting, constipation and continual abdominal pain, in many cases occurring after major surgery.

Malabsorption syndrome
Malabsorption syndrome is the condition of deficiency in protein, carbohydrate, fat, minerals and vitamins, even though the affected person is eating an adequate diet. The patient is thin and, if the disease occurs in childhood, may also be of short stature. He or she may pass frequent stools with a very high fat content, a condition known as steatorrhea; the stools are pale, bulky, offensive and difficult to flush away. In addition there may be abdominal pain or distension.

A number of conditions can lead to malabsorption. The failure of the pancreas to produce its digestive enzymes, as for example in chronic pancreatitis, can cause a failure to break down food. In coeliac disease the lining of the intestine becomes thin and wasted because the sufferer is sensitive to gluten, a protein found in wheat and rye flour. Once the condition is diagnosed, the person must avoid eating anything that contains gluten, such as wheat, rye, barley and malt; but maize, rice and oats can be eaten safely.

Tropical sprue is another disease where changes occur in the lining of the intestine, and it can be treated with B-vitamins, folic acid and sometimes antibiotics. It occurs only in tropical and subtropical regions. Other causes of malabsorption include diseases of the liver and blockage of the lymphatic channels that carry products of digestion from the intestine.

Hernias
A hernia is a lump or swelling that occurs when a tissue or organ moves out of position and pushes against adjacent tissues, as when a part of the intestine protrudes through a gap in the muscle wall of the abdomen. In many cases treatment involves surgery, so-called hernia repair.

Inguinal hernia
Inguinal hernias occur in the groin and are the most common type of hernia. They often occur in men, where the

hernia may extend into the scrotum. The hernia, formed from part of the small intestine, lies in front of the inner part of the inguinal ligament, which separates the thigh and abdomen at the groin. Coughing, straining at defaecation and severe muscular effort may all predispose to its development.

Femoral hernia

Femoral hernias pass behind the inguinal ligament and extend into the thigh. They are most common in the elderly. Both inguinal and femoral hernias may trap part of the intestine and block blood supply. These are known as strangulated hernias and require immediate surgery, because if not treated straight away they may become gangrenous.

Umbilical hernia

In umbilical hernias in newborn babies there is a weakness in the abdominal wall where the umbilical cord falls off after birth. This normally disappears by itself, but occasionally the defect can be larger and a considerable part of the gut may protrude into the thin sac formed out of umbilical cord tissue, in a condition known as exomphalos or omphalocele, which needs surgery.

— umbilical hernia

Umbilical hernia in a newborn infant: treatment is not usually necessary.

In adults, an umbilical hernia (para-umbilical hernia) is a different disorder from that in infants, and it typically occurs in overweight women who have borne many children; treatment is essential and usually involves surgery.

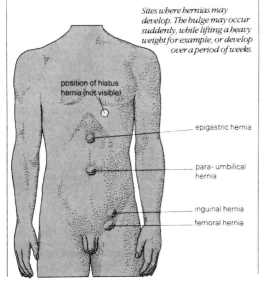

Sites where hernias may develop. The bulge may occur suddenly, while lifting a heavy weight for example, or develop over a period of weeks.

position of hiatus hernia (not visible)

— epigastric hernia

— para- umbilical hernia

— inguinal hernia
— femoral hernia

Hiatus hernia

Hiatus hernia occurs when part of the upper region of the stomach becomes trapped above the diaphragm, the sheet of muscle separating the chest from the abdomen and through which the oesophagus passes. In many cases, the herniated part of the stomach can slide into and out of the chest when the person stoops or lies down, and the main symptom is heartburn. In a few cases, the hernia remains fixed above the diaphragm and the main symptom is discomfort when eating. Hiatus hernia can occur at any time of life. It may be caused by muscle weakness or by an injury producing a tear in the diaphragm. It is quite common, particularly in the obese and in women who have had children, although the symptoms may begin after the menopause. Loss of weight can often improve the symptoms and so can care with the posture, for example bending at the knees rather than the hips.

Appendicitis

Inflammation of the appendix, appendicitis, occurs in both sexes and at all ages, although it is twice as common in men and rare in the very young and very old. If left untreated, an acutely inflamed appendix forms pus, becomes gangrenous and finally bursts. This releases the contents into the cavity around the gut (the peritoneal cavity), causing peritonitis (inflammation of the peritoneal cavity).

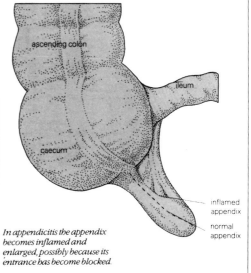

ascending colon

ileum

caecum

inflamed appendix

normal appendix

In appendicitis the appendix becomes inflamed and enlarged, possibly because its entrance has become blocked.

The first symptom is vague pain, generally in the centre of the abdomen near the navel, which gradually becomes more severe. There may be vomiting, and after a time the pain usually moves to the right lower quarter of the abdomen, as the appendix irritates the inside of the abdominal wall. The temperature rises, and the stomach is tender to touch (but sometimes the tenderness is inside the pelvis, so examination always includes feeling inside the rectum).

The number of white cells in the blood increases. In most cases surgical removal of the inflamed appendix is needed, and the sooner this is done the lower is the mortality rate from this condition.

Recurring spells of pain are often blamed on 'grumbling' appendicitis, but this condition is extremely rare, and these recurrent mild attacks usually have their origin in some other condition.

Disorders of the large intestine

Colitis
Colitis is inflammation of the colon, the main part of the large intestine. The commonest forms of the disorder are mucous colitis and ulcerative colitis.

Mucous colitis, or spastic colon, is thought to be brought about by stress, and symptoms include abdominal pain and diarrhoea alternating with constipation. Treatment is primarily psychological.

Ulcerative colitis may occur in the rectum as well and affects both sexes and almost any age group, although it is most common in the twenties and thirties. It is a tissue reaction in which the body damages its own tissues. The symptoms are blood-stained diarrhoea, abdominal pain and distension, fever, loss of weight and general ill health. During the severe stages of the disease the treatment is bed-rest, which may reduce the intestinal pain and diarrhoea. Omitting milk and milk products from the diet may also help. Corticosteroid drugs given by injection, by mouth or in the form of an enema may also give some relief. If the patient does not respond to this treatment, or if the disease worsens, surgery to remove the diseased bowel may be needed.

In megacolon, where the colon is badly dilated, the cause may be an obstruction, such as in severe constipation, but it normally results from Hirschsprung's disease, an abnormality of the colon inherited only by boys. This requires surgical treatment.

Diverticulosis (diverticular disease)
Diverticulosis occurs when pouches of the mucous membrane in the colon protrude through weakened regions of the wall. The condition is painful and there is a disturbance in bowel rhythm. Diverticulosis appears to occur more often in people who take a low fibre diet, and the symptoms can be eased by increasing the amount of roughage eaten. Diverticulitis occurs if one of the pouches becomes inflamed, often because a small piece of faeces has become lodged in it; there is tenderness in the abdomen and fever. Antibiotic treatment is usually required. Surgery does not always cure the patient completely and is not often performed.

Prolapse of the rectum
Prolapse of the rectum may occur in several forms. In internal prolapse or concealed prolapse, the upper part of the rectum and the sigmoid colon fold in on themselves and are carried down into the lower rectum. More often, the prolapsed rectum comes out of the anus and has to be pushed back inside. It is caused by poor muscle support, often due to undernutrition, from the floor of the pelvis, in combination with overactivity of the rectum during diarrhoea or constipation. Surgery is sometimes needed if the prolapse is severe.

Haemorrhoids (piles)
Haemorrhoids are dilated veins in the rectum and anus, usually referred to as piles, and there are two types, internal and external. Internal haemorrhoids are situated just above the sphincter muscle that keeps the anus closed, and consist of enlarged veins covered by a thin layer of the mucous membrane that lines the bowel. External haemorrhoids occur below the sphincter and initially they also consist of a collection of dilated veins, but covered by skin instead of mucous membrane. Frequently, the veins in external haemorrhoids shrink, so that the pile consists of a tag of skin containing a little fibrous tissue.

About one in four of all adults suffer from haemorrhoids at some time in their lives. The majority of haemorrhoids occur spontaneously, although some are related to other conditions such as pregnancy, fibroids, obesity, liver disease or cancer of the rectum. Diets low in roughage may also lead to piles. Bleeding is the most common and usually the earliest symptom, but itching or pain is also present. Blood is seen at defaecation and is usually first noticed as streaks of bright red blood on the faeces or toilet paper. A thrombosed pile, in which the blood has clotted, causes severe discomfort for a day or two but heals spontaneously.

Treatment may be medical (by drugs and creams) or surgical. Medical treatment is usually used in mild cases and normally consists of the application of various sorts of suppositories and soothing creams, often in combination with a mild laxative. Internal haemorrhoids are sometimes treated by injection. Adding extra roughage to the diet, in the form of bran for example, often prevents piles recurring. Where the problem is more severe, surgical treatment is necessary. This may involve surgical incision, but an alternative is the procedure of anal dilatation, stretching the anal sphincter under a general anaesthetic. This helps to release some of the strain on the veins.

Haemorrhoids – the varicose veins of the rectum.

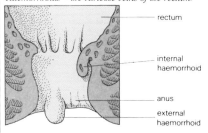

rectum

internal haemorrhoid

anus

external haemorrhoid

Anal fissure and fistula
Anal fissure is an ulcer in the anal canal; it becomes irritated on defaecation which causes the anal sphincter to go into spasm, with severe pain and sometimes bleeding. It may be cured by adding roughage to the diet, but a persistent or recurring fissure will usually require surgery.

Anal fistula is a rare condition in which an abscess in the

Colostomy and ileostomy

A colostomy is an artificial opening made in the abdominal wall so that the colon communicates directly with the outside as a new opening that replaces the natural anus. The operation is usually undertaken to bypass an obstruction of the gut below the colostomy or if the rectum has been removed (rectocolostomy). Temporary colostomy can also be carried out in the transverse colon to provide a temporary diversion when there is an obstruction to a part of the colon further along the tract. This may be needed where there is diverticulitis or cancer.

Ileostomy is a similar operation but is usually permanent, and performed at the same time as complete removal of the colon and rectum.

Although the thought of an artificial anus is distasteful, in reality even the friends of people with a colostomy usually cannot detect it, and these patients are perfectly able to undertake all forms of exercise. Social life is rarely affected once the techniques of changing bags and hygiene have been mastered.

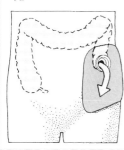

A colostomy does not allow defecation in the normal way; instead, the faeces are intercepted and collected in a colostomy bag attached to the surface of the abdomen. Control over bowel movements can usually, with time, become good.

anus causes erosion of the tissues of the bowel. This eventually leads to the formation of an abnormal channel between the body surface and the bowel wall. Watery faeces and pus pass through this channel, or fistula, irritating the skin and causing discomfort and itching. The usual treatment is surgical repair of the fistula after the abscess has been cleaned out. The wound is then dressed so that it will heal, but this may be a lengthy process.

Cancer

Cancer of the colon and rectum (colorectal cancer) is one of the commonest malignant tumours in the western world. Diet may play a role, although the evidence for this is not absolute. Pain, vomiting and weight loss are the main symptoms, although about one third of patients show no symptoms. The only treatment is surgery to remove the affected part, and success depends on the site and extent of the tumour.

Constipation

Constipation, the difficult or infrequent excretion of faeces, can be a symptom of illness but is more often caused by lack of fibre in the diet, or by emotional factors. A change of diet,

pregnancy, and some drugs can also cause constipation. Treatment should consist of removing the cause if possible. In the short term, laxatives, medicines that encourage the emptying of the bowel, can be useful, but should be used sparingly.

Some laxatives, such as mineral oil (medicinal liquid paraffin), act as lubricants. In the form of an emulsion they are reasonably palatable and suitable for occasional use, but regular use may cause deficiencies of the fat-soluble vitamins, which the oil carries out of the body. More commonly, laxatives stimulate the bowel. For example, cellulose, which is not digested, increases the bulk of material in the bowel. Some 'salts', such as Epsom salts and 'health salts' retain water and prevent the stored faeces from becoming dry, as well as increasing their volume. These types of laxative are very mild and are best for those who need to use laxatives frequently, such as some pregnant women. However, some laxatives irritate the bowel muscle or stimulate the nerves involved and can have violent effects, so are not suitable for regular use, since the colon can be damaged or weakened. Phenolphthalein and bisacodyl are examples; senna, rhubarb and cascara are among the many traditional vegetable laxatives of this type, and castor oil is notorious as one of the most objectionable.

Two tablespoons of bran every day can solve the problem, as constipation is often caused by a lack of roughage in the diet. Plenty of fruit and fluids also help.

Most enemas and suppositories act by irritating the rectum and should not be used unless the rectum contains hard faeces and their rapid removal is required. Severe or persistent constipation should always be investigated by a doctor, in case it is caused by obstruction in the bowel.

Diarrhoea

Diarrhoea, the frequent passing of soft or watery faeces, is not a disease but a symptom of any of several different diseases, and it is therefore important to find its cause. Diarrhoea is often a side-effect of taking drugs, especially antibiotics, which alter the levels of normal bacteria of the bowel, allowing abnormal types to multiply. Among some of the other causes of diarrhoea are: bacterial and viral infections; changes in diet and indigestion; inflammation of the intestine or colon; food poisoning; and malnutrition. Cases of acute diarrhoea should be treated by means of increased fluid intake to prevent dehydration. A bland diet may also help in mild cases. Green stools are of no special significance and only indicate that the contents of the bowel have passed along the intestine rapidly.

General infections of the digestive system

A variety of different organisms, including viruses, bacteria, fungi, and parasites, can either infect the digestive system or use it as a route to infect other organs. Food poisoning and dysentery are discussed here, and other infections in *Infections and Infestations* (page 206).

Food poisoning (gastroenteritis)

Food poisoning is a disturbance of the alimentary tract caused by the consumption of food or drink contaminated by bacteria. The symptoms are severe diarrhoea and abdominal pain which are frequently, but not always, accompanied by vomiting and fever. The three main types of bacteria responsible for food poisoning belong to the groups *Salmonella, Staphylococcus* and *Clostridium*.

Food poisoning caused by *Salmonella* (salmonellosis) results from eating food infected with these bacteria. They multiply in the body, and cause fever, headache, aching limbs, diarrhoea and nausea and vomiting, which may be mild or severe. Symptoms usually begin within twelve to thirty-six hours, although the incubation period may be longer. The illness may last up to eight days. Most sufferers then recover, but a few become carriers and continue to excrete the bacteria in their faeces and sometimes gall bladder, endangering others without experiencing any symptoms themselves. This type of food poisoning can be fatal, particularly in infants, the elderly and in people already suffering from other disease. Typhoid fever is the most serious of the *Salmonella* infections.

In staphylococcal food poisoning, certain strains of *Staphylococcus aureus* in food produce a poison (an enterotoxin) which they excrete into the food. Although the bacteria may be dead or killed during cooking, the toxin remains and causes the symptoms. These include nausea, vomiting, abdominal pain and diarrhoea, beginning soon after eating the contaminated food. The illness rarely lasts for more than a few hours and recovery is rapid.

Other major causes of food poisoning are the bacteria in the group *Clostridium*. These micro-organisms will only grow in the absence of oxygen, and can form spores which survive poor conditions such as severe cold, dryness and heat: the spores of some strains can survive boiling for as long as five hours. Large numbers of the organism *Clostridium welchii* must be consumed in food to cause food poisoning. The incubation period is eight to twenty-four hours and the illness may last up to twenty-four hours, followed by rapid recovery. The symptoms are usually mild abdominal pain and vomiting; the cause of the illness is thought to be a toxin released by the bacteria in the intestine.

Clostridium welchii is common in nature and is carried in the bowels of both humans and animals, on meat and poultry and in dust and soil. Illness only occurs after eating meat and poultry in which the organism has multiplied during slow cooking, or after eating cooked meats, stews and pies previously stored in a warm room. The spores are found in raw meat and come from the animal's gut and the surroundings during slaughter, and may survive heating to germinate and multiply after cooking.

Botulism is a rare form of food poisoning affecting the nervous system, and results from consuming toxins produced in food by the bacterium *Clostridium botulinum*. It is the most dangerous form of bacterial food poisoning. Raw, smoked and fermented fish products, home-bottled meat, fish and vegetables are the foods most frequently involved. Although the botulinum toxins are destroyed by heat, the bacteria's spores can survive boiling for several hours.

The incubation period of botulism can vary from a few hours to several days after eating contaminated food, but is normally from eighteen to thirty-six hours. Symptoms vary but may start with vomiting and diarrhoea, later changing to constipation, lassitude and general weakness. Later, other symptoms occur: blurred and double vision with fixed, dilated pupils, difficulties in speech and in swallowing, and a dry mouth. These are symptoms of gradual blockage of the nervous system caused by the toxin, which finally results in respiratory paralysis. Botulism is frequently fatal and when patients survive convalescence is slow.

Other, more common bacteria may also be involved in food poisoning when their numbers rise to high levels in certain foods. Types of *Streptococcus* cause food poisoning from time to time, and *Escherichia coli*, which was once thought to be harmful only to infants, may also cause diarrhoea in adults.

Treatment of food poisoning

Most people with food poisoning require little more than rest in bed and plenty of fluids to prevent dehydration. In cases of severe dehydration careful medical treatment is needed, with fluids such as saline or saline-and-glucose given intravenously.

In staphylococcal food poisoning, anti-emetic (anti-vomiting) drugs are useful if vomiting is prolonged and exhausting. Antibiotics should only be used for patients seriously ill from salmonellosis, as in typhoid fever, for antibiotics may increase the time bacteria remain in the bowel.

Dysentery

There are two principal types of dysentery, one caused by bacteria, mainly *Shigella* (bacillary dysentery) and one caused by single-celled *Entamoeba histolytica* (amoebic dysentery).

The bacillary form of dysentery is the most common type and often occurs in epidemics. If food or drink contaminated by the bacteria is taken, they multiply in the large intestine, causing damage to the bowel wall and, in severe cases, ulcers. Patients with bacillary dysentery pass large numbers of bacteria in their faeces, and under conditions of poor hygiene these may infect other people; after recovery from an infection the bacteria rarely remain in the faeces for more than a week or two. However, some infections cause no symptoms at all, and the infected person temporarily carries and spreads the infection without realizing it.

The microscopic single-celled animal that causes amoebic dysentery normally lives harmlessly on the inner surface of the large intestine. Sometimes, for a reason that is not understood, the *Entamoebae* invade the tissues of the intestinal wall and may be carried to the liver and other organs where they multiply and form an abscess. The infection is transmitted when the resistant form of the amoeba, the cyst, is swallowed. The thick-walled cyst is then passed in the faeces and can survive and reinfect for up to two months. Many amoebic infections cause no symptoms, but the tissue invasion can take place up to twenty-five years after the original infection has occurred.

For treatment of bacillary dysentery sulphonamide drugs and antibiotics are used, although some *Shigella* organisms are becoming resistant. For *Entamoeba* infections the drug metronidazole, taken by mouth, has been successfully used.

How to prevent food poisoning

Food stored at warm temperatures encourages the multiplication of the organisms that can cause food poisoning. All foods that might become infected should therefore be stored in a cold room or refrigerator, and this is particularly important in warm and hot weather, when the growth of most micro-organisms in food increases. Milk and cream should be pasteurized or treated in some other way, since outbreaks of staphylococcus infections have been caused by the growth of the bacteria in raw milk before it is heat-treated. Cheese and ice cream have also caused outbreaks. Processed peas and canned meats have caused outbreaks because staphylococci have been sucked in through minute holes in the seams of cans handled while still wet from the cooling water used after sterilization. Complete and rapid thawing of frozen foods, especially meat and poultry products, before cooking is also essential.

The hands are a very important element in the spread of infection, not only from the human bowel to food but also from raw foods to cooked foods during their preparation. The hands should be washed in hot, soapy water between preparing different kinds of food, and particularly after handling raw food such as meat and poultry. Uncovered raw and cooked food should be stored apart and separate surfaces and utensils used for the preparation of raw foods; all areas and equipment coming into contact with food should be in good condition and thoroughly cleaned after use. Disposable paper should be used instead of cloths.

animal feedstuffs

organic fertilizers

farm

poultry

pigs, cattle etc.

eggs

market and transport

egg products

Paths in the spread of salmonella. At each stage humans may be infected or become carriers. Preventive measures include: improved hygiene of production in the country of origin, on farms, in markets, in slaughter houses and in factories; and treatment of foodstuffs liable to contamination, including animal foodstuffs, by pasturization, dry heat and other methods.

slaughter house; meat and meat products

human salmonellosis

Rules of food hygiene

1 *Buy food only from clean places. Get the food home clean.*

2 *Use clean containers in your home.*

3 *Keep family foods away from pet food. Use special utensils and crockery just for pets and wash up separately from the family's equipment.*

4 *Always wash your hands before preparing food and after using the lavatory. See that your children do too.*

5 *Wash fruit and vegetables thoroughly under running water, especially if they are to be eaten raw.*

6 *Cover cuts and sores with waterproof dressings. If you are not well, and no one can take your place in the kitchen, be extra careful about personal cleanliness.*

7 *Keep food clean, covered and either cool or piping hot. Reheated leftovers must be made really hot right through. Do the same with ready-packaged foods intended to be eaten hot. Defrost all meat thoroughly before cooking it.*

8 *Keep working surfaces clean. Use really hot, soapy water; a wipe with a dishcloth is not enough.*

9 *Stack washed and rinsed crockery and pans to drain. If you use drying cloths, be sure that they are really clean.*

10 *Keep the lid firmly on the dustbin and kitchen bin.*

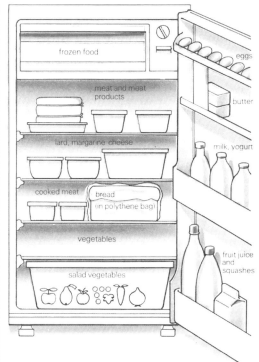

Above: the ideal place for storing most foods is in a refrigerator, in covered containers. Serve hot food as soon as possible after cooking or, if the food must be stored or eaten cold, cool it quickly.

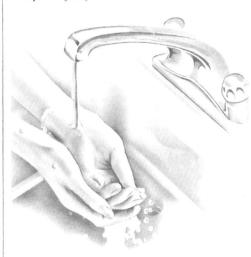

It is important to wash the hands after using the lavatory, and food handlers should be extra scrupulous. Those with staphylococcal infections, diarrhoea or cuts should not handle food.

Refrigerator rules

1 *Allow food to cool at room temperature before putting it into the refrigerator.*

2 *Do not keep cooked food or meat for more than three days in the refrigerator.*

3 *Keep raw and cooked food separate and covered so that drips from meat, for example, do not contaminate other food.*

4 *Do not overload the refrigerator. Allow space for air circulation so that it can work efficiently and economically to keep its contents sufficiently cool.*

5 *Ensure that the refrigerator is cooling to 3-5°C. Defrost it regularly for efficiency, and always keep it scrupulously clean, inside and out.*

Storing fresh food

The following are the recommended maximum storage times for a selection of common fresh foods.

One week in cool room	One week in cool dark place	Up to four days in refrigerator	Two to three days in refrigerator	Buy and eat on same day
apples	beetroot (beets)	cabbage	asparagus	blackcurrants
bananas	cheese	carrots	aubergine (egg plant)	broccoli
grapefruit	eggs	leeks	Brussels sprouts	fish
melon (three days when ripe)	Jerusalem artichokes	parsley	cauliflower	green beans
onions	lemons	parsnips	celery	lettuce
oranges	potatoes	peppers	courgettes (zucchini)	mushrooms
peaches (two days when ripe)	turnips	spring onions	globe artichokes	mustard and cress
pears (three days when ripe)		tomatoes	meat (poultry one day)	peas
pineapple (eat when ripe)			milk	raspberries
plums (two days when ripe)				spinach
				strawberries
				sweet corn
				watercress

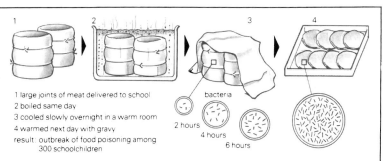

Right: bacteria multiply extremely fast in these conditions, and may cause an epidemic of food poisoning. Meat should be in cuts of no more than 3kg (6lb) and prepared, cooked and eaten on the same day, or cooled quickly and stored in a refrigerator. Cooked food should be reheated by thorough boiling, not simply by warming, which will not kill the bacteria but encourages their multiplication.

1 large joints of meat delivered to school
2 boiled same day
3 cooled slowly overnight in a warm room
4 warmed next day with gravy
result: outbreak of food poisoning among 300 schoolchildren

bacteria

2 hours
4 hours
6 hours

Hygiene on holiday

The commonest source of illness among travellers to foreign countries from the West is diarrhoea, caused by eating food contaminated with bacteria. The following hygienic measures should be taken in any non-European, non-Western country. Care should also be taken in Mediterranean countries. The more insanitary the conditions in the country you are visiting, the stricter hygienic measures should be.

1 Always use boiled or bottled water, not only for drinking but for cleaning teeth. Water can be sterilized with chlorine tablets or tincture of iodine, which should also be used to sterilize fruit and salad vegetables by immersing them in the water for half an hour.

2 Avoid cold, cooked foods and raw food unless it has been peeled or washed as described above.

3 Don't eat shellfish unless it is possible to see them alive first.

4 Make sure food is well cooked and has not been left standing for more than fifteen minutes.

5 Don't eat cream or milk unless it has been boiled; and do not eat raw cheese unless you know it is safe to do so. If in doubt, cook it.

6 Do not eat ice cream or other food from street vendors.

7 Avoid all foods that may have been open to flies.

8 Drink only soft drinks that have been made by a reputable international company; locally bottled soft drinks are not always subject to strict levels of hygiene during their manufacture.

The Urinary System

During many of the body's activities, substances are produced which are unwanted and even poisonous if allowed to accumulate. For example, carbon dioxide is a waste product of respiration, urea is an unwanted by-product of protein breakdown, and salts are often eaten in food in excess of the amount needed by the body. These have to be removed by the process of excretion.

The body has five organs of excretion: the skin, the lungs, the liver, the intestine and the kidneys. Each is important in its own way. The lungs (see pages 86-7) are the main excretors of carbon dioxide, and the liver (see page 103) is important in removing unwanted bile salts. The kidneys are, however, the most important organs of excretion. They filter the blood to remove toxic substances, including urea, salts and acids. They are also essential for regulating the amount of water present in the body. Linked to the two kidneys are the other parts of the urinary system: the ureters, the bladder and the urethra.

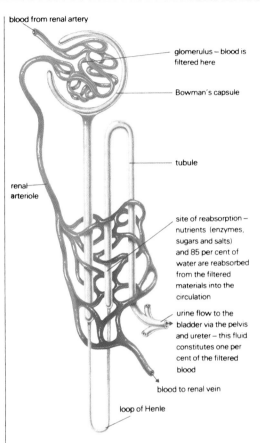

blood from renal artery

glomerulus – blood is filtered here

Bowman's capsule

tubule

renal arteriole

site of reabsorption – nutrients (enzymes, sugars and salts) and 85 per cent of water are reabsorbed from the filtered materials into the circulation

urine flow to the bladder via the pelvis and ureter – this fluid constitutes one per cent of the filtered blood

blood to renal vein

loop of Henle

The nephron, of which there are about a million in each kidney, is the kidney's filtering unit. Blood passing through the kidney is carried into each nephron, first to the glomerulus, a network of capillaries where water and dissolved substances are filtered out of the blood and forced into the tubule. Useful substances and most of the water are then reabsorbed into the blood vessels around the loop of Henle, and the wastes form urine, which is collected and excreted.

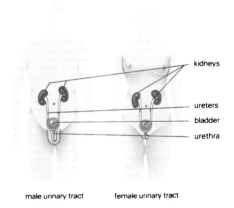

kidneys

ureters

bladder

urethra

male urinary tract   female urinary tract

The positions of the urinary system in the male and female.

The kidneys

The kidneys are situated on each side of the spine in the back of the abdomen behind the peritoneum (the membranous bag which contains the stomach, intestines, liver and spleen). The kidneys are well protected, lying under the diaphragm and lower part of the rib cage and embedded in a mass of fat. A normal adult kidney weighs approximately 150g (5oz) and is about 11cm (4in) long and 6cm (2in) wide.

Blood is supplied to the kidneys by two large renal arteries which arise from the aorta, the major artery carry-

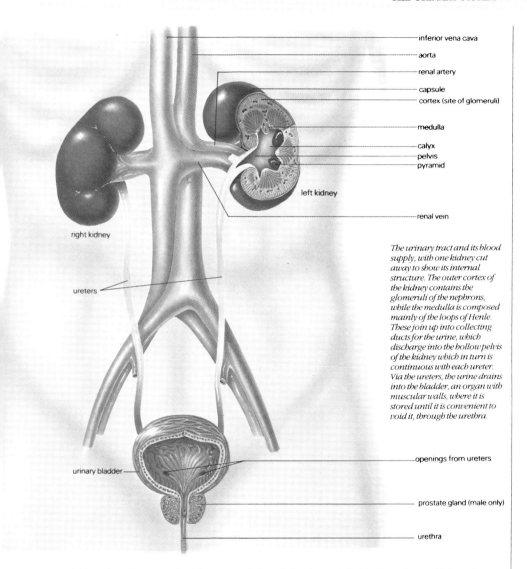

inferior vena cava

aorta

renal artery

capsule

cortex (site of glomeruli)

medulla

calyx
pelvis
pyramid

left kidney

renal vein

right kidney

The urinary tract and its blood supply, with one kidney cut away to show its internal structure. The outer cortex of the kidney contains the glomeruli of the nephrons, while the medulla is composed mainly of the loops of Henle. These join up into collecting ducts for the urine, which discharge into the hollow pelvis of the kidney which in turn is continuous with each ureter. Via the ureters, the urine drains into the bladder, an organ with muscular walls, where it is stored until it is convenient to void it, through the urethra.

ureters

openings from ureters

urinary bladder

prostate gland (male only)

urethra

ing oxygen-rich blood from the heart. Blood flows through these arteries at the rate of 1 to 1½ litres (1¾ to 2½ pints) each minute, or about one-fifth of the total output from the heart. This enormous blood supply to a relatively small part of the body highlights the importance of the kidneys.

The structure of the kidneys

The kidney can be divided into several regions. Each kidney is covered by a fibrous capsule. Beneath this is the outer area called the cortex, which covers the inner zone, the medulla. The medulla is built up of pyramid-shaped masses of tissue which point towards the five or six collecting sacs (calyces) of the kidney. These sacs finally merge to make the pelvis of the kidney.

The basic unit of the kidney is the nephron which itself consists of two parts, the glomerulus and the tubule. The glomerulus is a bunch of fine blood capillaries surrounded by a thin membrane, the Bowman's capsule. The renal tubule begins at the capsule and has several parts. The first part is called the proximal convoluted tubule. This then joins a long U-shaped part called the loop of Henle which itself is divided into descending and ascending parts. The ascending part of the loop of Henle joins the distal convoluted tubule which in turn is linked with a collecting duct (calyx). Several tubes are joined to one collecting duct which empties its contents at the pyramids of the medulla. Fine blood vessels and capillaries closely follow the course of the kidney tubule. These vessels absorb and secrete substances into and out of the tubule.

The length of a single nephron, straightened out, is about 5cm (2in), and the total length of all the tubules of both kidneys joined together would be 110km (68 miles).

How the kidneys work

Each of the nephrons of the kidney works as a filter that removes waste substances from the blood travelling through it, to produce urine. Blood under pressure is forced through the capillaries of the one million or so glomeruli. The pressure forces part of the fluid portion of the blood, the plasma, into the nephron and through the Bowman's capsule. About twenty per cent of the plasma is filtered away, through the capsule, and consists of water, salts, urea, sugars and amino acids. Larger substances, such as protein and cells, are not normally removed from the blood. The filtered fluid then passes along the tubule and many substances are absorbed by the cells lining the wall of the tubule and returned to the blood; most of the sugars, some salts, amino acids (the basic building blocks of protein) and a large part of the water is reabsorbed and taken back into the bloodstream. Other substances, such as some waste salts, are secreted into the tubule.

Each region of the tubule has a different function. In the proximal tubule, salts and some other substances are secreted. Sodium, other essential salts, glucose and amino acids are reabsorbed into the blood. The loop of Henle and distal tubule are involved with the reabsorption of water and the control of the delicate acid-alkaline balance of the body.

The resulting fluid from these processes is urine, a pale yellow, slightly acid mixture of salts, urea, uric acid, creatinine (a waste product of protein metabolism) and other wastes such as hormones and drugs. The exact composition and concentration of the urine varies enormously.

The kidney is important not only in excretion but also in ensuring that the amounts of certain substances within the body are kept at the correct levels. Water is one important example, and when large amounts have been drunk the urine will be diluted. The urine will be more concentrated if water is scarce, for example during hot weather when water has been lost by sweating. Also, excretion of acid or alkaline salts regulates and maintains the slightly alkaline nature of the blood.

The kidneys also have several other important functions. Erythropoetin, a protein-like substance secreted by the kidneys, stimulates the bone marrow to produce red blood cells. People whose kidneys are not functioning properly are therefore often anaemic (see pages 144-7). If the blood pressure falls, the kidneys may also produce a hormone called renin, which increases the blood pressure, to ensure that the kidneys continue to function.

Urine and the bladder

During a twenty-four hour period the average adult male excretes about 1½ litres (2½ pints) of urine. Women excrete a slightly smaller quantity.

The urine produced by the kidneys passes down two narrow tubes called the ureters. These lead down the back of the abdominal cavity and into the pelvis where they enter the bladder, a hollow bag about the size of a grapefruit. The bladder lies just behind the pubic bone, in front of the vagina in women, and in front of the rectum in men. Its elastic, flexible walls allow it to expand as it fills and then to contract as it expels the urine from the body through a tube called the urethra, leading from the bladder.

In women, the urethra is about 4cm (1½in) long and opens just behind the clitoris. In men, it is about 23cm (9in) long and passes through the prostate gland and the penis. Two tubes, the vasa deferentia, which carry semen from the testes (see pages 16-17) and ducts carrying secretions from the prostate gland also open into the urethra in men.

Urine is stored in the bladder until it is convenient to pass it (a process called micturition). Two rings of muscle, or sphincters, control the flow: one at the neck of the bladder, the internal sphincter, and another about 3cm (1¼in) further on, the external sphincter. The sphincter muscles keep the exit to the urethra tightly shut, so that urine cannot leak out, until a conscious decision is made to pass urine. The brain then sends two sets of nerve impulses to the bladder. The first of these causes the sphincter muscles to relax, opening up the way into the urethra. The second causes the powerful muscles of the bladder wall to contract and expel the urine. A voluntary contraction of the abdominal muscles gives added force to the stream of urine.

The desire to pass urine begins as a set of nervous impulses informing the brain that the bladder is full. If these messages are ignored, the bladder will enlarge in order to accommodate more urine, but as time goes by it will send impulses more frequently. If these are also ignored, the bladder can keep on enlarging but a point is reached at which it becomes impossible to prevent micturition.

It should be possible to eliminate the daily volume of urine produced by the kidneys in about four to six acts of micturition, since the bladder can easily hold 400 ml (14 fl oz) without discomfort. If urine is passed much more often than this, it may be due to infection or some other disorder of the urinary tract. Most of the urine produced during twenty-four hours is excreted during the day rather than the night, the normal proportion of day-urine to night-urine being 100:30. This means, in practice, that a healthy person should not have to get up often at night to pass water, and anyone who suffers from persistent nocturia – the need to urinate frequently at night – should consult a doctor.

When accident or disease interferes with the nerve supply to the bladder, the normal voluntary control of urination may be lost. Injuries to the backbone may cut through the spinal cord and prevent nerve impulses from travelling between the brain and the bladder. The victim of such an injury will at first be completely incontinent, but after a while a reflex action will take over, and the bladder will automatically empty itself of urine every few hours. This primitive reflex is exactly the same as the one which operates in infants: it is usually not until well into the second year of life that the brain can begin to impose any kind of voluntary control over the passage of urine (see page 48).

The urine

Urine is a yellow-coloured liquid with a faint odour. On average, ninety-six per cent of it is water, and the remainder consists of dissolved waste products. In a twenty-four hour period, an average adult will pass about 60 g (2 oz) of these solids in the urine, which includes approximately 30 g (1 oz) of urea and 15 g (½ oz) of common salt (sodium chloride). The rest is uric acid, hippuric acid, phosphoric acid, sulphuric acid, ammonia, creatinine and potassium. The main solid constituent of urine is therefore urea, a chemical compound produced by the breakdown of proteins in the diet. Although urea is not a very toxic chemical, its level in the blood provides a useful indication of the degree to which a patient is accumulating harmful waste products when the kidneys are not working properly. The condition in which there is a high level of urea in the blood is called uraemia.

The colour of urine in a healthy person is almost invariably some shade of yellow. This colour is caused by a pigment called urochrome. When a great deal of water has been drunk, however, the urine becomes very diluted and so the colour is much paler. It is darker when it is concentrated and only small volumes of water are being passed.

Very dark urine can have other causes, however. Blood in the urine can give it a dark, reddish-brown or smoky colour. In jaundice the urine may also be dark, often with an orange tinge. Black urine may be due to rare diseases or a complication of malaria known as blackwater fever. Many unusual urinary colours are, however, simply caused by the ingestion of chemicals such as medicines or food dyes. Often people who are passing urine of an alarming pink or red shade are quite healthy: all that has happened is that they have eaten beetroot or perhaps sweets containing an aniline dye. Nevertheless, anyone who notices his or her urine is an unaccountably odd colour should consult a doctor.

An important feature of urine is that in a healthy person it is sterile, that is, germ-free. This fact is not widely recognized, since most people are brought up from early childhood to regard both faeces and urine as being full of germs. In fact, it is almost impossible for urine to be a source of infection except during certain diseases.

Examining the urinary system

Urinalysis

Analysis of urine (urinalysis) can reveal much about the health of the kidneys and other organs. Tests for the presence of the protein albumin and of glucose in the urine can be done easily. Albumin appears in the urine in a number of conditions, particularly kidney disease (pages 120-23) and toxaemia of pregnancy (page 28). In women the detection of albumin may be of no significance unless the specimen has been obtained directly from the bladder with a tube (catheter), since secretions from the vagina,

which naturally contain protein, may get into an ordinary urine specimen. The detection of glucose in the urine forms a useful screening test for diabetes (see pages 185-7), but quite a high proportion of people who have glucose in their urine do not have this disease, so further tests are needed to make a firm diagnosis.

Most of the other common tests performed as part of urinalysis have to be carried out in a laboratory. Checks are made for abnormal substances resulting from various metabolic diseases and for drugs. The laboratory also carries out bacteriological culture of urine, a process essential for the correct diagnosis and treatment of any urinary tract infection.

Examination of the urine with a microscope may also provide information about the state of the kidneys. The cells, crystals and casts visible under the microscope in cases of urinary tract disease are a very valuable aid to diagnosis and treatment. Normal urine contains no more than one or two red blood cells, one or two white blood cells and epithelial cells, but when the urinary tract is infected there is an enormous increase in the number of white cells in the urine. The number of epithelial cells excreted is increased in many kidney diseases, particularly when the glomerulus is inflamed. Tubular casts, formed by the agglutination of protein, cells or cellular debris in the renal tubules and then flushed out, are also sometimes observed in the urine.

Small amounts of protein in the urine (proteinuria) are quite common, but large amounts may suggest a disease of the kidney, such as damage to the glomeruli.

It is also possible to test the ability of the renal tubule to concentrate urine or reabsorb water. If a person with normal kidneys is deprived of fluid or injected with a hormone known as antidiuretic hormone (see page 182), the volume of urine excreted falls and its concentration rises. The reverse of this – the ability of the renal tubule to produce a dilute urine and excrete a large volume of water – can be tested by giving the person a large amount of water to drink, and then measuring the volume and concentration of the urine.

X-rays and scans

X-rays and radio-isotope techniques are also used to study kidney structure and function. X-ray pictures of the abdomen may give information about the size and shape of the kidneys, as well as revealing shadows of renal stones (see page 122). If chemicals that are opaque to X-rays, such as iodine compounds, are injected into the veins of a patient (usually in the arm), the different parts of the kidney can be seen on the X-ray. This technique, known as intravenous urography, can reveal many kinds of kidney abnormality. Pictures are taken soon after the injection and may also be taken at timed intervals following the injection, to show the various parts of the urinary tract.

A similar technique, renal arteriography, involves the injection of the radio-opaque medium directly into the aorta above the renal arteries, and this gives good pictures of the blood vessels of the kidney. If a radioactive isotope is injected and the intensity of radiation measured, a continuous pattern of the blood flow through the kidney can be obtained. This is known as a renal scan or radioactive renogram, and is particularly useful in following the progress of a transplanted kidney. The patient is usually given a local anaesthetic before the test and may have to stay in hospital overnight.

Renal biopsy
Another test involves the removal of a piece of kidney for study under the microscope. This is done by introducing a special hollow cutting needle through the skin into the back and removing a small piece of the kidney (renal biopsy). The tissue can then be sectioned and examined microscopically for the presence of disease.

Cystoscopy
The bladder may be filled with radio-opaque solution and X-rayed (cystography) or studied by cystoscopy. A cystoscope is a long narrow tube with a light at one end and a magnifying eyepiece at the other. For a cystoscopy a general anaesthetic may be given, or the urethra anaesthetized by means of an anaesthetic jelly, and the cystoscope is passed into the bladder. An irrigation apparatus then runs water through the cavity down the centre of the cystoscope, thus filling the bladder. By alternately filling and emptying the bladder with fresh water, the surgeon cleans it out to make it easier to see its interior. After this procedure, the cystoscope is connected to a battery and the light adjusted for the best illumination. The surgeon can then look all round the bladder through the magnifying eyepiece.

The whole procedure should be painless, with only slight pain experienced when urine is passed immediately after the examination. Some cystoscopes have electrical cutting wires at the end to enable the surgeon to perform small operations in the bladder. Another, similar type of instrument has a cutting device which enables the surgeon to remove a piece of the prostate gland.

Cystoscopy is useful for several conditions. Firstly, any growth in the bladder can be clearly seen. Secondly, calculi (stones) in the bladder can also be seen, and if necessary broken up and removed. Thirdly, the openings of the ureters can be examined, and very fine plastic tubes can be inserted so that X-rays can be taken, or so that urine can be collected from each kidney separately for analysis. Finally, any person who has repeated infections of the bladder (cystitis) probably needs a cystoscopy to see if there is an underlying cause of the trouble that can be treated.

Diseases and disorders of the urinary system

There are many symptoms of disorders of the kidney and associated organs. Back pain can be a symptom of kidney disease and the presence of blood or protein in the urine is another important sign. Pain when urine is passed, an increase in the number of times the bladder needs to be emptied, or an increase in the volume of urine passed are symptoms of many disorders of the urinary system. Frequently, however, there are more general symptoms such as fever, anaemia, high blood pressure, heart failure or swelling (oedema).

Kidney failure
Kidney (renal) failure can be acute or chronic. Acute kidney failure is produced by any condition which leads to a sudden and prolonged period of low blood pressure, such as heavy blood loss or a heart attack.

There are numerous causes of chronic renal failure. A protracted case of acute renal failure or a renal disease may eventually become chronic. In some ten per cent of cases the cause is not discovered; and the patient may not notice anything wrong until the disorder is very advanced. At first he or she may notice an increase in the volume of urine excreted and general tiredness.

Treatment
The successful treatment of acute renal failure is complicated and, preferably, takes place in a specialized renal unit. The kidneys usually improve after several weeks. With chronic kidney failure, where symptoms appear gradually, the kidneys become less and less efficient as damage to them increases. Close medical supervision can slow the progress of the disease. When the kidneys fail completely the only satisfactory form of treatment is one that performs the kidneys' functions, either dialysis or a kidney transplant. Treatment of kidney failure has been revolutionized by haemodialysis.

Haemodialysis
Haemodialysis, in which the patient's blood is cleaned artificially to remove all waste products, depends on the ability of a machine to do the work of the kidney. Even if a kidney transplant is considered, an artificial kidney machine must be used first, so that the new kidney is grafted into a healthy body. The normal kidney is composed of living tissue, giving it a versatility which no machine can have, and the artificial kidney is much more simple in design and operation. Nevertheless, it is able to perform most of the essential functions of the normal kidney and is responsible for saving and maintaining many lives.

The principle on which it relies, called dialysis, depends on the ability of small molecules to be separated from larger ones in the blood, by passing the blood through a thin barrier. Starting with a mixture of small and large molecules on one side of the barrier and water on the other, the small molecules go through the barrier into the water while the larger ones are left behind. In haemodialysis, the patient's blood is on one side of the barrier and on the other is a prepared solution of salts, approximately the strength of normal, clean blood. The waste products in the patient's blood cross the membrane into the other solution, which is continually being replaced. In this way the blood is cleaned of all substances which the kidneys would normally remove, leaving essential substances behind. The membrane has to be semi-permeable; that is, permeable to substances such as urea, uric acid, creatinine, sodium, potassium and water – the main components of normal urine – but not to proteins and other relatively large molecules.

For information on the use of a dialysis machine and on portable dialysis, see page 123.

Kidney transplants
Many people dependent on dialysis look forward to the prospect of transplantation of a healthy kidney, from either

a living or a dead donor. Modern methods of identifying different tissue types mean that a compatible transplant can be made that will reduce the risk of the body rejecting the new organ. The patient's own kidneys are often left in place during the operation, and the donated kidney placed low down in the pelvis. Sometimes the new kidney works straight away, or it may take a few days to start functioning. After the transplant the patient must take drugs to suppress the immune system (see pages 202-3), and minimize the chance of the body's natural defence system rejecting the kidney.

Although kidney transplantation is a major operation, the success of the technique has grown dramatically over the last decade, to allow patients to lead a near-normal life.

Inflammation of the tubules (glomerulonephritis)

Glomerulonephritis occurs when the glomeruli become inflamed but are not directly infected by microorganisms. This condition, which takes several forms, is found more often in children and young adults, but is relatively uncommon.

In chronic nephritis (Bright's disease) the glomeruli become damaged over many years and are replaced by fibrous scars. This affects, and may eventually completely interrupt, filtration of the blood, leading to toxaemia and death. The cause is past kidney disease or arteriosclerosis (see page 160), and treatment consists of taking preventive measures to stop the progression of the disease.

When a kidney abnormality is associated with raised blood pressure, the combination of the kidney damage and the hypertension is often called arteriolar nephrosclerosis. The disease is very common in the western world but modern methods of treatment can control this very slow, progressive complaint.

In the nephrotic syndrome, another form of glomerulonephritis, the glomerulus becomes leaky and protein is lost into the urine (proteinurea). The condition usually starts between the ages of two and four, and affects slightly more boys than girls. The cause is unknown in many cases. About ten per cent of children with the syndrome will develop chronic nepritis as they grow up.

Symptoms
Symptoms of glomerulonephritis may include blood in the urine or excessively frothy urine, a symptom of proteinurea which can be detected by a simple urine test. Most of the protein lost is albumin, an important constituent of blood. The loss of albumin can result in the leakage of fluid from the blood vessels, and this in turn can cause accumulation of fluid in the tissues which results in puffiness of the face and swelling in the lower parts of the body. These symptoms may appear over a few days, sometimes after a sore throat caused by streptococci, or over a longer period. Glomerulonephritis may be discovered during a routine medical check, and in such cases the final diagnosis may require renal biopsy. A wide range of conditions can cause the syndrome.

Treatment
Many forms of glomerulonephritis are mild and require no specific treatment; other forms may be treated with corticosteroid or immunosuppressive drugs. Acute glomerulonephritis usually clears up completely. The chronic form, which may develop over months or years can, if it does not respond to any sort of treatment, lead to kidney failure.

Cystitis and urethritis

Inflammation of the bladder and urethra, called cystitis and urethritis respectively, is usually caused by bacterial infection. The bacteria involved are often normally harmless residents of the rectum, colon and vagina which for some reason invade the urinary tract and cause infection and inflammation. Sometimes the cause can be traced to an abnormality of the urinary system, in which case surgery will often cure the problem.

Cystitis and urethritis are more common in women, usually during the sexually active years, because the shortness of the female urethra and its close relationship to the vagina makes it highly accessible to bacteria. Urethritis can result if the urethra is bruised during sexual intercourse, when symptoms are caused by mechanical irritation rather than infection. Because symptoms are so similar to those of cystitis and are common in women who have just started having intercourse, it is sometimes called 'honeymoon cystitis'. Gynaecological conditions such as infected erosion of the cervix may also cause urethritis by affecting the types of organisms found in the vagina. Contraceptives and some tampons have also been thought to cause cystitis and urethritis because they change the environment in the vagina, encouraging the growth of certain strains of bacteria that may then invade the urinary system.

Cystitis and urethritis in men most often occur as a result of either obstruction to the urethra by the prostate or an infection of the prostate spreading to the bladder and urethra. Certain venereal diseases such as gonorrhoea (see page 21), can cause urethritis in both sexes. There may be a wide variety of other unidentifiable causes.

Symptoms
The symptoms of both conditions are similar: frequent passing of urine with intense, scalding pain. There may be pain in the lower abdomen and a frequent, urgent, desire to pass urine which, in the event, is only a small amount.

Treatment
Isolation and identification of the bacteria causing the infection are an important part of the diagnosis, and analysis of a urine sample obtained under sterile conditions is essential. Antibiotics effective against the specific organism identified as the cause of the infection will cure it in most cases. Unfortunately, some people, particularly women, have recurring infections which are resistant to treatment.

There are several simple measures which can be taken to reduce the risk of repeated attacks. First is attention to hygiene – particularly in washing around the urethra, vagina and anus after defaecating or sexual intercourse. Wearing loose-fitting, cotton underwear may also help, and nylon tights and tight jeans are best avoided. It is advisable to cut down on drinks such as coffee which tend to concentrate the urine and to drink plenty of water instead. If bouts of cystitis appear to be linked with sexual intercourse it may be worth using a lubricant such as KY jelly to minimize possible bruising.

Urinary incontinence

There are various forms of urinary incontinence. In true incontinence the bladder cannot retain urine, and there is a slight but continuous flow from a virtually empty bladder. Malfunction of the sphincter muscles which normally control the escape of urine can cause incontinence, perhaps as a result of nervous disease or injury to the muscles or nerves of the spinal cord (as in spina bifida). Another cause may be lesions in the urinary tract. In cases of tonic incontinence the bladder is emptied at normal intervals, but the desire to pass urine occurs urgently and the patient is unable to control it. This form of incontinence may be due to a shrunken or contracted bladder, or to inflammation of the prostate gland, the urethra or the bladder. It can often be treated once the cause has been found.

Stress incontinence occurs where emptying the bladder is directly stimulated by such things as coughing, sneezing, sudden exercise or movement, or any sudden contraction of the diaphragm resulting in increased abdominal pressure: once started it cannot be controlled. In these cases the sphincter muscles are usually either very weak or damaged, or there may be a disease of the nervous system. It is most common in women, particularly immediately after childbirth when there may be a weakened muscle in the floor of the pelvis.

Other causes of incontinence include tumours and enlargement of the prostate gland in the male. This can often be cured by removal of the prostate. Occasionally, a woman's urethra is damaged during childbirth, due to stretching of the vagina which lies very close to the outlet of the urethra, causing temporary incontinence. Incontinence occurring during sleep is known as enuresis and it is most common among children and adolescents. It is quite normal up to the age of five. Among older children it is often due to psychological problems or else to infection.

Treatment

Treatment of stress incontinence is to improve the function and condition of the sphincters by exercises in which the pelvic floor muscles are tightened. If the incontinence is caused by an underlying disorder, treatment of the disorder itself will usually solve the problem.

There are appliances and other aids that can be worn in cases of incontinence, either before or during treatment, or permanently where treatment is not possible for some reason. Several types of portable urinal are available for daytime use. For males, these take the form of a funnel connected to a bag, and fitting on to the penis with a sheath. The whole appliance is worn on a belt around the abdomen. During sleep the sheath and funnel are connected to a bottle by a long tube to prevent any urine spilling while the patient tosses and turns. A plastic dribbling bag may be useful where incontinence is only slight. Unfortunately, there are fewer satisfactory appliances available for women; one type takes the form of a wide funnel fitting over the entire vulva and draining into a bag. The best treatment for a woman may be a surgical operation to make a urinary diversion, which means creating a new system for expelling the urine by using another outlet. Where the incontinence is only mild, special padded pants may be all that is needed to counteract the problem.

Stones (calculi)

Stones in the kidneys, and elsewhere in the urinary system, form when substances normally dissolved in the urine, such as uric acid or minerals, precipitate out of solution. The precipitated substances condense on a tiny centre, such as a speck of protein or a bacterium, and then gradually form a stone as more material collects and clings to it. Why stones form in some people and not in others is not clearly understood. One cause may be an imbalance in metabolism which causes excessive amounts of a substance to be produced and excreted. There is a limit to how much of a substance can be dissolved, and once the limit is exceeded the substance will precipitate. An obstruction in the urinary tract which interferes with the flow of urine, prolonged immobility or an infection may also cause stones to form. Stones vary in their composition, shape, size and colour: calcium oxalate and calcium phosphate stones are the commonest, uric acid stones less common.

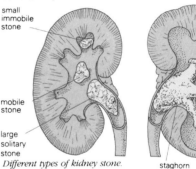

small immobile stone

mobile stone

large solitary stone

Different types of kidney stone.

staghorn stone

damaged kidney

Symptoms

Once formed, stones increase steadily in size. When they pass from the kidney into the ureter they can cause a dull, aching pain in the loin that is made worse by activity, although in some cases pain is slight or absent. Sometimes a kidney stone passing down the ureter causes renal colic, one of the most severe pains the body can experience. Waves of pain start in the loin and radiate round to the navel, or if the stone has reached the lower end of the ureter the pain passes down to the groin. About seventy per cent of stones pass into the bladder and out through the urethra. The remainder, however, because of their size or shape, become lodged.

Treatment

Treatment involves relieving the pain with drugs and removing the stone if the pain persists or if the stone is causing obstruction. Sometimes the stone will pass out of the body of its own accord, provided the patient drinks plenty of water. If there is obstruction, due to stones or some other cause, the pressure of urine flow above it will distend the pelvis of the kidney, forming a hydronephrosis. If extensive, this will damage the kidney tissue and stop it functioning. If the obstruction occurs lower down the ureter, the ureter itself will distend, as well as the pelvis, forming hydroureter as well as hydronephrosis. Specialist investigation and treatment are then required.

Dialysis

A person whose kidneys are unable to function is likely to be treated by means of haemodialysis. A dialysis machine is connected to the patient's blood system, usually by means of a 'shunt', an external joint between an artery and a vein which can be opened and the two ends connected to the dialysis machine. This shunt consists of tubing inserted by a simple surgical procedure under local anaesthetic. The arterial portion of the shunt can last two or three

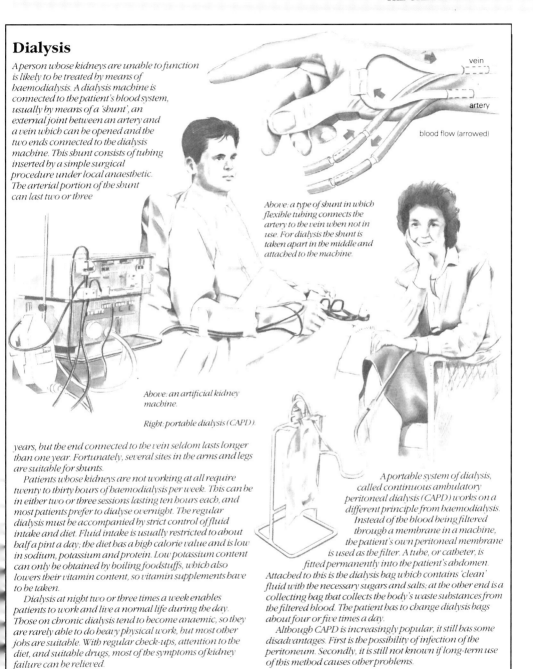

vein

artery

blood flow (arrowed)

Above: a type of shunt in which flexible tubing connects the artery to the vein when not in use. For dialysis the shunt is taken apart in the middle and attached to the machine.

Above: an artificial kidney machine.

Right: portable dialysis (CAPD).

years, but the end connected to the vein seldom lasts longer than one year. Fortunately, several sites in the arms and legs are suitable for shunts.

Patients whose kidneys are not working at all require twenty to thirty hours of haemodialysis per week. This can be in either two or three sessions lasting ten hours each, and most patients prefer to dialyse overnight. The regular dialysis must be accompanied by strict control of fluid intake and diet. Fluid intake is usually restricted to about half a pint a day; the diet has a high calorie value and is low in sodium, potassium and protein. Low potassium content can only be obtained by boiling foodstuffs, which also lowers their vitamin content, so vitamin supplements have to be taken.

Dialysis at night two or three times a week enables patients to work and live a normal life during the day. Those on chronic dialysis tend to become anaemic, so they are rarely able to do heavy physical work, but most other jobs are suitable. With regular check-ups, attention to the diet, and suitable drugs, most of the symptoms of kidney failure can be relieved.

A portable system of dialysis, called continuous ambulatory peritoneal dialysis (CAPD) works on a different principle from haemodialysis. Instead of the blood being filtered through a membrane in a machine, the patient's own peritoneal membrane is used as the filter. A tube, or catheter, is fitted permanently into the patient's abdomen. Attached to this is the dialysis bag which contains 'clean' fluid with the necessary sugars and salts; at the other end is a collecting bag that collects the body's waste substances from the filtered blood. The patient has to change dialysis bags about four or five times a day.

Although CAPD is increasingly popular, it still has some disadvantages. First is the possibility of infection of the peritoneum. Secondly, it is still not known if long-term use of this method causes other problems.

The Muscles

Muscles are involved in all types of movement made by the body and within it; they are responsible for the very obvious movements of lifting and running to the tiniest movement of the eyes. Muscles also control internal movements, such as the beat of the heart and the propulsion of food through the digestive system. Because they are involved in such a wide range of functions, different groups of muscles have to be able to contract by different amounts and at different speeds.

Right: front and back views of the skeletal muscles.

Below: an exploded view of skeletal muscle shows how it is made up of fibre bundles, each fibre consisting of myofibrils. The myofibrils contain millions of microscopic protein filaments of two types – actin and myosin – which interact by sliding past each other when stimulated by a nerve impulse, causing the muscle to contract.

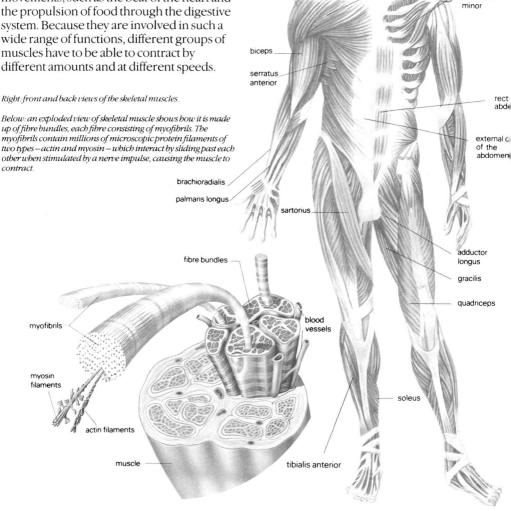

- frontal
- temporal
- levator scapulae
- sternocleidomastoid
- pectoralis major
- deltoid
- pectoralis minor
- biceps
- serratus anterior
- rect abd
- external c of the abdomen
- brachioradialis
- palmaris longus
- sartorius
- adductor longus
- gracilis
- quadriceps
- fibre bundles
- blood vessels
- myofibrils
- myosin filaments
- actin filaments
- soleus
- muscle
- tibialis anterior

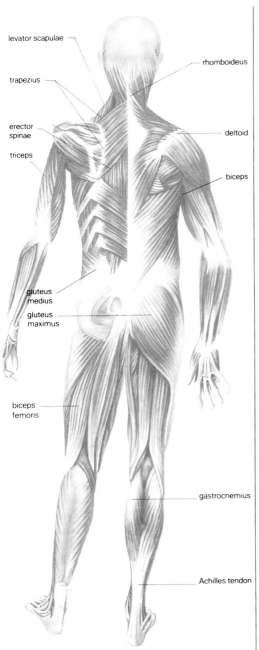

levator scapulae

rhomboideus

trapezius

erector
spinae

deltoid

triceps

biceps

gluteus
medius

gluteus
maximus

biceps
femoris

gastrocnemius

Achilles tendon

It is the skeletal muscles – those muscles attached to the skeleton – that make up the majority of muscle in the body. They account for about half of our body weight and are the main users of energy. Even the gentlest exercise, such as walking, increases the energy output of the body five to six times compared with the resting rate. The energy comes from a series of chemical reactions within the cells. Muscles, however, are only twenty-five per cent efficient in converting energy to movement (mechanical work). Some of the energy is wasted and lost as heat.

Everyone has the same basic number of muscles and muscle fibres in their body. These are all formed before birth. However, exercise of various muscles causes them to enlarge so that, for example, the biceps muscle in the arm of a blacksmith looks different from that of a ballerina.

The structure of muscles

There are three types of muscle: visceral, cardiac and skeletal. Visceral muscle is found in organs of whose movements we are usually unaware, such as the stomach, intestines, blood vessels, bladder and womb. These organs are controlled by the autonomic nervous system (see page 192). Visceral muscle has the simplest structure of all the muscles, consisting of flat sheets of spindle-shaped cells a few thousandths of a millimetre in length, each with a nucleus at the centre. It can contract automatically, spontaneously, and often rhythmically. It is capable of sustained contraction and responds to stretching by contracting. Hormones are also important in the control of these muscles (see pages 180-87). For example, during pregnancy the visceral muscle of the womb is stimulated by oestrogen and inhibited by progesterone. During childbirth, the hormone oxytocin released from the posterior pituitary gland provides a powerful stimulus for the contractions of the womb.

Cardiac muscle is the specialized type of muscle that forms the heart, enabling it to pump blood around the body continuously. It is similar in structure to visceral muscle but the cells are often branched, and there may be several nuclei in one cell. It contracts rhythmically, but hormones and the nerve supply from the autonomic system control the rate and force of contraction. Cardiac muscle has to contract and relax more than once a second; it has to function from the first days of embryonic existence up to the end of life, which may well involve some two and a half thousand million contractions.

Cardiac muscle cells are unique in their branching and interconnections, which allow waves of contraction to spread over the heart (see pages 152-5). Cardiac muscle is not capable of regenerating if it is damaged. Thus, after the blockage of a coronary artery in a heart attack, the muscle then deprived of oxygen dies and is replaced by scar tissue. Adjacent cells may be able to increase their size, a process known as hypertrophy, but not their number, to take on the additional load. The enlarged heart of a person with high blood pressure, which has to make more effort to pump the normal volume of blood around the circulation, contains the same number of (or fewer) muscle cells than that of an infant.

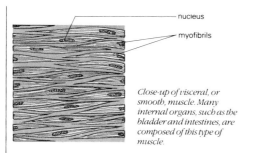

Close-up of visceral, or smooth, muscle. Many internal organs, such as the bladder and intestines, are composed of this type of muscle.

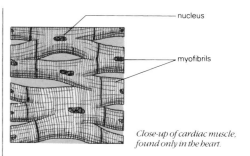

Close-up of cardiac muscle, found only in the heart.

Skeletal muscle is designed so that it can contract rapidly when it receives a message from a nerve. However, this type of muscle tires more easily than visceral muscle. It is involved mainly in producing voluntary, deliberate movement. It is also involved in stabilizing joints – that is, it holds the joint in its normal position, preventing undesirable movement and maintaining posture. For example, most of the short muscles at the head of the humerus (the large bone in the upper arm) act to stabilize the shoulder joint.

In general, skeletal muscles work in pairs. When a person decides to move part of the body, one muscle contracts whilst an opposing muscle relaxes. An example of this is seen in bending and straightening the arm. The biceps in the front of the upper arm contracts to bend the arm while the triceps at the back of the arm relaxes. To straighten the arm, the triceps contracts and the biceps relaxes.

Skeletal muscle is striated, that is, when viewed under the microscope the cells are seen to have dark stripes crossing their surface. These individual striated muscle cells are arranged into bundles. Sometimes, as in the case of the sartorius muscle in the thigh, the cells lie in parallel and merge to be inserted into a tendon at either end. The tendon attaches the muscle to a bone or joint. This arrangement enables a relaxed muscle 15cm (6in) long to contract to about 10cm (4in). Alternatively, the cells may be inserted into a tendon at an oblique angle so that a large number of muscle fibres can be packed into a given bulk of muscle. The attachment of muscle fibres to a tendon enables them to pull directly on a small area and so gives a fine control of movement.

The force of contraction of a muscle depends on the number of fibres involved, so that the arrangement that packs a lot of fibres into a small area offers strength at the expense of movement. Some of the muscles of the hand are located in the forearm and only a thin tendon goes into the hand. This allows the muscles to exert their pull from a distance, and does away with the wasteful inertia that would come from placing all the muscle in the fingers.

Skeletal muscle can be subdivided into red and white fibres, although some muscles contain both types. The red fibres contain higher concentrations of the protein myoglobin, similar to haemoglobin in the blood. Myoglobin stores oxygen from blood in muscles which have to act over long periods of time, such as those muscles involved in holding the body in its correct posture. White muscle has a

smaller amount of this myoglobin and is associated more with a once-only, 'twitch' type of contraction; that is, a nerve impulse to the muscle causes a single muscle contraction. Thus, in the calf, one muscle, the soleus muscle, is mainly composed of red fibres and is used in posture; whereas the gastrocnemius muscle is much paler and is used in movements such as jumping.

How muscles contract

Muscle consists of thick and thin protein filaments (myofilaments) arranged lengthwise in the muscle cell. The thin filaments are composed of a protein called actin, and the thick ones of the protein myosin. Of the three types of muscle, these myofilaments are most regularly arranged in skeletal muscle. Here the actin and myosin filaments form

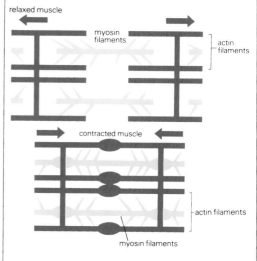

Voluntary muscles contract when the ratchet-like movement of the myosin filaments along the actin filaments causes the muscle fibres to shorten.

overlapping series, with crossbridges between the actin and myosin allowing them to move over one another in a ratchet-like fashion. The basic contractile unit of a muscle cell lies between two discs (Z-discs) of a substance known as tropomyosin (inactive myosin). The unit itself, called a sarcomere, is about three and a half thousandths of a milli-metre long when relaxed. In the biceps muscle of the arm, with individual fibres about 6cm (2.5in) long, there are about 20,000 such units along one muscle fibre.

When the muscle is stimulated by a message from a nerve, chemical reactions in the muscle unit cause the actin and myosin filaments to slide over each other, shortening the length of the unit. Energy is required for this con-traction, and for the relaxation that follows. The muscles store energy in the form of glycogen and other compounds. Glycogen is usually converted to glucose, and this in turn is converted to energy by a chemical reaction in the cell involving oxygen, a process called cellular respiration. The oxygen for respiration is brought from the lungs to the muscles by the blood, but if, during heavy exercise, not enough oxygen is supplied to the muscles, glucose is only partly broken down. This can lead to a build-up of certain compounds, such as lactic acid, and it is the accumulation of these acids that causes cramps.

Skeletal muscle contraction is controlled by the close integration of the muscular and nervous systems. Skeletal muscle is stimulated by long thread-like processes called axons that originate from nerve cells lying in the grey matter of the spinal cord. Terminals from the nerve cells divide and splay out as the nerve nears its muscle. In a powerful muscle exercising coarse movement, such as the biceps muscle in the arm, the axons from a single cell may connect with a hundred to a thousand individual muscle fibres. But in the small muscles of the eye, where delicate movement is essential, only about ten muscle cells are controlled by a single nerve cell. Every muscle cell receives a branch of a nerve fibre, however. Each muscle cell contracts to its full extent following a nerve impulse. The tension developed in a whole muscle depends on the number of nerve-muscle units stimulated to contract.

Muscles are supplied with two types of sensing device, one responding to the length of the muscle and one to the tension within it, which relay information to the cerebellum of the brain. Here the information is processed and appro-priate impulses sent back to the muscle.

Muscle fatigue

We are all familiar with muscle fatigue – when the tired muscles of limbs cease to contract effectively. In the laboratory, if an isolated muscle is stimulated repeatedly, the contractions get smaller and smaller. This is a sign that the muscle has become fatigued. Such fatigue may be caused by potassium (a vital component of all cells) passing out of the active muscle cells into the surrounding fluid. One function of the circulation during exercise is to carry potassium to the cells and take breakdown products away from muscle. In muscle fatigue a lack of potassium in the muscle prevents it from contracting, but as soon as the muscle is rested potassium is actively pumped back into it from the blood, and it is able to contract again.

Muscle disorders

Compared with other organs, skeletal muscles do not often become diseased. They rarely produce tumours themselves and are hardly ever affected by cancer spreading from other parts of the body. Bacterial infections of muscle are rare, although muscle is susceptible to gas gangrene if wounds become infected by the bacterium *Clostridium welchii*. There are several uncommon degenerative diseases involv-ing muscles, which are described below.

Paralysis

The skeletal muscles while not damaged themselves may be affected by damage to the nerves controlling them. For example, a nerve running to a muscle may be cut acci-dentally, or nerves may be damaged by inflammation (peripheral neuritis). Not only will movement cease, but the muscle becomes limp; this is called flaccid paralysis. The same effect is produced by death of the nucleus of the motor nerve in the spinal cord, as in poliomyelitis which is caused by viral infection (see page 209). Nerve cells are also destroyed in progressive spinal muscular atrophy, a disease of middle-aged men, and in the inherited disease of pro-gressive spinal muscular atrophy of infancy (motor-neuron disease). There is another inherited disease, peroneal muscular atrophy, in which these nerve cells are diseased along with the muscles. Paralysis of the muscles of the pelvis and legs is also seen in spina bifida (see page 195).

The effect is different if the nerve fibres which run from the brain down to the spinal cord, rather than those running directly into a muscle, are the site of disease. For a short time the muscles in the affected limb become slack, but within a few days they become stiff, or spastic. Some move-ment may return although it may not be under conscious control. The commonest cause of this condition is a stroke (see pages 196-7).

Muscular dystrophy

Muscular dystrophies include several inherited conditions in which there is progressive weakening of the muscles. There are about six main types of muscular dystrophy, and several rarer forms. The different types are characterized by how the disorder is inherited, the age of onset of the disease, the changes occurring in the muscle structure, and the groups of muscles affected.

The common feature of all forms of dystrophy is the way the muscles become weakened: individual fibres within the muscles begin to break up and degenerate, and the damaged tissues are removed by the body and replaced by non-muscular fibrous tissue and fat cells. A few undamaged muscle fibres remain between the destroyed fibres but these, too, may later become affected.

Of the many forms of dystrophy known, the most im-portant are Duchenne (pseudo-hypertrophic) dystrophy, facioscapulohumeral dystrophy and myotonic dystrophy.

Duchenne dystrophy

This is the most common and most severe form of the disease. It is an inherited sex-linked condition, which means that it is passed to offspring on the X chromosome.

Since girls have two X chromosomes, an abnormal one is masked by the second, so instead of suffering the disease girls are carriers; they can pass the disease on to their sons. Since boys have only one X chromosome its effect cannot be counteracted, so that if it is abnormal the symptoms of the disease will be manifested; therefore only boys have this type of muscular dystrophy. The disease may actually begin in the fetus, yet it does not develop fully until the second or third year of life. Before this age it can be diagnosed by an enzyme test.

Symptoms

At first the boy's muscular development may appear normal. But when the disorder begins the child will experience difficulty in getting up from the floor and has an awkward walk because the muscles in the thighs and pelvis are the first to be affected. Later the muscles in the trunk become involved and the weakness increases. The forearm, hands and feet remain strong, and the face is unaffected until late stages of the disease. By the age of ten, however, the child is usually confined to a chair or to a bed; death usually occurs from heart failure, obesity or pulmonary infection by the age of twenty.

Facioscapulohumeral dystrophy

This disease is less severe than Duchenne muscular dystrophy and appears later in life. The average age of onset of the disease is thirteen years (it varies between nine and twenty) and sufferers have a normal lifespan, being incapacitated only in their later years.

Symptoms

The muscles affected are those in the face and shoulders. Facial muscles are usually involved first, with a general flattening of features, difficulty in performing certain tasks, such as whistling, and involuntary mouth movements. The first real difficulty that sufferers encounter is in lifting their arms. Fortunately, though, the forearms remain strong. Facioscapulohumeral dystrophy, though inherited, is not sex-linked, and women and men may be equally affected.

Myotonic dystrophy begins early in adult life and also affects both sexes. Its main feature is the inability of muscles to relax after a contraction, so that, for example, the sufferer is unable to let go after shaking hands. Although symptoms often differ from person to person, weakness typically occurs in the face and neck muscles. As well as muscular defects, other disorders such as cataracts, degeneration of the testes or ovaries, and mental retardation can occur.

Treatment of muscular dystrophy

Although there is no cure for muscular dystrophy, an affected person can be greatly helped by physiotherapy, aimed at keeping unaffected muscles healthy and aiding mobility. Psychological support for both the sufferer and his family is also essential.

Doctors and scientists are carrying out research to find a possible drug or treatment that will help those with Duchenne muscular dystrophy, but at the moment the main approach is to prevent the birth of such children. A satisfactory test may become generally available which, if positive in an unborn child, would offer the chance of abortion.

Couples at risk of having a baby with Duchenne muscular dystrophy (if the woman is a carrier, for example) have to decide whether to take that risk or to remain childless. They are helped in this decision by experienced genetic counsellors who can tell them not only their chances of having such a child but also what it would mean in terms of treatment and their future life-style. Some couples decide to go ahead with a pregnancy, but may have an abortion if the fetus is discovered (by amniocentesis) to be a boy.

Myasthenia gravis

Myasthenia gravis is a disease characterized by muscle weakness, the individual easily tiring, with recovery of strength after rest. It occurs more frequently in women than men, usually between the ages of fifteen and fifty years. There is an inability to sustain muscular activity, which progresses over a period of a few weeks. The muscles of swallowing, speaking and chewing, and also the muscles of the eye, are those most often involved, but any muscle or group of muscles may be affected. Myasthenia gravis may be associated with various diseases such as rheumatoid arthritis, pernicious anaemia, cancer or an overactive thyroid gland; usually, however, no underlying disease is found.

Symptoms

Initially strong movements of the muscles quickly become weaker, resulting in such symptoms as double vision, dragging eyelids, difficulty in swallowing or slurring of the speech, and these symptoms are often worse at the end of the day. Muscles of the limbs or trunk may be affected, and if the shoulder muscles are involved, such activities as combing the hair become impossible without frequent rests. There is usually no loss of reflexes or sensation, and wasting of the muscles becomes apparent only after a long time. Occasionally the muscle sphincters that control the bladder or bowel may be involved, causing incontinence.

Treatment

There is no cure for myasthenia gravis but treatment with special drugs can usually control the symptoms, which sometimes remit spontaneously. In selected cases removal of the thymus gland is effective. Most people with this disease can live a fairly full and normal life.

Muscle and tendon injuries

Muscles and their tendons, especially those in the leg, are often torn or stretched during vigorous sports and games. The muscles of the lower back may be strained after incorrectly lifting a heavy object, and those in the ankle may be damaged when footing is missed on stairs or on a slippery floor.

Symptoms

A severe sprain or strain causes a sudden acute pain and inability to use the affected area. If the ligaments are affected, swelling and bruising also occur.

Treatment

The affected part should be immobilized for a day or so, with an elasticated bandage in severe cases, and then gradually exercised back to normal use. Application of hot or cold compresses, and pain relievers, may help. If a tendon is actually severed surgery will be needed.

Exercises for muscle flexibility

The exercises shown on this and the following two pages are designed to loosen, stretch and strengthen the muscles of various parts of the body. They should be performed at a leisurely pace, without straining, on a regular basis. People not used to taking regular exercise should start off slowly and gently, gradually building up the number of repetitions of each exercise as they become fitter.

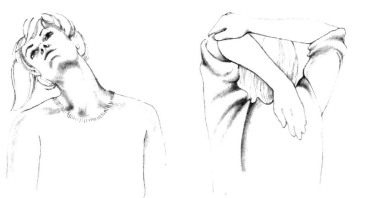

Head and shoulders
Neck rolls (right): slowly roll your head round in a circle, flexing your neck so that you face upwards and then downwards. Repeat five times in each direction.

Shoulder and arm stretches: clasp one elbow as shown and reach as far down your back as possible (far right). Hold for fifteen seconds, and repeat for the other arm. Place the palms together and raise your arms as high as possible above your head (below). Hold for fifteen seconds.

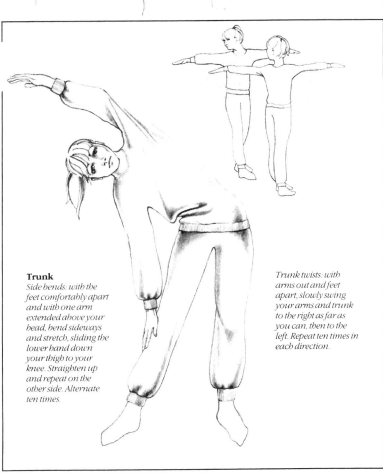

Trunk
Side bends: with the feet comfortably apart and with one arm extended above your head, bend sideways and stretch, sliding the lower hand down your thigh to your knee. Straighten up and repeat on the other side. Alternate ten times.

Trunk twists: with arms out and feet apart, slowly swing your arms and trunk to the right as far as you can, then to the left. Repeat ten times in each direction.

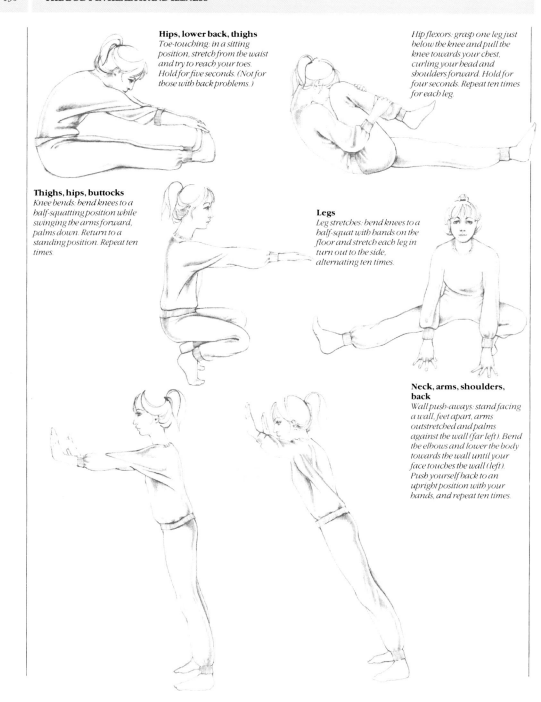

Hips, lower back, thighs
Toe-touching: in a sitting position, stretch from the waist and try to reach your toes. Hold for five seconds. (Not for those with back problems.)

Hip flexors: grasp one leg just below the knee and pull the knee towards your chest, curling your head and shoulders forward. Hold for four seconds. Repeat ten times for each leg.

Thighs, hips, buttocks
Knee bends: bend knees to a half-squatting position while swinging the arms forward, palms down. Return to a standing position. Repeat ten times.

Legs
Leg stretches: bend knees to a half-squat with hands on the floor and stretch each leg in turn out to the side, alternating ten times.

Neck, arms, shoulders, back
Wall push-aways: stand facing a wall, feet apart, arms outstretched and palms against the wall (far left). Bend the elbows and lower the body towards the wall until your face touches the wall (left). Push yourself back to an upright position with your hands, and repeat ten times.

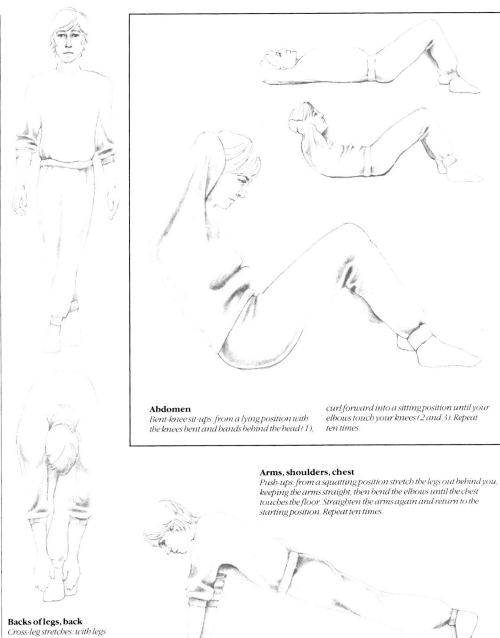

Abdomen
Bent-knee sit-ups: from a lying position with the knees bent and hands behind the head (1), *curl forward into a sitting position until your elbows touch your knees (2 and 3). Repeat ten times.*

Arms, shoulders, chest
Push-ups: from a squatting position stretch the legs out behind you, keeping the arms straight, then bend the elbows until the chest touches the floor. Straighten the arms again and return to the starting position. Repeat ten times.

Backs of legs, back
Cross-leg stretches: with legs crossed at the ankles (top), try to touch the floor in front of your toes (above). Hold for five seconds.

Bones and Joints

The bones of the skeleton form a supportive framework for the body. The skeleton combines strength and rigidity with resilience and mobility, providing attachments for muscles and ligaments so that movement can take place. The bone marrow makes the precursors of cells that are passed into the bloodstream. Bones also act as a store of minerals and salts that may be transported and used elsewhere in the body. In fact, though bone is thought of as hard and dry, it is an active living tissue.

The structure of bone

Bone makes up about sixteen per cent of total adult body weight. For its weight, it is an extremely strong material. The secret of its strength lies in its microscopic structure – a combination of the protein, collagen, fibres and minerals such as calcium phosphate. The protein fibres are laid down in a spiral arrangement which is repeated in an orderly fashion, giving toughness and pliability to the tissue. The whole system is then made rigid by deposits of calcium phosphate along the collagen fibres.

In a single bone there are in fact two different types of bone tissue: hard (or compact) bone; and spongy (or cancellous) bone. Within the skeleton, bones are classified as long bones, short bones and flat bones. A long bone is composed of an outer tube of hard bone tissue enclosing a cavity filled with marrow, and each end is made of spongy bone. Short bones have a thin layer of hard bone covering spongy bone, and flat bones are a sandwich of two layers of hard bone with a spongy centre. All bones are covered by a tough membrane called the periosteum.

Bone contains cells which are important for its own growth, maintenance and repair. Bone cells are supplied with blood through a network of small canals, and there are also nerve fibres in bone which are involved in the detection of pressure and pain.

At birth, a baby measures about 50cm (20in) long and already has about 30g (1oz) of calcium in its bones. When physical development is complete, growth and the re-modelling of bone will have taken the individual to three or more times this height, with about 1kg (2.2lb) of calcium in the body. In addition to this quantity of calcium, almost all of which is in bone, the adult body contains about 500g (1.1lb) of phosphorus, also mostly in bone. These stores can be added to or used as the body requires. The demands for

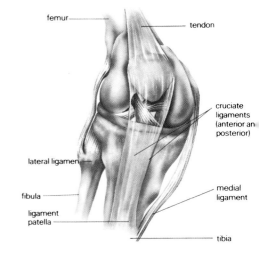

Bone tissue is made up of spongy, or cancellous bone surrounded by a layer of hard, or compact bone which protects and supports the lighter, spongy bone and the bone marrow within it. Within compact bone is a network of microscopic Haversian canals (shown here greatly enlarged) containing nerves and blood vessels.

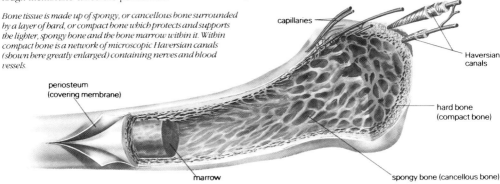

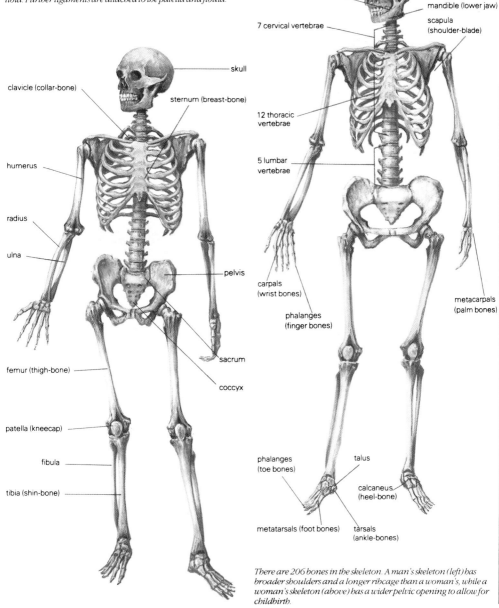

Left: the movements of joints are controlled by ligaments, strong bands of fibrous tissue which hold the bones together. Internal ligaments help to stabilize the knee joint, shown here. They cross within the joint and are attached at each end to the femur and tibia. Further ligaments are attached to the patella and fibula.

maxilla (upper jaw)

mandible (lower jaw)

7 cervical vertebrae

scapula (shoulder-blade)

skull

clavicle (collar-bone)

sternum (breast-bone)

12 thoracic vertebrae

5 lumbar vertebrae

humerus

radius

ulna

pelvis

carpals (wrist bones)

metacarpals (palm bones)

phalanges (finger bones)

sacrum

coccyx

femur (thigh-bone)

patella (kneecap)

fibula

phalanges (toe bones)

talus

tibia (shin-bone)

calcaneus (heel-bone)

metatarsals (foot bones)

tarsals (ankle-bones)

There are 206 bones in the skeleton. A man's skeleton (left) has broader shoulders and a longer ribcage than a woman's, while a woman's skeleton (above) has a wider pelvic opening to allow for childbirth.

calcium and phosphorus are many. Calcium is essential for the contraction of muscles, for the transmission of impulses along the nervous system, and for the prompt clotting of blood on injury. Phosphorus, in the form of phosphate, plays a key role in the metabolism of all cells, especially in those chemical reactions concerned with provision of energy.

Vitamin D controls the absorption of calcium and phosphorus from food and their deposition in the skeleton. An excess of vitamin D may cause kidney damage, calcium deposits in body tissues, lack of appetite and constipation. When the blood calcium is lower than normal parathyroid hormone is secreted from the parathyroid glands in the neck. This hormone acts on bone, the kidneys and the gut, to cause an increased calcium flow into the fluid around the cells, which results in a rise in blood calcium back to normal. If, on the other hand, the blood calcium rises above its normal level, a second hormone, calcitonin, is produced. This hormone acts to decrease the amount of calcium passing from bone into the fluid around the cells, and the blood calcium falls back to normal. Thus the two hormones exert opposite effects, allowing for the fine control of blood calcium levels.

Growth and repair of bone

Most bones are built on a cartilage framework formed in the fetus. Cells within the cartilage secrete the components of bone and eventually become part of the bone structure itself. The first type of bone to be laid down is immature or woven bone, in which the collagen fibres are irregularly arranged and the calcium deposits are scanty. In an adult this type of bone is seen at the repair site of a fracture. Gradually the immature bone is replaced by mature bone, which has a regular structure with large amounts of calcium salts. The first centre of bone formation, or ossification, is in the diaphysis, or shaft, of the bone, the diaphyseal centre. Other centres of ossification in long bones are at each end, at the epiphyses. The areas of growth at each end of a long bone are separated from the rest of the bone by a layer of cartilage, and it is not until about the age of twenty that this layer is finally replaced by bone, and growth stops.

Bone growth is controlled by many factors. Severe illness can halt growth, and hormones, such as those produced by the pituitary and thyroid glands, also affect bone growth (see *Growth*, pages 38-51). Throughout life, old bone tissue is continuously being dismantled and replaced by new bone, enabling the skeleton to adapt to the changes that occur with growth and the demands of physical activity. With age there is a gradual loss of minerals, particularly calcium, from the bones, which causes brittleness (osteoporosis) and accounts for the increased number of fractures in older people, particularly women who may be deficient in the hormone oestrogen.

Cartilage

Cartilage ('gristle') is a translucent, pearly-white substance, firm in consistency. It is a highly specialized type of connective tissue, and its fibres give it the ability to withstand pressures and strains that would damage other tissues. When fully developed, cartilage has no blood vessels,

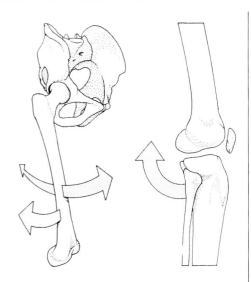

Two different types of joint are the ball and socket joint, found at the hip (above left) and shoulder, and the hinge joint, found at the knee (above right), the elbow, the ankle, and between the bones of the fingers and toes (phalanges).

nerves or lymphatics but is penetrated by numerous small canals. Because of wear and tear, cartilage is always being replaced.

The skeleton

The adult skeleton is composed of 206 bones. Twenty-six are in the spine, or vertebral column. In a child's spine there are thirty-three separate bones, called vertebrae: seven in the neck (cervical vertebrae), twelve in the chest (thoracic vertebrae), five in the lower back (lumbar vertebrae), five attached to the hip bone (sacral vertebrae) and four very small bones at the bottom of the spinal column (coccygeal vertebrae). In an adult the five sacral vertebrae fuse to form one bone known as the sacrum, and the four coccygeal bones fuse to form the coccyx. Each of the remaining vertebrae is separated from those above and below by a fibrous washer of tissue, the intervertebral disc.

A lumbar vertebra is fairly typical of vertebral structure. It consists of a main block through which runs a hole, the vertebral foramen, that contains the spinal cord. Each vertebra has three bony projections or processes; one points backwards (spinous process) and two point sideways (transverse processes); these processes are for the attachment of muscles and ligaments. You can feel the spinous processes easily if you bend forwards and run your finger down the middle of your back.

Each of the twelve thoracic vertebrae connect with a pair of ribs. The ribs arch forward from the vertebral column and attach to the breast bone (sternum) at the front of the chest, forming the rib cage. This cavity is called the thorax (chest) and in it are the heart and lungs. The twelfth or lowest pairs of ribs are short and arch halfway round the chest, and are therefore known as the 'floating' ribs. The diaphragm, the main breathing muscle attached to the ribs, separates the thorax from the abdominal cavity.

The skull is a bony case protecting the brain. In a baby the skull bones are widely separated by gaps (fontanelles), which can be felt. As the child grows the fontanelles fuse together to form a continuous protective covering. The front of the skull is formed by the bones of the face. The lower jaw, or mandible, is attached to the rest of the skull by joints just in front of the ears.

Joints

Joints are formed where bones meet; most of them allow the different parts of the skeleton to move in relation to each other. There are several different types of joint, which vary in the amount of movement they allow. The joints between the skull bones permit no movement; these bones are united by a layer of fibrous material which forms about two years after birth (slight movement does occur during birth and early development). Joints which allow little movement are those in the ankle, breast bone and spine.

The hip is a typical ball and socket joint. The head of the thigh bone (femur) is almost spherical and fits into a deep socket in the pelvis, allowing a wide range of movements. The knee is a typical hinge joint, permitting movement in one plane only; and strong ligaments prevent the joint going beyond its limit of movement. The patella, or knee cap, lies in the tendon of a muscle in front of the knee joint.

These mobile joints have a similar structure: the adjacent bone surfaces are smooth and rounded, and covered by a layer of smooth cartilage which facilitates movement without friction. Where the cartilages meet (but do not actually touch) a membrane, the synovial membrane, secretes a lubricating fluid that fills the gap like oil in a car engine. A fibrous capsule surrounds the joint and ligaments, muscles and tendons control movement.

Certain large joints contain extra cartilage pads, as in the knee where there are two moon-shaped discs, one on each side of the joint. These act as shock absorbers, capable of withstanding impact that would damage other tissues, and help to provide a closer and more stable fit for the bones.

Disorders of bones and joints

Fractures

Broken bones are a common occurrence in sports, road accidents and falls. As the bones become thinner and more brittle with age, they fracture more easily.

Symptoms

It can often be difficult to distinguish between a fracture and a sprain. With serious damage, the broken ends of bone may become displaced and cause an obvious deformity; occasionally the separate ends of a fractured bone may grate on one another, producing a noise (crepitus). Tenderness and pain can be useful in distinguishing between a serious sprain, which has a diffuse painful area, and the pain of a break, which is localized. Confirmation of a fracture is made by X-rays.

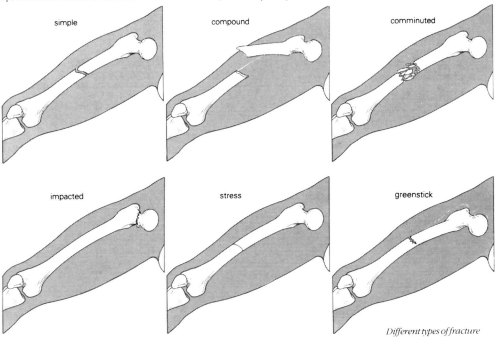

simple   compound   comminuted

impacted   stress   greenstick

Different types of fracture

There are several types of fracture. In the simple type, the bone breaks in one place. A compound fracture is one in which the broken bone has pierced the surrounding tissues to emerge through the skin. It is open to the air – a hazardous situation because it may become infected. A comminuted fracture is one where the bone is broken in two or more places; an impacted fracture is one where the bony fragments are pushed into each other. In some impacted fractures of the upper thigh bone the victim may manage to hobble about with a slight limp and pain, unaware of the nature of the injury. A stress fracture is a fine crack appearing in bone after repeated minor injury. A greenstick fracture occurs only in children; the bone bends and stays bent and, as the name suggests, the inside of the bend cracks and crumples in the same way as when a supple green twig is bent.

Treatment
Although there are different kinds of fracture, and there are many different bones that can fracture if they suffer enough damage, the basic treatment is straightforward. The first stage is to immobilize the fractured bone and the joints above and below the fracture. This will prevent the free ends of the broken bone from causing any more damage to surrounding tissues, and also prevent the severe pain that comes with movement of the fragments. In an emergency, a fractured arm can be strapped or splinted against the body, a leg against the other leg.

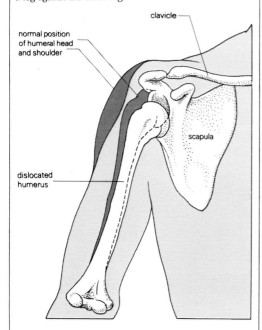

normal position
of humeral head
and shoulder

clavicle

scapula

dislocated
humerus

Dislocation of the shoulder. Because the shoulder is a very manoeuvrable joint it is more liable to dislocation than other joints.

As bone is a living tissue with a blood supply, bleeding can occur when it breaks. Prompt medical attention is important to prevent shock. Bone also contains marrow and fat in its central core, and in major fractures marrow and fat can be squeezed out into blood vessels and occasionally cause a blockage (embolus) elsewhere in the system.

In hospital, the aim is to 'reduce' the fracture – that is, to move the broken pieces into a good position so that the bone will heal and function again. The bone is held in this position by a plaster cast, although sometimes it is necessary to screw or nail the fragments together with a pin or plate to keep them in place. In some situations the muscles, particularly in the upper leg, are so strong that they pull the reduced fracture apart again, unless the limb is put in traction, that is, by weights suspended from pulleys attached to the limb and arranged to counteract the muscle pull.

Once the bone fragments have united the next stage is to return the injured person to full activity in the shortest time possible. This rehabilitation phase requires effort from both patient and physiotherapist to maintain circulation, minimize the wasting of muscles and reduce joint stiffness.

In elderly patients, particularly if they are bedridden, pneumonia may develop following fractures. Another complication is the slow or ineffective healing of the bone. Union of the fragments can be very slow, and although it should be complete in six to ten weeks it may take up to six months. Occasionally it may never occur, and surgery is then needed to join the fractured ends with a plate or metal pins. Surgery may be necessary for another complication, 'mal-union' when the bone heals in the wrong position.

A 'fracture dislocation' is a fracture complicated by a dislocation (see below), when both result from the same injury.

Dislocation
In a dislocated joint the surfaces of the bones between which movement takes place become displaced. Dislocation is also known as luxation and an intermediate condition, where the surfaces are partly displaced but retain some contact, is called subluxation. There are three types of dislocation; congenital, spontaneous and traumatic (due to injury).

Congenital dislocation is present at birth. Congenital dislocation of the hip is one of the most common in western races. Girls are affected five times more often than boys, and in a third of cases both hips are involved. If detected at birth, the deformity may be corrected by extra nappies or splints worn for three to six months. If the baby does not attend screening tests or the diagnosis is missed, the typical waddling gait becomes obvious once he or she starts to walk. Congenital dislocation of the hip is almost unknown where the offspring are carried astride the parent's back. This custom may prevent the head of the thigh bone from moving upwards and outwards from its socket in the pelvis.

For spontaneous dislocation to arise, there must be a defect in the structure of the bone or joint: for example, the stability of a joint may become impaired by arthritis.

In a traumatic dislocation, the joint is disrupted by external forces (as in a car crash) or awkward movements. It is often difficult to distinguish between a dislocation and a fracture; if in doubt, a fracture is assumed until proven otherwise. The treatment of traumatic dislocation is much the same as that described above, for fracture. The prompt treatment of a dislocation, before the muscles go into a protective spasm, can prevent pain, a possible operation, and even permanent disability. For example, immediately pulling on a finger which has been dislocated will usually return it to its normal position.

Prolapsed (slipped) disc

The intervertebral discs in the spine act as shock-absorbing washers, allowing the entire vertebral column to twist and bend. Each disc is made of a tough, outer, bag-like layer enclosing a soft, jelly-like inner core. Sometimes a portion of the internal soft material pushes through a weak point in the outer layer to form a bulge or prolapse. This is commonly called a 'slipped' disc, though the term is misleading since the disc itself has not slipped out of position but has acquired a bulge at some point; a more accurate name is prolapsed disc.

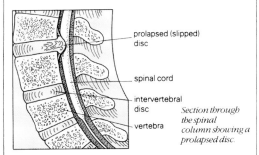

prolapsed (slipped) disc

spinal cord

intervertebral disc

vertebra

Section through the spinal column showing a prolapsed disc.

Causes of prolapsed disc

The causes of prolapsed disc are numerous and complex. In most cases the basic problem lies in a combination of poor standing and walking posture, bad lifting technique, general lack of fitness (which leaves back muscles flabby and weak), seating that does not support the lower back adequately, and a soft bed that allows the entire spine to assume an unnaturally bent profile during sleep. All these factors can be remedied. In a small proportion of cases actual disease is present, when the bony vertebrae fuse together (ankylosing spondylitis) or in degeneration of the discs. The condition is most common in the lumbar region. There is stiffness and low back pain. Pressure on adjacent nerves that run down to the legs may produce sciatica, pain spreading down the back of the leg (see *The Nervous System*, pages 188-201).

Spondylolisthesis is another condition affecting the vertebral column, usually in the lumbo-sacral region, as a result of injury or a congenital malformation in which a vertebra slips out of alignment with the one below. The vertebrae most often involved are the fifth lumbar and the sacrum, and low back pain results.

Treatment

Treatment for these conditions is basically bed rest and physiotherapy. To prevent recurrence, the patient must learn how to take care of his or her back by remedying the causative factors already mentioned. In more serious cases traction or surgery is required. Many other treatments have been successful in a proportion of sufferers, such as osteopathic and chiropractic manipulation, acupuncture, yoga exercises, and even hypnosis and herbal medicine.

Bone deformities

A number of bone deformities affect the foot. Some are present at birth, others are caused by strain or unsuitable footwear. Club foot (talipes) is a congenital condition where defects in shape and alignment of bones prevent the foot being placed flat on the ground, and may affect one or both feet. If treated soon after birth, by manipulation and the use of splints or casts to maintain position, the results of treatment are good. If not treated early, surgical correction is required.

In flat foot (pes planus), the arches show varying degrees of collapse. (Flat foot in children is normal and should not be treated.) Foot strain resulting from prolonged standing or walking may develop into chronic flat foot, seen frequently in people who spend many working hours on their feet. Foot strain should be treated by rest, followed by the use of correctly moulded arch supports and exercises. The opposite of flat foot is claw foot (pes cavus), characterised by excessively high arches. In most cases the reason for it is unknown.

A deformity of the big toe joint, made worse by wearing tight shoes with pointed toes, is hallux valgus, where the big toe is bent round towards the other toes, and may eventually come to lie under them. A painful swelling frequently develops over the side of the prominent big toe joint and is known as a bunion. Wearing soft shoes can provide some relief, but surgical correction of the deformity is often needed.

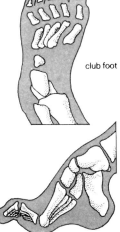

club foot

In club foot, the affected foot is bent downwards and inwards or outwards and upwards because the bones are misshapen and out of alignment. The condition is usually successfully treated by manipulation and the use of splints.

Claw foot, characterized by excessively high arches, may be corrected surgically in severe cases.

claw foot

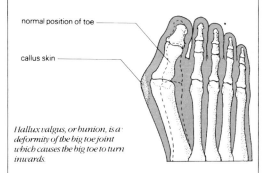

normal position of toe

callus skin

Hallux valgus, or bunion, is a deformity of the big toe joint which causes the big toe to turn inwards.

Pigeon breast is a deformity of the chest in which the rib cage protrudes at the front but is squashed in at the sides, giving a top-heavy appearance, rather like a pigeon. This is caused by the ribs being straightened and the breast-bone being pushed straight outwards in childhood, before the bones are properly set. The deformity can be a consequence of the vitamin deficiency, rickets, but it is also found in asthma and congenital enlargement of the heart.

Osteoarthritis

Arthritis has come to mean any disease affecting joints. However, since the word ending – *itis* means a process leading to inflammation, the word arthropathy is better used for all joint diseases, and arthritis only for conditions involving inflammation.

Osteoarthrosis (osteoarthritis) is a group of conditions that involves the wearing away, or degeneration, of the joints as the body ages and becomes less efficient at repairing itself. The disease begins in the cartilage forming the smooth inner surface of the joint, and can occur for a variety of reasons. The cells that replace the cartilage as it wears down may stop functioning, and injury or over-use may speed up the process. The cartilage loses its smooth surface, and friction within the joint increases. The bone underneath then becomes thickened, and spur-like projections of bone form around the joint. Creaking may be heard, both by the sufferer and others, as the joint moves. The most severe result is a joint with no cartilage and thickened, worn-down bone ends. This makes the joint both inefficient and painful

The typical appearance of an arthritic hand.

and, although at first the pain is only present when the joint is used, it may eventually be continuous. Osteoarthrosis does not affect all joints to the same degree. Joints which have the greatest stresses, such as the hips, knees, lower spine and big toes, are usually most affected.

A common form of osteoarthrosis, particularly in women, involves the joints of the fingers, where knobbly lumps called Heberden's nodes appear at the sides of the end joints and knuckles. Several fingers may become involved, causing pain and general discomfort. The condition affects the fine movements of the fingers.

As yet, there is no known way to prevent osteoarthrosis. The disease is most common in overweight people with poor posture, and those who use particular joints to excess (the footballer's knee, for example). Treatment involves exercise to strengthen surrounding muscles, and physiotherapy to train the patient to use the joint in the least painful way. Drugs can help relieve the pain and reduce inflammation. Joints such as the hip or knee can now be replaced by artificial ones, but this involves surgery and may not be suitable for all sufferers.

Rheumatoid arthritis

Rheumatoid arthritis is part of general rheumatoid disease that involves the connective tissues of the body and may affect many organs. However, in most people the most noticeable effect is on the joints.

The cause of rheumatoid disease is not known. It occurs in about three per cent of people, and can appear at any age but more commonly starts between forty and fifty years of age. About sixteen per cent of women over sixty-five are affected, and six per cent of men over seventy-five. Still's disease is an allied disorder, in children.

Symptoms

The first signs of general rheumatoid disease are tiredness, malaise, aches and pains and stiffness of the joints on waking in the morning. The disease involves the lining of the joints (synovial membrane) which swells and thickens and may produce excess synovial fluid. The result is swelling, stiffness, and pain when the joints are moved. Over a period of time, the cartilage lining the joints may be destroyed and the underlying bones damaged. Eventually the bones may fuse together and the joint becomes rigid.

The disease may remit spontaneously, at any time, leaving only minor changes in the joints, as happens in about forty per cent of cases. However, about ten per cent suffer from a persistent form of the disease which leads ultimately to destruction of the joints and deformity. Although the cause is unknown, there is evidence to suggest that the body's immune system is involved (see *The Immune System and Allergies*, pages 202-5). A protein (the rheumatoid factor) is present in the blood of many patients with rheumatoid arthritis, and this protein is a form of antibody, stimulated by an antigen which is an altered form of a normal blood protein. The exact significance of the rheumatoid factor is as yet unclear.

Treatment

No cure is yet known, but there are various ways of treating rheumatoid arthritis and rheumatoid disease. Rest can be useful in the early stages, to prevent damage to the joint, and is often required in combination with drugs and other treatment. Pain-killing drugs which may relieve inflammation (aspirin) and anti-inflammatory drugs, such as corticosteroids, are often effective in reducing swelling, pain and stiffness. However, there are side-effects which need to be carefully monitored. In severe cases, drugs that suppress the immune response of the body may control the disease.

Physiotherapy and occupational therapy can be useful in coping with day-to-day living. Surgery is performed in some cases, either to try and prevent damage to the joint by removing the swollen synovial membrane or by reconstructing or replacing damaged joints.

Gout

This disorder, most often affecting middle-aged men, is caused by the accumulation of uric acid salts (urates) in the body, and is often inherited. Uric acid is a naturally occurring substance, an end-product of cellular breakdown, which is normally excreted by the kidneys. Overproduction or under-excretion of uric acid salts, results in a build-up of urates in the body. In some circumstances urate crystals form in and around the joints.

It used to be thought that gout was caused by overindulgence in rich food and drink, and although certain foods, and alcohol, can precipitate an attack this only happens in people who already have the predisposition.

Symptoms
The symptoms of a gout attack are sudden inflammation of a joint, swelling, redness, and extreme pain. The joint most commonly affected is the base of the big toe. The attacks often recur, urates build up in the body in other joints, and visible lumps known as tophi may arise in soft tissues in the skin of the hands, feet and ears.

Treatment
The attack can be treated by drugs which reduce inflammation, and by altering the diet if this is particularly rich or alcoholic. The basic chemical defect can also be treated with drugs which prevent the accumulation of uric acid. Several such drugs are available, and often have to be taken for the rest of the patient's life.

Ankylosing spondylitis

In this chronic progressive disease, inflammation occurs in the lower joints of the spine. It often occurs in young men, and in extreme cases can result in a total stiffness of the spine as the bones fuse together, although the disease usually stops before this stage, leaving a stiff lower back and hips. Early symptoms include pain in the lower back and buttocks, moving from one to the other. Treatment involves anti-inflammatory drugs and exercises.

Bursitis

Bursitis is inflammation of a bursa, one of the fluid-filled sacs in a joint or tendon. The cause is often excessive use of the part concerned, as in 'housemaid's knee' (caused by over-use of the knees by kneeling) and 'tennis elbow'. Bursitis can be extremely painful, and treatment involves resting the joint and relieving the pain and inflammation with drugs, either as tablets or by injection into the joint.

Diseases of bone

Deficiency diseases

Bone may be affected by a diet deficient in one or more components. For instance, lack of vitamin D in children, either because there is not enough of the vitamin in the diet, or because of lack of sunshine (which helps to make vitamin D in the skin), or because of loss in chronic diarrhoea, can cause rickets (decalcification of the bones). Inherited resistance to vitamin D or chronic kidney disease can also cause rickets. The chief effect on bones is to disorder and slow down growth, resulting in deformities such as bow legs and misshapen pelvis. A similar deficiency of vitamin D in adults causes softening of the bones (osteomalacia). In children a deficiency of vitamin C also affects bone, causing scurvy in which there is bleeding into the growing ends of long bones and under the membrane (periosteum) surrounding the bones.

Osteoporosis

Osteoporosis, or thinning of bone, occurs as a result of inadequate replacement of the collagen framework in which calcium salts are deposited, so that the calcium is lost. The basic cause is a hormone deficiency, although poor nutrition, poor absorption of nutrients, prolonged inactivity and other diseases such as rheumatoid arthritis can contribute to the condition. The bones become porous and brittle, and fracture easily, often because of a slight injury. Osteoporosis is to some extent part of the ageing process and is commonly found in women after the menopause. Treatment involves taking certain hormones and a diet high in minerals and vitamin D.

Paget's disease

In Paget's disease (osteitis deformans) the normal degeneration and replacement of bone tissue is disordered, causing slow progressive thickening and deformity of several bones, particularly the skull, spine, pelvis and shin bones. It is sometimes accompanied by softening which causes the legs to bend. The condition is relatively common in people over forty, more often in men, but severe cases are rare. Treatment consists in maintaining good health, using pain-relieving drugs if necessary, and dealing with any fractures or deformities surgically as they arise.

Osteomyelitis

Bones may become infected, usually by *Staphylococci* bacteria, which cause severe illness, often with septicaemia. There is high fever, with intense and localized pain. Antibiotics are usually effective but surgery may be necessary to drain the affected sites. Much less commonly, the bacteria produce a chronic bone abscess.

Tumours

Tumours arising in bone tissue are rare but tend to be malignant. More common are secondary growths (metastases) spreading into bone from malignant tumours elsewhere in the body. Leukaemia is a malignant disease of the cells of the bone marrow and, in its later stages, Hodgkin's disease involves the bones (see page 150).

Taking care of your back

The flexible spine, containing twenty-four separate vertebrae, causes more problems than almost any other part of the body: back pain is the most common reason for adults in both the USA and Britain to consult a doctor, and millions of working days are lost each year because of back pain.

The spinal column has to support the weight of the upper half of the body and is the pivot of all movement. The muscles linking the vertebrae to each other and the muscles of the abdomen all support the spine, and so it follows that if these are weak or damaged for any reason the spine loses its alignment and stability and back pain is the result. If the spine is then subjected to a heavy strain while the vertebrae are misaligned, the shock-absorbing discs between the vertebrae may slip out of position, or prolapse (see page 137).

This situation can, however, often be prevented by proper care in movement—by using your back correctly; especially for activities that put particular strain on your back, such as lifting heavy loads. The muscles of the back should also be kept in good condition by regular exercise. Walking, swimming and gentle stretching exercises are all beneficial even when the back muscles are already damaged; complete rest will make the muscles even weaker. Being overweight also puts a strain on the back.

Posture

Good posture will improve health as well as the general appearance, by allowing the muscles to work to their best advantage at all times, thus making the body more efficient and less liable to damage. When standing, for example, slouching and hunching the shoulders will not only strain the back muscles but will not allow the lungs to expand properly. The aim should be to maintain the natural curves of the spine, and to achieve this the feet should be slightly apart with the weight evenly distributed between them; the shoulders should be relaxed and the pelvis tilted so that the abdominal muscles are held in.

When sitting, the feet should be flat on the floor, the buttocks well back in the chair and the back supported if possible. When lying down, the back should remain straight with the neck in line with the rest of the spine. This means investing in a firm mattress. When bending or lifting, keep the back straight and bend at the knees. Hold the object being lifted close to the body and take its weight equally in both hands.

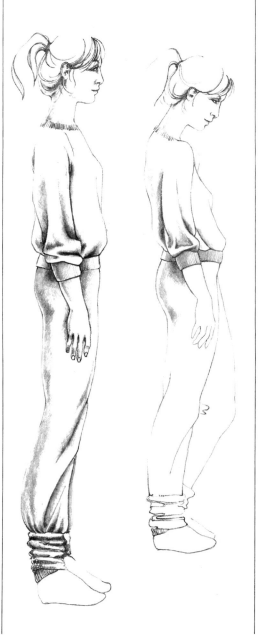

To stand correctly, imagine being pulled upwards by the hair of your head, this should automatically balance your spine so that it is held in the correct curve (right). Look in the mirror as you do this and compare it with your usual posture – if it is anything like that illustrated (far right), you should make a conscious effort to improve it.

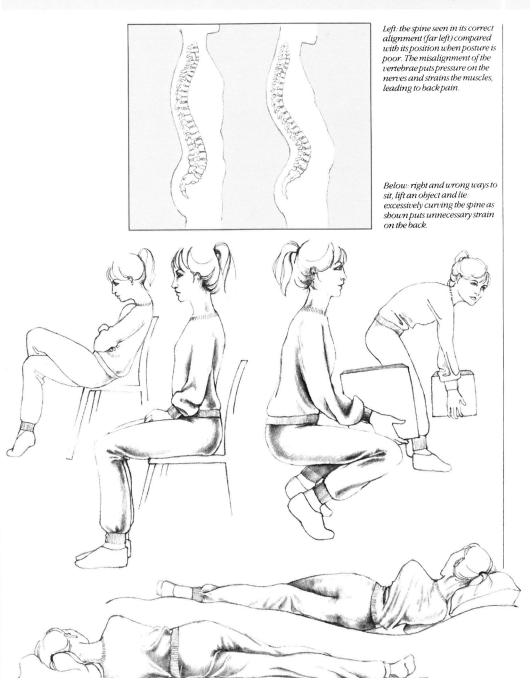

Left: the spine seen in its correct alignment (far left) compared with its position when posture is poor. The misalignment of the vertebrae puts pressure on the nerves and strains the muscles, leading to back pain.

Below: right and wrong ways to sit, lift an object and lie: excessively curving the spine as shown puts unnecessary strain on the back.

Blood and Lymph

Blood is a complex mixture of liquid and cells that is pumped around the body in the vessels of the circulatory system. The important functions of blood include the transport of oxygen, nutrients and hormones, and the defence of the body against infection.

Lymph is the colourless fluid that bathes the cells of the body; it has many similarities to blood. The lymphatic system is a network of channels that returns lymph to the blood circulation, and is an essential part of the body's defences against disease.

Blood

Blood is composed of plasma, red cells, white cells and platelets. The total blood volume in an adult is about 5 litres (8 pints); over half of this is plasma, about forty-five per cent is red cells, and about one per cent white cells and platelets. The cells are only visible under a microscope.

Red cells

There are about 25 billion red blood cells in the blood of one person. Each one is shaped like a biconcave disc, thinner in the middle than at the edges. The surface area of this shape is larger than that of a flat disc or sphere of the same size, and so the maximum amount of oxygen and waste gases can be exchanged between the cells in the lungs and tissues (see *The Respiratory System*, pages 84-7).

Red blood cells contain haemoglobin which is a protein containing iron that gives the cells their red colour. In adults, red cells (also called erythrocytes) are formed in the bone marrow, mainly in the bones of the ribs, sternum (breast-bone), spine, pelvis and skull. In newborn babies all the bones contain marrow capable of manufacturing blood cells, and in the fetus red cells are also made in the liver and spleen. A hormone manufactured by the kidneys, erythropoietin, stimulates the bone marrow to produce red cells. Production of red blood cells takes four to five days, and then the cells are discharged into the circulation. Each cell has a lifespan of about 120 days, after which it is broken down, mainly in the spleen and liver. The iron from the haemoglobin can be reused, and part of the haemoglobin turned into bilirubin by the liver.

To produce normal red cells, the marrow needs large amounts of amino acids (components of protein) and iron. Traces of certain vitamins and minerals are also needed, principally vitamin B_{12}, folic acid, riboflavine, vitamin C, vitamin E, vitamin B_6, cobalt and copper. A varied diet will normally provide all these in amounts adequate for red cell production.

The most important function of red blood cells is to transport oxygen to the tissues, where it is needed for cell respiration. The haemoglobin of the red cell combines with oxygen to become oxyhaemoglobin. In this way seventy-five times more oxygen can be transported than if the oxygen were simply dissolved in the blood. When the blood flows through areas rich in oxygen, such as the lungs, the haemoglobin takes up oxygen. But in the body's tissues, which continually need oxygen, the haemoglobin gives up its oxygen which is taken up by the tissue cells.

When haemoglobin is combined with oxygen, in oxygenated blood, it appears bright red, but becomes a darker red when it releases its oxygen. Thus arterial blood, which is coming from the lungs, is bright red, while venous blood, which is returning to the lungs from the tissues, is dark red.

White cells

The white cells, or leucocytes, are the largest particles in the blood but are about 1000 times less numerous than red cells. There are three main types: granulocytes (also called polymorphs), monocytes and lymphocytes. The granulocytes can be subdivided into three further types of cell, each with a different function: neutrophils (the most numerous), eosinophils and basophils. Granulocytes and monocytes are formed in the bone marrow, and lymphocytes are made in the lymph glands and other lymphoid tissue.

Granulocytes and monocytes have a lifespan of about a week. They can leave the blood vessels and move through the tissues, and are part of the body's main defence against infection, since they engulf and digest bacteria and viruses. Dead and dying neutrophils make up the bulk of pus at the site of wounds. The function of eosinophils is still not fully understood, but they are known to play a part in allergic reactions (see *The Immune System and Allergies*, page 202).

Lymphocytes have an important role in the immune system, principally in rejecting foreign substances (including skin grafts and transplants), and are also a source of antibodies. The lifespan of lymphocytes varies widely: some live for only a few weeks, others for as long as ten years.

Platelets

Platelets are colourless, disc-shaped or irregular bodies, the smallest particles of the blood, and are closely involved with blood clotting. They are produced by special cells in the bone marrow and live only a few days. If blood is stored for more than a day before transfusion, the platelets in it become worthless, and when there is a severe shortage of platelets bleeding can occur. This may be treated by transfusing concentrated platelets or using blood in which the platelets are still viable.

Plasma

The plasma is a clear, straw-coloured fluid which serves as a nutritional medium for the tissues, and contains a wide variety of substances. Sometimes the plasma and blood cells work together: for example, oxygen diffuses from the lungs into plasma before diffusing into the cells, while plasma proteins are involved in blood clotting. White cells and plasma antibodies function together in the body's defence against infection (see page 202). For other functions, the plasma acts alone, transporting sugars, fats and many drugs, which are absorbed in the intestine, to the liver, and from the liver to the rest of the body. The plasma is purified of waste products by the kidneys which excrete unwanted materials in the urine.

The main substances dissolved in plasma are proteins, which comprise six to seven per cent by weight of the plasma. The proteins differ from each other in many ways, and are specialized for various functions including the transport of metals (such as iron, copper and zinc), vitamins (such as vitamin B_{12}), fats and carbohydrates. Many of the plasma proteins are antibodies which, together with white cells, provide protection against infection. Yet another group of proteins, which includes heparin, is involved in blood clotting. Hormones are also circulated in the plasma to exert their influence on many tissues or 'target' organs (see *Hormones*, pages 180-7).

Blood groups and transfusion

Although red cells from different people look the same, there are, in fact, many different blood types. The most important way in which blood types are classified, especially for the purposes of blood transfusion, are the ABO and Rhesus systems. White cells also have their own blood group system which is becoming more important now that the matching of white cells between donor and acceptor is used in the transplantation of organs such as the kidney or heart.

The ABO system

In the ABO system, there are four groups: A, B, AB, and O. The surface of the cell in each group is different and will react with substances in plasma of blood from another group. This causes the cells to stick together (agglutinate), and may also cause them to burst and release their haemoglobin (haemolysis). This is an antibody-antigen type reaction where the red cell has the antigen on its surface and the plasma contains the antibody.

People in group A cells carry the A antigen on the red cell surface and the B antibody in their plasma; and vice versa for group B. People in group AB carry neither antibody in the plasma, and those in group O have both types of antibody. This means that blood from any group (if correctly cross-matched) can be transfused into someone with AB blood, since it does not carry either type of antibody. A person with type AB blood is therefore called a universal recipient. A group O person can only receive blood from a group O donor but can give blood to anyone and is called a universal donor. Type A can donate to types A and AB but receive only from types A and O. Type B can give to types B and AB but receive from only types B and O.

The Rhesus system

The Rhesus blood group was first discovered in the Rhesus monkey, hence its name. In humans, individuals either have Rhesus factor antigen on their cells and are Rhesus positive

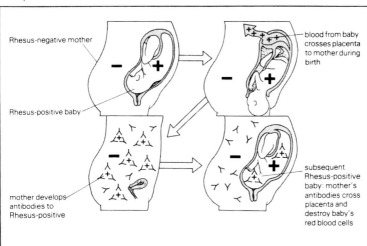

How Rhesus incompatibility affects the fetus. If the mother's blood is Rhesus negative and her first child's is Rhesus positive, she may develop antibodies to the Rhesus antigen if some of the fetal blood mixes with her own during birth as the placenta comes away. This does not affect the health of the first child, but if the second also has Rhesus positive red blood cells (carrying the Rhesus antigen), they will be attacked by the mother's anti-Rhesus antibodies. These molecules are able to cross the placenta as they are much smaller than whole cells. In this situation, the child is born anaemic and needs a transfusion of Rhesus-negative blood at birth.

Rhesus-negative mother

blood from baby crosses placenta to mother during birth

Rhesus-positive baby

mother develops antibodies to Rhesus-positive

subsequent Rhesus-positive baby: mother's antibodies cross placenta and destroy baby's red blood cells

The ABO blood groups and their antigens. People with blood group O can donate blood to all four blood groups; someone with type AB can receive blood from all four.

blood group	A	B	AB	O
antigen on red blood cell	A	B	A and B	neither A nor B
antibody in plasma	anti-B	anti-A	neither anti-A nor anti-B	anti-A and anti-B

(Rh+ve), or lack it and are Rhesus negative (Rh−ve). Antibodies are not found in Rhesus negative people unless they have been transfused with Rhesus positive blood at some time.

Particular problems can occur during pregnancy in a mother who is Rhesus negative and whose developing baby is Rhesus positive. During the last weeks of pregnancy small numbers of the red cells of the fetus may escape through the placenta into the mother's blood system. Although this is not dangerous in the first pregnancy the mother becomes sensitized so that in further pregnancies the mother's antibodies may invade the fetal circulation, destroying the red cells to cause haemolytic anaemia in the baby. When this occurs the baby's blood has to be exchanged for Rhesus negative, by transfusion, at birth. Mothers can now be given injections which remove the Rhesus positive cells leaking from the fetus before there is a chance of producing the antibody.

Blood transfusion
Any adult who is in good general health and free from disease which can be transmitted by blood transfusion (such as infective hepatitis) can donate blood if the amount of haemoglobin in the blood is adequate. Blood can be given safely two or three times a year. It is removed from a vein in the arm, and the amount taken normally does not exceed 420 ml (15 fl oz). It is stored at 4°C (39°F), and has several chemicals added to prevent it clotting and to increase its life. The donation of blood does not involve any major discomfort to the donor. After blood has been collected it is checked for safety, and the ABO and Rhesus groups are determined.

Before blood is given to a patient, several investigations have to be carried out. The first involves the determination of the blood group of the recipient in both the ABO and Rhesus systems. These tests are carried out on the recipient's red cells. Tests on the recipient's blood are also performed, to detect blood-group antibodies. Direct cross-matching, or compatibility, tests are then carried out, mixing the recipient's and the donor's blood and studying the mixture for signs of agglutination, or clumping together of the red blood cells, which destroys them.

The blood transfusion is given via a hollow needle, or cannula, inserted into a vein near the surface of the skin, usually in the arm, from a container suspended above the patient. The blood is allowed to flow slowly by gravity, so that it does not take more than four hours for each litre (2 pints) of blood to be given.

The main reasons for giving blood by transfusion are: to replace blood lost by bleeding from an accident or during an operation; and to replace blood not being manufactured by the patient in cases of anaemia which do not respond to treatment, or when underlying disease affects red cell production.

Blood clotting
When a blood vessel is damaged the blood clots in the wound and prevents excessive bleeding (haemorrhage). The clotting process is complex, involving factors in the blood and tissues, as well as platelets and a protein, fibrino-gen. Firstly, platelets gather at the site of the damaged vessel, and certain factors in the surrounding tissues are released into the blood, triggering a reaction between the platelets and the blood plasma. The result is that fibrinogen, a soluble protein in blood, is converted to an insoluble protein, fibrin. This forms a meshwork at the site of the wound which traps platelets and cells to form a jelly-like mass. Gradually, this contracts to form a clot.

Probably at least twelve factors in blood are involved in the clotting process, and the lack of any one of them may affect clotting.

Blood disorders

Because of its important functions and its intimate association with all the cells, tissues and organs of the body, disorders of the blood can have a profound effect on health. Changes in the blood occur in many diseases, and examining the blood is a routine diagnostic test.

Blood tests
A sample of blood is usually taken with a syringe from a vein at the front of the elbow. In babies, whose veins are small and difficult to puncture, blood may be obtained from scalp veins or by making a small cut in the heel. Very small amounts of blood can be obtained by pricking the end of a finger with a special needle.

The numbers and appearance of the blood cells can be checked by examining a thin film of blood under a microscope. This blood film can be stained with dyes to show up characteristics of both red and white cells. Either a microscope slide or an electronic machine can be used to count the number of cells in a sample of blood. Other tests can determine the amount of haemoglobin in the red cells and the quantities of other substances in the plasma. The time blood takes to clot (coagulation time) is another important test, as is the bleeding time.

Examination of the bone marrow with a microscope is important in determining what is wrong when the blood is abnormal. Marrow is obtained through a needle introduced under local anaesthetic, into the cavity of either the breast bone or the hip bone. Smears of marrow are stained and examined to assess the number of cells, the amount of iron, immature white cells, cells which produce blood platelets (megakaryocytes) and the presence of abnormal cells or micro-organisms. Of these, the most important applications of marrow examinations are in the diagnosis of megaloblastic anaemia and leukaemia (see below and page 147), and in assessing the treatment of leukaemia and multiple myeloma.

Anaemia
Anaemia is any disorder characterized by below-normal concentrations of haemoglobin in the blood, either because there is a reduced number of red cells or because the individual red cells are deficient in haemoglobin. Men normally have a haemoglobin concentration of at least 13.5 g (½ oz) per 100 ml (3½ fl oz) of blood; in women the level is usually fifteen per cent lower, while in newborn babies it is forty per cent higher.

Anaemia may be classified according to cause, according to the size and appearance of the red cells or according to whether the disease is primarily one of the blood, or is due to disease elsewhere in the body. Types of anaemia may also vary between different races and between different regions of the world.

Iron-deficiency anaemia

The most common anaemia throughout the world is iron-deficiency anaemia, a condition that in some tropical areas may be present in up to half the population.

Iron is essential for haemoglobin production and is present in many foodstuffs, particularly meat and liver, eggs, yeast, wheatgerm, oysters and green vegetables. It is more efficiently absorbed from some foods than others, but a normal, balanced diet provides enough iron to meet the body's requirements.

Iron deficiency is most common in women because of blood loss from menstruation (see page 11) and the greatly increased demands for iron in pregnancy. Iron deficiency is also common in infants before mixed feeding begins. In adult men, the most common cause of iron deficiency is

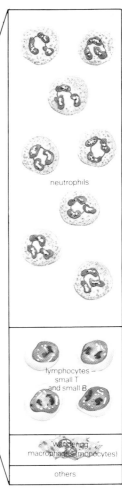

neutrophils

lymphocytes – small T and small B

wandering macrophages (monocytes)

others

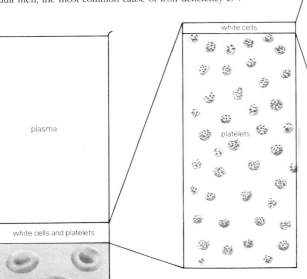

white cells

plasma

platelets

white cells and platelets

red cells (erythrocytes)

Blood is composed of about fifty-five per cent plasma and forty-five per cent formed elements (cells and cell-like structures). Plasma is about ninety per cent water, the rest being dissolved proteins, including those which help in blood clotting. The formed elements may be divided into red cells, white cells and platelets. The red cells transport oxygen and carbon dioxide

around the body in their haemoglobin. White blood cells, unlike red blood cells, have nuclei but no oxygen-carrying haemoglobin. They are important in recognizing bacteria and viruses and in fighting infection. Platelets play an essential role in clotting the blood when a blood vessel has been breached, by sticking together and forming a plug which prevents more blood loss.

There are many different types of white cell. The neutrophils and monocytes ingest bacteria and cellular debris during infections. The lymphocytes, both T and B cells, recognize foreign material such as a transplant or bacterium and produce antibodies, proteins which destroy the invader.

chronic blood loss, due to diseases of the stomach or in-testine, such as peptic ulcers or haemorrhoids, or hook-worm where this is endemic. It may also occur in aspirin addicts, because this drug can cause haemorrhage from the stomach. A single large haemorrhage will not cause anaemia immediately but over the following days. The lost red cells in an otherwise healthy individual will be replaced in about six to eight weeks by increased bone marrow activity. But loss of red cells due to haemorrhage will also result in loss of iron, and a large loss of blood or smaller repeated haemorrhages, deplete the body's iron to an extent that cannot be coped with by a normal diet. Iron-deficiency anaemia is the inevitable result. Prolonged loss of blood will cause chronic anaemia.

Symptoms
Symptoms generally include fatigue, irritability, and the skin may become pale. If the anaemia is due to internal bleeding, blood may be detected in the faeces.

Treatment
Treatment of iron-deficiency anaemia usually involves taking extra iron in the form of tablets, although some people, who cannot take iron orally because of intestinal disorders, may have to be given injections. It is important to make sure that the diet includes plenty of iron-rich foods.

Pernicious anaemia (megaloblastic anaemia)
Pernicious anaemia is caused by a deficiency of vitamin B_{12} or folic acid. One of its characteristics is that there are fewer red cells but these are large and packed with haemoglobin. The lifespan of the cells is short and they disintegrate easily; this can lead to a build-up of yellow pigment in the skin (caused by the accumulation of breakdown products of haemoglobin).

A normal diet provides plenty of vitamin B_{12}, but vegetarians who do not eat meat or other animal produce may not get enough of this vitamin. The usual cause of vitamin B_{12} deficiency in western societies, however, is the stomach's failure to secrete a particular substance called intrinsic factor which is needed for normal absorption of the vitamin in the intestine. Vitamin B_{12} deficiency can also arise after operations to remove part of the stomach and from other diseases of the stomach or small intestine which cause the inability to absorb this vitamin.

Folic acid is another B-group vitamin present in most kinds of food, but prolonged cooking, particularly in large volumes of water, destroys the vitamin. Folic-acid de-ficiency is common, particularly in elderly people on a poor diet lacking fresh vegetables and fruit. If the deficiency is severe it causes an anaemia very similar to that caused by vitamin B_{12} deficiency. Alcoholics are frequently sufferers, partly because of their poor diet and partly because alcohol seems to have an anti-folic-acid action. Infants fed solely on goat's milk may develop 'goat's milk anaemia' which is due to the milk's low folic-acid content. A deficiency of folic acid also usually accompanies scurvy (vitamin C deficiency) since the two vitamins tend to occur in the same foods. Deficiencies may also arise through failure of absorption in some disorders of the intestine, such as coeliac disease and tropical sprue (see *The Digestive System*, pages 100 and 108). Anaemia may also occur at times when folic acid is

needed in large quantities by the body, for example in pregnancy, in rapidly growing newborn infants, and as a side-effect of serious diseases such as cancer.

Symptoms
Besides fatigue, weakness and pallor, symptoms include depression and a smooth, red, sore tongue. A serious effect may be deterioration of parts of the nervous system, result-ing in numbness and tingling in the limbs.

Treatment
Treatment of pernicious anaemia caused by lack of vitamin B_{12} consists of regular injections of small amounts of the vitamin for the person's lifetime, and this alone will usually ensure good health. Treatment of folic-acid deficiency involves giving supplements of the vitamin in the short term and improving the diet in the long term.

Aplastic anaemia (aplasia of bone marrow)
Anaemia may arise from diseases that affect the bone marrow. The red-cell-forming tissue in the marrow may be injured by radiation, chemicals, drugs, and diseases such as cancer and leukaemia. In rare cases the red-cell tissues may just waste away for no apparent reason (primary aplastic anaemia). Anaemia due to poor marrow function also occurs in many other diseases such as tuberculosis and chronic kidney disease.

Haemolytic anaemia (including sickle-cell anaemia and thalassaemia)
The excessive destruction of red cells in the human body leads to a condition called haemolytic anaemia. The re-duced lifespan of the cells may simply be due to increased destruction of normal cells, or it may be due to abnormali-ties of either the cells or their haemoglobin.

Abnormal haemoglobins are all due to genetic defects which cause a fault in the globin part of the molecule. The best-known example of this is sickle-cell anaemia, so called because the red blood cells lose their normal disc shape and become crescent- or sickle-shaped when the level of oxygen in the blood falls. This causes the blood to become more viscous and the cells to become fragile and easily damaged. The blood supply to the organs becomes dis-turbed. If a person inherits the defect from both parents the condition is severe, and death usually occurs before the age of thirty. If the defect is inherited from one parent only, anaemia may be mild or even absent and is called sickle-cell trait, which is not fatal. This disease and trait are common in Negro races. The presence of the trait gives some protection from a common type of malaria. Sickle-cell anaemia is incurable, but the symptoms – those of anaemia and pain in the bones – can be treated.

Another fairly common type of haemoglobin disorder is thalassaemia. A person with this condition is unable to make enough haemoglobin and the red cells are very pale. If the sufferer inherits the defect from both parents he or she will have severe anaemia that may cause death in childhood, but a person who inherits the defect from only one parent will have either a mild form of the disease or no symptoms at all. The highest incidence of the condition is in people from the Mediterranean countries of Italy, Greece, Cyprus, Syria and Turkey, but it also occurs in other regions where people of

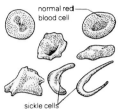

normal red blood cell

sickle cells

Sickle-cell anaemia is so called because many of the red blood cells, which should be round, are elongated and in the shape of a crescent, or sickle.

Mediterranean origin have settled. There is no satisfactory treatment, except for periodic blood transfusions in the most severe cases.

Defects in the red cells and their metabolism (rather than in the haemoglobin) include congenital spherocytosis and congenital elliptocytosis, in which the cells are spherical and elliptical respectively. There is another group of defects of red-cell metabolism, in one of which anaemia only occurs after exposure to certain drugs to which the red cells are particularly susceptible.

Defects in the red cells may also be caused by antibodies which for some reason attack the person's own red cells, causing an autoimmune haemolytic anaemia. In the case of haemolytic disease of the newborn, antibodies are produced by the mother against the Rhesus factor in the cells of the fetus.

Bleeding disorders

Haemophilia

Haemophilia is a relatively rare inherited disease caused by a lack of one of the clotting factors in the blood. It is characterized by uncontrolled bleeding even from a minor wound, leading to a dangerous loss of blood. Ordinary activities can cause spontaneous internal bleeding into a joint, causing swelling and eventually deformities.

The disease varies in severity: about two-thirds of all haemophiliacs have the severe form of the disease and one-third a milder disorder where the blood does clot, but very slowly. The disease appears in males and also, rarely, in women deficient in factor IX (haemophilia B; see below). The condition is inherited from the mother ('sex-linked'); she carries the gene without developing the disease herself. In approximately a third of all haemophiliacs no family history of the condition can be detected. This may be because it has been transmitted through several generations of female carriers without an affected male appearing, all record of a previously affected male having been lost to the memory of that family; alternatively, the disease may have arisen by a mutation (change) in the mother's genes.

The parents of a child with haemophilia may not become aware of the problem until the child starts to toddle, falls and cuts himself. The parents' suspicion of an abnormality may be raised by the appearance of unduly large bruises caused by a minor injury or even without an injury.

In the commonest form of haemophilia the blood of the person lacks a substance called factor VIII; and in another form, factor IX (sometimes known as Christmas factor) is lacking. Both factors VIII and IX are vital to the blood clotting mechanism.

Treatment

Since there are five times more haemophiliacs who lack factor VIII than factor IX, interest has been centred on obtaining factor VIII from the blood of normal people and injecting this into the circulation of the haemophiliac patient to correct, temporarily, the clotting abnormality of the blood. In order to supply enough factor VIII to stop bleeding, the missing factor extracted from 3-6 litres (5-10 pints) of normal blood may be needed. Once injected into the circulation, the factor VIII remains in the blood for only a few hours, and it can take as long as ten days of intravenous infusion of factor VIII to produce wound healing. The principles of treatment of factor IX deficiency are similar. Factor XIII can now be manufactured synthetically.

Haemophiliacs should carry with them an identity card or disc giving details of name, address, doctor's telephone number and the hospital dealing with them, their blood group, factor deficiency and the level of the factor in the blood. Patients with severe haemophilia should not take part in contact sports, although swimming is considered safe. It is very important for haemophiliacs to have frequent dental care so that dental decay can be treated by fillings instead of extraction. Sometimes the loss of milk teeth can cause bleeding, and hospital care is needed.

Since aspirin may cause internal bleeding in the stomach, it should not be taken. Haemophiliacs should not receive deep injections into the muscles; injections into the skin surface, however, do not usually result in undue bleeding.

Purpura

Purpura is a general term for bleeding from small blood vessels in the skin and mucous membranes, causing purple patches and bruises to appear under the skin. This bleeding may occur spontaneously or after minor injury. One cause of purpura is a reduction in the number of platelets, vital in the clotting mechanism, because of a disorder in their production in the bone marrow (thrombocytopenia). Other causes include deficiency in platelet function, disorders of the blood vessels, and vitamin C or K deficiency. Treatment depends on the cause of the purpura. If blood loss is severe, transfusions may have to be given.

In immune thrombocytopenic purpura (ITP), bleeding occurs because the platelets are damaged and then destroyed by an antibody reaction. The antibody may arise for no known reason or as a result of infection. If the cause is an autoimmune response – a reaction of the body against its own cells – blood transfusions and steroid drugs are given. With this treatment most cases are cured in a few weeks, but sometimes surgery to remove the spleen may have to be carried out before there is any improvement.

Leukaemia

Leukaemia is a cancer of white blood cells, the body's main defence mechanism against infection. It occurs when the developing cells fail to mature properly and multiply abnormally fast; these immature cells accumulate in large numbers in the bone marrow, eventually spilling over into the bloodstream. The most important effect of this growth of leukaemic cells in the marrow is that production of red cells, normal white cells and platelets is disturbed, and their displacement by the abnormal cells is responsible for the serious effects of the disease. Leukaemia most commonly affects the development of lymphocytes (acute or chronic lymphatic leukaemia) or the granulocyte white cells (acute or chronic granulocytic, or myeloid, leukaemia), but other cells may be affected as well. Apart from excessive exposure to radiation, in almost all cases the cause is unknown.

Leukaemia affects between fifty and sixty people per million each year. Unlike many other forms of cancer it often attacks children and young adults as well as older people. The commonest form of leukaemia in children is the acute lymphatic type. Chronic forms are rare before adulthood, but acute myeloid leukaemia occurs at all ages, with a peak in early adult life. Slightly more women are affected than men.

Symptoms
The main features of the disease are a combination of the symptoms and signs of anaemia (lack of red cells), multiple infections (due to lack of protective white cells) and bleeding (due to lack of platelets). Disorders ranging from boils, small bruises or nosebleeds, to pneumonia or severe internal haemorrhage can all be the first feature of acute leukaemia (myeloid and lymphatic). Weakness, fever, shortness of breath and palpitations are also frequent symptoms.

Patients with chronic myeloid leukaemia complain of weakness and fatigue, and discomfort due to an enlarged spleen. Serious infections and bleeding usually occur when the disease becomes acute. Anaemia and enlargement of the lymph glands and spleen are usually the initial symptoms in chronic lymphatic leukaemia. The leukaemic lymphocytes affect the production of antibodies and this makes the person prone to infections.

The disease is occasionally found in elderly people who have no symptoms at all, and it may persist for many years and never cause trouble, or change into an acute form.

One of the most remarkable features of the acute forms of leukaemia is the occurrence of what is called remission, when the patient feels well again for a time. This develops either following treatment or may occur spontaneously following an infection such as measles or a blood transfusion.

Treatment
The aim of treatment in acute leukaemia is to induce a remission and to maintain it indefinitely. In acute lymphatic leukaemia of childhood, remission regularly occurs in about ninety per cent of cases and may sometimes be permanent. The remission rate in acute myeloid leukaemia is much lower, about thirty to fifty per cent.

Drugs can suppress the multiplication of leukaemic cells, but also suppress the formation of normal cells by the bone marrow, so that during the early stages of treatment the patient will almost always pass through a dangerous stage which requires blood transfusions to replace the red cells and also platelet transfusions to control bleeding. After this danger period, the condition usually improves dramatically. Treatment may also involve bone marrow transplants and radiotherapy.

True remission does not occur in chronic leukaemia as it does in acute leukaemia. Drugs are used to suppress the cell multiplication and these can control the disease for many years, the patient returning to normal health.

The lymphatic system

The lymphatic system consists of lymph glands linked by channels called lymphatics that carry the fluid called lymph around the body. Most of these converge to form the thoracic duct which runs along the descending aorta and connects with one of the main branches of the superior vena cava vein carrying blood to the heart. Lymph is formed from the fluid that has left the blood circulation at the capillaries. It therefore has many similarities to blood, except that it is transparent and contains fewer cells, most of which are white blood cells. The lymphatic system collects fluid from the tissues and returns it to the blood.

The structure of the lymphatic system
The lymphatic system begins in the tissues as a three-dimensional meshwork of small blind-ended tubes, the lymphatics, near the blood capillaries. The lymphatics then pass towards the centre of the body alongside the arteries and veins, and join together to form channels of ever-increasing diameter, which empty into veins in the neck.

The lymph nodes or lymph glands are swellings of lymphoid tissue containing lymphocytes. The most easily recognizable groups of lymph nodes are the cervical (in the neck), the axillary (in the armpit) and the inguinal (in the groin). When an area of the body becomes infected, the nodes draining that area may become swollen, painful and easily felt under the skin (lymphadenitis) because they are responding to the infection by producing antibodies.

The spleen is the largest single collection of lymphoid tissue within the body. About the size of a fist, it lies below the ribs on the left side near the stomach. The spleen differs from the lymph nodes, however, because there is no direct flow of lymph through it, and whereas the lymph nodes filter lymph, the spleen filters blood to remove foreign materials and worn-out red cells. The thymus, which lies in the chest in front of the heart, is another important lymphocyte-producing organ, but exists only in childhood: at puberty it gradually shrinks and is replaced by fat.

Functions of the lymphatic system
The lymphatic system has several functions. It returns the fluid that has left the blood at the capillaries to the circulation. And in the intestine (see *The Digestive System*, page 100) specialized lymph vessels (lacteals) in the villi are important in transporting fat absorbed from food.

The lymph nodes filter the lymph, removing and destroying bacteria and other infectious organisms before they can reach the blood. When foreign particles enter the body they stimulate production of antibodies. The lymphatic system plays the major role in producing antibodies, both the type bound to the lymphocytes and those present free in solution in the body fluids. The antibodies bound to lymphocytes are called cell-bound and the cells that produce them start life in the thymus during childhood. These cells migrate to other parts of the lymphatic system, mainly the spleen. The antibodies in the body fluids are produced by lymphocytes which, when stimulated by invading organisms, turn into another type of white cell called plasma cells.

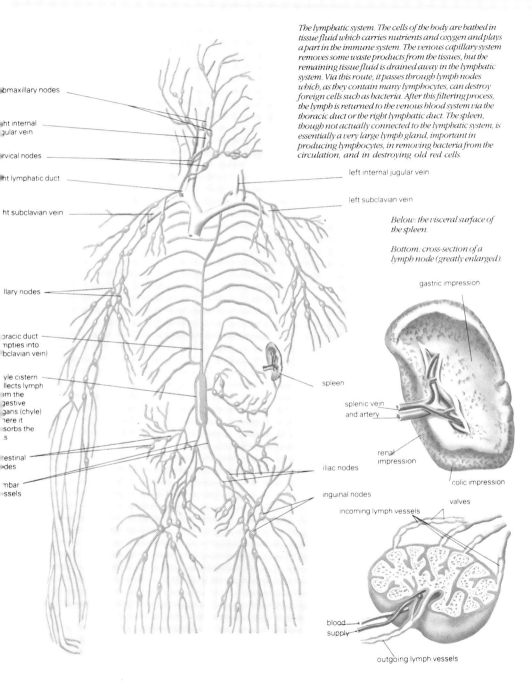

The lymphatic system. The cells of the body are bathed in tissue fluid which carries nutrients and oxygen and plays a part in the immune system. The venous capillary system removes some waste products from the tissues, but the remaining tissue fluid is drained away in the lymphatic system. Via this route, it passes through lymph nodes which, as they contain many lymphocytes, can destroy foreign cells such as bacteria. After this filtering process, the lymph is returned to the venous blood system via the thoracic duct or the right lymphatic duct. The spleen, though not actually connected to the lymphatic system, is essentially a very large lymph gland, important in producing lymphocytes, in removing bacteria from the circulation, and in destroying old red cells.

bmaxillary nodes

ht internal
gular vein

rvical nodes

ht lymphatic duct

ht subclavian vein

llary nodes

oracic duct
npties into
bclavian vein)

yle cistern
llects lymph
om the
gestive
gans (chyle)
here it
sorbs the
s

testinal
des

mbar
ssels

left internal jugular vein

left subclavian vein

Below: the visceral surface of the spleen.

Bottom: cross-section of a lymph node (greatly enlarged).

spleen

iliac nodes

inguinal nodes

gastric impression

splenic vein
and artery

renal
impression

colic impression

valves

incoming lymph vessels

blood
supply

outgoing lymph vessels

Disorders of the lymphatic system

There are several specific diseases of the lymphatic system, and also generalized disorders and infections that can lead to oedema (swelling) caused by the accumulation of lymph in the body tissues.

Hodgkin's disease (lymphadenoma)

Hodgkin's disease is a malignant condition in which the lymph nodes and other lymphoid tissue gradually enlarge, locally at first and then throughout the body. It is usually painless and, in most cases, the first symptoms of the disease are the enlargement of one or more lymph nodes in the neck. As the disease becomes more widespread there may be loss of weight, weakness, generalized itching and fever. In the later stages of the disease there is often very severe anaemia, requiring blood transfusions. Many patients in the later stages of the disease show a decreased resistance to infection.

As with all forms of cancer, successful treatment depends on early diagnosis (see *Cancer*, page 218). If the disease is limited to one node or group of nodes, then with early treatment by radiation or chemotherapy and surgery about ninety per cent of sufferers can eventually be completely cured.

Lymphoma

Lymphoma is a general term for any malignant tumour of the lymphoid tissues, including Hodgkin's disease. Unlike Hodgkin's disease, the other lymphomas are very malignant and more likely to be fatal. Burkitt's lymphoma is a rare type of lymphoma characteristically affecting the bones of the jaw; it occurs in well-defined areas of Africa, and there is evidence that it is caused by a virus.

Lymphangioma

This is a rare condition in which excessive growth of lymphatic vessels forms benign tumours, which are characteristically watery, cystic growths. Sometimes blood vessels or fat are also involved in the growth, which has to be removed surgically.

Lymphosarcoma

Lymphosarcoma is a malignant growth arising in the lymphatic tissue of the body, especially of the stomach or intestines. It is usually fatal eventually, but may run a slow course lasting many years. Early detection of its symptoms – enlargement of the lymph glands and spleen – frequently enables treatment with radiation and drugs to be effective.

Macroglobulinemias

This a very rare group of diseases characterized by an increase in the number of certain proteins, macroglobulins, in the blood. This is due to their over-production by lymphocytes or plasma cells. The symptoms include anaemia and enlargement of the liver and spleen. The abnormal protein interferes with the normal processes of blood coagulation, and haemorrhage may occur, particularly into the skin, leading to purpura (see page 147).

How white blood cells fight infection

One of the body's most remarkable attributes is its ability to distinguish between its own and foreign tissues. This provides the body with a sensitive defence mechanism which maintains the integrity of the organism in its potentially hostile environment. The white cells of the blood – neutrophils, lymphocytes, macrophages and others – are part of the body's main defence against infection, since they engulf and destroy foreign particles. When a harmful organism breaches the body's first line of defence against it – the skin and mucous membranes – the white cells increase rapidly in number and attempt to isolate it from the rest of the body by enveloping it and then consuming it. The white cells are shown in action in these photographs, magnified thousands of times.

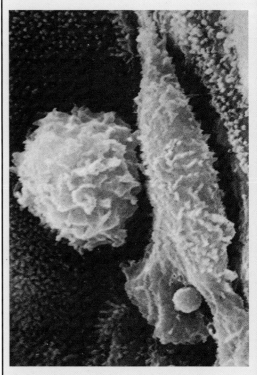

The scavenging macrophages wander freely in the bloodstream, consuming any debris they come across, such as bacteria, pollen, dust and other particles. These macrophages are in the lungs: the large round cell on the left of the picture is a macrophage, and so is the lower elongated one on the right which can be seen attacking a foreign body, the small round particle being enclosed by it at the bottom right of the picture.

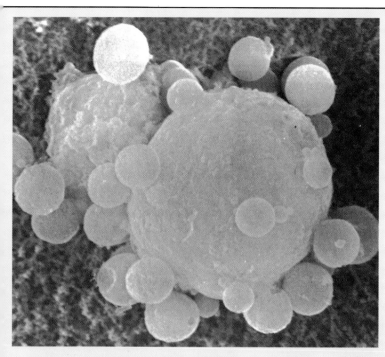

Lymphocytes, which are made in the lymph glands and other lymphoid tissue, attack invading cells, in this case cancer cells. The smaller lymphocytes cluster round the larger tumour cells, causing dramatic changes to occur on the surface of the tumour cells. Blisters form and turn into vesicles which become detached from the tumour cell and attach themselves to the lymphocyte, hindering it from doing more damage to the cancer cells.

White cells can be seen here engulfing a bacterium (centre).

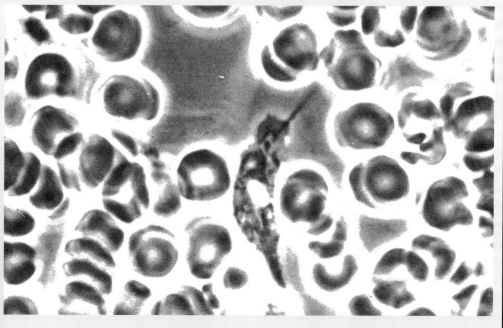

The Heart and Circulation

The circulatory, or cardiovascular, system consists of the heart and a network of blood vessels that take blood to and from the heart. The heart is the pump of the system and the main force behind the blood flow. The vessels consist of arteries, capillaries and veins. Arteries usually carry oxygenated blood, that is, blood rich in oxygen, to the organs and tissues of the body. Capillaries are very fine, thin-walled vessels through which exchange of materials between the blood and tissues occurs. The veins usually carry blood low in oxygen (deoxygenated blood) back towards the heart, from where it is pumped to the lungs.

There are two main networks of vessels which are joined and cross over at the heart. One of the networks supplies the body with oxygen-rich blood and returns the blood low in oxygen to the heart. This is the systemic circulation. The other network carries blood in a circuit from the heart to the lungs, where the deoxygenated blood releases carbon dioxide to the air, takes up fresh oxygen, and then returns to the heart. This is the pulmonary circulation.

The heart muscle itself is supplied with blood from two main coronary arteries that branch off from the aorta, the main artery leaving the heart. They are particularly important vessels since any disease in them can directly damage the heart.

The heart

The heart produces the force that propels blood through the vessels to all parts of the body. It beats steadily about seventy times a minute (2,500 million beats in an average lifetime), and during normal activity it pumps about 5 litres (9 pints) a minute, but this can increase to 30 litres (about 53 pints) a minute during exercise.

The heart is cone-shaped, roughly the size of a closed fist, and weighs about 300 g (11 oz). It is situated on the left side of the chest between the lungs and above the diaphragm, and is surrounded by a thin double-layered membrane called the pericardium. The two layers of this membrane are separated by a small amount of fluid that lubricates them as the heart contracts and relaxes.

The heart consists of special cardiac muscle (see *The Muscles*, page 125) divided into four hollow chambers, two on each side. Each pair of chambers is basically a pump, consisting of a thin-walled chamber, or atrium, at the top,

and a thicker-walled chamber, or ventricle, below. The chambers on the right are separated from those on the left by a muscular wall, the septum, which prevents blood from each side mixing.

Between each atrium and ventricle is a valve which controls the flow of blood between the two chambers. On the right side is the tricuspid valve, so called because of its three flaps, and on the left side the mitral valve, which has two flaps. Blood flows into and out of the heart in large arteries and veins, and valves in these, close to the heart, also control the flow.

Blood flows into the heart through the atria and is pumped out of it by the ventricles. Blood from the lungs, rich in oxygen, is delivered to the left atrium by the pulmonary veins which carry oxygen-rich blood. The pressure in the atrium forces the blood through the mitral valve into the ventricle below. This then contracts to push the blood through another valve into the aorta, and then to the rest of the body. Blood low in oxygen returns from elsewhere in the body to the right atrium of the heart through large veins called the vena cavae, and is then pumped by the right ventricle out through the pulmonary artery, to the lungs. Once it has exchanged carbon dioxide for oxygen, the blood returns to the left side of the heart. The left ventricle pumps the oxygenated blood to all parts of the body, and is the largest and most muscular part of the heart.

The heartbeat

When the heart beats, the cardiac muscle contracts and relaxes. Both sides of the heart contract and relax together, and the rhythm of the beat is regulated by nerve impulses (see below).

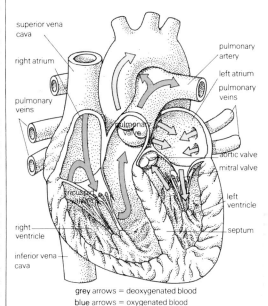

superior vena cava

right atrium

pulmonary veins

right ventricle

inferior vena cava

pulmonary artery

left atrium

pulmonary veins

pulmonary valve

aortic valve

mitral valve

tricuspid valve

left ventricle

septum

grey arrows = deoxygenated blood
blue arrows = oxygenated blood

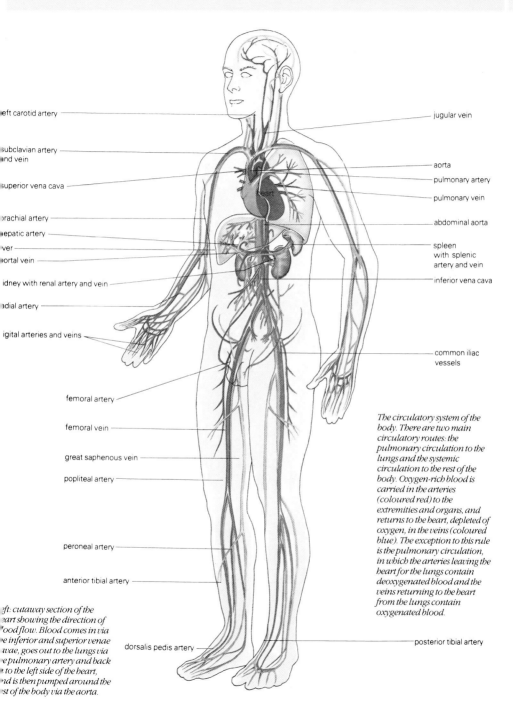

left carotid artery

subclavian artery
and vein

superior vena cava

brachial artery

hepatic artery

liver

portal vein

kidney with renal artery and vein

radial artery

digital arteries and veins

femoral artery

femoral vein

great saphenous vein

popliteal artery

peroneal artery

anterior tibial artery

dorsalis pedis artery

jugular vein

aorta

pulmonary artery

pulmonary vein

abdominal aorta

spleen
with splenic
artery and vein

inferior vena cava

common iliac
vessels

posterior tibial artery

heart

*The circulatory system of the
body. There are two main
circulatory routes: the
pulmonary circulation to the
lungs and the systemic
circulation to the rest of the
body. Oxygen-rich blood is
carried in the arteries
(coloured red) to the
extremities and organs, and
returns to the heart, depleted of
oxygen, in the veins (coloured
blue). The exception to this rule
is the pulmonary circulation,
in which the arteries leaving the
heart for the lungs contain
deoxygenated blood and the
veins returning to the heart
from the lungs contain
oxygenated blood.*

*left: cutaway section of the
heart showing the direction of
blood flow. Blood comes in via
the inferior and superior venae
cavae, goes out to the lungs via
the pulmonary artery and back
in to the left side of the heart,
and is then pumped around the
rest of the body via the aorta.*

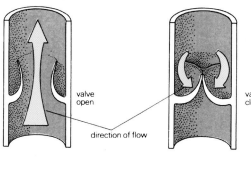

How the valves in the heart work. The valves are flattened against the side of each heart chamber as the blood enters it, but when the chamber contracts the backflow created causes the valves to open out. Thus, the only possible exit is in the forward direction.

valve open

valve closed

direction of flow

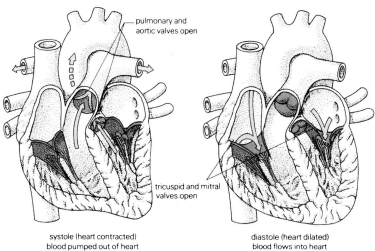

pulmonary and aortic valves open

tricuspid and mitral valves open

systole (heart contracted)
blood pumped out of heart

diastole (heart dilated)
blood flows into heart

At the start of a beat the heart is relaxed and blood flows into the atria from the veins. The valves in the heart are open at this time and some blood may flow into the ventricles. This period of relaxation is called the diastole. Both atria then contract, forcing blood into the ventricles and filling them further. Then both ventricles contract together and force blood out of the heart through the arteries to the lungs or body. When the ventricles contract, the pressure of blood shuts the valves and prevents blood flowing back into the atria. The valves at the opening of the arteries leaving the heart also open and close to allow blood through but prevent it flowing back. This period of contraction is called the systole. About 70 ml (2½ fluid oz.) of blood is pumped from each ventricle during systole.

When the heart beats, two sounds can be heard which resemble the words 'lub dub'. The 'lub' sound is caused by the valves between each atrium and ventricle snapping shut and by the vibration caused by ventricular contraction. The 'dub' sound is caused by the closing of the valves in the arteries leaving the heart.

Heart sounds can be heard with a stethoscope, and any changes in them can be a sign of disease or a disorder. For example, when the tricuspid or mitral valves become narrowed, a murmur can be heard.

The control of the heartbeat

The heart contains its own specialized conducting system which coordinates the contraction of the muscle during the heartbeat. Thus the heart can beat if it is isolated from the nervous system, although it cannot operate fully.

In one particular area of the heart, in the wall of the right atrium, the muscle cells have the ability to produce an electrical impulse at regular intervals. The electrical impulses spread from this area, called the sinoatrial node or pacemaker, throughout the heart and cause the muscle to contract. The impulses spread across the atria first, causing both of them to contract together. Because the ventricles are insulated from the atria except at one point, the impulses pass down a special bundle of tissues, the bundle of His, causing the ventricles to contract. If the pacemaker is damaged, the heart will continue to beat, but only about forty times a minute.

It is possible to measure the electrical activity of the heart, and this is an important method of investigating heart disease and disorders. Electrodes are attached to the skin over different parts of the body and are connected to the electrocardiograph (ECG), which displays a trace showing the electrical pattern of the heartbeat.

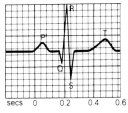

The trace obtained from an electrocardiogram (ECG) of a normal subject. The spikes indicate the pattern of electrical activity as it passes across the heart muscle from the atria (P) to the ventricles, which contract (QRS wave); the T wave represents the change in the ventricles as they prepare to contract again.

Heart rates

The rate of heartbeat (the pulse rate) may be increased (tachycardia) or decreased (bradycardia) for various reasons. Exercise and emotion are two well-known stimuli for tachycardia, but over-activity of the thyroid gland and disorders of the heart muscle can also cause the heart to beat as fast as 200 times a minute. The result of these very fast heart rates is that the heart cannot function efficiently and a symptom of this may be faintness because of in-sufficient blood supply to the brain.

Bradycardia may occur normally in highly trained athletes, whose heart rate at rest may be as slow as fifty beats per minute. Abnormally slow beats may also occur in jaundice, underactivity of the thyroid gland and in certain forms of brain damage.

Heart disease

Because the role of the heart is crucial in the circulation of blood, disorders or diseases of this organ can have drastic effects on life. Deaths from heart disease account for a third of all deaths in western countries today. Many different diseases affect the heart: it may become inflamed, as in endocarditis and pericarditis; valves may be diseased or damaged; any abnormality in blood flow to the heart can cause serious heart disease – coronary thrombosis, for example; abnormal heart rhythm can be a sign of heart disease; and some heart disease is congenital (present at birth).

Heart diseases may show themselves in several ways. Cyanosis, or 'blueness', is caused by an excess of de-oxygenated blood and usually indicates that something is wrong with the circulation. 'Blue babies', for instance, have abnormalities of the heart such as holes in the interatrial or interventricular septa which allow the mixing of venous and arterial blood. Another sign of cardiovascular abnormality is 'clubbing' in the fingers and toes, when the ends of the digits become swollen. The cause of this phenomenon is unknown, but it is found in endocarditis, inflammation of the endocardium (the lining of the heart), and in certain lung diseases.

Coronary heart disease

Coronary heart disease, the biggest killer in affluent countries, is also one of the most preventable causes of death, since dietary habits and smoking are major causes. Coronary heart disease is disease of the heart's own blood vessels, and it is also referred to as coronary artery disease or ischaemic heart disease.

Angina

Angina is a symptom of coronary heart disease rather than a disease in its own right. It can also be caused by high blood pressure, but the main problem is a lack of oxygen reaching part of the heart muscle. Angina pectoris, to give it its full name, is felt as a sharp pain in the chest, often occurring during physical exertion. Narrowing of the coronary blood vessels prevents sufficient blood and oxygen getting to the heart muscle.

Several drugs are used to control angina: beta-blockers are often prescribed to slow down the heart rate and so reduce the amount of oxygen the heart muscle needs. Other drugs work by increasing the blood supply, and therefore the oxygen available to the heart. When angina is found to be the result of severe narrowing of the coronary vessels, surgery may be used to overcome it. An operation that replaces narrowed vessels by grafting healthy blood vessels or artificial tubes – coronary artery bypass – is increasingly popular and successful.

Coronary thrombosis (heart attack)

If there is a sudden blockage of a coronary vessel supplying blood to the heart muscle, or myocardium, the portion of the heart affected will die (myocardial infarction). The seriousness depends on where the blockage or infarct occurs: only one small part of the heart may be affected, in which case the person may survive the heart attack even though a part of the heart does not work. If, however, the blockage halts the blood supply to a large area of the myocardium it may be fatal.

The main cause of coronary thrombosis is atheroma, a thickening of the blood-vessel walls by fatty and calcium deposits, or plaques. This thickening causes the blood to

common sites of coronary thrombosis

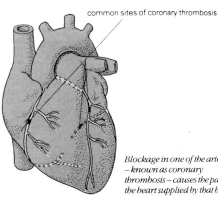

Blockage in one of the arteries – known as coronary thrombosis – causes the part of the heart supplied by that blood vessel to die.

slow down so that it clots and blocks the artery which may already be narrowed by arteriosclerosis (described below). Alternatively, a piece of the fatty material may break off and have the same effect. The causes of atheroma and its related conditions are described later in this section.

Coronary thrombosis is the largest single cause of death in the western world, and a major cause of illness. For every fatal heart attack there are two or more where the victims survive. Men are more likely than women to have a heart attack, and it is most common in the forty to forty-five age group. It can happen at any age, however.

Symptoms
A heart attack usually comes without warning, and the main symptom is likely to be pain. This is relatively constant and is felt in the centre of the chest beneath the breast bone, probably spreading out to one or both arms and sometimes the neck and jaw. Weakness, giddiness and breathlessness may accompany the pain, depending on how severe the damage is. The degree of pain may vary from a dull ache to a feeling of tightness to a crushing, vice-like gripping sensation.

Immediately after a heart attack, the victim is usually pale and still, but he or she may be restless, sweating or anxious. In a so-called 'silent' coronary thrombosis, which occurs mainly in the elderly, there is no pain, but there may be weakness, shortness of breath and giddiness. This may have been preceded by a period of unusual tiredness, lassitude and general malaise. Occasionally, though, even these symptoms are absent and the fact that a heart attack has occurred is only discovered during a routine medical examination, when abnormally low blood pressure or abnormal electrocardiogram traces indicate the possibility. The exact diagnosis relies on electrocardiograph examination and blood tests which may show chemical disturbances or changes in the white blood count.

Treatment and recovery
A heart attack is an emergency and needs prompt medical attention, even if symptoms are mild. One of the dangers of coronary thrombosis is cardiac arrest, where the heart stops beating. This may be caused by a sudden failure of the heart's conducting system (heart block). If the affected person is unconscious, external chest compression and artificial resuscitation should be started. In every case, stay with the heart attack victim until medical help arrives.

Most people are hospitalized after a heart attack, and treated according to its severity. Many who appear to have had a very severe attack make a smooth recovery and have no further signs of coronary disease. However, there may be complications and treatment is designed to anticipate these and to deal promptly with any that do arise.

Intensive care units, where the vital functions are monitored continuously, have revolutionized the treatment of coronary thrombosis. In these, specially trained medical staff are backed up by cardiac monitoring devices, respirators and apparatus for reversing any abnormal heart rhythm which may develop, and for stimulating the heart if it ceases to beat. However, although intensive care units are often essential, in some cases treatment at home may be preferred, particularly for elderly people.

The pain of a coronary attack, which seldom persists for long, can be treated with pain-killing drugs. In severe cases oxygen is given for the first few days, either in a tent or by face mask. Common complications during the early stages of recovery are disturbances in cardiac rhythm, shock and heart failure. The most dangerous arrhythmia is ventricular fibrillation, where the ventricles begin to contract very rapidly, and which may be fatal. Heart block, sudden cardiac arrest caused by a failure of the electrical conducting mechanism, is another hazard. Both of these conditions can be treated with electrical apparatus, heart massage and drugs. If they recur, drug treatment or the fitting of a heart pacemaker, which stimulates the heart regularly, can be useful.

The period of convalescence after a heart attack depends on the person's age and previous health, as well as the severity of the attack. Most people, once out of intensive care, are actively encouraged to take gentle exercise to speed their recovery. This can be positively beneficial to the damaged heart. Many people are, not surprisingly, shocked and frightened after having suffered a heart attack. But most can be encouraged to lead a normal life and do not have to feel they are invalids. It is, however, important to reduce the chance of a further heart attack by improving one's lifestyle. For most people, this means stopping smoking and losing weight, and in particular cutting down on the amount of fat in the diet (see *Preventing Heart Disease*, pages 164-7).

Congenital heart disease
A number of heart disorders may be present at birth, although some are not detected until later in life. These congenital heart defects range from small holes, which may heal of their own accord and cause few symptoms, to major abnormalities of the heart that are potentially fatal.

Patent ductus arteriosus
Patent ductus arteriosus is a condition in which a blood vessel that forms a short-cut in the fetal circulation does not close as it should immediately after birth. The vessel may close by itself a few weeks after birth, but if it does not surgery usually has to be performed. The outcome is good in almost every case.

Surgical correction is possible for both these congenital defects.

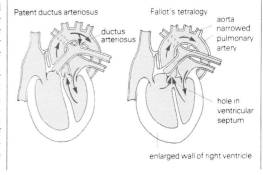

Patent ductus arteriosus

ductus arteriosus

Fallot's tetralogy

aorta narrowed

pulmonary artery

hole in ventricular septum

enlarged wall of right ventricle

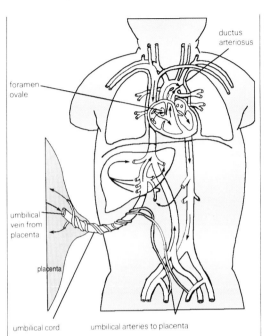

ductus
arteriosus

foramen
ovale

umbilical
vein from
placenta

placenta

umbilical cord   umbilical arteries to placenta

*Fetal blood circulation. The foramen ovale, an opening between
the right and left atria, allows some blood to go straight into the
systemic circulation. Blood that does reach the right ventricle
passes to the systemic circulation via the ductus arteriosus, a
connection between the pulmonary artery and the aorta.
Congenital heart disease is mostly because these openings fail to
close after birth.*

Septal defects

Two of the more common disorders are ventricular septal
defect and atrial septal defect. These are holes in the
septum, the muscular wall between the two ventricles and
the two atria. Surgery is needed only if there is a large hole
which fails to close of its own accord.

Fallot's tetralogy

Fallot's tetralogy, the commonest cause of cyanosis in
infants, is more serious. In this condition there are four
separate abnormalities: a narrowing of the pulmonary valve
(pulmonary stenosis), an enlargement of the right ventricle,
a large hole in the ventricular septum, and the septum
shifted farther left than it should be. Blood low in oxygen,
dammed back in the right ventricle, thus gets into the left
side of the heart and passes into the aorta to be circulated
round the body. The child looks blue because the blood
never becomes properly oxygenated. The condition may
not be diagnosed until almost a year old, however, but
unless symptoms are severe, surgery is usually delayed in
any case until this age, although it can be done earlier. In the
operation the ventricular septal defect is closed and the
stenosis eliminated. Most such children live to adulthood
and lead almost normal lives.

Damaged valves

If the valves of the heart become damaged or diseased, poor
circulation can result. Valvular incompetence means that
one or more of the heart valves becomes slack and does not
close properly. Mitral valve incompetence, for example,
when the valve separating the left atrium from the left
ventricle does not completely close, causes blood to leak
back into the atrium during contraction of the heart. If the
aortic valve becomes incompetent, blood will flow back
from the aorta into the left ventricle. This can be heard with
a stethoscope as a high-pitched murmur.

A more common condition is valve stenosis, when the
flaps of the heart valve stick together or the opening
becomes narrowed. Sometimes this can be treated with
drugs, but in severe cases surgery is needed. The damaged
valve may be replaced by an artificial one or by grafted
tissue from another part of the body.

Rheumatic fever during childhood is the chief cause of
damage to the heart valves, although it is far less common in
affluent countries than it used to be. The condition is caused
by streptococcal bacteria infecting the throat and working
their way down to the heart, but it rarely occurs now that
throat infections are treated effectively with antibiotics.
Symptoms of rheumatic fever include a high temperature,
painful joints, a skin rash and painless nodules under the
skin. In some cases the heart becomes inflamed, and this
initiates the process of valve damage, which may not cause
symptoms until as much as twenty years later. The mitral
valve is most commonly affected, although all the heart
valves may become either stenosed or incompetent because of the disease.

Heart failure

When the efficiency of the heart in its action as a pump is
reduced, by disease of the heart muscle or malfunctioning
of the valves, this is known as heart failure. It usually but not
always affects both sides of the heart, and fluid tends to
accumulate in the veins as a result. The term congestive
heart failure is given to the condition when the whole of the
heart is affected. In left-sided failure, blood returning from
the lungs accumulates. The lungs become waterlogged and
swollen, and this causes the main symptom of breathlessness. In right-sided heart failure, fluid tends to accumulate
in the rest of the body instead, especially in the legs, causing
swelling (oedema). In bedridden patients the swelling may
be most noticeable in the lower back. Right-sided heart
failure may also cause the internal organs to become
swollen, causing pain.

Treatment

All types of heart failure put a great strain on the heart which
can be fatal, but depending on its underlying cause, treatment of heart failure can in certain cases result in complete
recovery. Diuretic drugs remove excess fluid from the body
by increasing urinary output. Rest is also important, but care
must be taken to exercise the leg muscles to maintain
circulation and prevent thrombosis (page 160). With drug
treatment, the symptoms of breathlessness and swelling
should subside, but if the heart fails to respond to drugs and
rest, transplantation may be the only possible treatment
(see page 158).

Heart transplants

Heart transplantation is the ultimate therapy for someone with severe heart disease. Although results of transplants are better now than they used to be, the operation is still very dangerous and so is only performed on people who would otherwise certainly die.

As with all transplant operations, the main problem is rejection of the new organ by the body. When a person receives a new heart, it is immediately treated as an invader by the body's defence mechanism which sets out to destroy it (see The Immune System and Allergies, *page 202). Immunosuppressive drugs, those that suppress the immune system, therefore have to be taken for the rest of the patient's life, to prevent rejection of the new organ. Unfortunately they also leave the body open to attack by bacteria and viruses. The drug dosage must be carefully regulated and any infections promptly treated. Some heart-transplant patients have lived for several years after the operation, leading near-normal lives.*

Pericarditis

Viral infection or rheumatic fever may occasionally cause inflammation of the pericardium. Acute pericarditis is usually mild, but sometimes there is a build-up of fluid between the membrane and the heart, causing pressure on the heart itself. This fluid can be removed by a needle and syringe if it builds up to a dangerous level, but the inflammation usually subsides of its own accord within about two weeks or so.

Constrictive pericarditis is a more dangerous long-standing condition, usually the result of some chronic disease such as tuberculosis. Prolonged inflammation leads to heart failure, with swelling of the legs and abdomen caused by the accumulation of fluid. The only cure is surgery, to remove the thickening of the pericardium.

Cardiomyopathy

Cardiomyopathy (disease of the heart muscle) includes several uncommon disorders, some the result of nutritional failure including alcoholism, and others the result of inflammation as a complication of some infectious disease. Treatment depends on the underlying cause of the condition; cardiomyopathy is one of the main diseases for which heart transplantation is carried out.

Disorders of heart rhythm

Extrasystole

Alteration in the rhythm of the heartbeat (arrhythmia) occurs when contractions occur prematurely in the ventricles. This abnormal beat, or extrasystole, arises somewhere in the heart muscle other than the sinoatrial node. Because the beat occurs earlier than expected there is a long interval (the compensatory pause), while the heart recovers and then beats normally. This feels as if the heart has 'skipped a beat' and is not dangerous; it occurs in normal people after a stressful event such as anxiety, surgery or a feverish illness. Sometimes the extrasystole is not even noticed.

Sinus arrhythmia and paroxysmal atrial tachycardia

In some people the heartbeat varies in rhythm, especially with the breathing rate. This condition, called sinus arrhythmia, is particularly common in children and young adults, becoming less common with age. The heart rate may also suddenly become very rapid, up to 200 beats per minute, and this is termed paroxysmal atrial tachycardia. After a time, which can vary from minutes to days, the rate suddenly returns to normal. People with this disorder do not normally have heart disease in the usual sense; they often find that pressing on an eyeball or drinking iced water will stop the attack, and there are drugs available on prescription that can help.

Atrial fibrillation

Atrial fibrillation, occurring most frequently in arteriosclerosis, is a condition in which the sinoatrial node has lost all control over the heartbeat. The beat then originates from several parts of the atria, which gives rise to a completely irregular pulse. The ventricles are bombarded with more than 400 electrical impulses a minute, but cannot respond to each one and beat irregularly at 80 to 160 times a minute. Like the very similar condition of atrial flutter (which is much less common), it can be treated with drugs, and vast numbers of people lead normal lives with these conditions.

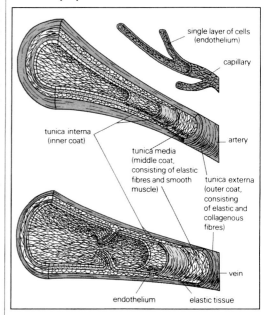

The fine structure of a capillary, an artery and a vein. In each case the structure is related to the vessel's function: capillaries are thin-walled to allow the exchange of nutrients and wastes between the blood and tissue cells; arteries have thick elastic and muscular walls to cope with variations in blood pressure; and veins, which carry blood of a more constant and lower pressure, have thinner walls as well as valves to stop blood flowing backwards because of gravity.

Heart block

If the conducting system joining the atria and the ventricles fails to function properly, this gives rise to a condition known as heart block. It may be partial or complete. If it is only partial, there may be no symptoms. In complete heart block the atria and ventricles contract independently at their own rates, known as idiopathic rhythm. Occasionally, the ventricles may cease to contract at all for a few seconds, and the consequent lack of blood supplying the brain causes brief loss of consciousness (Stokes-Adams attack).

Some people with this disabling condition can lead a normal life with the help of an artificial cardiac pacemaker. This device, implanted in the chest during a short surgical operation, replaces the irregular or absent heartbeat with a regular artificial one, by stimulating the atria with electrical impulses fed from it through electrodes. Most pacemakers have a life of up to twelve years. People with a pacemaker are checked regularly to ensure that it is functioning correctly. Pacemakers can correct bradycardia but not tachycardia, which is usually an abnormality of the patient's own heart rhythm rather than a fault of the pacemaker.

The blood vessels

The blood vessels – arteries, capillaries and veins – allow the continuous circulation of blood to every organ and tissue of the body. The blood leaves the heart through the aorta which then branches into arteries going to the arms, neck and head. As these arteries pass down the length of the body more branches come off them to supply the internal organs, legs and feet. Blood is returned to the heart through veins which finally join the superior and inferior venae cavae.

Arteries

Oxygenated blood is pumped from the left ventricle of the heart into the arteries of the systemic circulation. The arteries have thick walls that contain muscle and elastic tissue, which allows them both to contract and to expand. Arteries generally travel on the inner surfaces of bones where they are protected from possible damage.

Capillaries

In the organs and tissues the arteries branch into narrower vessels called arterioles, which in turn branch into the even narrower capillaries. At the entrance to each capillary is a ring of muscle which can shut off the blood flow through that capillary.

A capillary is a tube with a wall only one cell thick, with small holes, or pores, between the cells. Water and oxygen can easily diffuse through the cells to and from the tissues. Other substances, such as glucose, amino acids and proteins, pass through the pores. In the same ways substances such as hormones and waste products such as carbon dioxide and urea can pass into the capillaries from the tissues.

Veins

After passing through the capillaries, blood returns to the heart through the veins. Veins have thinner walls than arteries, containing less muscle and elastic tissue. The blood in veins is, with the exception of the pulmonary vein, low in oxygen and under low pressure. Veins are wider than arteries and many contain valves to prevent blood flowing backwards and to help return blood to the heart. When the muscle of the skeleton surrounding the veins contracts, the blood is squeezed along the vessels towards the heart. When the muscle relaxes, the valves close and prevent the blood returning the way it has come. Thus, if the muscle contracts frequently, as during walking or exercise, blood is forced back to the heart.

The portal system

A particular part of the systemic circulation is the portal system which, unlike all the other blood vessel systems in the body, does not take blood either to or from the heart. Instead, the portal vein drains blood from the intestine and its associated organs (the spleen, pancreas and gall bladder) and conveys it to the liver (see *The Digestive System*, page 100). This blood is rich in food substances absorbed from the intestine which are metabolized in the liver by many enzymes. From the liver, this blood enters the hepatic veins which, in turn, drain into the normal venous system.

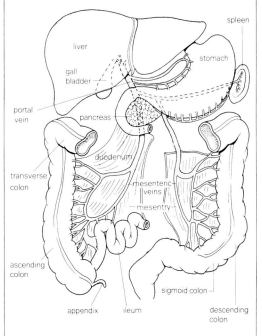

The portal circulation: the portal vein drains deoxygenated blood, rich in nutrients from digested food, from the alimentary canal, and carries it to the liver. There, many nutrients are metabolized, into a form in which they can be stored, for example, and harmful substances detoxified. The portal vein is the only vein in the body to carry deoxygenated blood to rather than from an organ.

Diseases of the blood vessels

Arteriosclerosis and atherosclerosis

Arteriosclerosis (hardening of the arteries) describes several types of changes in the arteries. The arteries of middle-aged and old people often become hardened and narrow and thus less efficient at pumping blood around the body. Arteriosclerosis in association with atheroma is called atherosclerosis. This disease, which principally involves the large and medium-sized arteries, is characterized by the deposition of fatty deposits (in patches or plaques) on the arterial walls. As these patches develop, calcium is laid down in them, tissue is destroyed and bleeding occurs into the wall of the artery. These changes lead to a gradual narrowing of the channel which results in a reduction of blood flow to the tissues supplied by that artery.

Under the age of sixty, atherosclerosis is commoner in men than women, for the female hormone oestrogen protects women against it. Obesity, diabetes, a sedentary life, large amounts of animal fats in the diet and smoking are all associated with atherosclerosis. But it can and often does occur in young adults and even children. Very rarely are there any symptoms, however. If this condition affects the heart vessels it leads to coronary artery disease (described on page 155).

With increasing age, fatty deposits can also appear in the arteries of the brain. Because these vessels are small in diameter, any narrowing of their bore reduces the blood flow considerably. Since the brain is very sensitive to any reduction in its blood supply, it responds immediately, producing attacks of dizziness, faintness, tingling in the arms and fingers, muscular weakness and visual disturbances. Although these attacks usually last only a short time, they tend to recur, as transient ischaemic attacks. In older people the symptoms progressively worsen and will eventually be permanent. Thus, although it used to be thought that all strokes (see page 196) were caused by clots blocking brain arteries, it is now known that many are caused by this slow narrowing.

Two procedures are now available to overcome these blocks in the arteries supplying the brain. One is an operation called endarterectomy in which the diseased inner layers of the artery are removed. The other procedure involves bypassing the blocked segment of the diseased vessel with a tube of plastic or other synthetic material. Such bypasses are very successful in suitable cases.

Thrombosis

Thrombosis is the clotting of blood in a blood vessel or an organ; the clot of blood is known as a thrombus. Both arteries and veins can be affected by thrombosis.

In arteries, it can be caused by atheroma or damage as a result of an accident or surgery. The disruption of the blood flow to the organ or tissue supplied by the affected artery may lead to the death of that part of the body, as in coronary thrombosis (see page 155) and cerebral thrombosis (see page 197).

Thrombosis in veins is much more common than in arteries. If the thrombus remains in the vein it can cause inflammation (phlebitis) of the vein wall and surrounding

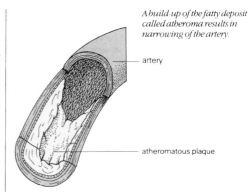

A build-up of the fatty deposit called atheroma results in narrowing of the artery.

— artery

— atheromatous plaque

tissue. Prolonged confinement in bed, a long and debilitating illness or the period after surgical operations all produce conditions that promote the development of thrombosis, particularly in veins, by affecting the blood flow and the clotting mechanism of blood.

Deep vein thrombosis (DVT) occurs when the thrombus forms in a vein deep inside the body, most commonly in the legs. The calf or thigh may become swollen because the clot prevents blood and fluids draining away. The condition can lead to a potentially fatal pulmonary embolism (see below). As with all types of thrombosis, to prevent DVT developing it is important to keep one's weight down and to be as active as possible. DVT is treated with drugs which prevent clots extending.

Thrombus formation also occurs in certain blood disorders (see *Blood and Lymph*, page 142). Oral contraceptive pills, particularly those with high levels of the hormone oestrogen, may cause venous thrombosis, and as low an oestrogen dose as possible is recommended for all women taking the Pill. Venous thrombosis may also occur as a complication of infectious diseases such as typhoid fever, tuberculosis, poliomyelitis and encephalitis.

Once formed, a thrombus may gradually break down naturally and a new network of blood vessels (collateral circulation) develops around the blockage and helps to keep the tissues alive.

Embolism

An embolus is any clump of material – a globule of fat, gas bubble or a clump of blood cells – that is carried in the bloodstream until it lodges in a vessel, blocking the flow of blood. An embolus originates in a different part of the body from the place where it actually blocks a vessel. A thrombus stays at the site where it originates, but a piece can break off to form an embolus, and venous thrombosis is particularly dangerous because of this possibility.

An air embolism – a bubble of air in the veins – can be fatal, since it is churned up with the blood in the venous circulation to form an air-lock in the heart and blood vessels. This may occur through, for example, a cut throat or through injection with a syringe, or if there are great changes in pressure such as when a deep-sea diver surfaces too quickly (bubbles of nitrogen are set free throughout the tissues and blood, causing the 'bends'). Excruciating pain occurs in the muscles and joints, and death may result if the blood supply to essential organs is disrupted.

Many other forms of embolism may occur. Multiple fractures can push fat from the bone marrow into the bloodstream, and clumps of bacteria may break away from the original point of infection and get into the bloodstream.

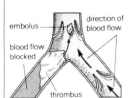

A thrombus is a blood clot within a blood vessel. If part or all of it breaks off and is carried in the bloodstream, it is known as an embolus.

direction of blood flow
embolus
blood flow blocked
thrombus

The effect of an embolus depends on its location. For example, an embolus lodging in a blood vessel in the brain will cause a stroke, and if the blockage is in the lungs – a pulmonary embolism – sudden death can result (see *The Respiratory System*, page 84).

Treatment
The best treatment for both thrombosis and embolism is prevention. Exercise after surgical operations helps to reduce the risk of venous thrombosis. People with arteriosclerosis should avoid injuries to the arteries by knocks or crushing. In some cases the blood vessel can be opened and the blockage removed, or a bypass operation can be performed in which an artificial artery is used to allow blood to flow around the obstruction.

Aneurysm
Sometimes an area of a blood vessel may balloon out like a weak area on a tyre. This is called an aneurysm, and it occurs at a point where the blood vessel is weakest. It may result from disease, injury or atherosclerosis. Although an aneurysm can occur in any vessel, it is most common and most troublesome when it appears in the arteries of the neck and head or in the aorta. An aneurysm may gradually

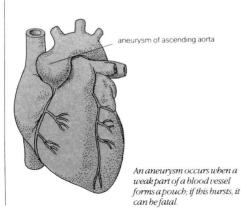

aneurysm of ascending aorta

An aneurysm occurs when a weak part of a blood vessel forms a pouch; if this bursts, it can be fatal.

enlarge and if it bursts will often cause fatal massive internal bleeding. Some aneurysms cause a throbbing sensation and a lump might be seen or felt. In the chest it may cause hoarseness and chest pain. Often the individual is not aware of the aneurysm until it bursts. If the aneurysm is detected early, it may be possible to tie off the distorted part of the blood vessel surgically.

Varicose veins
The flow of blood upwards against gravity in the legs is maintained by the pumping action of the leg muscles and by the presence of valves in the veins which allow blood to flow upwards but not downwards. In a varicose vein one or more of the vein's valves becomes faulty, so that blood collects in the vessel and causes it to swell.

Standing up a great deal does not in itself cause varicose veins but can encourage the condition to start. Similarly, in pregnancy, the extra demands put upon the circulation by the fetus can also trigger the development of varicose veins.

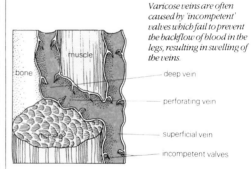

Varicose veins are often caused by 'incompetent' valves which fail to prevent the backflow of blood in the legs, resulting in swelling of the veins.

muscle
bone
deep vein
perforating vein
superficial vein
incompetent valves

Symptoms
The first symptom is a prominent, blue, swollen vein in the leg. Because of the stagnation of blood in varicose veins, tissue fluid is not absorbed properly and the leg also becomes swollen and discoloured. A complication is varicose eczema, caused by scratching of the irritated skin over the swollen veins (see *Dermatitis and eczema*, page 75).
The eczema causes further irritation and may spread to other parts of the body. Another complication of varicose veins is leg ulcers, which are a result of slow healing of a wound because of the poor blood circulation.

Because the blood in a varicose vein is moving slowly it may clot and form a thrombus, leading to phlebitis. This is dangerous because it can result in an embolus breaking off and blocking an artery elsewhere in the body.

Treatment
Treatment of varicose veins consists of resting with the legs raised to reduce the effect of gravity, and wearing firm-support elastic stockings or bandages. The only long-term cure for large varicose veins is surgical removal of the swollen veins (stripping) through small incisions in the skin. Smaller veins are treated by injections. The blood then returns through other veins in the leg, which take over the function of the removed vein. Any skin changes can be treated using a solution of the salt potassium permanganate.

Fainting

Fainting, a sudden and dramatic but temporary loss of consciousness, is caused by insufficient blood going to the brain. If blood becomes pooled in different parts of the circulation and is not available for pumping to the brain, fainting will result. Immediately after the person has fallen to the ground, he or she usually regains consciousness, since the pooled blood no longer has to defy gravity to flow back to the heart, and can readily return to be pumped to the brain.

There are many possible reasons why a person may faint. One cause is a sudden drop in blood pressure (see below); another is over-breathing because of stress or anxiety; and shock, when blood is diverted away from the brain to the muscles, is another. Hot, stuffy conditions may lead to heat exhaustion and fainting. Emotional upsets can also cause faintness.

Haemorrhage

This is the medical term for bleeding, the loss of blood from the vessels. It may be external or internal and can arise from arteries, veins or capillaries.

External haemorrhage

Arterial bleeding occurs in powerful jets, and each surge of blood is in time with the pulse. The blood is bright red because it is transporting oxygen to the body tissues. Arterial bleeding can be very dangerous because of the speed at which blood is lost. Haemorrhage from a vein is likely to be very dark red or almost bluish, and tends to be a continuous dark flow from the depths of a wound. Capillary haemorrhage is rarely serious: it is merely the ordinary type of bleeding seen when the skin is cut or grazed.

Internal haemorrhage

Internal bleeding is uncommon and usually occurs in accident victims. It can also be the result of disease and usually needs rapid medical attention. Vomiting of blood (haematemesis) may be caused by intestinal bleeding from an ulcer or peritonitis, for example. Blood which is coughed up (haemoptysis) is usually either bright red or pink and frothy. Although the amount of blood actually lost is small, medical advice should be sought. Blood in the sputum could be a sign of pneumonia, pulmonary embolism, pulmonary oedema, lung cancer or TB (see pages 92-5). Haemorrhage from the urinary passage almost invariably involves passing blood-stained urine, but severe blood loss in urine is almost unknown, and is not an emergency, though a doctor should be consulted.

In hidden internal haemorrhage, the only signs and symptoms may be those of loss of blood. A sudden but relatively slight internal blood loss (up to ten per cent of total blood volume) will probably produce no more than a feeling of faintness. After a loss of up to forty per cent the patient turns extremely pale and feels light-headed. The skin is cold and clammy, and the pulse fast and difficult to feel because the blood pressure will have dropped quite markedly. Internal haemorrhage of over forty per cent of

blood volume produces restlessness, extreme pallor, and rapid, gasping breathing and breathlessness. There is intense thirst and fear at first, followed by apathy as blood loss increases and death approaches.

Blood pressure

The force of the heart beating propels blood through the blood vessels, so that the moving blood exerts pressure on the walls of the arteries and veins, and this is what is known as the blood pressure. If the force with which the heart pumps the blood is too great or too little to maintain a steady blood flow, blood pressure is too high or too low.

Measuring blood pressure

Blood pressure is measured in an artery, usually the brachial artery of the arm, using an instrument called a sphygmomanometer. This consists of an inflatable rubber cuff attached by a tube either to a column of mercury or to a dial which measures the pressure. The cuff is positioned above the elbow and is inflated until the brachial artery is squeezed shut. A stethoscope is then placed at the bend of the elbow over the artery, or the pulse at the wrist is felt. At this stage, no sound can be heard in the artery or pulse felt. As the air in the cuff is released slowly, reducing the pressure, a point is reached when the blood begins to flow through the artery and this can be heard as a sharp sound in the stethoscope, or felt at the pulse. The pressure at this point is the highest in the artery, the systolic blood pressure, and occurs as the heart's ventricles contract and push out blood. As more air is released, the cuff pressure falls further and more blood flows through the artery, the sound in the artery disappears. The pressure at this point represents the diastolic or resting pressure in the artery.

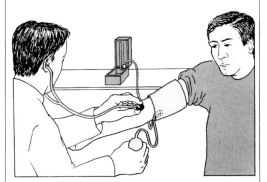

Measurement of the blood pressure is a simple procedure which involves inflating a cuff around the upper arm, and then gradually releasing the pressure of the cuff while the appropriate sounds in the artery are heard with a stethoscope.

The pressures are measured as millimetres (mm) of mercury (Hg), and a 'normal' blood pressure for a twenty-to-forty-year-old person is 120mm Hg systolic pressure and 80mm Hg diastolic pressure. This is expressed as

120/80mm Hg, or '120 over 80'. Blood pressure tends to increase with age and is usually higher in men than in women, but can vary considerably between healthy people. Systolic pressure in a healthy person is estimated as age in years plus a hundred.

Low blood pressure (hypotension)

Chronic low blood pressure, or hypotension, is rare and can be considered to occur when the systolic pressure is less than 105mm Hg. It is hardly ever serious unless it is a feature of an underlying disorder such as Addison's disease (see page 184). The most common type of low blood pressure is postural hypotension, which sometimes occurs if a person rises quickly from a sitting or lying position, causing dizziness or faintness. Sometimes this happens if a drug being taken to treat hypertension (high blood pressure) is taken at too high a dose. It can also occur in pregnancy and diabetes.

High blood pressure (hypertension)

High blood pressure is very common and is generally considered to be present when the blood pressure is more than 140/90 (except in the elderly), although at this level treatment is not always necessary. It is a disease mainly of middle and old age, rarely occurring before the age of twenty. If it does occur in the young age group, it is usually caused by kidney disease. Over the age of twenty, hypertension is very common, especially in the western world. As much as twenty-five per cent of the population may be hypertensive in some countries, and the incidence rises with age.

High blood pressure puts a strain on the heart and may cause heart disease. People with high blood pressure are also more likely to suffer a stroke. For these reasons it is important that hypertension is treated, even though there are often no obvious symptoms.

There are two types of hypertension. In essential hypertension, the most common type, the blood pressure is raised for no obvious reason. Secondary hypertension occurs as a side-effect of some other diseases such as an hormonal disorder or kidney disease. The contraceptive pill and some other drugs can also cause hypertension. Treatment of the underlying condition is needed to relieve the hypertension in these cases.

Essential hypertension often runs in families; a child of a hypertensive parent has a considerably greater chance of developing hypertension than children with no such family history. It is also more common in overweight people and in diabetics.

Symptoms

Hypertension usually develops slowly without symptoms over several years. Very rarely, it develops rapidly and can be dangerous unless promptly treated. This is sometimes known as 'malignant' hypertension although it has nothing to do with cancer.

In hypertension the diastolic blood pressure is more significant than the systolic pressure. A person with a diastolic pressure of more than 90mm Hg might be considered mildly hypertensive; a pressure of between 100 and 110 is moderately hypertensive; above this, hypertension is generally considered severe and potentially dangerous.

Hypertension eventually results in the small arteries throughout the body becoming constricted, and the walls may become thickened. This decreases the amount of blood they can carry, so that organs requiring a very large volume of blood in order to function properly also become diseased.

As the blood vessels narrow, the heart has to pump harder to push the blood round the circulatory system, and it soon increases in size to cope with this extra work-load. Eventually, however, the strain may be too much for the heart, which becomes less and less efficient at pumping the blood through the arteries, leading to heart failure (see page 157). Hypertensive heart disease is frequently associated with atherosclerosis of the arteries supplying blood to the heart, and hypertension also hastens the progress of atherosclerosis. With this combination, there may be a chest pain brought on by physical exertion, and the affected person runs a greater risk of a heart attack.

Hypertension can also damage the kidneys, and this may first show itself by blood in the urine, and later by kidney failure and uraemia, the accumulation of waste products in the blood. Since this dangerous condition often goes undetected, it is important for people with high blood pressure to have regular medical check-ups.

Treatment

Although in many people hypertension does not show any obvious symptoms, because of the severity of possible complications arising directly from high blood pressure it is essential that it is treated. Sometimes this means taking a life-long course of drugs.

There are several self-help measures that can be taken to reduce blood pressure without drugs. The most important is to stop smoking, since this is a major cause of atherosclerosis and leads to high blood pressure. If you are overweight, go on a diet; in any case reduce the amount of fat in your diet. Salt has been found to be linked to high blood pressure, so reduce your salt intake as much as possible, by not adding salt to food at the table and giving up highly salted foods such as pickles. In addition, relaxation exercises and yoga-type techniques help reduce stress and anxiety and so lower blood pressure.

Whether drugs are given or not depends on the degree of hypertension. If you have mild or moderate hypertension you may simply be monitored regularly by your doctor, without drug treatment. Hypertension is usually treated if the diastolic pressure is above 105mm Hg.

Several different types of antihypertensive drugs might be prescribed, including beta-blockers which lower blood pressure by acting directly on the heart, slowing the heart rate. These are sometimes combined with diuretic drugs that increase the amount of water excreted from the body in the urine, preventing the build-up of fluid caused by the slowing of the heart rate. Other drugs widely used to treat high blood pressure include those that block the flow of calcium through blood-vessel walls, calcium ion antagonists. New drugs are being developed to treat hypertension, without the side-effects produced by the drugs now commonly used.

Preventing heart disease: what you can do

Researchers have studied entire populations to try to discover what it is that increases the risk of heart disease. Their results show that there is no single cause but several different factors that together may contribute to heart disease. Some people are more likely to suffer from heart disease than others: for example, the tendency can run in families; and older people are at risk because the narrowing of the arteries which can lead to angina and heart attacks tends to increase with age, although it may start in youth.

In general, men are more at risk from heart disease than women. A man in his late forties is five times more likely to die of heart disease than a woman of the same age. After the menopause, however, a woman loses the protective effect of her hormones and her chances of suffering from heart disease become almost as high as a man's. And in the last twenty years or so there has been an increase in the incidence of heart disease among women in their thirties and forties. Nevertheless, even though age, sex and family history are all beyond individual control, there is still a lot you can do to keep your risk of heart disease as low as possible.

High-risk living

When people think of taking risks they usually think of going hang-gliding, driving too fast or even crossing a busy road. But you might be taking a life-and-death risk every day without realizing it. By smoking, eating too much of the wrong food and not getting enough exercise and relaxation you could be gambling with the health of your heart.

Smoking

Cigarette smoking can double the risk of dying from a heart attack, and heavy smokers are even more likely to die young from heart disease. A person of fifty who smokes more than twenty cigarettes a day is four times more likely to suffer from heart disease than a non-smoker of the same age; and the risk for a woman is particularly high if she is over thirty-five and on the pill.

Smoking affects the heart by increasing the pulse rate and raising the blood pressure. The carbon monoxide content of cigarette smoke cuts down the amount of oxygen in the blood, so the heart has to work harder but gets less oxygen. Smoking also accelerates the 'furring up' of the coronary arteries. For more information on the dangers of smoking, see pages 96-7.

The obvious answer is to give up smoking. As soon as you stop smoking you will start to reduce your risk of a heart attack, and you could be almost back to a non-smoker's risk level within a few years. Giving up altogether is not easy but it is certainly worth it. By stopping, not only do you improve your chances of avoiding heart trouble, but you also gain in other ways: you will be able to breathe more easily, for example when climbing stairs or running for a bus; you will suffer fewer colds and infections; you and your home will smell fresher; and you will save money.

Diet

Another way to reduce your risk of heart disease is to watch what you eat. Your daily choice of food can be a key factor in the health of your heart. First, consult the chart on page 229 to see what you should weigh. The more overweight you are, the more likely is the possibility of developing high blood pressure or diabetes, both of which can lead to heart attacks and angina.

The most likely reason for overweight is that you are simply eating too much of the wrong sorts of food, that is, too many fatty and sugary foods and not enough fibre. Fat and sugar are loaded with calories, and fat can also push up your blood cholesterol level, accelerating the build-up of atheroma that eventually leads to heart disease. (Use the opposite table to help you decide where you can cut down on the fat in your diet.) Fibre, a whole range of complex plant substances, provides roughage, which not only aids digestion and helps prevent constipation but also seems to stop too much fat and sugar getting into the bloodstream too quickly, and to help keep the blood cholesterol level down. In addition, fibre can give satisfying bulk to a meal without adding too many calories. The lists below show sources of fibre.

High-fibre foods	Medium-fibre foods	Low-fibre foods	No-fibre foods
Bananas	Apples	Cucumber	Butter
Beans, like baked beans	Brown bread	Grapefruit	Cheese
Bran and bran cereal	Celery	Lettuce	Eggs
Brown rice	Cornflakes	Porridge	Fish
Dried fruit	Most green vegetables	Potatoes, boiled	Meat
Leafy vegetables, like spinach	Most nuts	Tomatoes	Milk
Peas	Muesli	White bread	Sugar
Potatoes, with skins	Oranges	White rice	
Rye crispbread			
Stewed prunes			
Sweetcorn			
Wholemeal bread and flour			
Wholewheat pasta			

Assessing your risk of heart disease

The table below* can be used to calculate your chances of suffering from heart disease at some time in the future, taking into account all the known risk factors. The degree of risk depends on the combined total of several separate factors, one shown at the top of each column in the table. Within each column are six risk categories.

SEX	BLOOD PRESSURE	FAT IN DIET	EXERCISE	TOBACCO SMOKING	WEIGHT	HEREDITY	AGE
Female under 40 1	100 (upper reading) 1	Diet contains no animal or solid fats 1	Intensive work and recreational exertion 2	Non-user 0	More than 5 lb below standard weight 0	No known history of heart disease 1	10 to 20 1
Female 40-50 2	120 (upper reading) 2	Diet contains soft margarine, no fried food 2	Moderate work and recreational exertion 2	Cigar and/ or pipe 1	−5 to +5 lb standard weight 1	1 relative over 60 with cardiovascular disease 2	21 to 30 2
Female over 50 3	140 (upper reading) 3	Diet contains some butter or hard margarine, some fried food 3	Sedentary work and intense recreational exertion 3	10 cigarettes or less a day 2	6-20 lb overweight 2	2 relatives over 60 with cardiovascular disease 3	31 to 40 3
Male 5	160 (upper reading) 4	Diet contains a lot of butter, or hard margarine, or fried food 4	Sedentary work and moderate recreational exertion 5	20 cigarettes a day 4	21-35 lb overweight 3	1 relative under 60 with cardiovascular disease 4	41 to 50 4
Stocky male 6	180 (upper reading) 6	Daily diet contains butter, or hard margarine, or fried food 5	Sedentary work and light recreational exertion 6	30 cigarettes a day 6	36-50 lb overweight 5	2 relatives under 60 with cardiovascular disease 6	51 to 60 5
Bald stocky male 7	200 or over (upper reading) 8	Daily diet contains butter, or hard margarine, and fried food 7	Complete lack of all exercise 8	40 cigarettes a day or more 10	51-65 lb overweight 7	3 relatives under 60 with cardiovascular disease 7	61 to 70 and over 8

How to use the table

Study the different risk categories in each of the eight columns, mark the box in each one that applies to you, and then add up your score. In addition add one to your total if you are a smoker who inhales deeply and smokes to a short stub. It is thought that personality type also plays a part in the risk of heart disease, but this cannot be accurately gauged on a points system.

© Michigan Heart Association

Scores:

6 to 11 – well below average risk

12 to 17 – below average risk

18 to 24 – average risk

25 to 31 – moderate risk

32 to 40 – dangerous risk

41 to 63 – imminent danger: see your doctor

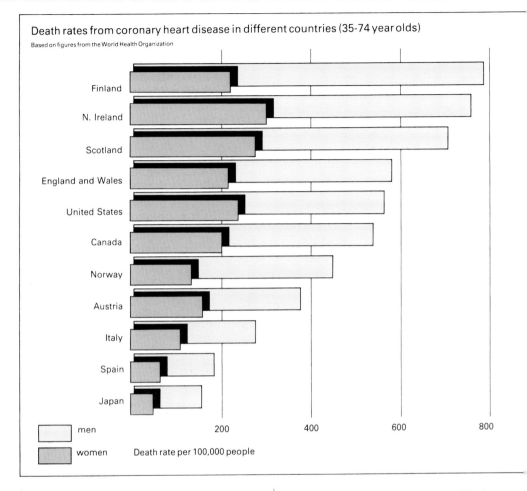

Death rates from coronary heart disease in different countries (35-74 year olds)

Based on figures from the World Health Organization

Finland
N. Ireland
Scotland
England and Wales
United States
Canada
Norway
Austria
Italy
Spain
Japan

200   400   600   800

men

women   Death rate per 100,000 people

High blood pressure

High blood pressure (see page 163) makes the heart work harder and increases the 'furring up' of the arteries, making angina or a heart attack more likely. The following are some of the things that might give you high blood pressure:

- *being overweight*
- *smoking*
- *drinking too much alcohol*
- *lack of regular exercise*
- *eating too much salt*
- *too much stress*

To help keep your blood pressure at a normal level, it therefore makes sense to take the following steps:

1 *Keep your weight at its correct level for your height.*

2 *Restrict alcohol consumption. Try not to drink more than two or three pints of beer or equivalent two or three times a week.*

3 *Take some exercise (see pages 98-9).*

4 *Eat less salt. Make it a habit not to salt your food, either during cooking or at the table.*

5 *Try to avoid too much stress, and learn how to relax (see pages 70-71).*

6 *Have your blood pressure measured regularly, especially if you are over thirty-five.*

How to reduce fat intake

There are two types of fat, saturated fat and unsaturated fat. All the different fats we eat are made up of different combinations of different fatty acids, most of which are high in saturates. Dietary experts believe that too much fatty food high in saturates can push up blood cholesterol, a factor that increases the chance of getting heart disease, and that we should cut the amount of saturated fats we eat by up to a half. Instead, we should choose food low in saturates, or 'high in polyunsaturates'. The following guidelines and the table of the fat in food, below, are designed to help you do this.

● *Eat less meat. Try fish or vegetable dishes. When you do eat meat, choose a leaner cut if possible, or eat chicken which has less fat than other meat. Always remove the visible fat from meat.*

● *Do not fry food; grill it instead.*

● *Switch from using lard and butter to polyunsaturated margarine and cooking oils, and use sparingly.*

● *Choose low-fat cheese, yogurt and milk rather than those high in fat.*

THE FAT IN FOOD

MEAT	PERCENTAGE FAT	CHEESE	PERCENTAGE FAT
Fried streaky bacon	45%	Cream cheeses	50%
Grilled streaky bacon	36%	Stilton	40%
Grilled lamb chops	29%	Cheddar	34%
Pork pie	27%	Parmesan	30%
Luncheon meat	27%	Processed cheese	25%
Liver sausage	27%	Camembert	23%
Roast lamb (shoulder)	26%	Edam	23%
Fried pork sausages	25%	Cheese spread	23%
Roast leg of pork	20%	Cottage cheese	4%
Fried beefburgers	17%		
Grilled rump steak	12%	**MILK, BUTTER, OILS**	
Casseroled pig's liver	8%	Oil (all kinds)	100%
Stewed steak	7%	Lard	99%
Casseroled chicken	7%	Butter	82%
Fried lamb's kidneys	6%	Margarine (all kinds)	80%
Tinned ham	5%	Double cream	50%
		Dairy ice-cream	7%
FISH		Gold-top milk	5%
Smoked mackerel	16%	Silver-top milk	4%
Fried fish fingers	13%	Yoghurt	1%
Grilled kippers	12%	Skimmed milk	Less than 1%
Cod fried in batter	10%		
Steamed plaice	2%		
Steamed haddock	1%		

The Senses

The world around us is full of different stimuli: lights, sounds, smells, tastes, heat and cold, contact, pressure and pain. Our senses enable us to detect the events occurring around us and to send this information to the brain, so that we can take suitable action. Of the five main senses, sight and hearing are probably the most important in daily living, and blindness and deafness are both severe handicaps.

Sight

The eyes are remarkable organs: they work in very bright and dim light; they can clearly see objects close to or far away; and they can distinguish an enormous variety of colours and shades.

The structure of the eyes

Each eye is a sphere about 2.5 cm (1 in) in diameter, filled with a jelly-like fluid that gives it its firmness. The eye is positioned in a bony socket, called the orbit, in the skull, and a ridge of bone above it (beneath the eyebrow) gives protection against blows. The movements of each eye are controlled by six muscles attached to each eyeball.

Each eye consists of three layers. The outermost layer is the sclera, visible as the white of the eye. It surrounds the eye except for the very front where there is a transparent window called the cornea, which bulges out slightly. The middle layer, called the choroid, is a thin pigmented layer rich in blood vessels that help to nourish the eye. At the front of the eye the choroid forms the iris which, depending on the way different pigments are deposited in it (as a result of genetic inheritance), determines the colour of the eye. The iris is made of muscle fibres that, by contracting or relaxing, can change the size of the pupil, the gap in the front of the eye. The choroid also forms the ciliary body, which, like the iris, consists of muscle, and is attached to the lens (suspended just behind the iris) by ligaments. The ciliary body alters the focusing shape of the lens.

The innermost layer of the eye is the retina, which consists of over a hundred million light-sensitive cells called rods and cones. Each rod and cone has its own nerve fibre and these fibres together form the optic nerve, which connects to the brain.

Inside the eye are two chambers. The larger one, behind the lens, is filled with a transparent jelly-like fluid, the vitreous humour. The smaller chamber in front of the lens is filled with a watery liquid, the aqueous humour. In the groove or angle between the cornea and iris a narrow passage allows excess fluid to drain away and acts as a safety valve to prevent pressure building up in the eye.

The blood vessels of the choroid are the only ones in the body readily available for direct visual examination under normal conditions, by looking into the pupil with a special light (an ophthalmoscope). Examination of these vessels can provide important information about the state of health of the blood-vessel system as a whole.

Diagrammatic cross-section of the retina, the innermost layer of the eyeball.

ganglia

light

rods

cones

nervous layer of retina

pigmented layer

optic nerve fibres

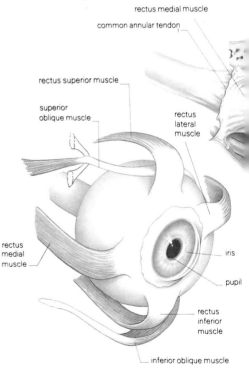

rectus medial muscle

common annular tendon

rectus superior muscle

superior oblique muscle

rectus lateral muscle

rectus medial muscle

iris

pupil

rectus inferior muscle

inferior oblique muscle

The left eye seen in cross-section (below), and the eyeball with the muscles extended (below left). The transparent cornea covers the pupil and the iris, the muscular band that controls the size of the pupil. The lens focuses light rays on to the retina at the back of the eyeball; the retina transforms these rays into impulses and transmits them via the optic nerve to the brain. The optic disc, where

the optic nerve leaves the eye, is called the blind spot because it contains no rods or cones and cannot perceive images. The rectus superior muscle rolls the eyeball upwards; the rectus inferior rolls it downwards; the rectus medial and the rectus lateral muscles roll the eyeball from side to side; and the oblique muscles rotate it on its axis.

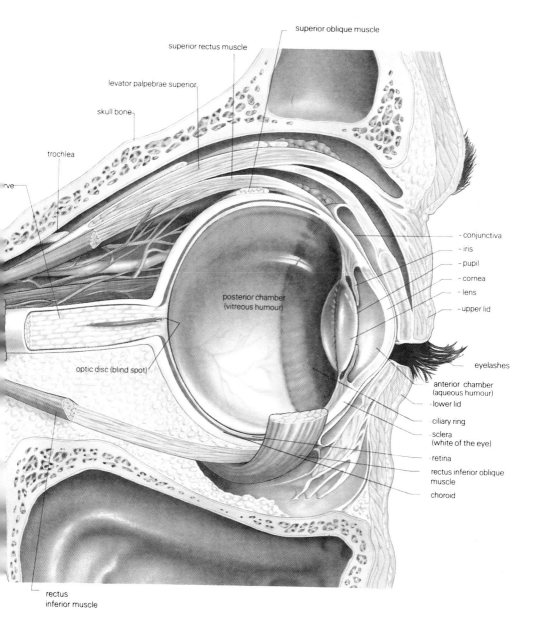

superior oblique muscle

superior rectus muscle

levator palpebrae superior

skull bone

trochlea

rve

conjunctiva

iris

pupil

cornea

lens

upper lid

posterior chamber
(vitreous humour)

optic disc (blind spot)

eyelashes

anterior chamber
(aqueous humour)

lower lid

ciliary ring

sclera
(white of the eye)

retina

rectus inferior oblique
muscle

choroid

rectus
inferior muscle

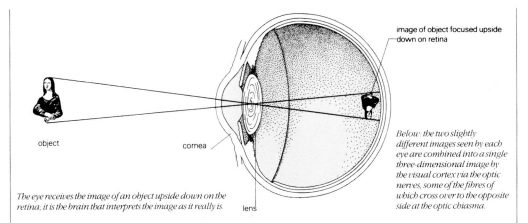

The eye receives the image of an object upside down on the retina; it is the brain that interprets the image as it really is.

object

cornea

lens

image of object focused upside down on retina

Below: the two slightly different images seen by each eye are combined into a single three-dimensional image by the visual cortex via the optic nerves, some of the fibres of which cross over to the opposite side at the optic chiasma.

Focusing

The eye works like a camera: the lens focuses light rays, the iris controls the amount of light entering the eye and the retina receives the focused image. Unlike a camera, however, the image is only interpreted when the nerve impulses from the retina reach the brain.

Light rays striking the eye are first roughly focused by the cornea, which is curved and acts like a fixed lens. Fine focusing is carried out by the lens, which can change in thickness by contraction or relaxation of the ciliary muscles attached to it. When the muscles contract, the ligaments attaching the lens to the ciliary body relax, the lens becomes thicker and close objects are brought into focus. For focusing on objects more than 6 m (20 ft) away, the muscles relax and the lens becomes stretched and thinner.

Light falling on the retina is converted into nerve impulses by a complex photochemical process involving chemical changes in the rods and cones. Objects that you look straight at come into focus on an area of the retina called the fovea. Surrounding this is a larger area, the macula lutea. It is in these areas that you can see the finest detail in images. The fovea is composed only of cones, which are much more sensitive than rods, and there are over 150,000 to each square millimetre here.

Colour and night vision

Within the retina the rods and cones react differently to both the amount and the colour of light. The rods are very sensitive to light but cannot distinguish colours or fine detail. Since cones work best in bright light and only cones can distinguish colour, in dim light colours cannot be distinguished, and detail is blurred. The part of the retina most sensitive to detail, the macula lutea, is composed mainly of cones. In dim light it is better to look to one side of an object so the image falls away from the macula lutea which is not sensitive to low light levels.

Colour blindness of various kinds affects about eight in every 100 men, but only about four in every 1000 women. Colour blindness is not actually blindness in any important sense, but a deviation from the usual colour vision. People

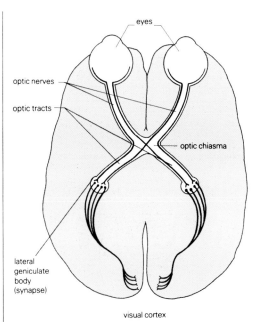

eyes

optic nerves

optic tracts

optic chiasma

lateral geniculate body (synapse)

visual cortex

who are colour blind simply do not agree with most other people about colour matching.

Testing for colour blindness is generally done with a series of cards (called Ishihara cards, after their Japanese inventor) which carry patterns of coloured dots. On some cards a colour-blind person cannot see the colour differences between the dots, whereas someone with normal colour vision makes out a letter or a number from the dots that do not match. On other cards there is a pattern with coloured dots that those with one kind of colour blindness can see, but which the rest of us cannot make out.

Nerves and vision

Although the healthy working of the eyes is vital in the formation of an image, what we actually see is created by the brain from the nerve impulses produced by the retina. Even though the eye might be functioning perfectly, blindness can still occur if the optic nerve to the brain is damaged.

The optic nerves are bundles of fibres connecting the rods and cones of the retina to the brain. Each eye has its own optic nerve which, on its way to the brain, changes course at a point called the optic chiasma. Here, some fibres from the left side join the right side, and vice versa. The nerve bundles then continue to the occipital lobes at the rear of the brain. It is here that the nerve impulses are interpreted to give a mental image of what the eyes see.

The cornea and lens of the eye project an upside-down image on the retina. We do not actually see things upside down, because of the way the brain interprets the impulses from the eyes. Although we take sight for granted, we actually have to learn to see and to understand the images that the eyes form, and this learning process takes place during the first months of life.

Tears

Tears are produced by the lacrimal apparatus. This consists of the lacrimal gland which secretes the tears, the ducts which convey the fluid to the surface of the eye, and two lacrimal ducts (upper and lower) which drain the tears away into the lacrimal sac. This in turn empties into the nose. Tears have three main functions: to keep the surface of the eye moist; to act as a mild antiseptic, helping to destroy bacteria; and to trap and wash away dust and other small particles. Irritating substances, infection and emotion cause a rapid increase in the production of tears, often to the extent that they overflow and cause weeping.

Eye disorders

Refractive errors and their correction

There are four common abnormalities of the eye that impair vision and make images blurred. These are called errors of refraction, and they can usually be corrected by spectacles or contact lenses.

Long sight

In long sight (hypermetropia) the image of an object is focused behind the retina rather than on it (that is, the eyeball is too small for the focusing power of the lens). The result is indistinct vision at all distances unless an effort is always made to focus the lens, and this can lead to eye fatigue. Long sight can be corrected by convex lenses.

Similarly, in presbyopia (from the Greek word presbus meaning old man), the ability of the lens to focus decreases steadily with increasing age because of a gradual hardening of the material making up the lens. This condition causes long-sightedness and is corrected by convex lenses.

Short sight

In short sight (myopia) the image is brought to a focus in front of the retina. The most obvious symptom is the inability to distinguish distant objects clearly, such as the blackboard in school or road signs. This type of refractive error can be corrected by concave lenses.

Astigmatism

In astigmatism, the curvature of the cornea is irregular and the image is blurred because some of the light rays are focused and others are not. This is similar to the distortion produced by a wavy pane of glass. Astigmatism is corrected by using a lens that bends light rays in one plane only.

Refractive errors and their correction with lenses of different shapes.

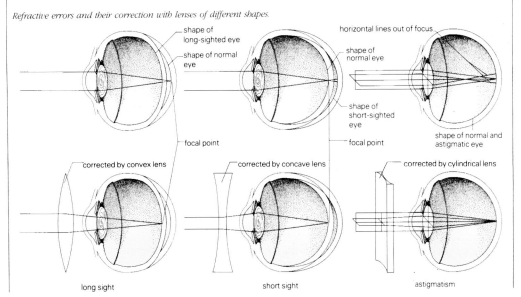

long sight   short sight   astigmatism

Infections and inflammations

Conjunctivitis
Conjunctivitis is inflammation of the conjunctiva, the transparent covering on the inside of the eyelids and the surface of the eye up to the cornea. The condition may be acute or chronic.

Acute conjunctivitis, commonly called 'pink eye', is infectious and usually caused by bacteria that can be transferred from one eye to the other as well as from one person to another. The eye becomes red and sore, and there may be a yellow discharge. Antibiotic drops or ointment are usually prescribed to treat the condition. Allergies such as hay fever can also produce non-infectious acute conjunctivitis.

Styes and chalazions
If the root of an eyelash becomes infected, a painful swelling known as a stye (or hordeolum) occurs. A stye should be bathed with warm salt water to encourage it to discharge and to clean away the pus. Blockage of an oil-producing gland on the eyelid causes a small, hard, painless lump called a chalazion or meibomium cyst, which should be treated by a doctor.

Trachoma
Trachoma is an infection of the eyelids and surface of the eye which may, if not treated in the early stages, cause scarring of the cornea. The eyelids swell and produce a discharge, and the sufferer cannot tolerate bright light. Trachoma, which can be successfully treated with antibiotics, is a common cause of blindness in countries in Africa and South America where general hygiene is poor.

Iritis and iridocyelitis
The cause of both iritis (inflammation of the iris) and iridocyelitis (inflammation of the iris and the ciliary body) is usually unknown, although it may be related to a general disease such as rheumatoid arthritis. Both these conditions cause pain, redness and discharge from the affected eye. Inflammation of the sclera (scleritis) also usually has no known cause. All these conditions may be treated with eye drops.

Foreign bodies
An embedded foreign body in the cornea can cause serious infection and result in an ulcer. If not treated, this can perforate the eyeball, and the infection may spread to other parts of the eye, causing blindness. Use a piece of clean gauze to remove a superficial particle; for an embedded particle seek medical advice.

Glaucoma
Glaucoma, a condition in which the pressure of fluid inside the eye is increased, may be caused by gradual blockage of the narrow canal through which excess fluid inside the eye drains away. The amount of fluid, particularly the aqueous humour in the front chamber, then builds up, causing the pressure inside the eye to rise. Glaucoma may be painful, and eventually there is damage to the retina and optic nerve, possibly causing partial or even complete loss of sight, if not diagnosed and treated early. This condition often starts very slowly and insidiously, so that the person affected may not seek medical advice until a late stage, when the damage has been done. An ophthalmic optician may detect signs of glaucoma before the victim has noticed any symptoms, which is one reason why you should go to the optician for a check-up every year or two. Glaucoma is treated with drugs (eye drops and tablets) or, if these fail, surgically to release the fluid and relieve the pressure, through a new channel.

Muscle imbalance
If the muscles of the eye are not functioning correctly, problems with vision may occur because both eyes are not pointing together at the same object. The eyes may be crossed or divergent from birth, or may become so later in life. Treatment, which may involve surgery, is often successful.

Squint (strabismus) may be due to weak eye muscles or to other eye problems. The result is lack of proper stereoscopic vision, which can be improved by exercises and training, or surgery. If squint is not treated it may lead in one eye to ambylopia (diminished vision). 'Lazy eye' is a form of squint which may be treated by covering the healthy eye with a patch to encourage the affected eye to work.

Blindness
Although most people think of blindness as the complete loss of sight, the legal definition of a blind person is one who is 'unable to perform any work for which eyesight is essential'. Some people who are registered as blind have, in fact, enough vision to walk about, to look after themselves in their homes and to do their shopping and other domestic tasks.

There are many causes of blindness and they can be roughly grouped into eight types: congenital, traumatic, inflammatory, neoplastic, degenerative and neurological; and glaucoma or diabetes.

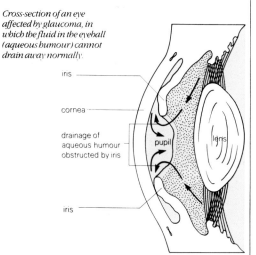

Cross-section of an eye affected by glaucoma, in which the fluid in the eyeball (aqueous humour) cannot drain away normally.

iris

cornea

drainage of aqueous humour obstructed by iris

pupil

lens

iris

Congenital causes of blindness, occurring before or soon after birth, include very small eyes, glaucoma (buphthalmos), misshapen cornea, gaps in the iris or other parts of the eye (colobomata), absent iris, cataract, or an abnormal optic nerve. Trauma, a common cause of blindness, may occur as a result of explosions, car accidents and gunshot wounds. Damage from splashes of caustic chemicals and staring at the sun may also greatly reduce vision.

Inflammation of the iris or the choroid is another common cause of blindness. Corneal inflammation (keratitis) can cause serious damage to sight, and, as one of the consequences of infection with trachoma, is a major cause of blindness in the world. People who develop corneal opacity, when the normally clear cornea becomes milky-coloured, can be treated by corneal grafts, which involve the removal of a disc of the patient's opaque cornea and its replacement with healthy cornea taken from a cadaver.

Cataract is a degenerative form of blindness in which the lens gradually becomes opaque and vision mists over. Cataract can occur as a result of other eye disease, or of a more generalized condition, but the commonest type is senile cataract that develops with age. It usually affects both eyes, but one eye may be affected before the other. Cataract can be successfully treated by removing the diseased lens surgically, provided the eye is otherwise healthy, and replacing it with an implant or a contact lens.

Another common cause of blindness results from a condition called macular degeneration, in which the nerve cells of the macula (part of the retina) change so that the individual is unable to perceive fine detail. A person with this condition, although technically blind, can get about with a reasonable amount of independence. Neurological disease such as disseminated sclerosis, neuromyelitis optica, and brain tumours may cause blindness by affecting the optic nerves or another part of the optic pathway.

In detached retina, a hole or tear in the retina allows fluid to seep beneath this layer and lift it up. The symptoms involve painless change in or loss of vision, often preceded by sparks or flashing lights. It may result in blindness if left unchecked, but can be treated quite successfully by surgery.

Coping with blindness

Most children who are blind were born so. It is difficult to tell whether a new baby can see or not, but there are special tests that are designed for the purpose. During about the first two years at least, a blind baby should live with the parents if possible, and quickly be taught to talk. Attention should be given to developing the senses of touch and hearing to compensate for the loss of vision. After the age of two, if the parents cannot undertake the necessary care and management, the child can go to a special school.

Adults who become blind have usually been educated and may have trained for a career, which they may be able to continue, depending on what is involved. Often retraining is required, and some degree of special training is necessary for all blind people. It takes about three months to learn basic items such as one of the embossed alphabets (Braille, Moon), how to type, and the principles of living, moving about and coping with everyday chores without the use of the eyes.

Taste and smell

Taste and smell are closely linked. Humans can actually taste only four sensations – salt, sweet, sour and bitter – and each is detected by nerve endings in tastebuds located in the hair-like projections (papillae) on the surface of the tongue. There are different types of taste buds for each of the four sensations, and each type is concentrated on a different part of the tongue. The rear of the tongue is most sensitive to bitter tastes, the front to salty tastes, the front and side edges to sweet tastes and the centre to sour tastes. More subtle tastes than these are detected by smell, not taste.

The sense of smell is 10,000 times more sensitive than the taste buds. Small receptors project into the top of the nasal cavity. They consist of several million tiny hair-like endings of the olfactory nerves, which pass through a perforated plate of bone to join the olfactory bulb of the brain. Smells are appreciated when odoriferous particles are breathed in through the nose and detected by the olfactory nerves which pass the information to the brain. When the nose is congested, during a heavy cold, for example, air is prevented from reaching the smell receptors.

Touch, pain and other receptors

There are special nerve endings in the skin for touch, pressure, heat, cold, and pain. Pain receptors are present in the greatest numbers, followed by those of touch, pressure, heat and cold. The numbers of each receptor vary in different regions of the body; there are many touch receptors, for example, on the tongue, lips, fingertips, hair roots, nipples and orifices of the body, but few in the back.

Pain receptors record different qualities of sensation depending on their position in the skin. Those in the epidermis produce the feeling of an itch when stimulated, those in the upper dermis produce sharp pain, those in the deep dermis the sensation of ache. More than any other sensation, pain is affected by one's mental state and the sensation of pain can vary in intensity according to such factors as anxiety, imagination, tradition and training.

Inside the body there are two main types of sense organ; proprioceptors and visceral receptors. Proprioceptors include sensors in muscle fibres (muscle spindles) and receptors in joints and tendons. They respond to the state of contraction or the position of the structure they are in, and by sending information to the brain they contribute to the system whereby posture and tone are maintained to keep the body steady. Visceral receptors are nerve endings in the organs of the body. They normally form a link in the reflex system whereby the brain controls the organs' activities, a part of the autonomic nervous system (see page 192). Pain from an organ may be 'referred'; that is, felt to be in another part of the body.

One special type of internal receptor is the chemoreceptor, found in the large blood vessels near the heart. This type of receptor is sensitive to the level of carbon dioxide in the blood and, by sending impulses to the respiratory centre in the brain, helps control the rate of respiration (see pages 86-7). Other receptors are sensitive to pressure of the blood vessels (baroceptors).

An otoscope is used for examining the ears (right). It consists of a light which illuminates the inside of the external ear and a magnifying lens, and can reveal any changes in or infections of the outer ear canal and eardrum.

Even if there seems to be nothing wrong with your eyes, you should have regular sight tests because some eye disorders produce no symptoms in their early stages. A visit to an optician (left) will include reading letters from a standard chart which is viewed through a mirror so that its letters are reflected the right way round. If glasses are needed, the prescription is worked out by means of trial frames like those shown, in which the lenses can be changed until suitable ones are found. Other tests include an examination of the back of the eye with an ophthalmoscope which can reveal any internal eye disorder.

Types of hearing aid

All modern hearing aids are powered by a small battery to increase the volume of sound reaching the ear. A microphone transforms sounds into electrical signals which are increased in strength by an amplifier. The stronger signals are then turned back into sounds and transmitted to the ear through the earpiece. There are three main types of electric hearing aid. The behind-the-ear aid consists of a small plastic case worn behind the ear, containing the microphone, amplifier and battery, attached by a short tube to the earphone which fits snugly into the outer-ear canal. The body-worn type is used when more power is required; the battery and amplifier are contained in a larger plastic case worn on the body and attached to the earphone by a thin wire. In cases of conductive deafness a bone-conduction aid is required: sound is transmitted through a pad touching the mastoid process behind the ear instead of through an earphone.

Non-electric hearing aids are also available, for people who find it difficult or impossible to use modern aids, and they include ear trumpets and conversation tubes with swivel-joint earpieces.

No hearing aid can cure deafness, but of the many models available, one is sure to prove helpful in most cases. If your first hearing aid is not successful, say so to the technician who dispensed it, so that he or she can make any adjustments necessary.

A behind-the-ear hearing aid, showing the volume and tone controls. This type of aid is popular because it is inconspicuous and comfortable to wear.

Hearing and balance

Sound consists of vibrations, usually in the air, and the ear is the organ that detects these vibrations, converts them into electrical impulses and transmits the information to the brain. The ear is very sensitive and can detect and discriminate between a wide range of different sounds. As well as being the organ of hearing, the ear is also very important in the sense of balance.

The structure and function of the ears

The ear can be divided into three main parts: the external ear, the middle ear and the inner ear, each of which has a different function. The external ear consists of the fleshy external pinna (the ear flap we can see) which collects sound vibrations and directs them into the external auditory canal. The eardrum is at the far end of the external auditory canal, about 2.5 cm (1 in) from the outside. The skin of the outer half of the canal secretes wax which helps to lubricate the canal and trap dust. This wax is moved to the outside of the canal by the movement of the jaws and is washed away when the face is cleaned. Sometimes a ball of hard, old wax collects close to the eardrum and does not move. This can cause discomfort and may affect hearing. However, it can easily be removed by the doctor using a syringe and warm water.

The middle ear begins at the eardrum (tympanic membrane). It is an air-filled cavity connected to the Eustachian tube, which opens into the throat. The air pressure between the two sides of the eardrum has to be kept the same, and the Eustachian tube, by allowing air to flow between the throat and middle ear, ensures this. The familiar clicking of the ears when swallowing or going up in an aircraft or lift is this equalization of pressure working.

Sound waves travelling along the auditory canal strike the eardrum and cause it to vibrate very slightly. An amplifying system consisting of three small bones in the middle ear is connected to the eardrum. These three bones, the ossicles, are the smallest bones in the body, and are called the malleus, incus and stapes (hammer, anvil and stirrup) after a faint resemblance to these objects. As the eardrum vibrates, its movements are transmitted and amplified by the movements of these bones, to the inner ear.

The inner ear, a fluid-filled structure set in the bones of the skull, is where the vibrations of sound waves are converted into nerve impulses. The conversion takes place in the cochlea, a spiral tube shaped rather like a snail-shell. In the cochlea, in a part called the organ of Corti, there are thousands of hair-covered cells. These hairs are 'tuned' to vibrate at the different frequencies (pitches) of sound vibrations; these vibrations are then converted into nerve impulses and transmitted to the brain along the acoustic nerve. If the cochlea were uncoiled it would be about 4 cm (1½ in) long. Different pitches of sound are detected along its length, bass notes at the outer end and very high notes at the inner end of the spiral. The stapes touches on the surface of the cochlea at a point called the oval window, and movements of the stapes cause the fluid in the cochlea to vibrate.

Vibrations can reach the cochlea through the bony structures of the head as well as through the eardrum. This conduction is particularly important for hearing our own speech and is the reason why one's own recorded voice, heard from a tape recorder, sounds quite different from what one hears while actually speaking.

Balance

In the inner ear, behind the cochlea, is the organ of balance, called the labyrinth. It consists of three semi-circular canals, each situated in a different plane at ninety degrees to the other two. The fluid in these canals moves as the head moves, and sensitive hair cells, with small crystals of the mineral calcite attached to them, detect this movement. Impulses are then sent to the brain that indicate the position of the head and body.

Testing hearing

The human ear is able to appreciate sounds over a limited range of frequencies. The lower threshold is about 16 Hz (cycles per second) and the upper threshold is 20,000 Hz. Frequencies above 20,000 Hz are above the limit of human hearing. Such high-pitched sounds are known as ultrasounds.

Hearing becomes less sensitive after puberty. As we get older our hearing for the higher tones, especially, deteriorates.

Disorders of the ear

Earache

About ninety-five per cent of all cases of earache are due to infection. The three parts of the ear that are specially prone to infection are the auditory canal, the middle ear and the mastoid bone.

Otitis externa

Frequently the lining of the ear canal becomes inflamed (by a fungus, bacterium or virus), a condition known as otitis externa. Symptoms include pain, which is increased when the jaw is moved, and there may be a discharge of fluid from the ear. Anyone who uses earpieces or headsets for their job should have their own set, which should be kept scrupulously clean to prevent infection.

Treatment of outer ear infections is usually simple, but should be carried out by a doctor. The ears should be kept dry, so that swimming or other water sports should be stopped until the condition clears up, since damp favours the spread of infection.

Children may insert their fingers or small objects such as beads into their ears. Occasionally, insects fly into the ear and become trapped. Any of these foreign bodies, apart from causing earache, can result in otitis externa, as can the practice of removing wax with paper clips, long fingernails, hairgrips or a crochet hook. Removal of foreign bodies is a job for the doctor, as inexpert hands can cause damage.

Otitis media

The most common ear infections in children are those of the middle ear (otitis media), which can only be seen with an auriscope, an instrument used to view the eardrum.

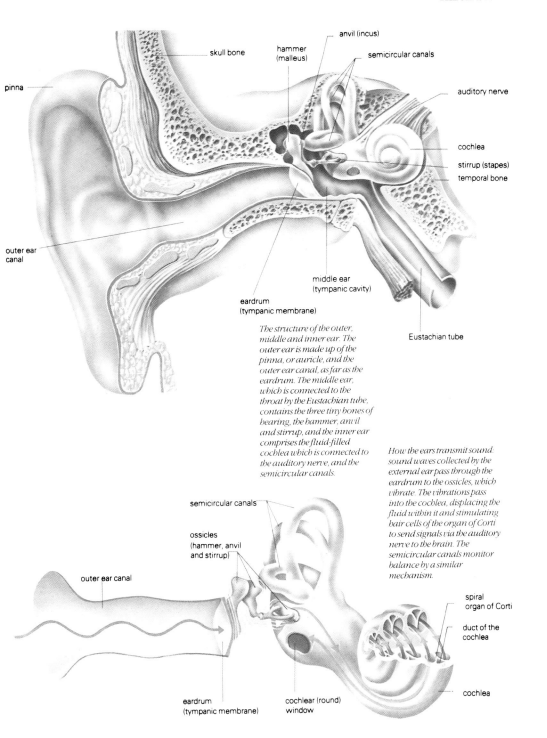

anvil (incus)

skull bone

hammer (malleus)

semicircular canals

pinna

auditory nerve

cochlea

stirrup (stapes)

temporal bone

outer ear canal

middle ear (tympanic cavity)

eardrum (tympanic membrane)

Eustachian tube

The structure of the outer, middle and inner ear. The outer ear is made up of the pinna, or auricle, and the outer ear canal, as far as the eardrum. The middle ear, which is connected to the throat by the Eustachian tube, contains the three tiny bones of hearing, the hammer, anvil and stirrup, and the inner ear comprises the fluid-filled cochlea which is connected to the auditory nerve, and the semicircular canals.

How the ears transmit sound: sound waves collected by the external ear pass through the eardrum to the ossicles, which vibrate. The vibrations pass into the cochlea, displacing the fluid within it and stimulating hair cells of the organ of Corti to send signals via the auditory nerve to the brain. The semicircular canals monitor balance by a similar mechanism.

semicircular canals

ossicles (hammer, anvil and stirrup)

outer ear canal

spiral organ of Corti

duct of the cochlea

cochlea

eardrum (tympanic membrane)

cochlear (round) window

Severe throbbing earache is the main symptom of middle-ear infection. Unless checked, the drum ruptures and a discharge appears, which is initially watery but characteristically becomes thick yellow pus, which has collected in the middle ear.

The causes of infection of the middle ear are numerous: the common cold, influenza, tonsilitis, measles, and scarlet fever may all spread to involve the middle ear. Children are most prone to this type of ear disease, since infection spreads more easily up their shorter Eustachian tubes. Treatment usually involves the use of antibiotics, as tablets or ear drops or spray, to fight the infection. Another drug can be given to shrink the lining of the blocked Eustachian tube.

Inflammation of the mastoid bone at the back of the middle ear is called mastoiditis. It may result in some degree of hearing loss, but since the introduction of antibiotics has become rare.

Poor hearing due to recurrent middle-ear infection is a major cause of learning difficulty in young children. Partial deafness should always be considered in such circumstances.

Hearing loss and deafness

There are two types of deafness. The first type, known as conductive deafness, is due to some abnormality or disease of the part of the ear which conducts the sound waves to the internal ear. This may be a plug of wax, a perforated eardrum, or disease or abnormality of one of the tiny bones of the middle ear which conduct the sound waves from the eardrum to the fluid of the internal ear. The other type of deafness is due to some abnormality or disease in the part of the ear which actually perceives the sound waves. Disease in the area of the brain concerned with hearing will also produce deafness, of the type known as perceptive deafness, inner ear deafness, or nerve deafness. Deafness may also be due to a psychological disturbance, when it is termed psychogenic deafness.

There is a simple tuning fork test which indicates which type of deafness is present. A person with normal hearing can hear the tuning fork better when it is held in front of the ear than when it is touching the bone behind the ear. If the tuning fork is heard better when it is placed on the bone behind the ear, it is an indication of conductive deafness. If the tuning fork can be heard by conduction of sound through the air, but not by conduction through the bone, it is a sign of perceptive deafness.

In order to find out accurately the degree of hearing loss, measurements may be made by audiometry. A pure sound at one pitch is produced by a machine and the intensity of the sound is altered until it can just be heard. The test is repeated with different frequencies of sound, and a graph of the results relates the frequency to the intensity of sound required for it to be appreciated by the person being tested. The record is called a pure-tone audiogram.

Injuries can cause deafness, and include explosions or a direct blow on the ear, which may lead to injury of the eardrum. (A 'box on the ear' should never be used as a form of punishment as it can rupture the eardrum, causing conductive deafness.)

Coping with deafness

The investigation of hearing defects in young children is very important because, unless deafness is recognized and treated early, speech development will be poor or absent and general development will be retarded. Special units exist for testing hearing, where various measurements of hearing are carried out, advice is given about hearing aids, and help in methods of auditory training is offered to parents of deaf children.

The deafness of old age usually comes on gradually over many years, and the first signs may be a failure to notice high sounds and increasing difficulty in hearing speech when background noise is present.

If you think that you or your child may be going deaf, first consult a doctor. A preliminary examination with an otoscope may reveal wax blocking the ears; after this is removed the hearing returns to normal. If deafness *is* diagnosed, make sure that you have a suitable hearing aid fitted; do not buy one at an exhibition, for example. Careful investigation of the nature of the deafness will be necessary before an appropriate type can be selected. For information on types of hearing aid, see page 175. Other aids may also be available, such as an amplifier fitted to the telephone receiver; approach your local centre for the deaf for help and advice on ways of coping. Help others to help you by asking them to speak while facing you, slowly and clearly, and not while eating or smoking.

Otitis barotrauma

Otitis barotrauma is damage caused by pressure differences between the air in the middle ear and the atmosphere outside it. The Eustachian tube, which connects the middle ear to the back of the nose, is important in preventing pressure differences developing during, for example, an aeroplane flight. If air does not enter the middle ear cavity to equalize pressure differences, for example if the Eustachian tube is blocked by infection, this can cause severe pain in the ears, accompanied by deafness as the eardrum is gradually drawn inwards. Usually, the condition clears within twenty-four hours without treatment. If the condition continues, blood vessels rupture and the ear cavity becomes filled with blood. It will then be necessary to consult a doctor who may perforate the eardrum to allow fluid to drain from the ear.

'Glue ear'

Deafness may develop suddenly, as a result of the accumulation of fluid in the middle-ear cavity. The cause of this is not always known, but it can be the result of an infection of the ear or a cold, causing blockage of the Eustachian tube. This type of deafness can often be cured quite easily by a specialist, who will make a small hole in the eardrum with a fine instrument to allow the fluid to escape, and hearing returns to normal. The eardrum soon heals naturally. The condition is common in children but is often difficult to treat, as the fluid may be so thick and viscous that an operation is necessary to remove it. Known as 'glue ear', this is one of the most common causes of conductive deafness in young children. If untreated, it may lead to permanent damage.

Otosclerosis

A common cause of chronic deafness in young adults and older people is a disease known as otosclerosis. The cause of this form of deafness is the stiffening of the middle-ear bones by a new deposit of bone. If the bones cannot move, the sound waves are not transmitted to the fluid of the internal ear, and deafness results. Fortunately, it is possible to treat this type of deafness by surgery.

Chronic otitis media

Chronic inflammation of the middle ear – chronic otitis media – is found most commonly among poorer members of the community living in industrial areas. The symptoms, discharge from the ear and deafness, can be worsened or caused by smoke pollution, living in overcrowded conditions and poor hygiene.

Perceptive deafness

Perceptive deafness is caused by disease, injury or congenital abnormality of the mechanisms concerned with the perception of sound, and one cause is a fracture of the base of the skull. Certain drugs and chemical poisons can also lead to deafness; among the most common are alcohol, tobacco and quinine.

The only treatment for nerve deafness is the wearing of a hearing aid which may not always be very helpful in this type of hearing loss.

Deafness present from birth is a most serious disability. Few such children have absolutely no hearing present, however, and if it is possible to stimulate them by the wearing of a hearing aid, even at six months old, the results of treatment are likely to be good. By the age of two, a deaf child should, if possible, be with other (preferably normal) children in a nursery class. If this is not possible, the child should attend a nursery class in a special school for the deaf.

Deafness that accompanies old age is known as presbycusis. Most people over the age of sixty-five have some loss of hearing in the higher tones. Presbycusis is a degenerative condition and is caused by the wasting away of some of the cells in the cochlea. It is not usually possible to treat except by a hearing aid.

Even with a hearing aid, a deaf person is unlikely to hear quite as well as a normal person, because there is often a loss of the ability to distinguish between different tones, so that amplification of volume alone does not improve intelligibility of speech.

Vertigo and dizziness

There are many causes of dizziness and vertigo, which can be a result of infections and disorders of the semicircular canals of the labyrinth or of the nerves and parts of the brain associated with balance. In Menière's syndrome, there is an increase of fluid and a build-up of pressure inside the labyrinth which disturbs the sense of balance. It is most common in middle-aged people, and symptoms include deafness, noises in the head and vertigo. There may also be nausea and vomiting. Treatment depends on the severity of the problem and may involve drugs or surgery. In most people, however, the disorder is mild and clears up spontaneously.

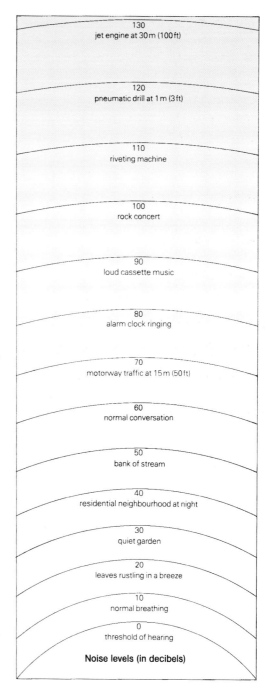

130
jet engine at 30 m (100 ft)

120
pneumatic drill at 1 m (3 ft)

110
riveting machine

100
rock concert

90
loud cassette music

80
alarm clock ringing

70
motorway traffic at 15 m (50 ft)

60
normal conversation

50
bank of stream

40
residential neighbourhood at night

30
quiet garden

20
leaves rustling in a breeze

10
normal breathing

0
threshold of hearing

Noise levels (in decibels)

Hormones

Hormones act as chemical messengers which exert a powerful influence on the body, yet we have no conscious control over them. These substances play a vital part in growth and development, as well as in controlling a wide range of activities within the body, such as digestion, excretion and sexual activity.

Hormones are secreted by glands known as endocrine glands. These glands, unlike others in the body (such as the salivary glands), secrete directly into the bloodstream rather than through a duct (and are also known as ductless glands). Because they are transported by the blood, the messages in the hormones travel more slowly than nervous impulses and are usually involved in processes that take place over a relatively long period.

There are seven major endocrine glands in the body. The most important, the pituitary gland, controls the activity of the other endocrine glands. It is situated at the base of the skull in a bony hollow. The thyroid gland is in the lower neck, curving round the windpipe in the shape of a horse-shoe. Four small parathyroid glands lie close and may be embedded in the surface of the thyroid. The pancreas, lying just behind the stomach, in addition to its role in digestion (see pages 102-3), contains groups of endocrine cells called the islets of Langerhans. Lying on top of each kidney are two more glands, the adrenals. Other endocrine glands are the testes in men and the ovaries in women. The pineal and thymus glands are also endocrine glands, but their function is not clear. Certain tissues with other functions produce hormones, too: the stomach, for example, produces the hormone gastrin and the kidneys produce renin.

Many of the endocrine glands act together in a finely regulated way, and a hormone released from one gland often influences the release of another from a different gland. The pituitary gland produces several hormones that either stimulate or inhibit the release of other hormones from distant glands and has been compared to a telephone exchange. The pituitary itself is regulated by a part of the brain called the hypothalamus.

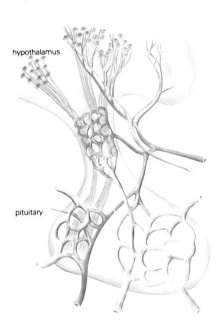

The pituitary, a pea-sized gland at the base of the brain, is connected to the hypothalamus by a slender stalk. Through the pituitary, the hypothalamus regulates most of the functions of the body, by releasing a variety of hormones which act on several 'target' organs which in turn release other hormones.

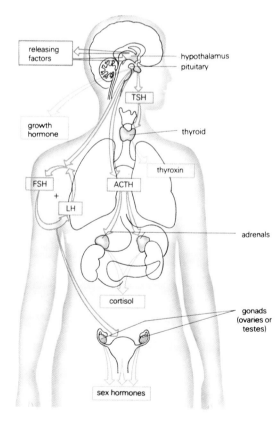

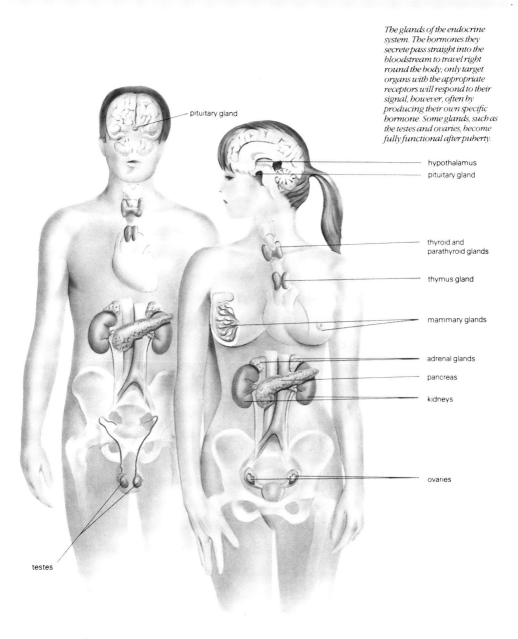

The glands of the endocrine system. The hormones they secrete pass straight into the bloodstream to travel right round the body; only target organs with the appropriate receptors will respond to their signal, however, often by producing their own specific hormone. Some glands, such as the testes and ovaries, become fully functional after puberty.

pituitary gland

hypothalamus
pituitary gland

thyroid and parathyroid glands

thymus gland

mammary glands

adrenal glands

pancreas

kidneys

ovaries

testes

The hypothalamus

The hypothalamus is about the size of a walnut, and situated at the base of the brain near the part that controls many of the body's automatic (involuntary) functions. Centres within the hypothalamus control, via the pituitary gland, activities such as appetite, sleep and waking, thirst, sexual activity and body temperature. The hypothalamus also acts as a nerve centre, and since some of its functions are via nerves and others via hormones, it links the nervous system with the endocrine glands.

Disorders of the hypothalamus

Because the hypothalamus controls so many of the body's automatic functions, any disorder of this structure can have serious effects: extreme obesity may occur because of uncontrollable hunger; lack of temperature control may cause the body to become too cool or hot; the menstrual cycle may stop or become irregular; and puberty may occur abnormally early or be delayed. The hypothalamus can be damaged by tumours, injury or inflammation, but its function may be impaired without any damage to its structure.

The pituitary gland

The pituitary is in two parts, or lobes. The rear, or posterior, part is connected to the hypothalamus by nerves, and secretes two hormones actually produced in the hypothalamus, vasopressin and oxytocin. Vasopressin, also called antidiuretic hormone (ADH), is involved in controlling water excretion from the kidneys (see *The Urinary System*, pages 116-20). Oxytocin stimulates the uterus to contract during birth and is also involved in the secretion of breast milk (see *Prenatal Development and Birth*, pages 24-8).

The front part (anterior lobe) of the pituitary is connected to the hypothalamus by blood vessels. Several hormones, called trophic hormones, are secreted by the anterior lobe and affect the action of other endocrine glands. There are two gonadotrophins (luteinizing hormone, LH, and follicle-stimulating hormone, FSH) which control the gonads, thyrotrophic hormone (thyroid-stimulating hormone, TSH) which affects the thyroid, and adrenocorticotrophin (ACTH) which controls part of the adrenal glands. There are also two hormones that act directly on the body: growth hormone, also called somatotrophin, which stimulates growth and is involved in controlling the rate at which the body uses energy, and prolactin, which stimulates breast-milk formation during and after pregnancy.

The release of these hormones is controlled not only by the brain, but also by other glands in the body. This means that, for instance, if there is too much thyroid hormone in the blood, the pituitary will reduce the amount of thyroid-stimulating hormone it releases. If there is too little hormone in the blood, the pituitary produces more of the trophic hormone needed to stimulate its production by the gland.

Disorders of the pituitary gland

Because the pituitary controls other endocrine glands, any disorder of this gland can have wide-ranging effects. If the anterior part of the pituitary is damaged (for example, by tumours or cysts) the glands under its control – the thyroid, adrenal cortex, and testes or ovaries – will also be affected. The results of this may include impotence, fatigue, loss of appetite and low blood pressure. This severe, and possibly fatal, condition can be treated by giving artificially the various hormones normally produced by the glands affected.

If too little growth hormone is secreted, a form of dwarfism can occur; too great a secretion may result in gigantism and acromegaly (see *Growth*, pages 42-3). Premature sexual development can be caused by the gonadotrophins being secreted too early in life because of a fault in the hypothalamus, which times a person's development. The opposite condition, failure of sexual development, may be due to failure of the pituitary to secrete gonadotrophins, although there may be other reasons such as failure of the ovaries or testes to produce sex hormones.

Excessive secretion of prolactin can cause abnormal milk production (in a woman who has not just given birth), and also failure of menstruation and infertility. Tumours of the pituitary (and in rare cases, certain tranquillizing drugs and contraceptive pills) can cause high prolactin levels.

Failure of ADH (antidiuretic hormone) secretion causes diabetes insipidus (see page 187).

The thyroid and parathyroid glands

The thyroid gland, in front of the windpipe, consists of two lobes joined together by a bridge of tissue. At each of the four corners of the thyroid is a parathyroid gland.

The thyroid produces two hormones, thyroxine (T4) and triiodothyronine (T3). Both of these are essential for normal growth and development. They require adequate amounts of the trace element iodine for their production, and this is absorbed from food and transported to the thyroid in the bloodstream. Other functions of these hormones include regulation of metabolism (that is, how the body uses energy) and its oxygen consumption.

A special group of cells in the thyroid produces another hormone, calcitonin, which plays an important part in calcium absorption. If the amount of calcium in the blood rises above a certain level calcitonin reduces it, by increasing the rate of calcium absorption from the blood into bone, the amount of calcium excreted through the kidneys, and by slowing the absorption of calcium from food passing through the intestine (see *Bones and Joints*, pages 132-6).

Parathormone, produced by the parathyroid glands, has the opposite effect to calcitonin, raising the amount of calcium in the blood.

Disorders of the thyroid gland
Hyperthyroidism

Hyperthyroidism, also known as thyrotoxicosis or Graves' disease, results from an increase in thyroid activity, which leads to an increased metabolic rate. The disease, which is most common in women in early adult life, causes extreme nervousness and irritability, sweating, and loss of weight in spite of voracious hunger. Other symptoms are palpitations and muscle weakness. Protrusion of the eyeballs (exophthalmos) is often obvious. The pulse is rapid and there may be a fine tremor of the hands. The thyroid gland is usually enlarged (exophthalmic goitre). Treatment includes drugs which reduce thyroid activity, radioactive iodine and surgery to remove part of the gland.

Hypothyroidism

Hypothyroidism, also called myxoedema, is the opposite of hyperthyroidism, and causes general slowing of metabolism. Symptoms include reduced physical and mental activity and a gradual increase in tiredness, weakness, sensitivity to cold, and constipation. Deafness and vague muscular and joint pains are common; hair loss may also occur, speech becomes slow, hoarse or croaking, and the skin is pale and dry. Mental apathy can be so severe that friends or relatives may notice the deterioration in health well before the sufferer does. The face appears swollen, with puffy eyelids and thickening of the lips. The pulse is slow, and anaemia (a loss of red blood cells) is also common. The gland is not usually enlarged. The cause of primary hypothyroidism is unclear. A person with severe hypothyroidism is in danger during severely cold weather because the deficiency in body temperature control may result in coma.

Hypothyroidism may also be congenital (present at birth), and an infant born with this defect will become a cretin if untreated. The symptoms of early cretinism include inactivity, loss of appetite, constipation, dry skin, and poor muscle tone. Later, puffiness of the skin, low body temperature, a thick, protruding tongue, a pot belly and umbilical hernia may appear, and eventually dwarfism and mental retardation will result.

Successful treatment of hypothyroidism depends upon early diagnosis. Treatment involves replacing the deficient hormones with thyroxine which must be taken for life. Now that every newborn baby is chemically screened for the disease, cretinism is fortunately rare.

Goitre

A goitre, caused by an enlarged thyroid, is a sign of many different thyroid conditions. Simple goitre, as shown here, is due to lack of iodine, which can be corrected by taking iodine-enriched salt in the diet.

If there is an iodine deficiency in the diet because water and food supplies lack iodine, the thyroid compensates by enlarging to form a visible swelling in the neck, called a goitre. These often occur in areas lacking in iodine, and the condition is then termed endemic goitre. Most of the major mountainous districts of the world are endemic goitre regions, including the Andes, but the condition may be prevented by adding iodized table salt to the diet.

Disorders of calcium metabolism

Abnormality of function of the parathyroid glands or of calcitonin production usually causes either too much or too little calcium (hyper- or hypocalcaemia) in the blood. If the parathyroid glands produce too much parathormone hypercalcaemia results, with possible loss of calcium from the bones; occasionally there may be kidney stones, and tiredness and lethargy. Treatment depends on the main symptoms; sometimes surgery is needed, while the excess calcium can sometimes be rectified by certain drugs.

The opposite condition, parathormone deficiency or hypocalcaemia, is most often caused by accidental removal of one or more of the parathyroid glands during thyroidectomy. Treatment involves supplements of calcium which may have to be taken for life.

The adrenal glands

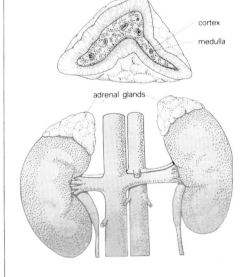

The adrenal glands, showing their internal structure and their position over the pole of each kidney. The adrenal cortex secretes steroid hormones involved in sugar metabolism, response to stress, control of salt balance and sexual development. The internal medulla produces adrenaline and noradrenaline which act on the autonomic nervous system.

The two adrenal glands are situated just above each kidney. Each adrenal consists of two parts, the inner medulla and the outer cortex, each with distinct functions. The medulla, part of the autonomic nervous system (see *The Nervous System*, pages 188-92), secretes the hormones adrenaline and noradrenaline, which are important in activating the body during periods of danger or stress. Both hormones have wide-ranging effects, increasing heart rate, altering blood flow to the organs and releasing energy stored in the liver. All these effects allow the body to reach maximal efficiency when faced with an emergency.

The outer part of each gland, the cortex, secretes hormones concerned with sugar metabolism and stress (glucocorticoids), salt balance (mineralocorticoids) and sexual development. These are all steroid hormones, being made from cholesterol, a type of fat. Cortisol is the main hormone concerned with stress. It increases blood sugar levels and causes a breakdown of fat in the body. In very high levels, cortisol also inhibits the body's natural defence mechanisms, suppressing the immune system and reducing inflammation in damaged tissues (see *The Immune System and Allergies*, pages 202-3). The main mineralocorticoid produced by the adrenal cortex is aldosterone. This regulates the levels of sodium and potassium, minerals important in many of the body's functions. The adrenal cortex also produces the sex hormones, androgens and oestrogens (see page 11). The adrenal cortex is under the control of the pituitary through the hormone adreno-corticotrophin (ACTH), which stimulates the production of these corticoid hormones.

Disorders of the adrenal glands

Addison's disease
Addison's disease is caused by destruction of the adrenal glands as a result of disease, which may be tuberculosis, cancer or by failure of the pituitary gland to produce ACTH. It occurs equally in males and females and is most common in mature adults. The main symptoms are anaemia, an incapacitating lethargy, both mental and physical, attacks of diarrhoea and vomiting, and darkening of the skin, especially in exposed areas such as the face and hands. Low blood pressure may cause fainting and giddiness, and there may in some cases also be abdominal pain and considerable weight loss.

The way in which deficiency of the cortical hormones causes the many different symptoms of Addison's disease is complex, but particularly important are the effects on the kidneys of the lack of mineralocorticoid hormones. Without these hormones, excessive amounts of salts and water are lost in the urine so that blood volume is greatly reduced. The pulse becomes weak, the circulation deteriorates and the capacity for even slight exertion is reduced. Gluco-corticoid hormones play a less important role in the disease, but their absence brings about loss of weight, low levels of sugar in the blood and disordered metabolism in general. Their absence is also the cause of anaemia and depression.

Treatment of Addison's disease consists of replacing the missing hormones with synthetic hormone preparations, and adding extra salt to the diet.

Cushing's syndrome
Cushing's syndrome is the result of abnormally high levels of cortisol in the bloodstream, caused either by overactivity of the adrenal cortex or by overproduction of ACTH by the anterior pituitary (the commonest cause). Cortisol affects a great number of metabolic processes, including water balance, carbohydrate and fat metabolism, bone formation, the central nervous and cardiovascular systems, and muscle activity. For example, the obesity and 'moon face' typical of a person with Cushing's syndrome are due to redistribution of body fat, while purple streaks on the abdomen and easy bruising may be due to effects upon blood vessels. Effects upon bone include a calcium-deficiency bone disease, osteoporosis. General weakness and inability to perform exercises, with extreme tiredness, are also symptoms. The growth of unwanted hair of a fine silky nature is also common. Treatment depends upon identifying the under-lying cause of the excess cortisol secretion. If overpro-duction of ACTH is the cause, for example, surgery or irradiation of the pituitary gland may be undertaken.

Hormones of growth and development

Hormones have considerable influence on growth and development. Life begins with a genetic blueprint which sets out the individual's basic pattern for growth. It is on this blueprint that hormones such as growth hormone (somato-trophin), insulin, thyroxine and the sex hormones act.

Growth hormone (GH) exerts its influence by affecting the assembly of protein molecules for new tissues. The level of GH secreted by the pituitary is of critical importance, as is shown by the effects of under- or over-production: during active growth too little GH produces dwarfism; an excess results in gigantism (see pages 42-3). The output of GH from the pituitary is controlled by messages from the hypo-thalamus, but, for its normal activity, GH needs to interact with insulin, thyroxine and testosterone. The effect of thyroxine on growth is striking. Its absence before birth results in cretinism (see page 43), in spite of the presence of growth hormone, and there is a subtle interaction between these two hormones in normal growth (see *Growth*, pages 38-42).

The dramatic mental and physical changes that occur in adolescence are brought about by the action of the sex hormones – oestrogen and progesterone in females and testosterone in males (see *Sex and Reproduction*, pages 11 and 16). These sex hormones produce the obvious physical differences between men and women, but also have an effect on bone growth. Before and during adoles-cence there is a rapid elongation of the long bones which slows up and then stops, earlier in girls and some years later in boys. The difference is the result of the difference in potency of the sex hormones: working in conjunction with growth hormone, oestrogen stimulates rapid bone-maturation in girls, resulting in relatively limited overall growth, while the influence of testosterone, being less potent than oestrogen, means that bone maturation is slower in boys and their bones therefore grow longer.

All the hormones involved in growth, with the exception of insulin, are secreted as a direct result of the influence of the hypothalamus, the chief motivator. The individual hormones then exert their specific effects on the different parts of the growing body.

Hormones and reproduction

The role of hormones in reproduction shows the wide-ranging effects of the endocrine system. As well as being involved in reproduction itself, the hormones produced by the ovaries and testes are important in the control of the reproductive cycle and in sexual development. (For a detailed account of hormones' effect on reproduction, see *Sex and Reproduction*, pages 8-20.)

Hormones and sugar metabolism

Sugar metabolism, the control of the glucose balance between blood and the tissues, is also controlled by the endocrine system. Glucose is a simple carbohydrate which is used by cells as an energy source; the nervous system in particular relies heavily on glucose. However inactive the body may be, the metabolism of all cells continues, and a constant supply of glucose is needed to keep the cells alive.

The pancreas has a dual role: it produces a mixture of digestive enzymes known as pancreatic juice, and it also secretes the hormones insulin and glucagon from the islets of Langerhans.

The body obtains glucose from food (see *The Digestive System*, pages 100-103). Carbohydrates such as starch are converted to glucose which enters the bloodstream. From the blood, the glucose can be temporarily stored as glycogen in muscles and the liver, and these stores can be used when extra energy is needed.

Since eating food is an intermittent activity, the influx of glucose into the blood is also intermittent. The endocrine system acts to keep the level of blood-glucose steady. Each time glucose pours into the bloodstream there is an increase in the secretion of the hormone insulin from the

pancreas, which causes the tissues of the body to absorb glucose from the blood. (Insulin also inhibits the breakdown of glycogen to glucose in the liver, and the breakdown of fat.)

If, on the other hand, there is too little glucose in the blood, other hormones come into play. The main one is glucagon which, like insulin, is produced by the islets of Langerhans in the pancreas. Glucagon encourages the release of glucose from the liver's glycogen store into the bloodstream, and the blood-glucose level is thereby increased. Growth hormone is also involved in raising blood-glucose levels, since an adequate supply of glucose is required for growing tissues.

The 'fight or flight' mechanism

Normally insulin acts with glucagon and growth hormone to maintain the energy levels of the body. But if the body has to face a crisis such as exposure to cold, danger or stress, three other hormones are secreted: adrenaline and cortisol from the adrenal glands and thyroxine from the thyroid gland.

The sick feeling in the pit of the stomach that is experienced in the face of danger is caused by the secretion of adrenaline. The crisis situation is recognized by the central nervous system – usually through sight or sound – which then alerts the autonomic nervous system (see *The Nervous System*, pages 188-92). The body is then made ready for action – 'fight or flight' – by adjustment of the tone of, and blood flow through, the relevant muscles; this happens by direct autonomic nervous stimulation. In addition, the autonomic nerves running to the medulla are stimulated, resulting in a massive flow of adrenaline and its close relation, noradrenaline. Cortisol, produced by the adrenal cortex, has a tendency to increase blood-glucose in conditions of physiological stress, such as inflammation.

Thyroxine is responsible for controlling the body's resting or basal metabolic rate (BMR). When the body is exposed to cold, the metabolic rate is increased in response to thyroxine, so that more heat is produced by metabolizing glucose.

Diabetes

Diabetes mellitus is a disorder of sugar and starch metabolism. In diabetes sugar is not taken up and used by the cells of the body, but instead accumulates in the blood and is excreted by the kidneys; hence the large quantities of sugar in the urine of diabetics.

There are two types of diabetes mellitus. The most common is non-insulin-dependent diabetes mellitus (NIDDM), sometimes called type-2 or maturity-onset diabetes. In this type, the pancreas produces some insulin but not enough to cope with the amount of glucose in the blood. This condition is often caused by obesity and excessive food intake, and can be treated by dieting alone.

In insulin-dependent diabetes mellitus (IDDM), also called type-1 or juvenile diabetes, there is a total or almost total failure of the pancreas to produce insulin. It usually starts before the age of twenty, and sufferers will need daily insulin injections for the rest of their lives in order to keep blood-glucose levels stable.

There are many causes of diabetes mellitus. Genetic factors are known to play a part, and diabetes can follow the removal or destruction by disease of the pancreas. Several diseases of other endocrine glands can also cause diabetes, and people taking steroid hormones or some diuretic drugs may develop diabetes as a side-effect.

Symptoms and diagnosis

Both types of diabetes mellitus cause the same main symptoms. Two of the first symptoms are excessive thirst and high urine output, the result of the accumulation of an abnormally high level of sugar in the blood which overflows into the urine. To keep the excess sugar dissolved in the urine, the volume of water excreted has to be increased. An affected person may find that the frequent need to pass urine occurs at night as well as during the day. This excess loss of fluid in turn causes dehydration, leading to constant thirst. Sugary urine is a breeding ground for microbes, which may cause urinary-tract problems such as cystitis (see page 121), or fungal infection such as *Candida*.

The diabetic's inability to utilize carbohydrate may lead to a breakdown of body protein and fat to supply essential energy needs, and this gives rise to a loss of weight and strength, and a need for much more sleep than usual.

Diabetes mellitus is easily diagnosed by testing the levels of glucose in blood and urine. Other conditions apart from diabetes can also cause high glucose levels in urine, however, so that if there is no clear result a glucose-tolerance test will be needed. In this, the blood-sugar level is measured during fasting and then at intervals after taking a measured dose of glucose.

Treatment

Diabetes mellitus used to be fatal, but since the discovery of insulin in the 1920s diabetics can lead a full and normal life. However, no cure has been found, and lifelong treatment is still essential for almost all diabetics. Treatment involves controlling the amount of blood-glucose by diet, insulin or drugs, the exact treatment depending on the individual.

Diet

Diet is often the only treatment needed for non-insulin dependent diabetes, but all diabetics should restrict the amount of sugar they eat. Small, regular meals high in unrefined carbohydrate and fibre, including vegetables, beans and wholemeal bread, are best, and the amount of food that can be eaten is usually determined by a dietician who plans a diet tailored to the individual. In cases of obesity, a strict weight-reducing diet will be required.

Insulin

For many diabetics, treatment with insulin is the main method of controlling the disease. Insulin has to be given by injection because it is a protein and so would be broken down by digestion if taken by mouth. Most types of insulin are extracted from the pancreas of cows or pigs, but human insulin, made by genetic engineering, is also available.

There are several different types of insulin, which vary mainly in how long they act in the body. Although using a long-acting insulin reduces the frequency of injection, this type often does not control the blood-sugar level accurately. Shorter-acting insulin, given twice daily, is often the best

treatment. Injections are given just under the skin, in the thighs, hips, abdomen or arms. (Insulin can also be given by a continuous infusion with a portable pump.) Insulin is usually self-injected shortly before a meal. Timing is important, since if the action of the insulin in lowering blood-glucose occurs before enough sugar has been absorbed from food into the blood, too low a blood-glucose level may occur and cause hypoglycaemia (see below).

Many diabetics on insulin therapy are encouraged to measure their level of blood sugar on a regular basis. This can be done by a simple test, which also helps the doctor decide whether the correct dose of insulin is being taken. By ensuring that blood-sugar levels remain as stable as possible, the risk of complications may be avoided.

Drugs

Certain drugs can be taken by mouth to control diabetes. They are often effective for those who develop diabetes in middle age. None of the oral diabetic drugs contains insulin, and each acts in a different way; the sulphonylurea type drugs, for example, stimulate the pancreas to produce more insulin and are therefore only effective when some pancreatic tissue is still producing the hormone. The biguanidine drugs can help lower blood-sugar levels but have serious side-effects and are rarely used.

Complications of diabetes

Hypoglycaemia

If the level of glucose in the blood is too low, perhaps after taking too much insulin, not enough food, or prolonged exercise, hypoglycaemia may result. Its symptoms are sweating, shaking, unsteadiness, double vision, slowness of speech and finally unconsciousness. Usually these symptoms occur gradually, and a diabetic can learn to recognize them and take some sugar to counteract the attack. More rarely, the attack can be sudden, which can be dangerous if the diabetic is driving or undertaking other potentially dangerous activities alone. Glucose must be given immediately, by injection into a vein.

Hyperglycaemia

If, on the other hand, not enough insulin is available, the diabetic may go into a coma, as the blood-sugar level rises above the normal level (hyperglycaemia). This may happen if an injection is missed or if the need for insulin is greater than normal, such as during an infection. Coma is sometimes the first sign that a person is diabetic. An early sign of hyperglycaemia is increased thirst, and if a urine test shows too much sugar, extra insulin should be taken.

Long-term risks

Eventually, diabetes can lead to long-term complications affecting the nerves, eyes, arteries and kidneys. Regular medical check-ups and strict control of the disease can help minimize the possibility of such complications developing.

The nerves most often affected are those in the legs, and pain and numbness in the feet are the most common symptoms. The autonomic nervous system can also be affected, giving rise to impotence and night-time diarrhoea. Microangiopathy, a disease of the small blood vessels, is peculiar to diabetics. Although vessels throughout the body may be affected, the kidneys and retinas are most frequently involved. Changes in the blood vessels of the retina (retinopathy) that occur in long-standing diabetics result in permanent reduction in vision. Although only a small proportion of people with retinopathy go blind, diabetes is a common cause of blindness in western countries because of the large diabetic population. Cataracts (page 173) and glaucoma (page 172) are two other conditions to which diabetics seem prone. All these conditions can be treated, and it is important for diabetics to have regular eye tests.

Impairment of kidney function may gradually develop in diabetics who have had the disease for twenty years or more. Kidney failure (see page 120) is now a more common cause of death in diabetics than diabetic coma.

Control of water balance

Approximately seventy per cent of the human body is water. Most essential biochemical reactions are carried out in solution in the cells, and the waste products are disposed of in solution in the urine. If there is too little water in the body the blood becomes over-concentrated. Special nerve receptors in the hypothalamus respond to this by stimulating the release of antidiuretic hormone (ADH) from the posterior pituitary gland. ADH is transported in the bloodstream to the kidneys and stops the excretion of water. The hypothalamus in its capacity as partial controller of the nervous system also initiates a drinking response.

The kidneys respond both to the messages from the hypothalamus and to the reduced volume of blood by producing a protein called renin. Renin interacts with a substance manufactured by the liver, and eventually the hormone angiotensin is produced. This hormone reinforces the drinking response induced by the hypothalamus and also enhances the release of ADH. At the same time, aldosterone is secreted from the adrenal cortex in response to stimulation by angiotensin. Aldasterone acts on the kidneys to prevent them excreting sodium ions, and this also further reduces urine formation. In the case of excess body water, the opposite mechanisms are set in motion.

Diabetes insipidus

Diabetes insipidus is a rare chronic disorder with symptoms of inordinate thirst and excessive output of dilute urine which does not contain sugar. It is entirely different from diabetes mellitus, and may arise because of a deficiency of ADH. Diabetes insipidus is occasionally caused by an hereditary defect in the pituitary gland but, more commonly, arises for no known reason. It may also be a secondary disorder, or occur after damage to the pituitary gland or the hypothalamus. The disease is treated by supplying the missing hormone by injection.

Another form of diabetes insipidus is caused not by a deficiency of ADH but by the kidney tubules not responding to the hormone. This form of the disorder, known as nephrogenic diabetes insipidus, appears mainly in infants who, because of the large amounts of urine which they pass, have been termed 'water-babies'. The outlook for these infants is poor because they do not respond to ADH, although some other drugs may be effective. In these cases the main treatment is to give sufficient fluid to counteract the constant loss of water in the urine.

Living with diabetes

Being a diabetic is not simply a matter of suffering from a disease; it involves an entirely different way of life. In general, the diabetic has to plan activities more carefully than a normal person, and to do this successfully needs to learn as much as possible about the disease – how the body controls blood sugar, and the effects not only of insulin and other drugs, but also of exercise, illness and different foods. Nevertheless, it is important that diabetics do not let the condition rule their lives. Provided they follow the simple rules and procedures they have been taught, few activities will have to be restricted, and they will be able to follow active and productive lives.

If you are a diabetic, the following guidelines should prove useful to you in coping with your disease so that you can lead a normal life.

- *If you plan to go on a long walk or partake in some vigorous sport, you need to make sure by eating extra food beforehand that your blood sugar level does not fall so low that you pass out.*

- *Regular mealtimes are important: if you miss a meal or a meal is delayed, eat some sugar or a biscuit to restore blood sugar levels. It is useful always to carry sugar lumps or sweets with you. Your blood sugar level may also fall if you have taken too much insulin by mistake; again, some sugar will restore it to normal.*

- *Make sure that friends and associates know that you are diabetic and understand that you cannot take irregular meals or drinks, or go on binges. They should know, too, the symptoms of low blood sugar (hypoglycaemia) – faintness, sweating and paleness, unsteadiness and disturbed behaviour that may resemble drunkenness – so that they can offer sugar and send for medical help should your blood sugar level drop.*

- *Avoid operating machinery or driving unless you have eaten in the previous two hours.*

- *Children and those particularly prone to hypoglycaemic attacks should carry a card or wear a bracelet giving details of their condition and instructions for treatment in an emergency.*

- *To help prevent foot problems to which older diabetics are especially prone, attention should be paid daily to the condition of the feet. Wash them and wear clean socks or tights every day, and make sure that shoes are comfortable and do not pinch or rub the skin. Have any corns, calluses or ingrowing toenails treated promptly by a chiropodist. Do not risk making a foot problem worse by treating it yourself.*

The Nervous System

The nervous system controls, coordinates and monitors the activities of the body. It is responsible for sending messages to the various muscles to produce movement – both consciously, for those movements we are aware of and 'will' to happen, and unconsciously, for 'automatic' activities such as breathing, heartbeat and digestion. The nervous system also receives and interprets information from the senses, to tell us about our surroundings. Above all, the nervous system is responsible for behaviour, thought and personality.

The nervous system has three main parts. First is the central nervous system (often called the CNS) which consists of the brain and spinal cord. Second is the peripheral nervous system (PNS) which takes messages to and from the CNS and all other parts of the body. Third is the autonomic nervous system, which controls the 'automatic' functioning of the body.

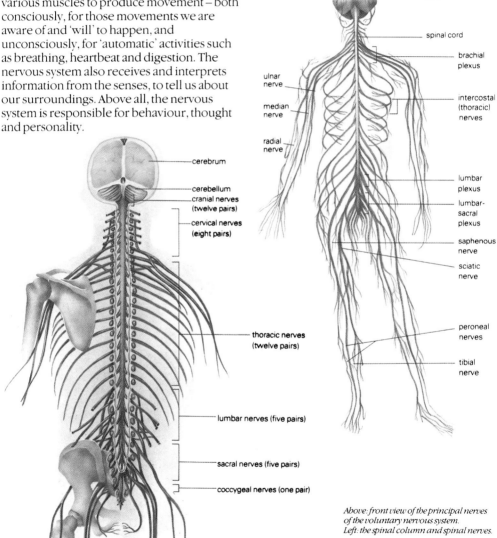

cerebral cortex

spinal cord

brachial plexus

intercostal (thoracic) nerves

ulnar nerve

median nerve

radial nerve

lumbar plexus

lumbar-sacral plexus

saphenous nerve

sciatic nerve

peroneal nerves

tibial nerve

cerebrum

cerebellum

cranial nerves (twelve pairs)

cervical nerves (eight pairs)

thoracic nerves (twelve pairs)

lumbar nerves (five pairs)

sacral nerves (five pairs)

coccygeal nerves (one pair)

Above: front view of the principal nerves of the voluntary nervous system.
Left: the spinal column and spinal nerves.

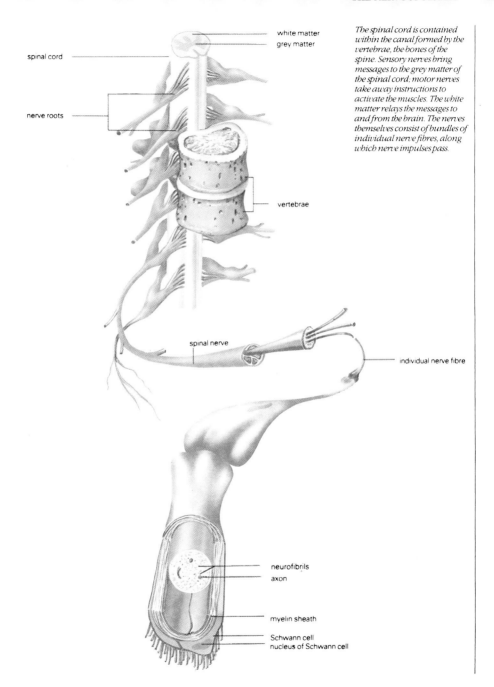

white matter

grey matter

spinal cord

nerve roots

vertebrae

spinal nerve

individual nerve fibre

neurofibrils

axon

myelin sheath

Schwann cell

nucleus of Schwann cell

The spinal cord is contained within the canal formed by the vertebrae, the bones of the spine. Sensory nerves bring messages to the grey matter of the spinal cord; motor nerves take away instructions to activate the muscles. The white matter relays the messages to and from the brain. The nerves themselves consist of bundles of individual nerve fibres, along which nerve impulses pass.

Nerve cells (neurons)

All parts of the nervous system consist of special nerve cells called neurons. Each neuron consists of a cell body from which there are many slender projections. One of these projections, called an axon, is usually longer than the others, and may be several feet long. The axon is often called a 'nerve fibre' and it normally carries nerve impulses away from the cell body. The shorter projections, called dendrites, usually carry nerve impulses towards the cell body. Some dendrites may also be very long. Neurons communicate by passing nerve impulses between their axons and dendrites, though these projections do not actually touch each other. At the junction between the axon of one neuron and the dendrites of another is a special connection called a synapse, and there is a tiny gap (the synaptic gap) between the axon and dendrite.

There are many different kinds of neurons throughout the nervous system, and their structure varies with their particular function. For example, sensory neurons, which carry impulses from receptors to the central nervous system, usually have a single long dendrite and a single long axon. Motor neurons, which carry impulses from the central nervous system to a muscle, often have very short dendrites and a single long axon. Sensory neurons are responsible for collecting information about the surroundings and the workings of the body and sending it to the brain and spinal cord; motor neurons carry instructions from the brain and spinal cord to the muscles in various parts of the body, to produce movement. Neurons are not simply wires through which nerve impulses travel: between the point where a nerve impulse starts and where it finishes there may be very many neurons, connected by synapses.

Nerve fibres are covered by a sheath of white fatty material called myelin, and the 'white matter' of the brain and spinal cord consists of fibres covered by myelin. The myelin covering is important both in nurturing the nerve fibre within and insulating the nerve impulse from adjacent fibres. The white, shiny, cordlike structure known as a nerve is, in fact, a collection of many individual nerve fibres and cells. Some nerves consist entirely of sensory neurons taking sensory information to the brain; others consist wholly of motor fibres taking information to the muscles to instruct them on how to contract. Some nerves contain both sensory and motor neurons.

Nerve impulses

A nerve impulse, a special kind of electrical pulse, is brought about by the movements of chemicals into and out of the neuron. These produce an electrical current which flows along the nerve. When the electrical impulse reaches the synapse it is transmitted by chemicals produced at the end of the axon, which travel across the gap to the dendrites of the next neuron to start an impulse. These chemicals are called neurotransmitters.

Because of the way the nerve impulse travels, it moves relatively slowly – about 320 kph (200 mph) – compared with, say, the speed of electricity, which is about 17,956,000 kilometres (11,160,000 miles) a minute. For this reason nerve reactions are never instantaneous.

The brain

The human brain controls not only our thoughts and conscious actions but also all the unconscious functions of our bodies, through the rest of the nervous system.

The brain has the consistency of thick blancmange, and is contained and protected within the rigid bony skull or cranium. At the base of the skull is a hole, through which the spinal cord passes. The brain and spinal cord are protected by three covering layers of tissue called the meninges. The outermost of these layers, the dura mater, is the thickest; it lines the skull, and is very fibrous. The intermediate layer and the innermost layer, called the arachnoid mater and the pia mater, adhere closely to the brain and spinal cord, and are thin and delicate. Between the dura mater and the arachnoid mater there is a tiny space that contains fluid – the cerebrospinal fluid. This fluid bathes the whole surface of the brain and the spinal cord.

The brain consists of the two cerebral hemispheres and the midbrain, and behind them the cerebellum and the brainstem. The brainstem consists of the pons and the medulla oblongata, and connects the brain and the spinal cord.

The cerebral hemispheres

The cerebral hemispheres form the largest part of the brain. The right hemisphere controls the left side of the body, and vice versa. Each hemisphere is divided into four lobes, called the frontal, parietal, temporal and occipital lobes. If a brain is cut open it appears greyish at the outer edges, and white inside. The grey outer layer is called the cortex and contains many thousands of nerve cell bodies, whereas the white areas contain mainly nerve fibres. These nerve fibres connect nerve cells with one another in various parts of the brain. Some of the nerve fibres are very long indeed, running from the brain all the way down the spinal column, carrying impulses as far as the feet and toes.

The surfaces of the hemispheres are made up of flattened folds, or convolutions. These have small, rather narrow, valleys between them, termed fissures. Some areas of the hemispheres have become specialized; for example, the area of the brain that deals with body movement, the motor cortex, is in front of the cleft called the Rolandic fissure. The area immediately behind this large fissure deals with sensation, and the occipital lobe, at the back of the hemisphere, with vision. Large areas of the frontal lobes have functions which are not well understood, but which are concerned with personality and emotional attitudes.

One area of the cerebral hemispheres is responsible for integrating the many complex nervous pathways that deal with speech. Many nervous interactions are necessary for understanding words and for controlling the muscles that enable us to speak. The speech centre is near the motor cortex; it is always in the left hemisphere in right-handed people and in the right hemisphere in nearly all left-handed people. The hemisphere containing the speech centre is known as the dominant hemisphere.

In the speech centre 'memories' are stored for the combinations of muscular movements necessary to speak each word. Each word requires a unique combination of

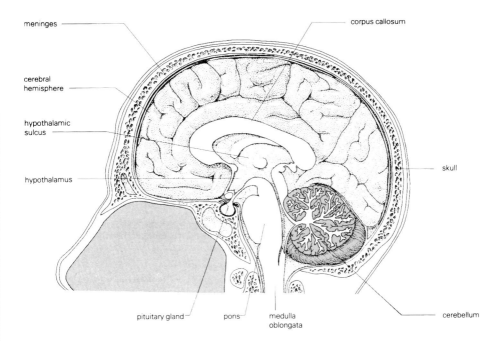

Above: sectional view of the middle of the brain.

Below: external view of the brain.

muscular contractions for its utterance, and depends upon the coordinated action of vocal cords, throat and tongue muscles, soft palate, lips, chest wall and diaphragm. The cells in the speech centre do not themselves send impulses to the speech muscles, but influence the motor cells for these muscles which lie in the motor cortex. These centres are so near each other that disease of one area frequently affects others. Since nerve fibres from one side of the brain cross over and act on the other side of the body, a stroke that produces paralysis on the left side will not affect the speech centre if the person is right-handed. Should paralysis occur on the right side, however, the chances are very high that the ability to speak normally will be lost.

Within the cerebral hemispheres are paired cavities, called ventricles, which are filled with cerebrospinal fluid (CSF). This fluid also flows into the space between the arachnoid and pia mater – the subarachnoid space (as mentioned earlier) – and bathes and cushions the brain and spinal cord along its whole length. The CSF is normally clear and watery, and a healthy adult has about 140 ml (5 fl oz) of it. It is constantly being made, circulated and re-absorbed.

Deep in the cerebral hemispheres lie the thalamus and basal ganglia. The thalamus is a relay station for the sensory pathways from the body to the cerebral cortex. The basal ganglia are involved with the control of movements and it is here that Parkinson's disease, or paralysis agitans (slow progressive trembling), may arise.

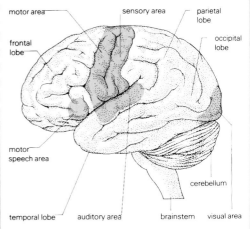

The brainstem is concerned with the essential mechanisms of the body, such as respiration, blood pressure, heart-function, alertness and sleep. The lower end of the brainstem, called the medulla oblongata, is where sensory and motor nerve fibres of the spinal cord cross over. At the upper end of the brainstem there are connections with the centres in the cerebellum concerned with consciousness.

The spinal cord

The spinal cord extends from the brain all the way down the vertebral column. In cross-section the cord is seen to contain an H-shaped area of grey matter and a surrounding area of white matter. The grey matter contains the nerve-cell bodies while the white matter consists of nerve fibres conveying information to and from cells higher up the cord or in the brain.

The peripheral nerves

From the spinal cord run thirty-one pairs of nerves that branch and ramify to reach every part of the body. Motor nerves leave from the front of the cord, and sensory nerves join at the back of the cord. The part of the nerve where it joins the cord (the nerve root) runs through or between the bones of the spine; this portion may be pressed on or damaged by a prolapsed (slipped) disc (see page 137) or by a collapsed vertebra.

In addition to spinal nerves, twelve pairs of cranial nerves run to and from the brain and branch out into the muscles and sense organs of the head, face, neck and chest.

Reflexes

The information that sensory nerves supply to other parts of the nervous system can have several results. Between a stimulus being received and action being taken there may be several complex connections. One of the simplest connections between the sensory and motor parts of the nervous system is the reflex, the most basic being a spinal reflex. An example is the knee-jerk reflex: if the point just below the kneecap of one leg is tapped when it is hanging over the other leg, a stimulus passes along a sensory nerve to the spinal cord. Here, a straight-through connection is made to a motor neuron which then stimulates the muscles in the leg to jerk. At the same time, the brain is informed of what is happening but is not involved in the response.

There are many other types of reflex, most of them including quite complex nerve pathways, such as sneezing, urination and digestion. Some of these can be modified by 'training' and conditioning. For example in a famous experiment carried out by Pavlov, a dog was conditioned to associate the ringing of a bell with being fed. After a while, when the bell was rung the dog salivated even though no food was present. Salivation, both in dogs and humans, is not under conscious control, and the pathways had been established which associated the bell with food. This is called a conditioned reflex.

The autonomic nervous system

The autonomic system controls 'automatic' functions of the body. These include controlling most glands, the heart, and organs controlled by the action of involuntary muscle such as the bronchi, arteries, stomach and intestines. There are two parts of the autonomic system, the sympathetic and para-sympathetic, which work in opposite ways. For example, stimulation of the sympathetic system increases heart rate and stimulation of the parasympathetic system slows it. The sympathetic system mainly uses the neurotransmitter adrenaline while the parasympathetic system acts through the chemical acetylcholine.

Sympathetic nerve cells are collected together in structures called ganglia in the neck and chest, and in the nerve trunks that lie on either side of the spinal column to connect with the spinal nerves. Parasympathetic nerves arise in the brain and also in the lower part of the spinal cord.

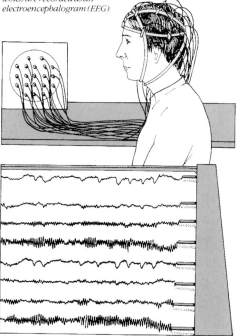

An electroencephalograph is used to record the electrical activity of the brain. Electrodes attached to the scalp detect the brain waves which are recorded as an electroencephalogram (EEG).

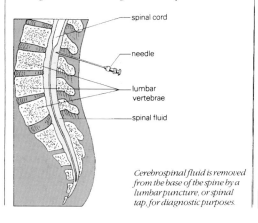

spinal cord

needle

lumbar vertebrae

spinal fluid

Cerebrospinal fluid is removed from the base of the spine by a lumbar puncture, or spinal tap, for diagnostic purposes.

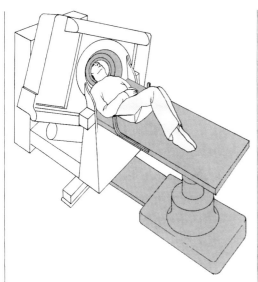

The CAT (computerized axial tomography) scanner takes photographs of soft tissues such as the brain for diagnostic purposes, to detect abnormalities such as a tumour.

Examining the nervous system

Investigation of nervous disorders involves looking for general symptoms as well as testing motor and sensory function, sensation, coordination, the eyes, and blood pressure. Three particular types of investigation that can be useful in diagnosis are lumbar puncture, electroencephalography and X-rays.

In lumbar puncture a sample of the cerebrospinal fluid is withdrawn through a needle inserted between the vertebrae in the small of the back. By examining the constituents of the fluid much can be learnt about the state of the nervous system. The electroencephalograph (EEG) is a machine that records the electrical currents produced by the brain cells. Changes in the pattern of electrical activity occur during certain disorders such as epilepsy.

X-rays of the head can often show abnormalities of the skull or its contents. A radio-opaque liquid is injected into the arteries supplying blood to the brain, or air is introduced through a lumbar puncture, to show up certain structures. CAT scanners have recently made these procedures less common.

Consciousness and unconsciousness

Consciousness is the state of being awake and aware of oneself and one's environment. Fluctuations in the level of consciousness normally occur during the day, from full alertness and deep concentration on the one hand to drowsiness and thought wandering, often after a meal, on the other. Sleep is the state of physical and mental inactivity from which a person can rapidly be aroused to full consciousness. There are several levels of unconsciousness: in coma, the deepest level, the person lies as if asleep but does not respond to external stimuli; in the deepest coma the subject will not even respond to painful stimulations, and reflexes are absent. In lesser depths of unconsciousness these reflexes are present and the patient will stir or moan if shouted at or if the skin is pinched.

Stupor is a condition which may precede the development of coma. If stimulated vigorously, the patient will open his eyes and look round, but responds slowly to spoken commands. Frequently, in conditions such as liver or kidney failure, for example, a sequence through confusion, stupor, light unconsciousness, and ultimately to deep coma can be traced. In other cases, for example following a head injury, the subject passes instantly from normal consciousness to deep coma.

The areas of the brain most concerned with consciousness are the brainstem and the thalamus. The cerebral cortex must be severely and extensively damaged before consciousness is lost, but damage to the upper brainstem can also produce deep unconsciousness. The most important part of the brainstem, as far as consciousness is concerned, is the reticular formation. This is composed of widely scattered nerve cells whose processes form a net-like (reticular) mesh. The formation extends from the lower medulla upwards through the midbrain to the thalamus, and has wide connections with the cerebellum, the cerebral cortex, the spinal cord, and other areas of the central nervous system.

Coma

The main causes of coma are head injury, poisoning by alcohol or drugs or other chemicals, stroke, epilepsy and diabetes. The cause of unconsciousness may be obvious, for example where there is a head injury, but the situation is often not as simple as it seems at first. A person in an apparently drunken state may also have a head injury, or a stroke victim may also be diabetic. Diabetics and epileptics carry a card or wear a necklace or bracelet indicating the disease from which they suffer and what is needed in case of emergency, so routine examination of an unconscious person should include a search for these items.

Coma is a medical emergency, and it is essential that the airway is clear and that breathing is not obstructed. Once under medical care, the insertion of a tube into the mouth and down the windpipe, and possible the assistance of a breathing machine, may be necessary. The doctor also makes sure that blood pressure is satisfactory and that the patient is not bleeding (internal bleeding is often difficult to detect).

Anyone who is unconscious for any length of time depends on others for survival and should be in hospital. He or she must be fed either by a stomach tube or by injecting nutrients directly into a vein (parenteral nutrition). The deeply unconscious patient is unable to pass urine or faeces and so nursing must take this into account. Other problems are the prevention of pressure sores if the patient lies in one position for long, and the risk of pneumonia because stagnant fluid collects in the lungs.

Concussion

Anyone who has received a minor blow to the head knows the momentary stupor and the unpleasant sensation of bright lights and stars before the eyes. If the impact of the blow can be clearly recalled, however, and there is no confusion associated with the injury, concussion has not occurred.

Sometimes the victim of a head injury, as the result of an accident or a fall, appears to be dead: he or she has become completely paralysed and lax, with hardly any pulse, and no breathing. Yet within a few seconds the person gets up, 'comes to', makes a complete recovery, and may be unaware of any injury, being unable to remember the impact of the blow or the immediate events leading up to it, although of course he or she can feel the bruised head and recall the general circumstances. This transient state (retrograde amnesia) has been explained as a momentary cessation of the brain's activity, and an example of true concussion. Because of the possibility that damage to the skull or brain may have occurred, concussed people should be examined by a doctor, preferably in hospital, and kept under observation, at least overnight.

Diseases and disorders of the nervous system

Headache

Headache is a very common symptom with many different possible causes, most of them minor and self-limiting. One particular type of severe, recurrent headache – migraine – is dealt with separately below.

A number of different parts of the head and neck may be responsible for causing the pain of a headache, and the types of pain they produce differ. The brain tissue itself cannot feel pain, but the membranes surrounding the brain (the meninges) and the arteries passing through the brain may be sources of pain if they become infected, inflamed or abnormally stretched. The bones of the skull, like the brain itself, cannot feel pain, but like other bones they are covered by the periosteum, a thin 'skin' which is sensitive to pain if stretched or inflamed. Within the skull-bones are several air-filled spaces, including the sinuses of the respiratory tract and the cavity inside the middle ear; we are conscious of changes in air pressure inside these spaces, and if the pressure changes are sudden or extreme then pain will result.

Over the periosteum and skull lie the scalp muscles, covering the skull at the forehead and temples, and spreading over the top of the head to the back of the neck. These muscles contract when we wrinkle our brow or scalp, and can be felt contracting at the temple when the jaws are clenched. Like other muscles, scalp muscles may produce very severe pain indeed. Cranial arteritis is most common in the elderly, and diagnosis is important because if the arteries at the back of the eye become affected blindness may result.

Meningitis, an infection of the meninges, is a rare but important cause of severe headache. Bleeding inside the head, which has spread into the cerebrospinal fluid, may also irritate the meninges and cause pain.

Pressure inside the skull causes headache and this may occur for a number of reasons. The brain itself may swell if its blood supply is damaged or if it becomes infected, a condition known as encephalitis. Tumours, blood clots and abscesses in the brain will also increase pressure and cause headache.

Mild injuries rarely cause headaches, but a more severe injury to the head is often followed by headache, the cause of which is uncertain. The pain may not occur at the site of the injury but may be a general throbbing ache, often becoming worse on exertion, sudden movement or bending forward. Headaches such as these nearly always get better in due course. Very rarely, a head injury may result in slow bleeding inside the head, producing a blood clot (subdural haematoma) which slowly enlarges and increases the pressure inside the skull. A headache associated with a blood clot is usually accompanied by other symptoms such as drowsiness, vomiting or confusion.

Treating headaches

A doctor should be consulted if a headache starts suddenly and is very severe, particularly if it is followed by vomiting or neck stiffness. These signs, and not being able to look at a bright light, may indicate irritation or inflammation of the meninges. A continuous headache which starts gradually and increases steadily in severity over the course of several days or weeks may be due to rising pressure inside the skull; any headache associated with drowsiness, confusion or loss of consciousness may have a serious cause, as may any failure of vision associated with headache; all these cases should be investigated by a doctor.

A simple, occasional headache with no obvious cause, or one associated with fever, a slight bang on the head or a cold, may reasonably be treated with a pain-killer such as aspirin or paracetamol.

Tension headaches and those associated with anxiety or depression are best dealt with by relieving the tension or depression. If headache is a feature of depression and it is not possible to treat or find the cause of the depression, then antidepressant drugs may help the headache (see *Mental Health and Illness,* pages 64-71).

Headache is one of the conditions in which alternative (complementary) therapies have had some success. Acupuncture and herbalism are effective for some people; likewise, relaxation and yoga-type techniques can ease tension and induce relaxation, which is often all that is needed to cure a tension headache. One other procedure that has been effective against headache is biofeedback, where the person is able to see his or her own brain waves (EEG traces) on a machine and consciously try to alter them, often with relief of the ache.

Migraine

Migraine is a particular type of severe and recurring head pain. The exact cause of the pain is not known, though it has been linked with muscular spasm of arteries in the head. The arteries first narrow, then widen, though why they do this is not clear. Somewhere between one in five and one in ten of the adult population are said to suffer from this condition. It is more likely to occur in energetic, lively people and some sufferers report that it is triggered by overwork, stress or the release of stress, taking the contraceptive pill, flashing lights, or certain foods such as chocolate, cheese, fruit and fried items.

Symptoms

Before a migraine attack there is often an aura, a warning sign such as flashing lights or zig-zag patterns before the eyes, or a tingling feeling in the face or limbs. Then comes the headache: a severe, throbbing pain usually on one side of the head, accompanied by feelings of nausea or actual vomiting and possibly dislike of bright lights. The sufferer is virtually incapacitated by the pain. Other symptoms include redness and watering of one eye, and possibly a runny nose. The attack may last from a few hours to a day or more, and may recur after a few days, or not till months or years later.

Treatment

A first attack of migraine is a frightening event and a doctor should be consulted who may order special tests such as X-rays to eliminate other causes of the headache. One common fear is that the pain is caused by a brain tumour, but as doctors have been known to say, 'You cannot have a brain tumour on Wednesdays and Saturdays and not for the rest of the week.'

Once the pain is diagnosed as migraine, there are several self-help procedures the sufferer can carry out (see also pages 200-201). For example, lie down in a darkened room and relax; trying to carry on as normal will probably make the attack last longer. Keep a diary of attacks and try to ascertain whether there are any trigger factors such as particular foods or stressful events; if so, take action to remove them. Worry about the migraine (which is an extremely unpleasant but not inherently dangerous condition) can itself bring on further attacks, so discuss the situation fully with your doctor until you are satisfied and understand the problem. Several types of drug may help certain migraine sufferers; some help to prevent the attacks, others reduce the severity of an attack once it begins. These drugs do not work for everyone, and should be taken exactly as prescribed.

Congenital malformations of the nervous system

If a large part of the brain is missing at birth, the result is usually fatal. Two other congenital disorders of the nervous system are spina bifida and hydrocephalus.

Spina bifida

Spina bifida is caused by the imperfect development of the vertebrae of the spinal column. Instead of forming a complete ring of bone through which the spinal cord passes, some of the vertebrae remain open so that the nerves of the spinal cord are unprotected, and may also be defective. The child is born with the spinal cord exposed through gaps left in the skin and malformed vertebrae. The site and extent of the defect has an important influence on the outlook. Hydrocephalus (see below) is often present in children with spina bifida.

If untreated, the majority of children with severe spina bifida will die soon after birth. The cause of death is often infection of the exposed spinal cord, or complications that arise from hydrocephalus. Closing the gap by surgery greatly increases the survival rate, but any defect in the formation of the spinal cord cannot be rectified, and patients can expect a restricted life with paralysed legs, rectum and bladder.

The degree of paralysis varies greatly, though the area affected is always situated below the spinal deformity. As well as paralysis, fractures and dislocation of hips and other joints can affect the degree of mobility that can be achieved. Incontinence affects about eighty-five per cent of patients to some degree, and this can also lead to serious kidney conditions. Kidney failure is one of the main causes of death in spina bifida patients.

Spina bifida tends to run in families. A test can be done in pregnancy to find whether it is present, by examining the amniotic fluid surrounding the fetus for the presence of alphafetoprotein, which if positive indicates spina bifida.

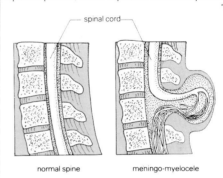

spinal cord

normal spine   meningo-myelocele

Section of a normal spine compared with one affected by meningo-myelocele, a severe type of spina bifida.

Hydrocephalus

Hydrocephalus is enlargement of the head of an infant because more cerebrospinal fluid is produced than is absorbed; as a result, fluid builds up in the ventricles of the brain causing pressure that enlarges the head. Usually something obstructs the flow of cerebrospinal fluid between where it is produced and where it is absorbed, distending the part above the obstruction. The blockage

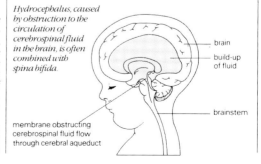

Hydrocephalus, caused by obstruction to the circulation of cerebrospinal fluid in the brain, is often combined with spina bifida.

brain

build-up of fluid

brainstem

membrane obstructing cerebrospinal fluid flow through cerebral aqueduct may be due to congenital malformations, a cyst or tumour, or scarring from infection or accidental injury. Hydrocephalus occurs in about three per 1000 births.

The only treatment is surgery, after which the outlook is quite good. Operations attempt to bypass the obstruction by shunting the fluid elsewhere along a tube, usually to a vein in the neck or near the heart. Without surgery, about two-thirds of affected infants would die at an early age.

Infections of the nervous system

The brain, the spinal cord and the peripheral nerves may all become infected and inflamed. When the brain is involved it is called encephalitis; and infection of the meninges is called meningitis. Infection of the spinal cord is myelitis and infection of the nerves is neuritis.

Encephalitis

Encephalitis is usually caused by a virus infection and may cause headache, fever, nausea, drowsiness, or coma. Paralysis, numbness, blindness and deafness may also result. Although a full recovery may be made, some infections can be fatal or lead to permanent disability.

Meningitis

Meningitis is inflammation of the membranes that cover the brain and spinal cord. The symptoms of meningitis include headache, which may be very severe, either in the front of the head or all over. There is also often pain in the back and limbs, and fever which may be accompanied by vomiting or, in children, by fits. Bright lights hurt the eyes, and the sufferer has to lie still, and wants to be left alone; if untreated his or her mental state gradually deteriorates, through confusion and drowsiness, to coma.

Viruses are a common cause of meningitis. The meningitis may be the only sign of infection or it may be a rare complication of mumps, measles, glandular fever, infectious hepatitis, or other viral infections. Meningitis may also be caused by bacteria, either spreading from elsewhere (for example, pneumonia, osteomyelitis, or tuberculosis), or sometimes, as with a virus, it may be the only sign of infection. One form is meningococcal meningitis, the result of infection with the bacterium *Neisseria meningitidis*, with which there may also be a skin rash.

In all cases of suspected meningitis, a lumbar puncture is performed and the cerebrospinal fluid examined. There is usually an increase in CSF pressure; pus in the fluid will be evidence of bacterial infection. Treatment depends on the infecting organism. For bacterial infections, the appropriate antibiotics must be used. In viral meningitis the patient is rested and nursed; complications are watched for and treated if they arise. Most patients recover.

Neuritis

Neuritis is a term covering a large group of disorders affecting the peripheral nerves anywhere in the body. It is not necessarily due to inflammation; pressure on a nerve or nerve root is a common cause. Occasionally other nerves are involved, and in addition to pain, there is widespread muscular weakness and sometimes paralysis. This is called polyneuritis which can have many causes. A common form of polyneuritis occurs in the alcoholic who may, in addition to pins and needles and numbness, experience severe, cramp-like pains in the calves, particularly at night. Polyneuritis may be caused by infections, diphtheria and leprosy in particular, or it may be a result of untreated diabetes or vitamin B deficiency.

Shingles *(Herpes zoster)* is caused by the infection by a virus of a group of nerve cells. Irritation and pain are the first symptoms, followed by blisters in the area of skin supplied by the nerve. The pain can be very severe and last several weeks, and discomfort may last for months. This disorder is described in more detail in *The Skin*, page 78.

Sciatica causes pain in the buttock, thigh or leg, produced by pressure on the sciatic nerve or on its roots as they emerge from the spinal cord. The most common cause is an intervertebral disc protruding and lying in contact with one or more nerve roots. There are, however, other causes of sciatica, including disorders within the spinal canal, such as collapse of a vertebra, tumours affecting nerve roots and the meninges; and disorders within the nerve canal.

The pain of sciatica begins in the back and shoots down the back of the leg to the sole, or over the top of the foot. There is often a spasm in the muscles of the back, and movements such as lying down or undressing become difficult. The treatment of sciatica includes bed-rest and physiotherapy. Those who must be active may obtain relief from a surgical corset or a plaster cast, although these tend to weaken the muscles of the back. For further information, see the description of prolapsed disc on page 137.

Neuralgia is a term used to describe stabs or surges of pain felt in one or more nerves, and there is often no known cause. The trigeminal nerve, which supplies the skin of the face, is commonly involved (tic douloureux). The pain, felt in severe, almost unbearable stabs which can last one or two minutes, occurs in the cheek, jaw or forehead depending on which division of the nerve is affected. It can usually be controlled by drugs but if this treatment is not successful it may be necessary either to cut or inject fibres of the affected nerve, to destroy it.

Stroke

Stroke is the popular term for the condition of apoplexy, or cerebro-vascular accident (CVA). It is caused by a disturbance in the brain's activity due to interference with its blood supply. Stroke victims are usually middle-aged, often over sixty, but younger people may suffer from the condition, which is a major cause of death in the West.

If a blockage occurs in one of the arteries supplying oxygenated blood to part of the brain, that part of the brain will stop functioning and the cells concerned may die if the stoppage continues more than a few minutes. The blockage may be caused by a clot forming in the artery itself (thrombosis) or from a clot forming elsewhere in the blood system and travelling to the brain (embolism). There are also several types of haemorrhage which may cause stroke, as described below.

A person who suffers a major stroke on the right side of the brain, and survives, will be left with a left hemiplegia, that is paralysis of the left arm and leg and lower half of the face. There will also be diminished sensation in the same area of the body, and loss of awareness of objects in the left half of the field of vision. A stroke in the left side of the brain will cause similar disturbances but on the right side of the body and, in addition, interference with speech function, varying from total loss (aphasia) to some difficulty in finding correct words (dysphasia).

Recovery from a stroke is usually slow, and encouragement of the patient from doctors, nurses, physiotherapists, relations and friends is the most important part of the treatment to restore bodily function and help the return to normal life.

A temporary condition that may resemble a mild stroke is called a transient ischaemic attack. The cause is usually a temporary blockage of a small artery in the head, as with a stroke, but this soon clears and the symptoms fade after a few hours. Someone who experiences a transient ischaemic attack should consult a doctor, however, since there is an increased risk of a stroke in the future.

Cerebral haemorrhage
Cerebral haemorrhage is the most serious form of apoplexy. It usually occurs in elderly people whose cerebral arteries have been subjected to the strain of prolonged high blood pressure. The artery ruptures deep within the brain, and the tissue is damaged by the flood of blood under high pressure; the patient loses consciousness and may die with-

blockage in artery

area and artery
deprived of
blood

temporal lobe
cut away to
demonstrate
blockage

The brain seen from below, showing the area affected by a stroke caused by an arterial blockage.

in a few minutes of the onset of the attack. If the patient survives the initial stroke, a clot of blood forms in the brain and the increased pressure inside the skull stops the bleeding. This increase in pressure, however, will lead to interference with the brain's control of respiration, so that breathing becomes more laboured and stops unless helped artificially. In this small minority of cases, surgical treatment can be effective: the skull is opened and the clot removed. Life is saved but severe disability usually follows.

Subarachnoid haemorrhage
Subarachnoid haemorrhage is a disease of younger people, and occurs when a small abnormal, balloon-like swelling on an artery, called an aneurysm, bursts into the subarachnoid space between the meninges. The contact of blood with the sensitive meninges causes sudden intense headache and stiffness of the neck. There may be loss of consciousness, depending on the volume of blood which leaks from the aneurysm, and the deeper the degree of unconsciousness, the worse is the outlook for the patient. The diagnosis is confirmed by lumbar puncture, revealing blood in the cerebrospinal fluid. Patients who survive the initial attack usually require further investigation.

Cerebral thrombosis
Cerebral thrombosis is found in older people whose cerebral arteries are the site of atherosclerosis (see *The Heart and Circulation*, page 160). It is often a less dramatic event than cerebral haemorrhage. Consciousness may be preserved, and it is not unusual for the patient to wake from sleep to find that one arm and leg are weak, and the mouth distorted by the pull of the unopposed face muscles on the non-paralysed side; if the left side of the brain is involved, there is difficulty in speaking. In such cases recovery may be expected in a few weeks or months.

Epilepsy
Epilepsy is a disorder of the brain in which there is a tendency to suffer from fits (seizures or convulsions). It has been estimated that one in every two hundred people may be affected. Epilepsy may begin at any age, and seizures may occur with a frequency varying from once in a lifetime to many times a day. The general health of the individual may be perfect, both mentally and physically, or there may be severe mental and physical retardation. With treatment many epileptics are capable of leading a completely normal, productive life, while others are so severely affected that constant care is necessary. Mental defect, though often a feature of the disorder, is in many cases a result of the condition interfering with education rather than inherent mental inadequacy. There is a slight tendency for epilepsy to run in families.

Symptoms
Epilepsy can be divided into two basic varieties, described by the French words *petit mal* and *grand mal*. Both these forms of epilepsy are characterized by loss of consciousness, but they differ enormously. Petit mal consists of a brief break in consciousness without a convulsive seizure and lasts for seconds only. It may not even be apparent to the casual observer, since the subject does not usually fall to the

ground and simply appears to be daydreaming. If this type of seizure occurs frequently however – and it may happen in serious cases up to hundreds of times a day – the implications are obvious. This type of epilepsy has been termed 'absences'.

Attacks come without warning; the patient is motionless, and either a failure to respond to commands or a staring expression is the only sign of abnormality. In its more severe forms, petit mal may cause more prolonged periods of unconsciousness and there may be involuntary urination. Convulsion, in the sense of a fit, however, does not happen. This form of epilepsy is more common in childhood and adolescence and often disappears at puberty.

Grand mal, the commonest form of epilepsy, can occur at any age. It is a loss of consciousness with a convulsion (also called a fit or seizure) which may affect only one side of the body. Typically there is an aura, a warning signal which may be a feeling or a physical movement in the form of twitching muscles or limbs. It may precede the actual fit by a matter of hours or seconds. When the fit starts the patient falls to the ground completely unconscious, and the body first stiffens and then jerks. At the beginning of the attack, because of the muscle stiffness, breathing may stop and the face become blue. There is often incontinence of both urine and faeces. As the muscles relax, the breathing is resumed, often noisily, and froth may appear at the mouth, frequently mixed with blood if the tongue or lips have been bitten. Gradually the whole body relaxes as the convulsion dies away.

After regaining consciousness, the individual usually has a headache and an overwhelming desire to sleep. There may be mental confusion for some hours, with an incoherence of speech similar to drunkenness, but this post-fit period varies considerably from person to person. In this state, known as post-epileptic automatism, or the epileptic fugue, the affected person is apparently fully conscious, but behaves in an odd manner, sometimes violently or abusively or otherwise anti-socially and at variance with his or her normal behaviour. Paralysis of one or more limbs (Todd's paralysis) may last for a few hours. A severely epileptic person may have several fits without regaining consciousness between each one. This condition, called status epilepticus, requires urgent treatment.

Sometimes a fit can be triggered by external factors such as watching a flickering television screen, or hearing church bells or a particular piece of music. It is not clear why the brain of an epileptic reacts to external stimuli in this way.

Diagnosis and treatment
The most important aspect of diagnosing epilepsy is to determine whether the cause of the condition is unknown (which is the case in about two-thirds of sufferers) or the result of organic disease of the brain, such as a tumour. The history of the case, type of fit, past medical history and family medical history all contribute to a diagnosis, but much depends on the result of electroencephalography (EEG), to record the electrical impulses from the brain. The normal brain has a characteristic pattern of impulses and an expert can interpret abnormal changes. The EEG can be almost normal in epileptics and abnormal in people who have never had fits, but absence of certain nervous-system signs combined with abnormalities in the EEG tend to confirm a diagnosis of epilepsy.

Although epilepsy is a handicap, epileptics must be encouraged to maintain their general health by means of social activities, sport and exercise of all kinds. In other words, epileptics must try to lead as normal a life as possible. Moderation, however, should always be exercised, particularly if the sufferer is having some form of drug treatment. About seventy-five per cent of cases can be controlled by anti-convulsant drugs.

Finding work can be a problem, depending on the frequency of fits and general mental capacity. Fits occur less often when the attention of an epileptic is fully occupied and is not unduly tired, but working with unprotected machinery, at heights, and driving vehicles must be avoided in most cases. There are laws governing the issue of driving licences and car insurance to diagnosed epileptics. Happily, there are sympathetic and understanding employers and well-controlled epileptics of normal intelligence seldom have difficulty in obtaining suitable work.

An epileptic fit is almost always self-limiting, and if the epileptic is fortunate enough to experience warning signs of an attack, it is usually possible to arrange to be in the least harmful situation.

Cerebral palsy and spasticity
The word spastic is a general term used to describe someone suffering from cerebral palsy, a condition where movement and posture are disturbed and disorganized from early life, due to brain damage. The disorder of movements will vary, however, as the child grows. About two babies per thousand have cerebral palsy.

There are three main types of cerebral palsy: spastic, athetoid, and ataxic, though it is quite common to have a mixture of these. In the spastics group the cerebral cortex is damaged, in athetoids the basal ganglia and ataxics the cerebellum (see pages 190-91).

Children with spastic cerebral palsy have some weak and some stiff muscles. The stiffness, or spasticity, is due to the fact that the muscle is overactive and does not cooperate normally with the other muscles that move the joint. In the early stages, the affected muscles and joints can be moved passively through their full range of normal movements by another person, but if left untreated the muscles may become permanently contracted, and as a result normal movements become impossible. Different parts of the body may be affected. In monoplegia one limb is affected, in hemiplegia the leg and arm on the same side of the body are affected, and in tetraplegia (quadriplegia) all four limbs are affected to a similar extent. The term spastic diplegia refers to the condition where the lower limbs are more affected than the arms, while double demiplegia describes the child who has more severely affected arms than legs, but in both cases all four limbs are involved. The word paraplegia is used to describe children who appear to have normal hands but whose legs are affected with paralysis.

Children with athetoid cerebral palsy have quite a different problem. At times their muscles and joints seem to be quite normal, but their control of them is poor. They frequently make uncontrollable movements when they do not intend to, yet when trying to carry out an action they are unable to coordinate it. Movements intended to involve only a small part of the body often seem to spread to the rest of the body, so that an attempt to move the hand will be accompanied by facial grimaces.

Ataxic children also suffer from an inability to control their movements. They do not have the involuntary movements of the athetoid, but they are clumsy and uncoordinated.

Since cerebral palsy results from brain damage, it is not surprising that other functions of the brain may also be disturbed in this condition. Speech disorders are very common: over half of all children with cerebral palsy have difficulties, and there may also be associated deafness or difficulty in interpreting sounds when they reach the brain. Epilepsy also occurs in about a third of affected children. A small number of cerebral-palsied children are blind, and other visual problems are much more common than in ordinary children. Many cerebral-palsied children's sense of touch and position in space is also affected.

Children with cerebral palsy may have specific learning disorders. They may have difficulty in comprehending shapes, for example, because of their disturbed sensory nervous system, and this could result in great difficulty in learning to read. Less severely affected children with cerebral palsy may be able to go to an ordinary school and do well there, while others will need to go to special school.

Parkinson's disease

This is a shaking palsy usually occurring in middle age and affecting about one person in a thousand. Shaking often begins in one hand and gradually spreads to the other limbs. Slowness of movement also occurs, and the affected person's walk may become slow and shuffling. There is also difficulty with delicate movements such as handwriting. The face becomes mask-like because the facial muscles become rigid, and other symptoms include severe constipation, heartburn, greasy skin, difficulty in eating and drooling from the mouth.

The cause is disease of the basal ganglia in the brain, and a number of drugs are available to treat the symptoms. Very rarely a drug given for some other disorder may cause Parkinson-like symptoms (Parkinsonism) and it may be necessary to stop the drug.

Multiple sclerosis

This is one of a group of diseases involving the loss of part of the myelin coverings of the nerve fibres. Any part of the brain, spinal cord or optic nerves may be affected. It is more common in women than in men, and most commonly arises between the ages of thirty and forty-five. About a third of cases start with an episode of partial or complete loss of vision in one eye. Other common early symptoms of multiple sclerosis include double vision, tingling or numbness in one limb, unsteadiness when walking or paralysis of the legs (paraplegia).

Usually, the first symptoms disappear within weeks or months, but recur over the course of several years, the same or different parts of the body being affected. This cycle of

recovery and relapse can go on for many years but there is a tendency towards partial or total invalidity. A great deal of research is being done into the causes of multiple sclerosis and a viral infection seems possible. No cure is known at the moment, but certain drugs may help. Several organizations exist to help and advise sufferers and their relatives.

Mental handicap

About one child in a hundred is born with a severe abnormality of the brain. About half of these infants die soon after birth or before the age of seven, so that after this age four children per thousand are severely mentally handicapped. Mild mental handicap is more common, and occurs in two to three per cent of the population. The mildly mentally handicapped are not very different in appearance and behaviour from ordinary people, but are poor scholars and the disability tends to be discovered at school.

Causes of mental handicap

The severer forms of mental handicap are usually due to an abnormality of brain structure. The condition may be hereditary – due to faulty genes or to an abnormal or additional chromosome – or congenital, caused by an infection in pregnancy such as German measles. The birth process itself is critical for the brain, which may suffer during delivery from lack of oxygen, or later from an excess of bile pigment or sodium in the blood. The importance of nutrition in the newborn child, especially the premature infant, as regards mental development is now recognized. After birth, infections such as meningitis can damage the brain. A few children become severely retarded following head injury, lead poisoning or other environmental factors.

Little is known about the causes of mild mental handicap. Social and cultural factors are important: children from underprivileged groups, those with ill mothers, those whose mothers are shorter than average, or those whose mothers smoked during pregnancy are at greater risk.

The parents of a backward child often first become concerned because of the child's delay in reaching the various stages of development. The baby may be quiet, sleep a lot, show little energy, take feeds without enthusiasm, or be slow to gain weight, take notice, smile, sit up and crawl, and later on, standing, walking and talking may not occur until well after the ages of the usual milestones.

Down's syndrome

Down's syndrome (trisomy 21) occurs in about one birth in 600, and is due to the presence of an additional chromosome in each body cell. The birth weight of such babies tends to be low, they are 'floppy', with the nose and facial skeleton poorly developed, and there may be a number of additional physical signs of the disorder. For more information, see page 18.

Errors of metabolism

There are several errors of metabolism (problems concerned with the body's chemical functioning) that may lead to mental handicap. Phenylketonuria, the most common, is the inability to break down a certain amino acid, phenylalanine, completely because of the lack of the necessary enzyme. By-products of the incomplete breakdown of the phenylalanine then accumulate in the body, eventually causing brain damage. The condition is diagnosed by testing the blood at birth (the Guthrie test), and is treated by a special diet low in the amino acid. PKU affects about one in 10,000 children and is inherited.

Another chemical abnormality is homocystinuria, which is also characterized by an excess of one particular amino acid in the blood and urine. The condition can be recognized by looking at the child; one of the characteristics is dislocation of the lenses of the eyes.

Treatment of mental handicap

There is little scope for curative treatment in the field of mental handicap because, to be successful, the treatment must be given before mental handicap has developed. Children with mild mental retardation should not, in general, be treated differently from normal children, even if they have other defects such as poor sight, hearing faults or epilepsy. Parents of the more severely handicapped need sympathetic advice from all concerned. The attitude of the obstetrician, the children's specialist, the general practitioner and the nurses and other professionals will set the tone and determine the parents' attitude. If these advisers are able to show sympathetic understanding and can find time for counselling, parents will be helped to accept their misfortune realistically and constructively. They may avoid the extremes of rejecting the child on the one hand and refusal to acknowledge his or her retardation on the other. Advice from a trained social worker should assist them in home care and in finding an appropriate school.

Backward babies have basically the same needs as other children, but develop at a slower pace; they remain babies longer. They demand infinite patience and a great deal of love. If parents can come to terms with the situation they can often achieve gratifying results: to see their child taking its first steps can be as rewarding for them as for other parents when their normal child has been awarded a scholarship or shows great sporting or music ability.

Prevention of mental handicap

The prevention of mild mental handicap is largely a social and national or community problem. The findings of studies in the United States and Britain suggest that anything that improves the health of the mother and the environment of the child is likely to reduce the incidence of backwardness. The quality of obstetrical care is important, as is the care of the newborn, especially for infants at risk; and visiting nurses may play an essential role here.

The prevention of severe mental handicap is only possible where the cause is at least partly understood. Would-be parents who know or suspect that some sort of inherited problem, such as Down's syndrome, runs in the family should ask their GP whether expert advice on genetic counselling is appropriate. When there are grounds for anxiety during pregnancy, the fluid surrounding the fetus can be sampled by the technique of amniocentesis to identify chromosomal and other defects; if the test is positive, the parents will be offered a termination of the pregnancy.

Coping with migraine headaches

Migraines, which tend to run in families, are a particularly severe form of headache accompanied by other symptoms such as disturbances of vision, nausea and sometimes even vomiting and diarrhoea. A migraine may last several hours (see also page 194), and the affected person is quite unable to carry on normally and so must rest. Bright lights and noise make migraines much worse and can also make them last longer, as can trying to cope as usual. There is no cure for migraine, but it can be treated with a variety of drugs.

Self-help treatment for a migraine attack consists of taking action at the earliest sign of its onset. It helps to splash your face with cold water and then to lie down, preferably in bed, with the room dark and quiet, and to relax. Stay in bed for at least two hours. Try to sleep if possible, or listen to soothing music. Do not try to read. Meditation (see page 71) has been found to help migraine sufferers because it aids relaxation and reduces stress.

At the first sign of a migraine attack, it helps to splash the face with cold water and then to lie down in a dark, quiet room and try to sleep. The migraine will then probably be much shorter than if you try to carry on normal activities.

Possible triggers

Anxiety

Depression

Over-exertion

Overwork

Tiredness

Excitement

Change of routine

Travel

Change in weather or climate

Bright light

Hunger

Noise

Contraceptive pill

Menstruation or the premenstrual period

Toothache

Alcohol

Certain foods: cheese, chocolate, milk, eggs, shellfish and citrus fruit are among the foods most likely to trigger attacks.

Triggering factors

Triggering factors, those which cause migraine attacks, may be discovered by studying the pattern of events preceding an attack. By noting the circumstances of an attack and recording activities and food and drink taken over the twenty-four hour period before it started, it may be possible to identify the cause or causes of your migraine. A combination of factors may have to exist in order to trigger an attack. They could include any of the items listed above. Once the likely trigger has been identified, it should be avoided if possible. Relaxation techniques (see page 70) can help you to reduce the stress that often contributes to the cause of an attack.

The Immune System and Allergies

The basis of the immune response is that the body recognizes foreign substances and reacts against them. These substances need not be living organisms; reactions to a wide range of chemicals can also occur. Allergy and hypersensitivity are two particular reactions of the immune system.

The immune system

Once the body has been infected by an organism such as a bacterium or virus, the next time it encounters the same type of organism it may resist reinfection; this immunity is brought about by the cells and tissues of the immune system. Immunity to disease often occurs naturally, and can also be created artificially by processes such as vaccination.

An important feature is that protection against one type of infection does not necessarily guard against another type; immunity to measles, for instance, is not effective in chickenpox. Immunity can be very strong and last for life, or it may be weaker and last for a shorter time.

Antibodies and antigens

Antibodies are protein molecules formed in response to invasion by a foreign substance. They are present in the bloodstream and play an important part in the body's natural defence mechanism, neutralizing, in various ways, the effects of the foreign invader. Babies born without the ability to make antibodies soon die from infection.

Any substance which causes the body to produce antibodies is called an antigen. Antigens are usually large, complex molecules such as proteins or carbohydrates, but some smaller molecules, called haptens, may become antigens by combining with larger molecules in the body. How antigenic a substance is depends to a large extent on the shape of the molecule, and the more foreign the substance is to the host the more likely it is to be a powerful antigen. An antigen stimulates the production of antibodies that react specifically with that antigen, to destroy it and any microbe that carries it.

The cells responsible for making antibodies are white blood cells, lymphocytes, in the spleen and lymph nodes (see *Blood and Lymph*, pages 142-9). A particular group of lymphocytes called B cells produces plasma cells which then make antibodies when they come into contact with an antigen.

Antibodies are proteins of the globulin type, with a roughly spherical shape, and are called immunoglobulins. There are five main classes of immunoglobin in the blood.

The most abundant, seventy-five per cent of the total, is immunoglobulin G or IgG, which is the most efficient at neutralizing viruses and toxins. The others each have a particular role, though they often overlap: IgA protects the surface of the body, IgM assists consumption of bacteria (phagocytosis), and IgE is responsible for allergic reactions. The function of the fifth group, IgD, is less clear.

The basic structure of the immunoglobulin protein molecule is the same in all types. But one part of the protein shows great variation in the sequence of its basic building-blocks (amino acids), and it is this variation that allows so many different antibodies with different antigen specificities to exist. Certain immunoglobulins are formed in the fetus. Adult levels of some types are reached at about one year of age but others not until about the age of six.

The most common antigens are those on the surface of micro-organisms. They are different in different species, although some types of bacteria that belong to a closely related family – such as the *Salmonellae* – do have antigens in common, so that infection by one kind of *Salmonella* can result in a certain degree of immunity to another. Some bacteria produce another sort of antigen, called a toxin, which, as its name suggests, is highly poisonous. Bacterial toxins are of two types, exotoxins, secreted by the living bacterium, and endotoxins, produced inside the bacterium and only released when it dies. The antibodies produced against toxins are called antitoxins. Some are required to fight very powerful poisons such as those produced by the bacteria which cause diphtheria (see page 212) and tetanus (see page 208). Endotoxins usually have relatively mild effects. Bacterial endotoxins, for instance, are responsible for the headache and general malaise that accompany some infections.

Other important antigens are those on the surface of the body cells. These differ from one individual to another, for example in the blood group system (see *Blood and Lymph*, pages 142-4), and a healthy person has no antibodies to his or her own antigens (see *Autoimmune disorders*, below). All cells in the body carry antigens, and when a transplant operation is planned it is very important that as many similar antigens as possible are present in both the donor and recipient, to minimize the risk of rejection when the organ is transferred. This is called tissue matching, and since antigens are inherited brothers and sisters often match quite well, so the best donors are normally close relatives. The only people who have exactly matching antigens are identical twins, whose tissues can be exchanged without rejection problems.

The response to the first contact with an antigen is called the primary response, and the antibodies are usually found in the bloodstream after about a week. The amount of antibody reaches a maximum a few days after this, and then declines. If the individual comes into contact with the antigen for a second time, even years later, antibodies appear in the blood much earlier, reach higher levels and are maintained for a longer period.

This improved response to a second contact, known as the secondary response, is an important part of the body's defence mechanism. It is why we only catch some diseases once; after the first infection antibodies remain in the blood for many years, giving immunity to a further attack, since the infection is wiped out before it can take hold. However, the length of time that antibodies stay in the blood varies with different infections.

Antibodies react with antigens by physically joining (binding) to them. When the antigen is on the surface of invading micro-organisms such as a bacterium, the antibodies can cause the bacterium to burst open or to clump with other bacteria (agglutinate), making it easier for the body to remove them. One method of removal is phagocytosis by certain types of white blood cell, in which the cells engulf the foreign organisms. Some antibodies react with and neutralize the toxins produced by some organisms. Also, when antibodies combine with antigens on the surface of a micro-organism, the organism might be prevented from attaching itself to and damaging the body cells.

Cell-mediated immunity
The system known as cell-mediated immunity is the second main arm of defence against infection. It is initiated by white blood cells called T-lymphocytes, which occur in the lymph fluid and lymph tissue as well as the blood. When they encounter a foreign organism or antigen they are stimulated to set into motion mechanisms aimed at destroying the invading organism. For example, they stimulate macrophages, large white cells that engulf micro-organisms. T-cells also stimulate the mother defence system, called complement. This is a complex series of reactions that ultimately results in activating white blood cells (polymorphs and macrophages) to engulf the foreign organism.

Other defence mechanisms
Virus infections activate another system in the body's defence armoury, interferon. Interferon has a generalized effect on all types of viruses, so if it is induced by one type of virus it can also inhibit the multiplication of other, unrelated viruses to which the body is normally susceptible. Interferon extracted from cells grown in the laboratory – or made by genetic engineering – has shown some promise as an antiviral agent, and may also prove useful in treating some cancers (see *Cancer*, pages 218-21).

Immunization
The process of producing resistance to a particular antigen, or immunization, may be active or passive, and both forms occur naturally or can be artificially induced.

Active immunization and vaccines
Active immunization occurs when a person is stimulated to make antibodies to an antigen. This occurs naturally during an infection, when the body makes antibodies against the antigens on the infecting bacteria or viruses. But the infection may not always produce symptoms, so it is possible to contract a disease and make antibodies against it without being aware of having suffered from it.

Active immunity can also be artificially induced, by an injection of the organism or a modified form of it that will not multiply and cause the infection. This procedure is called vaccination. The organism is usually killed by chemicals or radiation to render the vaccine harmless, but

care has to be taken that its power to produce antibodies is retained, as many organisms lose this when they are killed. Because of this possibility, some vaccines are prepared from living organisms which have been grown in the laboratory in unfavourable conditions such as high temperature. This process, known as attenuation, means that the organism is weakened and no longer harmful to humans. To immunize against an organism which produces a toxin, a modified form of the toxin – a toxoid – has to be produced. When this toxoid is injected, antibodies are formed which will protect against the active toxin; two examples are tetanus and diphtheria toxoids.

Vaccines against a whole range of viruses and bacteria are now available. For example, people can be vaccinated against whooping cough (pertussis), measles, German measles (rubella), tetanus, typhoid, paratyphoid, diphtheria, hepatitis, poliomyelitis, influenza and tuberculosis. Immunization against such tropical diseases as yellow fever and cholera is also possible.

Because of the great health benefits of vaccination, campaigns are frequently mounted to encourage people to be vaccinated. Better understanding of diseases and the organisms that cause them, together with new technology such as genetic engineering, mean that safer and more effective vaccines are always being developed.

Passive immunization
Passive immunization occurs when antibodies are transferred from one individual to another; this type of immunity does not last long compared with active immunity. It occurs naturally when antibodies cross the placenta from mother to fetus, and antibodies are also present in the mother's milk for a few days after birth; the baby is passively immunized in both these ways. The immunity protects the child during the first weeks of its life. Newborn babies are able to start making their own antibodies but in the womb they have met no antigens, so passive immunity gives them protection while they are building up a range of antibodies of their own.

Artificial passive immunization is used medically when it is too late for active immunization, for example during a tetanus or diphtheria infection. Usually an antiserum, the portion of blood which already contains the antibody or antitoxin is used. Sometimes antisera are obtained from humans – people who have suffered and recovered from an infection. This may be rare in some diseases and horses are used to prepare some antisera, although in rare cases there may be a reaction to the foreign substance in the horse serum.

Disorders of the immune system
Agammaglobulinaemia
Inability to produce antibodies, agammaglobulinaemia, can be a serious disorder. There are several forms of this condition, and some are congenital (present at birth). The commonest affects males: at birth the babies appear normal, and it is not until they are five months to three years old that they experience the frequent severe infections characteristic of the disorder.

The most severe form of the disease, fortunately extremely rare, is the so-called 'Swiss' type, in which the thymus gland (in the upper chest) is smaller than it should be. Affected infants have no resistance to infection, and soon develop infection of the lungs and gut. In spite of treatment, death almost always occurs before the child is a year old. Other varieties are rarer still. In some adults disease may be responsible for the failure to produce sufficient antibodies. Treatment consists of lifelong administration of antibodies by injection, bone-marrow transplants and treatment by antibiotics or other drugs for any infections that occur.

Acquired immune deficiency syndrome (AIDS)

AIDS is caused by human T lymphotropic virus type-III (HTLV-III) which affects the brain and certain cells of the immune system. As a result of the immunodeficiency a minority of infections and other diseases normally prevented from developing may take hold. The virus is transmitted in blood and blood products, and probably not in semen or saliva, as has been thought. It causes swollen lymph glands throughout the body, and in its severe form several months of ill-health, loss of weight, fever and general malaise, usually preceding the development of infections such as pneumonia, herpes simplex and candidiasis (thrush), and a rare malignancy, Kaposi's sarcoma, which usually arises in the skin. The mortality rate of this form of the disease is high, death being predominantly due to pneumonia. So far no cure is known. However, many people with antibodies to the AIDS virus merely suffer from weight loss, fever, fatigue, diarrhoea and swollen glands without developing the infections described above; others with antibodies in their blood have no symptoms. It is not yet known how many vulnerable people in these two groups will eventually develop the fatal form of the disease.

The number of people suffering from AIDS is thought to be doubling every six months. Three-quarters of all cases (in the USA and Europe) occur in homosexual and bisexual men. Other high-risk groups include intravenous drug abusers, the female partners of male intravenous drug abusers, the babies of infected mothers, haemophiliacs (who receive the blood product Factor VIII; see page 147), and the recipients of transfused infected blood. In central Africa, where AIDS is common and increasing, the virus appears to be transmitted by heterosexual intercourse, and some observers believe that it may soon become a common sexually transmitted disease among heterosexuals in the USA and Europe. Others, however, believe that the virus is more likely to be transmitted by anal intercourse between homosexuals than by vaginal intercourse, because, whereas the vagina is tough and thick, and bleeding rarely occurs during heterosexual intercourse, homosexual intercourse regularly causes bleeding from the lining of the rectum.

For haemophiliacs and blood-transfusion recipients, the introduction of heat-treated Factor VIII (a process which kills the virus) and a screening test for potential blood donors will cut the risk of contracting AIDS. The development of a vaccine against HTLV-III has not yet been developed.

Autoimmune disorders

Normally the body's immune system can recognize its own cells and does not attack them, but if this mechanism breaks down auto-antibodies are produced which react against parts of the body. The reaction may be specific against one particular organ or it can affect the whole body.

In Hashimoto's disease, antibodies are formed against the thyroid gland; in systemic lupus erythematosus damage occurs to the skin, kidneys, joints, blood vessels and blood cells. Other examples of diseases where autoimmunity may be involved are hyperthyroidism (page 182), pernicious anaemia (page 146), Addison's disease (page 184), ulcerative colitis (page 110) and rheumatoid arthritis (page 138).

Where a particular organ is affected, treatment involves replacing the substance that may be missing because that organ is damaged: the hormone thyroxine if the thyroid is damaged; vitamin B_{12} in the case of pernicious anaemia. Steroid drugs can help to suppress inflammation, and immuno-suppressive drugs which suppress the synthesis of auto-antibodies can also be useful.

Allergy and hypersensitivity

Allergies and hypersensitivity are harmful and unwanted reactions of the body's immune system to ordinarily harmless substances such as pollen, house dust and certain foods. In the same way that an infective organism carries antigens that cause antibodies to be produced, the allergic substance (allergen) also stimulates antibody production. Other reactions occur as well, and many of these are caused by body cells producing potent chemicals with wide-ranging effects. One of the best-known of these chemicals is histamine, which causes blood vessels to dilate (leading to redness of the skin), smooth muscle to contract, and fluid to be produced by cells, resulting in tissue swelling. These sorts of reaction can affect organs in different ways. There may be swelling in the throat, interfering with breathing; the mucous membranes in the nose also swell and produce fluid. In the skin, a common reaction is the production of weals (nettle rash or urticaria).

In order to become allergic to a substance a person must be exposed to it a first time when no allergic response occurs. It is only on a second or subsequent exposure that the allergy becomes obvious.

Anaphylaxis is a particular type of severe allergic reaction which can be life-threatening, since the lungs may be so badly affected that asphyxiation occurs; immediate medical attention is essential. Anaphylactic shock can occur as a response to certain drugs, such as aspirin and penicillin, and some foods, but fortunately is rare.

There are many different causes of allergy. Allergy to foods is common, with eggs, cow's milk, shellfish, cereals, vegetables, fruits and alcoholic drinks being particularly allergenic. Certain metals, nickel and chromium in particular, can affect the skin, causing allergic dermatitis, as can some chemicals and drugs. Aspirin can also cause worsening of asthma symptoms, while other drugs may cause either widespread rash or affect only a small area, which erupts in a rash in the same place each time the drug is given. Some people are allergic to substances they encounter at their place of work: for example, hairdressers handling chemicals may suffer dermatitis on the hands, builders may become allergic to cement and bakers may react to sugar- and bread-additives. Allergy to insect bites, plants and pollen also occurs.

Diagnosis and treatment

Although it is relatively simple to determine that a person has an allergy, it is often difficult to identify the particular substance responsible. Sometimes the allergy can be associated with eating unusual food or taking part in a certain activity. In other cases, if the allergen is common, it may be more difficult to identify.

Skin tests are widely used to identify allergens. There are two main types. In scratch tests the skin, normally on the forearm, is scratched or pricked and a solution of each different suspected allergen is placed on each scratch. A positive reaction – a red lump at the site of the scratch – will occur within twenty minutes if the person is allergic to that particular substance. With patch tests, the second type of skin test, different suspected allergens are held against the unbroken skin for up to forty-eight hours and the reaction examined. With both tests, if a reaction occurs it does not necessarily mean that this is the substance causing the problem, and further investigations may be needed.

Avoiding the substance that causes the allergy is one of the best forms of treatment. This can involve a change of diet, employment or residence; removal of pets or articles of furniture, or avoiding certain clothing or cosmetics.

Desensitization is another form of treatment. It consists of a series of injections, containing gradually increasing amounts of the allergen, given over several weeks or months and often repeated for three years. However, desensitization may not work; it also has to be carried out with great caution since it could be dangerous if a severe allergic reaction occurs, as happens very rarely. It is usually reserved for people who suffer badly from an allergy and where other treatment has failed.

Antihistamine drugs do not stop an allergic reaction but they do counteract some of the irritating symptoms produced by the chemical histamine. With some of the older types unwanted side-effects such as drowsiness occurred, but the newer antihistamines do not have these effects.

Steroid drugs that partially suppress the immune allergic reaction may also be used to treat allergies. 'Topical' steroids (applied to the skin, as creams) are often used to treat skin reactions such as allergic dermatitis. Sodium cromoglycate (Intal) is another drug sometimes prescribed for hay fever and asthma sufferers, and it is also available as eye drops for allergic conjunctivitis.

Further details of specific allergic disorders are given in the sections dealing with the systems they affect.

Either patch tests or scratch tests are commonly used to test for allergy, depending on the type of allergy being investigated. In patch tests (below), a battery of possible allergens is placed against the unbroken skin – usually the back – for a period of two days. A raised, reddened patch indicates a positive result, although it does not necessarily identify the substance causing the allergy. In scratch tests (right), the skin is scratched and solutions containing possible allergens placed on each scratch. Positive reactions develop within twenty minutes.

Infections and Infestations

A small proportion of the millions of different organisms in the environment live either in or on the human body. Some of them are harmless, or even beneficial, but others produce diseases, ranging from minor ones such as the common cold to severe or potentially fatal illnesses such as rabies. Most of these diseases are infectious, that is, they can be transmitted from one person to another.

Infections can enter the body in a variety of ways: through the mouth (in air or food) and then via the lungs or intestine; through the skin by contact, through open wounds or bites; from sexual contact; and during fetal development. Infective organisms inside the body may live either within the cells (intracellular) or outside them (extracellular). Any part of the body may be attacked by a disease-producing organism.

Human beings have many defences against infection, however. Some of these defences are part of the normal structure and function of the body, such as the skin and the acid in the stomach. Other defence processes only take place after infection occurs, and these are part of the active immunity of the body (see *The Immune System and Allergies*, pages 202-3).

Infective organisms come from several different groups. Many of them, such as bacteria, viruses, protozoa and fungi can only be seen with a powerful microscope (microorganisms). Others, such as parasitic worms and insects, are visible with the naked eye. The specific diseases that these organisms cause are described in other chapters of this book; this chapter describes the nature of the main groups of infective organisms, along with some of the generalized diseases that they cause.

Bacteria

Bacteria are one of the simplest forms of life. Neither plants nor animals, they are single-celled organisms which may grow in loose associations of chains or clusters. The cells cannot be seen without a microscope, although it is possible to grow visible colonies of bacteria on special growth media in a laboratory. A bacterium can reproduce rapidly by dividing and becoming two new cells which can then divide again, and so on.

A bacterium cell has a rigid wall that gives it its characteristic shape, which might be rod-shaped or spherical. When a bacterium divides, the cell wall grows inwards, forming a cross-wall which splits the cell to form two new cells; the cells of some bacteria may remain in contact with one another, forming chains. Some antibiotics (see pages 205-6) act by interfering with the manufacture of the cell wall during growth or division, and so killing the bacteria.

On the inside of the cell wall there is a plasma membrane which contains several enzymes and controls the movement of substances into and out of the bacterium. The bulk of the bacterial cell lies within the plasma membrane and consists of soft gel-like protoplasm containing several structures. These include ribosomes which are concerned with protein manufacture, mesosomes which are involved in the formation of the cell wall and spores, and the nucleus, containing genetic information in the form of DNA (deoxyribonucleic acid). Many bacteria have a capsule, outside the cell wall, made of complex carbohydrates. This can counteract some defence mechanisms of the body.

Some bacteria can move in fluids by twisting, or by using whip-like filaments called flagellae. Smaller threads – fimbriae – may make bacteria sticky so that they adhere to cells, and other threads – sexual fimbriae – are involved in passing genetic information during a form of sexual reproduction called conjugation.

When adverse conditions occur, such as high or low temperatures, some bacteria form resistant spores. These spores can remain dormant for many years, only germinating when conditions are suitable. Spores have an important role in the transmission of certain infections such as tetanus and anthrax. Other organisms, such as the one which causes syphilis, cannot survive outside the body for long and do not form spores; these types are often transmitted from person to person by specialized mechanisms.

Some bacteria can live and multiply in the absence of oxygen (anaerobes) while others require oxygen (aerobes); this distinction is often used to identify bacteria. Other ways of identifying bacteria include how the cell walls are stained by dyes, the shape and size of the bacteria, what substances they need for growth, and what antibiotics are effective against them. An important feature of bacteria is that they can often change some of their characteristics so that a new strain develops which may be difficult to identify and treat.

Bacterial infections

Anthrax

Anthrax is a severe and often fatal disease caused by *Bacillus anthracis*. Cattle, horses, pigs, goats and sheep may be attacked by anthrax, and human cases arise among people in contact with affected animals, or those concerned with the processing of animal products, such as leather, hair or bones, some of which may have come from an animal which died of anthrax. Transmission from human to human is possible but exceptionally rare. The bodies of animals which have died of anthrax contain countless millions of the bacilli, and these are deposited on the ground as the carcass decays. Before death, the animal will have spread the organism through its excreta, too.

The active form of the anthrax micro-organism cannot survive in the presence of oxygen, but once the active bacilli have come into contact with air they form spores which are

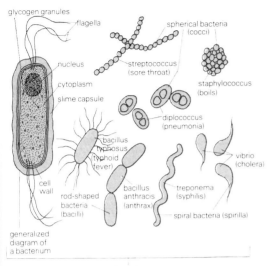

glycogen granules
flagella
spherical bacteria (cocci)
nucleus
streptococcus (sore throat)
cytoplasm
staphylococcus (boils)
slime capsule
diplococcus (pneumonia)
bacillus typhosus (typhoid fever)
vibrio (cholera)
cell wall
bacillus anthracis (anthrax)
rod-shaped bacteria (bacilli)
treponema (syphilis)
spiral bacteria (spirilla)
generalized diagram of a bacterium

bacteria

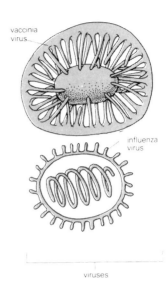

vaccinia virus
influenza virus

viruses

The structure of different types of bacteria and viruses (not to scale). Spiral bacteria and bacteria with flagellae can propel themselves forward; other round bacteria, known as cocci, characteristically form clumps or chains as they multiply by cell division. Much less is known about the structure of viruses, as they can only be seen under a high-powered electron microscope. All viruses, however, contain a nucleic acid and have a protein coat.

able to live for many years, to become reactivated when they enter the system of an animal.

The spores enter the human body through the skin, the lungs or the intestine. The characteristic reaction is a skin lesion called a 'malignant pustule', a reddened area of inflammation, and oedema (swelling). Other more general symptoms include uncontrollable shivering, headache and vomiting. If the infection is untreated, septicaemia can result, as the bloodstream becomes infected with anthrax bacilli. Treatment of the disease is with antibiotics. Those at risk because of their occupation can be immunized against the infection.

Cholera

Cholera is caused by the organism *Vibrio cholerae*, which is spread in contaminated faeces and water. It has been the cause of several widespread epidemics and is still common in parts of the world where hygiene is poor.

The incubation period of the disease is from five hours to three days. The vibrios live on the inner surface of the intestine, and produce a powerful toxin which causes profuse diarrhoea, nausea and vomiting. It is the massive loss of fluid from the body, resulting in severe dehydration, that is the main cause of death; replacing the lost fluids is the most effective treatment. People who intend to travel to parts of the world where cholera is endemic can be vaccinated against the disease.

Typhoid fever (enteric fever)

Typhoid fever is caused by *Salmonella typhi*. Infection occurs after contact with food, drink and objects contaminated by the faeces or urine of infected people. Poor hygiene, particularly among people who prepare food, can spread typhoid. Cooking food, pasteurizing milk and treating sewage all kill the typhoid bacteria, so the disease is rare in most developed countries. A complicating factor is that the disease can be transmitted by 'carriers' who exhibit no symptoms of the infection themselves but can nevertheless spread it. The bacteria spread rapidly from the intestines into the bloodstream via the thoracic duct to the internal organs, particularly liver and spleen, where they multiply.

About fourteen days after infection the first symptoms of typhoid fever appear: they include fever, severe headache and chills, abdominal pain and constipation. A faint rash of scattered pink spots may appear on the trunk and abdomen. Chronic infection of the gall bladder may result, and a severe complication may be ulceration of the bowel followed by perforation of the bowel wall leading to peritonitis, which may be fatal. Treatment requires hospital admission, where a course of antibiotics is given. If there are no complications such as pneumonia or perforation, recovery takes up to four weeks. (See also *Food poisoning*, pages 111-3.)

Paratyphoid fever

Paratyphoid fever is caused by *Salmonella paratyphi* A and B. It is related to typhoid fever but is usually a milder infection. Both typhoid and paratyphoid vaccines are normally given together as TAB (typhoid and paratyphoid A and B), sometimes combined with cholera vaccine, and can give some protection to travellers. Other types of salmonella bacteria cause food poisoning (see pages 111-3).

Tetanus (lockjaw)

Tetanus is caused by *Clostridium tetani* which is found as spores in the soil, and infects the body through wounds. The spores germinate in conditions of low oxygen, and deep puncture wounds are the most dangerous; tetanus has been contracted from a rose-thorn prick. The bacterium is also found in animal faeces, particularly from horses and other grass-eating animals. Soils that have been manured are therefore the most dangerous.

The bacterium produces a toxin which attacks nerve cells and causes the muscles to contract and go into spasm. The jaw muscles are the first to contract, hence the disease's common name. The muscle spasms spread to other parts of the body and can cause death if the muscles of the lungs are affected, preventing breathing. Treatment is with antibiotics and injections of antitoxin. Intensive care in hospital is usually needed so that equipment is available to maintain breathing. Drugs to relax the muscles are also given.

The incubation period for tetanus is usually eight to twelve days, but can be longer. Prevention by immunization with tetanus toxoid is simple, and a course of injections should be given in infancy, followed by booster doses every five years.

Plague

Plague (bubonic and pneumonic plague) is caused by the bacterium *Pasteurella pestis*. In the past there have been several major epidemics, including the so-called Black Death of the Middle Ages. The bacteria are carried by rats and other animals, and spread to humans by blood-sucking insects, particularly fleas. In the bubonic form of plague, the lymph nodes near the bite swell to form painful, pus-filled buboes, or boils. Bubonic plague has an incubation period of two to ten days and, if untreated, is fatal in thirty to ninety per cent of cases by the fifth day.

Pneumonic plague develops if the bacteria spread to the lungs. Unlike bubonic plague, it is highly infectious, as bacteria-laden droplets leave the body during coughing and sneezing. Treatment with antibiotics is successful in the early stages of the disease. The spread of plague around the world is controlled by keeping rats out of ships.

Leprosy

Leprosy is caused by the bacterium *Mycobacterium leprae*, which is related to the organism causing tuberculosis. It is commonest in tropical and subtropical countries. The exact means by which the disease is transmitted is not known, although close contact with an infected person is an important factor. It is not very infectious, and some people seem more susceptible than others.

Leprosy affects the skin and nerves. After an incubation period of between two to four years a slight change in an area of skin occurs, possibly where the bacteria invaded the body. There may be sensations of pricking or numbness in this area, followed by a slight redness or loss of pigment. After this stage, small nodules full of bacteria may develop, usually on the face. The skin may become thickened and folded. If the nerves are badly affected there is a loss of sensation and muscle weakness, which can lead to damage to fingers and toes. The muscles of the hands, feet and face

may become paralysed and contracted. Treatment with drugs such as dapsone can be successful if begun early enough. The drug kills the infection, but cannot reverse the tissue damage that has already occurred.

Leptospirosis

Leptospirosis is caused by bacteria in the Leptospira group, tightly coiled organisms which move by spinning and bending at the ends. The disease is transmitted by animals, and humans become infected if they come into contact with the tissues or urine of an infected animal. There are many types of leptospirosis throughout the world. In one common type, Weil's disease, rats are the animal host.

In severe forms of the disease there may be high fever, jaundice, bleeding, and liver and kidney failure. At an early stage of the infection, antibiotics may bring it under control. Dialysis may be needed if there is kidney damage (see *The Urinary System*, pages 116-23).

Psittacosis

Psittacosis is an infectious disease of birds (particularly parrots) that can spread to humans. It is caused by the bacterium *Chlamydia psittaci* and passes from birds in faeces and other discharges. In humans it affects the lungs, resulting in either a feverish illness with pneumonia (inflammation of the lungs), or a less serious, influenza-like illness. Severe cases can be treated with antibiotics.

Viruses

Viruses are the smallest and simplest form of life. Most are much smaller than bacteria, up to twenty times smaller, and have the unique feature of being able to multiply only within living cells.

All living matter contains nucleic acids, which form the genetic material. These nucleic acids belong to two categories, DNA and RNA (deoxyribonucleic acid and ribonucleic acid). Animals, plants and bacteria contain in their cells both kinds of nucleic acid; viruses contain either RNA or DNA, but not both. Nucleic acids are rather unstable chemicals but they can be protected by combining with protein, the combination being known as nucleoprotein. The smallest, simplest viruses are virtually made up of nucleoprotein; the larger ones contain numerous proteins, and carbohydrates, fatty materials and other substances.

During infection the protein coat of a virus makes direct contact with the outside of a body cell, which then engulfs the virus. Its nucleic acid is liberated by an enzyme which uncoats the virus, stripping off the surrounding protein. The viral nucleic acid then takes control of the cell. Virus particles may be mass-produced in the infected cell, which is immediately destroyed, bursting and liberating the particles. In other cases the virus particles may be made progressively, and gradually shed from the cell surface without immediately killing the cell.

Viruses can be passed from one person to another in several ways. The first form of transmission is by breathing, coughing or sneezing. The second is the faecal-oral route: viruses passed in the faeces, especially under conditions of poor hygiene, may get on to the hands or food and thence into the body via the mouth. This method is the most important one for poliomyelitis and related viruses. Insects and ticks form the third type of transmission: hundreds of different viruses are known to be transmitted by the bites of mosquitoes or ticks, including yellow fever, dengue fever and several varieties of encephalitis, which are most common in tropical and subtropical countries. The fourth mechanism of transmission is mechanical: for instance, the warts virus may be transferred from one person to another in this manner, and improperly sterilized syringes have been responsible for passing on the hepatitis virus.

The body reacts to viruses in the same way as to any other infection (see *The Immune System and Allergies*, pages 202-5), except that infected cells produce interferon which may bring the infection to an end as well as protecting against other viruses. Interferon is a complex protein produced in minute amounts; its mode of action is poorly understood. Modern methods of manufacture may enable it to be more widely used in treating viral infections. There are very few good anti-viral drugs.

Viral infections

Colds

The common cold can be caused by one of more than a hundred related viruses. The virus infects cells lining the upper respiratory tract, and most symptoms – streaming nose, coughing and phlegm – result from the body's re-action to the infection. The success of the virus in invading the cells determines the severity of the cold. The infection usually lasts only three to five days until the body's defences successfully resist the virus. Because of the large number of different cold viruses, which may also be continually changing in slightly different ways, immunity to the common cold is rare. Although colds are commoner in winter, temperature has nothing to do with how easily the infection is caught. It is more likely that in winter people tend to crowd together more and the chance of colds spreading is therefore greater, but the virus also grows best at a lower temperature. There is no specific cure for colds, and the best remedy is bed-rest with hot drinks and aspirin or paracetamol.

Influenza

Influenza, another common viral infection of the respir-atory tract, may be caused by one of three types of virus: influenza A, B or C. The A type is responsible for major epidemics, the B and C types for outbreaks between epidemics. Both A and B viruses can change their nature.

The virus infects the cells lining the upper respiratory tract, and causes a fever and symptoms similar to those of the common cold. If infection occurs further down the tract the symptoms of bronchitis occur, with a cough and pain on breathing, behind the breastbone. There is a general feeling of feverish illness lasting a few days, followed by a period of tiredness. Depression is quite common after influenza.

Complications can occur if bacteria infect the damaged cells of the respiratory tract, causing pneumonia or pleurisy (see *The Respiratory System*, pages 84-95). Influenza is rarely fatal now, but in the world epidemic of 1918-19

twenty million people died. Vaccination is available for those at risk, particularly the elderly and people with chronic chest conditions. Antibiotics are not effective, although they may be given to prevent a secondary bacterial infection. Treatment includes bed-rest and fluids. Aspirin or paracetamol may help to relieve symptoms.

Glandular fever (infectious mononucleosis)

Glandular fever is a viral infection which is spread through the bloodstream. Symptoms include fever, headache, sore throat and painful swollen glands. Some people are affected for only a week or so, but the illness may persist for much longer, with symptoms of general tiredness and depression lasting several weeks. The disease may also recur during the next few years. Antibiotics do not help since it is a viral disease; rest, and pain-killers if necessary, should be taken until it has run its course.

Poliomyelitis

The poliomyelitis virus (poliovirus), which attacks the motor nerves, enters the body through the digestive tract and multiplies in the glandular tissue of the throat, intestine and the lymph glands. In many cases there may be no symptoms, and the disease is severe only in a few instances. The first signs of this appear when the virus infects the central nervous system (see *The Nervous System*, pages 188-201), causing a severe headache and stiff neck. If nerve cells are destroyed, the resulting muscle weakness may lead to paralysis. The paralytic form of polio is fairly uncommon and occurs more in older children and adults than in young children, who seem to be more resistant to it.

The virus is probably spread from the lungs in droplets, or in faeces; poor hygiene contributes to its spread. In many countries, where children are routinely vaccinated against the disease, polio has been almost eradicated. It is still found in poorer countries and the tropics, however, and people travelling to a polio-risk area should arrange to have a booster dose of the vaccine.

Rabies (hydrophobia)

Rabies is a viral infection of animals such as dogs, cats, bats, squirrels and foxes. Humans become infected if they are bitten by an infected animal, although a lick on broken skin can also be dangerous. The disease affects the central nervous system, causing mental confusion, fever and paralysis, and there may also be a morbid fear of water or drinking (hydrophobia) as a result of the throat spasms that occur when the patient tries to drink. Once the symptoms have appeared the condition is always fatal, but anti-rabies injections usually prevent the onset of symptoms if given at once on contact.

The disease may appear between one and ten months after contact with an infected animal, although the usual incubation period is six to eight weeks. If contact is sus-pected, the animal should be isolated to see if it is rabid, and the antiserum or vaccine given to the affected person.

Rabies is rarely found in Britain because of strict quaran-tine regulations for animals imported into the country. Even in countries where rabies is endemic, it is not common.

Smallpox

Smallpox was a serious, often fatal, infection which has now been eradicated by worldwide vaccination. The symptoms of smallpox were a high fever with a characteristic rash, similar to that of chickenpox, principally on the limbs and face. The risk of preparing and giving the vaccine, although small, has led most countries to abolish the vaccination requirement for travellers. The virus now exists only in medical laboratories engaged in research.

Dengue fever

Dengue fever is an acute infection confined to tropical and subtropical areas. It is caused by a virus that is transmitted to humans by the bite of infected mosquitoes. The incubation period varies from five to ten days. The first signs are similar to those of a common cold, followed by a severe headache, pain behind the eyes, backache in the small of the back, and severe limb, muscle and joint pains. The temperature rises to 40°C (104°F) and then 41°C (106°F) within the first few hours; it subsides rapidly, but there is usually another rise to about the same level on the third to sixth day of the illness (when there may also be a rash), with a final drop to normal on the seventh or eighth day. There is no specific treatment except bed-rest and painkillers.

Lassa fever

Lassa fever is an uncommon viral disease occurring mainly in central and West Africa. It appears to be spread by small animals such as rats. Some forms of the disease are mild, others fatal.

Yellow fever

Yellow fever is an acute viral infection spread by mosquitoes among both monkeys and humans. It is common in tropical areas of Africa and America. Its severity varies from a mild influenza-like condition to a severe illness with jaundice, internal bleeding, and liver and kidney failure. The mortality rate is twenty-five per cent. The disease can be prevented by vaccination.

Rickettsia

The rickettsiae are classified as bacteria but have many of the features of viruses. They are small round bacilli with cell walls, and are visible under the microscope. They can live and multiply only within the cells of the infected host, on which they are totally dependent.

The rickettsial diseases affecting humans include the typhus fevers: epidemic louse-borne typhus (*Rickettsia prowazeki*), trench fever (*Rickettsia quintana*), borne by fleas, and tick-borne spotted fevers. These infections are harboured by wild animals and are continuously being transmitted and circulated among them by insects. Humans are only incidentally infected when they interrupt this cycle.

Epidemic louse-borne typhus is the most severe of this group of diseases. It can recur many years after an initial attack without any renewed contact with lice. The recurrence, which usually takes the form of a mild typhus attack, is known as Brill's disease. Sufferers can infect body lice and thus transmit the disease to others.

The symptoms of typhus are sudden fever, chills, headache, vomiting, cough, chest pains, aching muscles and a rash. Complications include pneumonia, gangrene and inflammation of the heart muscle. Antibiotics are effective against epidemic typhus and other rickettsial infections. Vaccination is also possible against some of the infections, and control of lice and tick infestations in both people and animals is important in controlling the spread of these diseases.

Fungi

Examples of fungi include mushrooms, yeasts, moulds and mildews. Some, like the yeasts, are single cells and grow by budding off new cells. Others consist of a branching, thread-like network of cells called a mycelium, which can grow rapidly and spread across or through an area. Human diseases caused by fungi are called mycoses. Common examples are thrush, caused by the yeast *Candida albicans*, and athlete's foot and ringworm, both caused by *Tinea* (see page 78).

Common childhood infections

Certain infectious diseases are most common in children, often occurring after a child first starts mixing with other children, at school or play group. With these diseases (mumps and measles, for example) one infection confers life-long immunity so that the disease is much less common in adults (see also *The Immune System and Allergies*, pages 202-5).

Measles

Measles is a highly contagious viral infection, appearing in epidemics. The virus, which is inhaled, multiplies in the respiratory tract. The incubation period varies from ten to fourteen days.

Symptoms

The early signs of measles are very similar to those of a common cold. There is a harsh cough, a runny nose, red eyes and sore throat; and exposure to bright light is often uncomfortable (photophobia). There may be headache, hoarseness and diarrhoea with a rise in temperature. A diagnosis of measles can usually be made by the early appearance inside the cheek of small white spots called Koplik's spots. The disease is at its most infectious at this early stage.

After the initial fever the temperature will often return to normal, and then rise again to about 40°C (104°F) on the evening before the skin rash appears. At first the rash is composed of distinct pink spots, but as it spreads to cover the whole body the colour intensifies to a reddish-purple and the spots become raised and pimple-like (papules). These papules become so numerous that they tend to join together at their edges, giving the impression of large, irregular blotches on the skin. After forty-eight to seventy-two hours, the temperature gradually returns to normal and the rash begins to fade, leaving a brownish stain which lasts about seven to ten days, after which time the affected skin peels off.

The danger of measles lies in the possibility of its complications such as bronchopneumonia (see pages 92-3), ear infection or otitis media (see page 179) and inflammation of the brain, or encephalomyelitis (see page 196).

Treatment
There is no specific treatment except to make the patient comfortable in bed; the illness has to take its course. Conjunctivitis can be eased by bathing the eyes with warm boracic acid or sodium bicarbonate solution several times a day, and if there is photophobia the amount of light entering the room must be reduced. If the tongue is furred the mouth can be cleaned by rinsing with a mouthwash. Antibiotics may be prescribed if there is a secondary bacterial infection.

Vaccination against measles is recommended for all children. It is usually administered at about fifteen months of age.

German measles (rubella)

German measles is usually a mild illness with a rash, often causing symptoms no more severe than those of a common cold. The virus has an incubation period of fourteen to twenty-one days. An infected child spreads the virus in droplets during talking, coughing and sneezing, probably from the time that the first symptoms appear until about three days after the rash has subsided.

Symptoms
The chief features are a rash and swollen lymph glands at the back of the head and in the neck. The rash appears within twenty-four hours of the onset of the infection and consists of small flat pink areas known as macules. Complications in German measles are rare, but encephalitis is not unknown.

Although rubella itself is a mild illness, infection of a pregnant woman may damage the fetus. About twenty per cent of babies born to infected mothers have some congenital abnormality such as deafness, a congenital heart defect or cataracts. After the end of the fourth month of pregnancy infection does not cause congenital deformity, but the baby may be born with chronic rubella. Vaccination against German measles is recommended for all girls aged eleven to fourteen who have not had the disease and is offered through the school medical service. Vaccination should not be given during pregnancy.

Scarlet fever

Scarlet fever is now much less common than other childhood diseases. It is caused by infection with strains of the bacterium *Streptococcus pyogenes*. The focus of infection is usually the throat, and once inside the body the bacteria produce a toxin which enters the bloodstream. After an incubation period of two to four days symptoms appear: high temperature, sore throat, shivering, headache and sometimes vomiting. The tonsils are enlarged, and often covered with a yellow exudate. The lymph glands in the neck are also enlarged. On the second day a generalized red rash appears, over which is a spotted rash of a deeper red that turns white when pressed. At the same time the temperature begins to fall and the tongue becomes bright red. The rash fades in about a week, and is succeeded by scaling and peeling of the skin. Complications are rare but include rheumatic fever (see page 157) and glomerulonephritis (see page 121). Antiobiotics are effective in treating scarlet fever, and most children recover completely.

Chickenpox (varicella)

Chickenpox is a common and highly infectious disease caused by the *Herpes zoster* virus, the same virus that may cause shingles after years of dormancy (see page 196). The incubation period of chickenpox is fourteen to twenty-three days, and the first symptoms are a slight fever and headache, followed within a day by a rash. The patient is infectious from one day before to six days after the rash appears. The rash consists of groups of itchy red spots with central blisters, mainly on the trunk of the body. After a few days the spots crust over and gradually fade. The main treatment is lotions to soothe the skin irritation: scratching the spots may infect them and cause scarring. Chickenpox is a mild infection and complications are rare.

Mumps

Mumps is a viral infection characterized by inflammation and enlargement of the salivary glands. Many people who become infected fail to develop any symptoms but nevertheless produce antibodies to the virus which, in most

Measles rash (left). The rash starts behind the ears and on the face, and then spreads over the trunk.

The rash of rubella (right). This is usually mild, with pale spots which merge into larger patches.

Chickenpox (far right), showing the characteristic fluid-filled vesicles which appear mainly on the trunk and face.

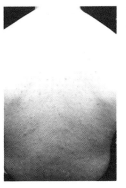

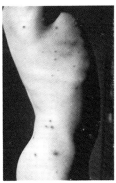

cases, gives them immunity for life. The infection is generalized and the virus often spreads to other organs, particularly the central nervous system and, after puberty, the testes, ovaries and breasts. The virus is present in the saliva and is spread by droplets. The incubation period is quite long – eighteen to twenty-eight days – and illness begins with the gradual development of fever. The glands most frequently affected are the parotid glands below the ears, which enlarge, first behind the angle of the jaw, then extending downwards and forwards. Sometimes the swelling appears first on one side of the neck and then on the other between one and three days later.

Provided there are no complications, the temperature returns to normal after about four days and the glandular swelling gradually subsides after about seven to ten days. Possible complications include pain and swelling in the testicles in men, and mild meningitis. Very rarely in adult men it may result in sterility. A mumps vaccine can be given to children at the age of one year.

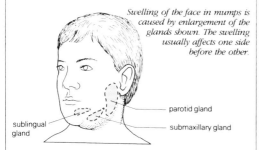

Swelling of the face in mumps is caused by enlargement of the glands shown. The swelling usually affects one side before the other.

sublingual gland

parotid gland

submaxillary gland

Diphtheria

Diphtheria is caused by the bacterium *Corynebacterium diphtheriae*. The organisms do not directly attack human tissues, but multiply in the throat and produce a toxin which is rapidly distributed throughout the body by the blood system. This toxin attacks nerve cells and the cardiac muscle cells. It may attack and destroy any form of nervous tissue; when the nerves controlling muscle groups are involved, paralysis can involve the throat, larynx, breathing muscles or limbs, up to seven weeks later.

The bacillus may invade the body at other sites. Cutaneous diphtheria can arise from any scratch or abrasion if the organism happens to be present. Another form is wound diphtheria. In western countries vaccination has abolished the disease but it is still a common cause of death elsewhere.

Symptoms

Often, before any signs in the throat are visible, an affected child becomes listless, pale and limp. Within a few hours white or cream-coloured specks can be seen on the tonsils. The specks rapidly join together and form a continuous membrane over the tonsils, which changes to yellow and then to brown or even black.

This laryngeal form of diphtheria usually occurs in children under five years of age who have not been immunized. As the growing membrane and swelling of the throat

obstruct the airway, breathing becomes difficult, or even impossible, and the affected child turns blue from lack of oxygen in the blood (cyanosis).

Treatment

In severe cases an urgent operation may be needed to make an opening into the windpipe below the obstruction (tracheostomy) so that the child can breathe. Early diagnosis, with the injection of antitoxins, is essential, but if the toxin has become fixed to cardiac or nervous tissues, the damage has been done and antitoxin can only prevent further damage.

Whooping cough

Whooping cough (pertussis) is an infectious disease of the respiratory system. It is caused by the bacteria *Bordetella pertussis*, in which the airways become clogged with mucus. It can be a dangerous and debilitating disease, carrying the risk of permanent brain damage, and often affects very young children. When the immunization rate falls, the disease occurs more widely. Early symptoms resemble those of a common cold but worsen over the first week, and severe bouts of coughing develop. These bouts gradually increase until each coughing attack lasts up to a minute. Since it is impossible to breathe during an attack, each one ends with a 'whooping' noise, caused by the sufferer gasping for breath. Phlegm or mucus and sometimes food is brought up with the cough. Antibiotics help prevent complications such as pneumonia, but the only other requirement is good nursing at home, with regular doctor's visits. Severe cases have to be admitted to hospital. Immunization should be started at the age of three months, except in cases where it is contraindicated.

Parasitic animals

A parasite is an animal or a plant which lives in or on another organism (the host), and benefits from the relationship at the expense of the host. In most cases, a parasite cannot live away from its host, although it may be able to survive in a dormant state. In this sense bacteria, viruses and fungi are all parasites, but there is also a variety of parasitic animals that infect humans. These include the single-celled protozoa, worms (nematodes and helminths), and insects and mites.

Parasitic animals are frequently very specialized, and have developed complicated life-cycles in which an animal may be the intermediate host and a human the final host; different stages of development occur in each host.

Parasitic protozoa

The protozoa are single-celled organisms whose structure is more similar to the cells of animals than to bacteria. There are many parasitic protozoa of animals, although only relatively few types infect humans.

Malaria

Malaria is caused by parasitic protozoa called plasmodia. There are several types of malaria infecting a wide range of animals, but the two most important human infections are *Plasmodium vivax* and *Plasmodium falciparum*.

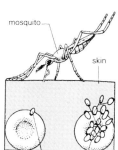

mosquito

skin

Malaria is spread by certain species of mosquito. The parasite (plasmodium) is injected when the mosquito bites, and reproduces inside the red blood cells. When these rupture the plasmodia are released into the bloodstream and may be passed on to another mosquito should it bite the affected person at that stage.

plasmodium enters red blood cell and multiplies

plasmodia released

The malarial parasite has a complex life-cycle involving both mosquitoes and humans. The plasmodium multiplies in the red blood cells and liver cells of humans, finally producing the sexual stages: male and female gametes. For these to develop further, a female anopheles mosquito must bite the infected person and take up the sexual stages in the blood it feeds on. In the gut of the mosquito, the male and female stages join and, after several stages of multiplication, produce many more infective stages. These reach the salivary glands of the insect and are injected into the blood of another human when the mosquito feeds again.

Malaria is widespread in many tropical and subtropical countries where the anopheles mosquito lives. It is the world's single greatest cause of death and disablement. Mosquitoes breed in still, stagnant water and one of the ways in which the disease is fought is to drain swampy areas, or to spray them with insecticides. Since the mosquitoes feed at night, sleeping under an excluding fine net can prevent them biting an individual.

Symptoms
The symptoms of malaria are a result of the damage caused by the multiplication of the various stages in the blood and liver cells. The diagnosis is made by microscopic examination of the blood for parasites. There is a chill with severe shivering, backache, headache and a dry cough. The skin is pale and the pulse rapid. After an hour the temperature begins to rise to as high as 41°C (106°F) with sweating, restlessness and dehydration followed by a fall in temperature. Blood cells are destroyed by the parasites, and this may cause anaemia (see page 144). Damage to the liver may result in jaundice.

Treatment
Treatment of malaria consists of a course of drugs which must be continued for several weeks, even though symptoms are usually relieved within a few hours. Several anti-malarial drugs, such as chloroquine and Paludrine, can prevent the infection developing; these must be taken continually in a malarial region, and for a month afterwards.

Trypanosomiasis
Trypanosomiasis is caused by several related types of protozoa. In Africa, two forms are transmitted by tsetse flies and affect the nervous system, causing sleeping sickness. In South America, *Trypanosoma cruzi* (Chaga's disease) is transmitted by the bites of certain insects. The infection affects the heart, intestinal muscles and the nervous system. It is effectively treated with drugs.

Leishmaniasis
Leishmaniasis comprises several diseases caused by protozoa. *Leishmania donovania* occurs in Asia and around the Mediterranean where it causes visceral leishmaniasis (kala azar), a prolonged serious illness with fever, anaemia and enlarged liver and spleen. *Leishmania brasiliensis* occurs in many South American countries as mucocutaneous leishmaniasis (espundia) and is transmitted by the bite of a sandfly. The disease attacks the mucous membrane and skin of the nose and spreads to the lips and mouth, producing blisters which ulcerate. The cartilage of the nose may be destroyed, resulting in severe facial damage.

Toxoplasmosis
Toxoplasmosis is caused by infection with the protozoan *Toxoplasma gondii*. Besides human beings, the parasite has been found in dogs, guinea pigs, horses, weasels, ferrets, rats, bats, certain monkeys, certain birds, cats, cattle and, in particular, mice. It is not certain how the disease is spread to human beings, but close contact with animals, particularly pets, may be one source of infection.

There are two distinct types of toxoplasmosis: congenital and acquired. If a woman develops the infection during the first four months of pregnancy, her baby will be born with the disease. Most such infants do not survive the first few weeks of life, since the nervous system is affected. With the acquired infection, the most common type affects the lymphatic glands, but symptoms are rare in adults. Diagnosis is by blood test or microscopical examination of one of the glands. Drug treatment is effective.

Parasitic worms
The three main groups of parasitic worms are the nematodes (roundworms), trematodes (flukes), and cestodes (tapeworms). Some are transmitted directly from person to person, while others have life-cycles involving one or two intermediate animal hosts.

Nematodes (roundworms)
Nematodes are generally small, thread-like, cylindrical animals, although some may be several centimetres long. There are many parasitic nematode infections of humans. Some of the most important are caused by a group called the filariae which infect the blood and tissues; elephantiasis and onchocerciasis (river blindness) are two serious tropical diseases caused by them.

Trichinosis is a disease caused by *Trichinella spiralis* which has an unusual life-cycle. The trichina larvae are eaten by pigs, become adult in the intestine, mate, and the female produces more larvae which migrate to the muscles, where they form cysts. If a person eats infected pork the same cycle occurs, causing muscular pain.

The other major group of roundworm includes the intestinal ones; in these infections the adults live in the intestines and mate, and the eggs (ova) or larvae leave the body in the faeces. The eggs get back into a human body via contaminated fingers, or via food contaminated by faeces used as fertilizer or carried to food by flies. The swallowed eggs hatch in the intestines. This occurs in ascariasis, caused by *Ascaris lumbricoides* and trichuriasis, caused by *Trichuris trichiura*.

The hookworms, *Necator americanus* and *Ancylostoma duodenale*, and a worm causing a similar infection, *Strongyloides stercoralis*, have free-living larvae which inhabit faeces-contaminated soil before they enter the skin of a person walking barefoot. In these diseases, adult worms in the intestine cause the symptoms. With *Ascaris* and *Trichuris*, the presence of a large number of worms may cause abdominal pain or even intestinal blockage. The hookworms and *Strongyloides* live on blood and tissue fluids, thus causing severe anaemia, blood loss and nutritional deficiency.

Enterobius vermicularis, the pinworm, threadworm or seatworm, is a common infection in children. The adult worms live in the lower bowel and deposit their eggs around the anus at night. When the females emerge to lay eggs they cause itching. A child scratching the anus gets eggs on the fingers which, if sucked, reinfect the digestive tract. Drug treatment is usually very effective.

Trematodes (flukes)
Trematodes have muscular suckers by which they attach themselves to their host. All trematodes spend at least one stage of their life-cycle in an intermediate host before they settle in a human, their final host; there may be a second intermediate host in some cases. The first intermediate host is a water-snail, while the second intermediate host may be a snail, crustacean, insect or fish.

The most important trematode infection is schistosomiasis (bilharzia) which is found in Africa, South America and the Far East. Picked up from infected water, it is caused by three main species, one of which enters the blood vessels of the bladder and the other two of which invade the blood vessels of the intestines and liver. In some areas up to sixty per cent of the population may be affected; it is the most serious parasitic infection after malaria. Drugs can be given to destroy the parasite, but these may have serious side-effects and must be given by injection. Prevention includes controlling water-snails and improving sanitation.

Either humans or sheep may be the final host of the liver fluke, *Fasciola hepatica*. Both can become infected by eating watercress grown in water infested by a type of snail, which is the first intermediate host. The flukes burrow through the liver to the bile duct, leaving cavities which become filled with fibrous tissue. In heavy infestations this causes cirrhosis (see page 107), damage to the bile duct and, if there is much bleeding, anaemia (see page 144).

The oriental lung fluke, *Paragonimus westermani*, is found all over the world, although the disease is most common in the Orient. From its first intermediate host, a snail, it infects crabs or crayfish. Humans become the final host by eating these. Some flukes settle in the lungs, causing coughing, bloody sputum and chest pain, while others spread elsewhere to cause low fever and irritation.

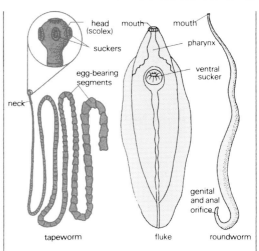

Parasitic worms (not to scale). Tapeworms and roundworms live in the intestine, while the fluke burrows towards the liver.

Cestodes (tapeworms)
Tapeworm live in the digestive system of vertebrates. The head (scolex) attaches to the intestinal wall by means of suckers or hooks. Behind the head a growing region produces a series of body segments (proglottids) which mature towards the tail end. There is no digestive system, as digested food is absorbed from the host's intestine, but each proglottid has both male and female apparatus, and is self-fertilizing. Ripe proglottids, each full of eggs, break off and pass out with the faeces. The egg develops into a ripe embryo, which is taken up by another host (usually a herbivorous mammal). The embryo bores through the host's alimentary tract and migrates to muscle or other tissues, where it forms bladder-like cysts. The cycle is completed when the final host eats infected meat and the cysts hatch and develop in the intestine.

The commonest tapeworm infection is by the dwarf tapeworm *Hymenolopsis nana*, which causes little disturbance. The second most common intestinal infection is caused by the adults of the beef tapeworm *(Taenia saginata)*, the pork tapeworm *(T. solium)* and the fish tapeworm *(Diphyllobothrium latum)*. The beef tapeworm may measure up to 6 m (20 ft) long, the fish tapeworm up to 10 m (32 ft) long and producing a million eggs a day. Thorough cooking of meat and fish will destroy any worms. In slaughterhouses, inspection of meat for cysts has greatly reduced the incidence of infection.

Tapeworm infections are often symptomless, or produce only vague digestive disturbances, and are discovered only when worm segments are found in the faeces. They seldom cause weight loss. The fish tapeworm, which absorbs vitamin B_{12} from the host's intestine, is the most likely one to cause pernicious anaemia, but this is rare. A drug to kill the worm may be prescribed.

There are two important varieties of human infection by

the larvae of tapeworms. Hydatid disease is caused by *Echinococcus ganulosus*, the adult of which lives in the intestine of dogs. Larvae may be picked up by handling the skin of infected animals, and form cysts in the liver and lungs. Symptoms are due to damage caused by the growth of the cysts, and rupture of the cysts may produce a toxic state. Cysticercosis is infection with the larval stage of *Taenia*, causing the skin, muscles, and brain to be affected by cysts. The skin and muscular lesions cause little discomfort, but brain cysts may cause epilepsy. There is no specific treatment.

Insects

Insects transmit disease by carrying bacteria and viruses on their bodies or by swallowing infected material. In the latter case the organisms survive and may multiply within the gut of the insect, eventually being excreted or regurgitated.

Flies

Apart from the blood-sucking insects transmitting fevers such as malaria, yellow fever, sleeping sickness and typhus, the greatest culprits in the spread of disease are houseflies *(Diptera)*, which may carry several million micro-organisms, of sixty or more types, on their bodies. These and other flies, such as bluebottles and fruit flies, are dangerous because they habitually visit both food and faeces. Many diseases, including typhoid, cholera, gastroenteritis, poliomyelitis, amoebic dysentery, yaws and trachoma, are transmitted by flies.

If the live maggots or eggs of a fly are swallowed with food, they can infect the intestine causing intestinal myiasis, a disease with symptoms of nausea, diarrhoea, vomiting and violent pain. Maggots may also infect the urine and skin wounds, although they actually help to keep wounds clean.

Mites and ticks

Mites and ticks (acarids) live as parasites on humans and animals. Probably the best known is *Sarcoptes scabiei*, the itch mite, which causes scabies in humans (see page 78). Some ticks carry typhus.

Lice

Lice are tiny but visible flat, wingless insects which parasitize birds and mammals, sucking their blood. Three species live on man: *Pediculus humanus*, variety *capitis* on the head, variety *corporis* on the body, and *Phthirus pubis* in coarse hair, usually in the pubic region. The lice live in hair or clothing and do not move about much outside their chosen area of the body. The eggs (nits) are also visible as tiny white grains attached to hairs or clothing. Lice live from two weeks to one month, and may survive for several days between feeds. When feeding, the louse injects saliva which irritates the skin and subcutaneous tissues, producing a raised itching red papula. Scratching may cause open, sometimes infected, sores. The body louse, and to a lesser extent the head louse, carries typhus, trench fever and European relapsing fever. Lice are effectively treated by special shampoos and lotions. Several applications may be needed to remove the eggs.

Antibiotics

The term antibiotic originally referred to a substance produced by one micro-organism which was harmful to another, but it is now also used to include synthetic agents which disable or destroy micro-organisms. Bacteria, but not viruses, are susceptible to various antibiotics. Antibiotics are generally used to treat established infections, though they are sometimes given to prevent disease.

Every antibiotic exerts its own chemical effects. Some antibiotics actually kill bacteria (bactericidal) while others only prevent bacteria multiplying (bacteriostatic). Specific bacteria are often more sensitive to one drug than another, although sometimes they become resistant to a particular antibiotic. Before an antibiotic is prescribed, unless time is important, sensitivity tests should be performed in a laboratory to show which antibiotic will be most effective.

Antibiotic resistance

There may sometimes be resistance to a particular antibiotic, perhaps because the organism is not susceptible to antibiotic action or produces an enzyme that destroys the antibiotic. An organism may acquire resistance to an antibiotic during its use, in which case the organisms will continue to multiply despite continuing treatment. This resistance may be transferred from a resistant organism to a sensitive one in the form of transferred genetic material.

Resistance is most common in hospitals where many patients in the same ward may be taking similar antibiotics. If a resistant organism develops it can then be passed to other patients taking the same antibiotic. If antibiotics are used indiscriminately a similar problem arises, and if antibiotics are not prescribed in a sufficient dose and for long enough the infection may not be eradicated and a resistant organism may develop.

Antibiotic treatment

The length of treatment varies enormously, depending on the type of organism and the severity of the infection. A simple infection of the upper respiratory tract may only require a week's treatment, whereas tuberculosis will require therapy for many months.

The route of treatment also varies. For instance, a localized superficial infection may be treated by applying the antibiotic directly to the skin (topical application). Many antibiotics are absorbed from the stomach and can therefore be taken by mouth, but others must be injected because they are destroyed by digestive enzymes. In the initial treatment of severe infections, injections may be given so that the antibiotic reaches the blood rapidly.

Side-effects of antibiotics

Probably the most common side-effect of antibiotics is bowel disturbance. The many beneficial organisms which normally inhabit the gut may be destroyed by antibiotics. If this happens, organisms such as the yeast *Candida albicans*, which is normally controlled by the bacteria in the gut flora, can proliferate, producing wind and diarrhoea. The yeast may also grow in other parts of the body such as the mouth or vagina, producing thrush (see page 78).

Allergy to antibiotics is quite common, and may develop during a first course of treatment or a subsequent one. Once someone has developed an allergy to a particular drug they should not use it again, as the reaction would be much more severe. Because the development of allergy is common, it is unwise to use antibiotics unless absolutely necessary. As with all drugs, there may be toxic side-effects.

Common antibiotics

The first antibiotic to be discovered was penicillin, which was produced from *Penicillium* moulds. Benzylpenicillin was the first synthetic variety to be made and is still one of the most powerful antibacterial preparations. Penicillin is a powerful bactericidal antibiotic acting against the cell walls of growing bacteria. Benzylpenicillin is destroyed by the acid in the stomach and so is usually given by injection. Another form, phenoxymethylpenicillin, can be given by mouth.

Some bacteria, such as staphylococci, produce an enzyme called penicillinase which destroys some forms of penicillin, but some other derivatives of the drug are resistant to this and so can be used against them. Some of the newer penicillins such as ampicillin and amoxycillin have a wide range of antibacterial activity (broad-spectrum antibiotics). Penicillins are not normally toxic in standard doses but allergic reactions, from mild skin rashes to serious general reactions, are common. The cephalosporins are similar to penicillin in structure and mode of action, but their range of activity is greater and they are not destroyed by penicillinase. They are useful for people who are allergic to penicillin and for penicillin-resistant infections. There are several tetracyclines with similar properties. They are bacteriostatic and are absorbed from the intestine but, because they bind to calcium, they should be taken before eating so that they do not bind to this mineral in food. They should not be given to children before they have their permanent teeth because they may bind to the calcium in growing teeth, causing damage and yellow discoloration. For the same reason, pregnant women should not take the drug because of possible damage to the bones and teeth of the fetus.

Other antibiotics include erythromycin, a bacteriostatic antibiotic with similar activity to benzylpenicillin, which is rarely toxic or allergenic but alters the development of resistant bacteria. Lincomycin and clindamycin are used for the treatment of bone infections, but are used only rarely because they produce severe side-effects including diarrhoea and colitis. Chloramphenicol also has a toxic effect on the bone marrow, and is now mainly used only for the treatment of typhoid fever, for eye and ear infections and where there is resistance to other antibiotics.

Antibiotics of the streptomycin group (streptomycin, neomycin, gentamycin and framycetin) are usually given by injection. Because they have toxic effects on the kidneys and the nerves involved in hearing and balance, they are used only as a last resort in serious infections.

The three commonest drugs used to treat fungal infections are nystatin, griseofulvin and amphotericin. Nystatin is usually used for fungal infections of the mouth and vagina (thrush), while griseofulvin acts against ringworm.

Nursing childhood infections

The principles of nursing a sick child are much the same as those that apply to the nursing of adults, except that extra skill is required to keep the patient from becoming uncomfortable or bored and to persuade the child to take medicines and accept other possibly unpleasant treatment. Many young children revert to more babyish habits when they are ill, and this should be taken into account, and allowances made for a child who is feeling less independent than usual.

The sickroom

The sickroom itself should be as pleasant and peaceful as possible, not necessarily a bedroom if the illness is likely to last more than a few days. Fresh air should be available but without causing draughts; the room should be cool in summer and of a constant warmth in winter; and there should be access to entertainment such as radio or television, toys and books within reach, and if possible a tray on legs or a table that can be swung over the bed for games, painting and drawing as well as for meals. For sitting up in bed, bolsters or a slanting board attached to the headboard makes a firm foundation for pillows.

Once children begin to feel better they should be allowed to get up if they wish, at least for part of the day, and perhaps a makeshift bed can be made up on the sitting-room sofa so that they can rest from time to time. As long as they do not become overtired, it is important that they are made to feel part of the family and its activities again as soon as they start to get better, since this will speed recovery.

Diet

Unless the sick child is required to be on a special diet, any light, easily digested foods may be offered, appetizingly presented. In the early stages of an illness, especially if there is fever, the child will probably not feel like eating anything and it is enough simply to offer plenty of drinks such as fruit juice. As the child begins to get better, toast, cereal, biscuits, ice cream and milk puddings may be offered along with simply cooked eggs, fish, fruit and vegetables. Do not insist that the child eats anything he or she does not want – even the convalescent may still not have much appetite because less energy than usual is being used. Offer food that you know the child likes.

Giving medicine and other treatment

Most children's medicines are made to taste pleasant and should not pose problems of refusal if they are given in a relaxed manner without a fuss. Otherwise, liquid medicines can be given in fruit juice; and tablets can be crushed in a little jam or honey and capsules put in soft food such as mashed banana or cream cheese. In cases of measles, if the child's eyes are crusted, a soothing eyewash may be used by dissolving a teaspoon of salt in half a litre (1 pint) of boiled cooled water and applied with cotton wool (a different piece for each eye to prevent cross-infection). The itching spots of chicken pox may be soothed with calamine lotion or by adding two cups of bicarbonate of soda to the child's bath. Mouthwashes can be given if the mouth is sore and dry. Reduce the discomfort of a fever by keeping the child cool with cold compresses, and sponging with tepid water.

Preventing boredom

Boredom becomes a problem as the child begins to recover from an illness, so it is a sign that the worst is over. It is at this time that most demands are made upon the parent, who should be prepared to devote quite a lot of time and patient attention to the child. Bear in mind that although plenty of the following items should be provided, a convalescent child tires easily and not too many things at one time should be given. Several new small toys, a different one given every day, are more fun than only one large one. A bag hung on a coat hanger and suspended from the bed or bedside table makes a useful place to keep small toys.

Ideas for play in bed

For children aged up to about four: large, simple jigsaws; fitting together toys; bricks; doll's house; toy telephone; bead stringing using pips, seeds and buttons; drawing and colouring.

For older children: jigsaws; models to make; cutting and pasting; constructional toys; weaving; knitting; collecting stamps.

Sand, paint, dough and clay can be played with in bed if the bedclothes are protected with plastic sheeting.

Companionship

Make sure that the child has plenty of visitors, who are prepared to talk and play. Puppets, card games and board games, guessing games, nursery rhymes and stories are all enjoyable activities for a child confined to bed or feeling less well than usual. Soft toys and dolls make good companions, and so do pets.

When they are ill, children usually need plenty of attention and absorbing but undemanding things to do.

Cancer

Cancer is not one, single disease but a term used to describe several hundred diseases with the same general characteristics. Their causes and treatments are many and varied: types of cancer that affect specific organs or systems of the body are described elsewhere in the book; this section deals with the general features of all cancers.

Features of cancer

The common characteristic of cancer is the appearance and uncontrolled multiplication and spread of abnormal types of body cell. Cell multiplication is a normal and essential process in the body; there is a constant turnover of cells in most tissues and organs, as the old, worn-out cells die and are replaced by new cells. But in cancer, for reasons not fully understood, a cell (or cells) becomes transformed and loses the control that cells normally have over their own function and multiplication. This 'renegade' or cancer cell causes the normal control of cell turnover to go awry – cell multiplication is no longer balanced by cell loss at a comparable rate. The cancerous cells accumulate, and are unable to carry out the functions of the original type of cell from which they arose.

The result of uncontrolled and rapid multiplication of abnormal cells is usually a localized lump which is referred to as a tumour or neoplasm. This tumour may be benign or malignant (cancerous). The cells of a benign tumour do not spread to other parts of the body, but remain confined to the tumour area, and as they multiply the lump grows. Benign tumours can usually be completely removed by surgery, but even without treatment are rarely fatal unless they interfere with some vital function such as blood circulation, or cause an intestinal or other blockage. But it is usually wise, on discovering a benign tumour, to have it removed since there is a small risk that it may become malignant.

The cells of a malignant tumour do not remain in the tumour area but grow into adjacent tissues and disrupt their functioning. Some malignancies (cancers) spread by a variety of routes to other parts of the body. It is this invasiveness that makes malignancies so potentially lethal. Normally, cells of different types remain in their appointed places in the body: liver cells stay in the liver, skin cells remain in the skin, and so on. Cancer cells colonize and destroy surrounding structures; if such cells invade a blood or lymph vessel, they may be carried to more distant sites and form new tumours there. This process of colonization of distant sites is known as metastasis. Many cancers – those of the cervix and skin, for example – can be detected early, before they have a chance to spread. If treated promptly, they can in most cases be completely cured.

In the USA and Britain, the five most common cancer sites in women are, in order of incidence: the breast, the large intestine, the uterus, the lung, and the blood and lymph. In men the five most common sites are: the lung, the prostate, the large intestine, the urinary tract, and blood and lymph.

Causes of cancer

It is not yet understood why cells suddenly start multiplying and behaving in a way that is of no benefit to the body. The fact that all the cells of a particular cancer have the same defect suggests that a cancer arises from a single cell. For some reason a previously normal cell suddenly changes (mutates) so that it becomes a cancer cell. The changes that occur involve the information stored in the genes of the cell. The genes consist of nucleic acid, DNA, which controls all living processes. The nucleic acid is delicate and its construction complex, and it is thought that damage to it, if not repaired, is the trigger that changes a normal cell into a cancerous one. Since the nucleic acid is copied and passed on to the daughter cells when an individual cell divides, it is easy to see how one cancer cell can give rise, over repeated division, to a whole group of cells that all bear the cancerous changes. Quite how the original damage happens to the DNA, or how the damaged DNA then causes the cell to act as a cancer cell, is poorly understood in most types of cancer.

In most common forms of cancer it is thought that environmental factors contribute to the appearance of the cancerous change. Many chemicals and certain types of

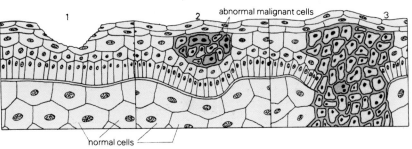

abnormal malignant cells

normal cells

Normally, damaged tissue (1) is reformed by nearby body cells replicating themselves by division. If something goes wrong with one cell and it becomes malignant, it starts dividing in an uncontrolled way (2). Unchecked, this group of abnormal cells eventually invades adjacent tissue (3).

radiation have been shown to be carcinogenic (cancer-causing) in laboratory animals exposed to them, and some of these factors have also been shown to have a similar effect on humans. There are many known carcinogens, a great number of which occur in industrial processes; and although much has been done to protect people against such occupational hazards, it is impossible to shield everyone completely. In addition, substances previously considered harmless are often discovered to be carcinogenic, perhaps after many years of people being exposed to them. One of the best-known carcinogens is cigarette smoke, and tobacco smoke in general. It is now clear that cigarette smoking is a major cause of lung cancer. There is also evidence that certain components in the diet may cause cancer, while other dietary constituents (such as fibre) may protect against certain types of cancer.

As described above, carcinogens probably act by damaging the structure of the DNA in the cell. Often the cell can repair this, which may explain why, if we are all exposed to the same carcinogenic chemicals, cancer is not more common. The fact that cancer is more common later in life may be related to the fact that the body has been exposed to carcinogens for longer, or that the ability to repair cell damage is slowly lost.

Cells normally recognize other cells as belonging to the same or different types by means of their surface antigens. Also, one type of white blood cell, the lymphocyte, is continually checking that all the surface antigens of cells are normal. If, as a result of mutation, a cell begins to show an abnormal antigen on its surface, lymphocytes gather round and destroy it. It is thought that this immunological surveillance is an important defence mechanism against cancer. Mutations of cells from the normal to the cancerous state are probably taking place at a slow rate all the time because of exposure to environmental carcinogens, but the abnormal cells are being destroyed as fast as they are formed, and most of us remain free of cancer. Many cancer sufferers have a malfunction of their immune response and this could be one cause of cancer; people who receive drugs which suppress immunity are more likely to develop cancer. Research in this area may reveal how cancer is caused, as well as possible ways of developing new treatments. (See also The Immune System and Allergies, pages 202-5.)

Although some types of cancer in animals are caused by viral infections, in humans there is little evidence to prove that viruses are commonly involved in cancer. The virus that causes infectious mononucleosis (glandular fever) in European countries, however, is interesting because in African people this virus (Epstein-Barr virus) can cause a cancer of the lymphatic system called Burkitt's lymphoma (see page 150). Another virus, human T-cell leukaemia virus (HTLV) may be one of the causes of leukaemia (see page 147).

Cervical cancer and liver cancer may also be caused by a virus, or at least a particular viral infection may increase the likelihood of that person getting cancer. Hepatitis B infection may increase the risk of developing liver cancer. Herpes virus or human papilloma virus (the virus that causes genital warts) may be involved in cervical cancer.

Classification of cancers

Tumours can arise from the epithelium (the covering tissues of the body and the lining of the digestive tract), from glandular or connective tissues.

The suffix '-oma' is used to indicate that a structure is a tumour. For example, benign epithelial tumours are called papillomas, and malignant epithelial tumours are called carcinomas or epitheliomas. Benign tumours that arise from glandular tissue are called adenomas. Benign tumours of connective tissue have the suffix '-oma' added to the cell type from which the tumour is derived, so that a benign tumour arising from fibrous tissue is a fibroma, and one from cartilage a chondroma. Malignant connective tissue tumours are termed sarcomas and a prefix indicates tissue of origin: malignant tumours of fibrous tissue are fibrosarcomas, and those of cartilage chondrosarcomas.

There are many unusual growths that cannot be neatly classified. Certain embryonic tumours, called teratomas, contain various different cell types: bone, muscle, glandular tissue and epithelial cells all within the same tumour. Some sarcomas contain a number of different elements so that a long compound word, chondro-myxo-fibrosarcoma, may describe it. Tumours of lymph nodes are given the general term lymphoma, although they, too, are extremely complex and difficult to classify. Cancer of the white blood cells is given the general term leukaemia. The type of blood cell involved in a particular case is added as a prefix, so that a patient may be described as suffering from monocytic or lymphocytic leukaemia (see pages 147-8).

How a normal cell becomes a cancer cell

A normal cell:
1 is immobilized by contact with neighbouring cells;
2 only divides if permitted to by various regulators;
3 has normal surface antigens and no abnormal ones;

but when environment or ageing lead to:

either a breakdown in cell regulation by
1 expressing information normally suppressed; or
2 failure in cell contact, or hormonal or nervous control; or
3 failure of lymphocyte surveillance after abnormal antigens have developed;

and/or an abnormality in genetic information because of
1 the presence of a virus; or
2 mutation, altering the cell's genes; or
3 loss of genetic information and therefore of normal surface antigens;

the result may be a cancer cell, which
1 moves freely around, as it has few or no cell contacts;
2 divides according to its own whim; and
3 has abnormal surface antigens, or has lost some of its normal ones.

Diagnosis of cancer

In diagnosis, cancer may be divided into three categories. The first includes those in which early detection and treatment is possible, such as cancer of the skin, breast, cervix, Hodgkin's disease of the spleen and lymph nodes, and possibly cancer of the lung and bladder. The second category includes cancers which can rarely be detected at an early stage, for example, cancer of the pancreas or stomach. The third, much smaller group comprises cancers which when first detected are already distributed throughout the body. Examples of these are the leukaemias.

It is not always easy to confirm a diagnosis of cancer. Frequently, symptoms are few and relatively vague in the early stages of the disease, and only cancers that arise in or just under the skin, or in the mouth, are easily discovered. A high proportion of cancerous tumours arise in tissues which cannot be examined directly, which makes them very difficult to detect. The smaller and more localized the cancer the easier it is to treat, and so early diagnosis is very important before it has spread too far.

Many factors combine to suggest the possibility of a cancer being present in a particular organ. Symptoms vary according to the site of the growth, but in general a doctor should always be consulted if any one of the following symptoms is present. Though by no means necessarily indicating cancer, they do suggest the need for further investigation.

1 Any sore, particularly on the face, that will not heal.

2 Any swelling or lump under the skin such as in the breast.

3 Unexplained rapid loss of weight.

4 A mole that begins to bleed or change in appearance.

5 A persistent dry cough.

6 Excessive menstrual bleeding or bleeding between periods; vaginal bleeding after the menopause.

7 Blood in the sputum, urine or stools.

8 Persistent indigestion or abdominal pain.

9 A marked change in normal bowel habits.

10 Difficulty in passing urine.

There are now successful diagnostic tests for the early detection of many kinds of cancer, and new techniques are being developed all the time. Tests range from X-rays to more complicated techniques such as contrast radiology (for the digestive or urinary tract), endoscopy (for stomach, bowel or bladder) and biopsy (removal of a sample for microscopic examination). In X-ray scanning (computerized axial tomography, or CAT scan), a special X-ray machine linked to a computer produces a series of pictures of thin sections of the body. Unlike conventional X-rays, which normally show only hard tissues such as bone, these X-ray scans show details of soft tissues and can detect the changes caused by tumours. A lump in the breast tissue, which is easy to detect by regular examination of the breast can be examined by means of a special type of X-ray technique called mammography, which will determine correctly if the lump is malignant in about 85 per cent of suspected breast cancers.

If a tumour comes into contact with the body surface, ulceration usually occurs and malignant cells become detached from the main part of the tumour. With a technique known as exfoliative cytology it is possible to recognize such cells. It is becoming an increasingly important and reliable technique, particularly in the diagnosis of cancer of the cervix (the neck of the womb), in the test known as the cervical smear or Pap test. Examination of the sputum may be helpful in diagnosing lung cancer, and kidney and bladder cancer can be often diagnosed by examining the urine for malignant cells.

Treatment of cancer

The methods of treating cancer include surgery, radiotherapy (radiation treatment) and drugs (chemotherapy), often in combination. There are also a number of unorthodox treatments, but their success has not been proved scientifically.

Surgery

Removal of a tumour by surgery can be successful, particularly when the cancer is diagnosed early and has not spread or invaded other parts of the body. To be successful, however, the surgeon must make absolutely sure that all the cancerous tissue is removed, otherwise the tumour may recur; therefore it is usually necessary to take away some of the surrounding tissue at the same time.

Even when tumours are quite widespread, surgery can relieve symptoms and treat complications. For example, cancer of the intestine may cause obstruction that would shortly lead to death without operation. Removal of a tumour allows the patient to return to a symptom-free and relatively active life despite the fact that metastases (secondary cancers) are present which may eventually cause death. Similarly, someone with cancer of the bladder may be in danger from local bleeding. Removal of the bladder will relieve the symptoms and improve the quality of the affected person's life, despite the presence of metastases.

Future developments in curative surgery seem to lie within the field of organ transplantation, particularly lung and liver transplants.

Radiotherapy

Radiotherapy, the treatment of tumours by exposing them to radiation, aims to kill tumour cells without causing undue damage to surrounding, normal tissues. Cancer of the skin and testes, and Hodgkin's disease, can be successfully treated by radiotherapy.

Most radiotherapy involves either X-rays, gamma rays or radioactive isotopes. X-rays and gamma rays are produced by machines which give a very fine beam of radiation that can be accurately directed at the tumour. Radioactive isotopes are usually positioned close to the tumour inside the body in a special container. A variety of different isotopes is used and, with some tumours, the isotope can be combined with a substance which the organ uses; for instance, radioactive iodine is used to treat cancer of the thyroid gland.

The use of radiation in treating cancer relies on the fact that cells that are dividing rapidly, such as tumour cells, are more sensitive to it than normal cells. Radiation can also destroy the small blood vessels supplying the cancer cells with nourishment, causing the cells to die.

Radiotherapy is usually carried out over a period of several weeks; sometimes it is given daily but in other cases less often. The aim is to spread out the treatment so that as little damage as possible is done to normal cells, while the cancer cells receive enough radiation to kill them. The frequency and length of treatment depend on the site of the tumour, since some sites absorb radiation more easily than others.

Side-effects are often experienced because it is almost impossible to prevent normal cells being affected. The most common side-effects are tiredness and a loss of appetite. The skin may also become reddened at the site of the radiation. The other side-effects tend to be specific to the area being treated. For example, the ovaries and the testes are both sensitive to radiation, so patients are likely to be made infertile if the radiation is directed towards these organs. Radiation to the abdomen may cause diarrhoea, and radiation to the neck may cause sore throat and difficulty in swallowing.

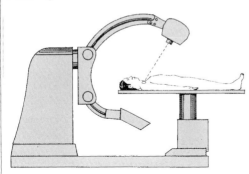

Radiotherapy for cancer. The radiotherapy machine can be finely adjusted so that an exact dose of radiation is delivered to a limited area of the body. Only certain cancers are radio-sensitive and suitable for this treatment.

Chemotherapy

Treatment with anti-cancer drugs (also called cytotoxic drugs or chemotherapeutic agents) is usually employed when a malignant tumour has spread too widely for effective surgery or when the cancer is distributed throughout the body, as in leukaemia. Unlike surgery and radiotherapy, chemotherapy involves the whole body, including all the healthy cells. The anti-cancer drugs are chemicals that act only on cells that are actively multiplying, relying on the fact that cancer cells multiply more rapidly than most other cells. (The word cytotoxic literally means 'cell poison'.)

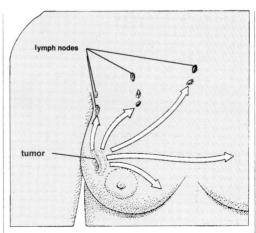

Metastases (secondary growths) from cancer commonly spread along lymphatic pathways to other parts of the body.

Drug treatment has been successful in some cancers of the blood and lymphatic tissue. These cancers are quite rare, however, and many of the more common cancers cannot be cured by drugs. But chemotherapy is often used in combination with radiotherapy and surgery and can help to kill any cancer cells that escaped the original treatment.

Any normal cells that are multiplying are also affected by anti-cancer drugs, particularly those in the bone marrow, ovaries, testes, intestine and skin. This can cause severe side-effects. Treatment with anti-cancer drugs requires a delicate balance between killing the cancer cells and minimizing the effects of the drug on normal cells. This is done by adjusting the type of drug, the dose levels, and the timing of doses. Side-effects may include nausea, tiredness, constipation and mouth ulcers. Other drugs can often relieve some of these side-effects however, and when there is a chance that cytotoxic drugs might cure or prolong the life of a cancer sufferer they are worth using. New drugs with improved effectiveness and reduced side-effects are continually being developed.

The antiviral agent interferon, a naturally occurring substance, has been used to treat some cancers, but results have been disappointing and for most cases interferon is no better than other drugs.

There is some hope that certain cancers might be treated in future by immunological means. The immune system of many cancer sufferers does not function properly, and if it could be artificially stimulated it might help the body itself to get rid of cancer cells and also help to prevent recurrences. Immunology might also be used to direct cytotoxic drugs directly to the cancer cells. This could be done by attaching poisons to a monoclonal antibody (see *The Immune System and Allergies*, pages 202-5) which recognizes molecules on the surface of cancer cells but not on normal cells. This technique might reduce the side-effects of chemotherapy.

Index